WAR TORN

Other Books from Daniel Thomas Chapman

There and Then: *A Summer to Remember*
Messages from Vallarta: *The Traveler Series*
Be Not forgot: *Remembrances of Life, Loves, and a Little Larceny* (Poetry)
Poetic Justice: *The Lost Art of Reason, Rhyme, and Meter* (Poetry and Prose)

Other Recommendations:

Deep Where the Octopi Lie by Jean McCord (Editing and Foreword by DT Chapman)
Bitter Is the Hawk's Path by Jean McCord (Editing and Foreword by DT Chapman)

WAR TORN

DANIEL THOMAS CHAPMAN

War Torn
Copyright © 2022 Daniel Thomas Chapman

All rights reserved. No part of this book may be reproduced, stored, or transmitted by any means—whether auditory, graphic, mechanical, or electronic—without written permission of both publisher and author, except in the case of brief excerpts used in critical articles and reviews. Unauthorized reproduction of any part of this work is illegal and is punishable by law.

ISBN: 978-1-957203-29-4 (sc)
ISBN: 978-1-957203-30-0 (hc)
ISBN: 978-1-957203-31-7 (e)

Because of the dynamic nature of the Internet, any web addresses or links contained in this book may have changed since publication and may no longer be valid. The views expressed in this work are solely those of the author and do not necessarily reflect the views of the publisher, and the publisher hereby disclaims any responsibility for them.

The Ewings Publishing LLC
One Galleria Blvd., Suite 1900, Metairie, LA 70001
1-888-421-2397

CONTENTS

Foreword ix

Part One

Family Disunity 3
Jean McCord 7
Roy "Bo" McCord, Jr. 11
Patricia "Patsy" McCord 16
"Bo" McCord 19
Mary "Sis" McCord 25
Colleen McCord 31
Lorraine Jannette "Jann" McCord 33
Joseph "Jackie-Boy" McCord 35
Marie Helms McCord 37
Stepmother Edith McCord 40
On the Farm 45
Rooster Roasting 101 49
Patsy, Come Home 55
Hand's Off 57
Reunion 62
Kindergarten Daze 66
Jerrold "Jerry" McCord 71
New Home, New Start 76
Bad Dad "Roy" 78
Abortion 82
Confessional 85
Cinderella Complex 89
Rolling Stone 101
Rejected Again 104
Yuletide Fever 109
Christmas Crunch 115

Home for the Holidaze 119
Conundrum 129
Religious Toil 134
Bombs Away! 142
Braggart 146
Heroic Injuries 148
Pearl Harbor 168
Change in the Air 172
On My Own Accord 176
Spreading Wings 182

Part Two

Sisterhood 191
Truancy Reports 196
Freighter Later 201
Elder Siblings Together 206
Search for Work 212
Sears & Roebuck Gas-Station 217
Robin Hoodlum 221
Convoluted 236
Promotions! 243
Time to Go 258
There's a Future Ahead 260
Crazy Driver 266
"Wendy the Welder" Jean 272
Go West, Young Woman! Go West! 277
Road Hazards 281
Scary Driver 283
Dirty Driver 292
More Road Hazards 297
Difference A Year Makes 303
"Flash" Learner 306
Team Terrific 308
Little Orphans 311
Kinnapping 316
New Adjustments 327

Whatever You Say, Jean	331
Mantras	335
Blushing Heroine	337
Sacrifices	342
New Shoes	346
Rebellion	351
On My Own	357
Sister Protector	360
More Family History	365
Wendy Does It All	371
Arc Welding 101	373
Warner & Swasey Armaments	377
"Mum" Was the Word	379
Latrine Queen	381
Hush Hush	385
'Wurzburg' Newsreel	388
Game Winner	393
Shiftwork	397
Traitor Among Us?	400
Spy Among Us?	404
Reacceptance	421
Dream Farm	424
G.I. Jean	427
Forget the Farm	430
Dog Gone Diligence	436
Good Ideas	444
New Welder	449
Showing True Colors	455
Bigots Among Us	463
No Support	465
Emotional Assault	471
Mental Escape	478
Devil Be Damned	481
Eeny Meeny Miny Moe	489
St. Patrick's Day	492
That "Guy" Is the One!	495

Guy Henry (Chapman) Dork 498
Basic Magnesium Plant, Inc. 504
War's End 514
Bay Area, Here We Come! 516
Wedding Reunion 521
Confirmation 523
End of the Beginning 525
Epilogue 528
About the Author 533

FOREWORD

Appreciatively, many WWII Home Front stories have been written to help celebrate all the wonderful contributions from countless American women involved in wartime, construction causes. Throughout the entire course of WWII years and across all of America a vast array of war-support operations was developed from many previously conventional, civilian-oriented facilities. These production sites included hundreds of armament factories, railroad-car manufacturing plants, military-vehicle construction plants, shipyards, aircraft assembly plants, and many other areas of important military support. At all those sites and especially including shipyards, aircraft manufacturing plants and armament factories across our country, women were hired to replace men and help fill the enormous, wartime-labor needs. Those women's efforts greatly and heroically supported and positively affected our war effort here at home.

With the onset of the *Emergency Shipbuilding Program* established in early 1941 to assist our British ally in their war struggle, efforts to greatly increase highly needed construction labor ultimately focused on encouraging women to take over on jobs previously held by men only. To help inspire, encourage, and motivate additional women in America to go to work in these *war-cause*, production operations, many US government agencies effectively advertised women's proud, heroic, and vital efforts who were already working in the aircraft manufacturing industries by calling them *Rosie the Riveter(s)*.

It is important to note that *riveting*, itself, is a specialized skill utilizing a small, bolt-like *rivet* and a gun-like rivet-tool to automatically hammer it into sheets of metal fabrics strongly fastening them together. During the war period, rivets were primarily used in aircraft production facilities to attach an airplane's fuselage to its frame. However, the nickname *Rosie* became so popular that its meaning expanded to symbolize all women working in any of the countless war-cause, manufacturing, and construction efforts.

Additionally, in many of those phases of production, arc-welding rather than riveting was often required to complete a variety of construction requirements. Welding is a unique and highly skilled field requiring specialized-training and often dirty, dangerous, and difficult work assignments. Many *Rosie's* and other women stepped forward choosing to receive that skilled-training and become arc-welders in primarily the shipyards and aircraft manufacturing plants. That unique group was also a tremendous asset to the war-cause providing serious dedication and service to our nation. Also, because of their highly specialized training and efforts, those workers were affectionately singled out from *the Rosie's* for their significant contributions and nicknamed, "Wendy the Welders."

Thus, still giving broad credit to all *Rosie*'s, the following story focuses on a tale of one such member from that special group of *Wendie's*. The Depression Era and onset of WWII provided ample stories of survival, diligence, responsibility, and genuine, heroic behavior from women across our nation. To single out one case story merely reflects and recognizes the vast array of other, unique lives and experiences which took place during that troublesome and critical period in modern, American history. To honor one is to honor all of them.

Therefore, that is the purpose of part of this story. Originally, it began as a single, biographical contribution to many other brief, *Rosie* vignettes available for review at the *Rosie the Riveter Museum* located in Richmond, California. The story grew and developed into this book which transitioned into a completer and more complex story of an entire family's struggles during the war period. It is also a family tale of brothers and sisters struggling during wartime to survive and remain together. In fact, several of those sisters did so by rising to volunteer for the ranks of *Rosie's* and *Wendie's*.

With so many American lives in conflict, this story reminds us of all the family struggles which existed during The Great Depression and WWII periods. The heroes and main characters of this story are the children of the Roy and Maria McCord family of Minnesota. But, they could be tales of countless other family members in constant crisis throughout those daunting and challenging periods. These lives' stories are offered-up, therefore, as tribute to all those families everywhere who faced hardship during those critical and challenging times. This tale of the McCord children's lives describes their ongoing struggles to reunite, salvage and repair their own, personal lives while remaining true to their sibling-code: *McCords stick together.* During the war years and its aftermath, they persisted with determination to grow, develop, and succeed as an extended and supportive family-unit.

True to its initial purpose, this book also serves as a form of acknowledgement for all *Rosie's* and *Wendie's* everywhere. However, the story's motivation necessitated the author to focus on the unusual life-and-times of primarily just one such *Wendy*. The story was originally developed as a special, singular tribute to our main *Wendy* character, Patricia McCord. Yet, the tale eventually grew to include supportive information of her courageous siblings' lives during those precarious and difficult times. However, and furthermore, I am especially proud to relate *Patsy's* story not just because she was the main, key character in this book. It is also because as a true, original *Wendy the Welder,* she was none other than *Patricia McCord,* my mother.

From Patricia's own recollections, then, including additional insight and material from some of her siblings, comes this personal, honest, and mostly genuine account of her story and that of her family during those challenging years of the Great Depression, WWII and shortly afterward. As the author, I chose the title "War Torn" to reflect upon those many destructive and damaging, yet unique and strengthening, events of my mother's family saga during both the angry, crippling depression years and tumultuous war years. Naturally, however, the story within includes facts and highlights of Patricia's and her sisters' unusual *Rosie* and *Wendy* experiences during WWII.

In fact, because of respect and appreciation for my mother's unique story, the book's initial working-title was reverently referred to as: "The Life and Times of '*Patsy the Welder.*'"

To: My mother, "Patsy the Welder"

Patricia Vera McCord
Age 15, Sioux Falls, South Dakota
10th Grade Class Picture
St. Michael's Catholic Highschool

WAR TORN

Depression and war seem cruelest of harms,
Yet abandonment's questions pose tormenting hurt.
Hunger and danger cause lasting alarms,
While unrequited love can smother a heart.

But resolute focus on managing schemes
Servicing minds and placating souls
As methods developed to satisfy means
Let siblings divided partake-in control.

Once reunited, sisters and brothers
Find strength in meetings of familial love.
Providing purposeful goals for each other,
They service their families and country proud of.

Life is a mystery with hollows and hills
Which challenge the strong and deny the weak.
Love's purpose in searching for that which fulfills
Gives mindful relations promises to keep.

No matter our journeys or trials-by-fire,
Departed siblings still define their bloodlines.
Regardless of partings, love never expires,
And war-torn reunions are families enshrined.

PART ONE
Sioux Falls, South Dakota

FAMILY DISUNITY

I was fifteen-years old when the war broke out. I can remember that ominous day very well, alright. My family was living in a relatively modest home in the small town of Sioux Falls, South Dakota. Our house was a typical wood and brick structure with two floors and a full basement. At that time, there were still four of us kids remaining at home with our parents, our dad and stepmother, living there. All three bedrooms were upstairs, and we kids shared two of them. We had a large family room downstairs along with a single bathroom, a pretty good-sized kitchen and a hallway leading to the other stairwell to the basement.

On that particularly gloomy day, with exception of our dad, we four remaining sibling members, along with our stepmother, had just returned home from church in the very late morning. Our three eldest siblings, two sisters and a brother, were no longer living at home. However, I had been allowed to return home a couple years earlier, so I was there along with our three youngest siblings, also two sisters and a brother. It had been really nice that day being home indoors because of all the snow outside. Fact is, it had been a chilly day all Sunday afternoon, and it was December 7, 1941.

When I really think about it, *chilly* isn't even the right word for it. It was downright freezing outside, and I was pleased-as-punch to be inside where it was all nice and toasty. Believe me, I knew all about cold weather and winters, too, having spent most of my previous years living with relatives in Minnesota. For sure, Sioux Falls, SD was just as bad in the wintertime, or worse, than there.

Outside, the leafless, tree-lined streets were all covered with hard-packed dirty-ice formed from vehicle discharges and fallen leaves from the nearly barren American Sycamores and Elms. Our suburban neighborhood had thick, white blankets of fluffy snow spread across all the lawns and rooftops. Many homes, including our own, had high stacks of piled snow around the front and rear yards due to layers of snow falling from the steep rooftops. Having just returned from Catholic Church mass and services, I know we McCord kids were grateful as hell to be inside our cozy, little oven of a home.

Besides, all of us having been chilled-to-the-bone inside that church during services we had just returned from, I remember thinking that those insensitive priests had kept that saintly building extra cold just to keep me alert and not slumbering-off during mass. I mean, heck, the whole darn mass was in Latin anyway, so I never knew much of what was going on except by following others' actions. *Stand. Kneel. Sit. Stand,* no, *kneel. Sit. Stand. Sit...* and on and on. Fortunately, at least that exercise helped to keep me warm, a little bit.

Plus, I never was much good at learning Latin in catechism, or even in school. It was like studying a foreign language, and that was all Greek to me. So, after hearing, "Dominus vobiscum" and responding with, "Et cum spiritu tuo," I was more lost than found, I guess. I really enjoyed English class at school, though, but that was hard enough. Paying more attention to movement and vocal cues from the congregation than understanding anything those priests were chanting was just too awkward and difficult for me to remain interested in and warm.

Anyway, walking to church and returning home, however, was not at all bad. It had been mostly fun trudging up those frozen, six blocks from our home to the small church and then back home again afterwards. We would trudge over snow-packed sidewalks and across ice-covered streets. It was crazy fun slipping and sliding along those sidewalks and then charging across the neighborhood's streets at the corners.

I'd hold my two, younger sisters' hands, and we'd take turns pulling each other across the frozen, slippery streets. Our little brother would laugh with delight at our antics, but nevertheless hold tightly onto our stepmother's hands for his own security and safety. I think our stepmother held onto little, Jackie-boy for her own stability too.

Yes, it had been fun for a little while, anyway, playing outside on our brief journeys to and from church. Yet, it had been way too-cool-for-comfort once we arrived inside that church building. Can you imagine steam bellowing from your mouth and nostrils every time you prayed or spoke? I mean, it was a little-bit entertaining, at first, but also pathetic watching prayers materialize right before your eyes whenever you exhaled.

It had become more interesting watching steam evolve into shapes from our exhaled breath than it had been for anything coming from those priests mouths. I believed that the priests must have had a special heater, besides all those candles, just to keep their *pulpit* area warm. Priests never spewed steam when they sermonized. That would have been sacrilegious, I supposed.

I recall, however, that on that one particularly terrible afternoon, once the cold, church-services had ended, we had hurriedly made our way back to our cozy, home sanctuary. I had felt especially fortunate that day to be inside our family's home, all warm and comfortable inside, and surrounded by my younger brothers and sisters. My younger siblings were there, and I had been grateful about that. I had only been allowed to return and live with my brothers and sisters a couple times in my whole life, and it had only been a brief, two years since I had been with them that last time, since our previous separation. Oh, yes, I was grateful.

Also, because of that fact, I treasured each day being with my siblings. Like I said earlier, I had two younger sisters and a baby brother still living at home there. The older three, two sisters and a brother, had already been forced out, or ordered, quite a while before. However, I was right in the middle, age-wise of our brood, and still at home with the youngest ones. I remember that day when they were also all lying about the living room just as relaxed as me while enjoying our quiet, so far, Sunday afternoon.

I loved all my brothers and sisters, and it was so comforting to be near any of them. I can remember looking-up from my textbook that I had been reading to watch each of my siblings busy at their own games or projects. Those few and precious times together, it had always made me smile. To be included with them made me feel special. So much time before in my life, I had felt insecurity, hurt, shame, and abandonment after being sent away, kept away, and forced to live with distant relatives. I had wanted nothing more than to return home and be joined with all my sisters and brothers. That had been a very special time when I had been allowed to return home, and we were all together at the same time. Special and unique, it was.

Unfortunately, though, all of us McCord children had not been living in the same house together for quite some time before the war's start. Terrible family issues, I guess you might say, had already taken its toll on us kids.

We were already involved in our very own *warfront* right there within our home. Because of so many previous battles and conflict among the older kids and our parents, especially our dad, circumstances had already split us apart. Gratefully, I was still allowed at home to be among the remaining. Yet, I *remained* very aware and knowledgeable of our family's precarious circumstances. Regarding the older ones absences, unfortunately, just like me several times already, they had all been forced-out to go live elsewhere, or with far-away relatives.

Altogether, however, there were seven of us McCord kids remaining, but living together and being *all together* had been a rare occurrence. By the war's start, the three eldest children of our family had been living East in other states with different relatives. At that terrible time, *Jean*, the oldest sister, and eldest of all of us McCord siblings, was living with our grandmother in Hayward, Wisconsin. After a while, they were both joined by our older brother, whom we all affectionately called *Bo*. The other missing sibling was Bo's twin, our sister Mary, or *Sis* as we nicknamed her, who had been living with an aunt in Duluth, Minnesota. All three of them, we had learned, had been kept busy going to school and working at odd jobs whenever possible to help earn their keeps…

JEAN MCCORD

It had been no secret that our eldest sibling, Jean, had been *ordered* out of the house at the ripe old age of seventeen-years. Shortly after my last *arrival*, when I had been allowed to return once again to the family nest, I was thirteen-years old, in fact, and I had been back just long enough to observe Jean being forced-out and sent away. Jean had been ordered to go and live with Grandmother Agnus Helms, on our deceased mother's side of the family in Hayward, Wisconsin.

It had been none too soon for Jean, either. I mean, I watched so many times when she used to have some God-awful battles with our dad. It seemed like Jean must have spent most of her youth arguing and fighting with our father. As a result, she almost always looked bruised and battered from continual, horrendous spats and brawls with him. It didn't help her case either that, for whatever reasons, she was an obstinate, stubborn, defiant, and rebellious teenager- a fighter who literally and physically *fought* with our dad so much of the time when necessary.

For some reason, Jean would get all upset over some issue and then she would never-back-down from her viewpoint. I mean, it was like she refused taking orders at all from our dad, and she would never give-in. *Compromise* was not in her vocabulary. We other youngsters used to watch in horror and gasp with anguished whimpers as the two of them tore around the house from room-to-room screaming and threatening each other. Both would be swinging punches, kicking out, grabbing, and clawing at each other's faces and throwing objects aimed to strike serious injury at their opponent.

Whenever one of them accidentally, or on purpose, broke something like a lamp or a thrown object, our dad would roar even louder and make all sorts of violent gestures and vile threats. He used to call Jean terrible, mean, cruel and vicious names too, and when she got him all riled-up, he would explode with his ever-so typical, nasty, and angry cursing.

"You miserable, ugly, nasty, little bitch queer," our dad would scream. "When I get my hands on you, I am going to tear you apart!"

We'd watch as Jean flashed-by yelling back over her shoulder, "Eat shit, you rotten old bastard! Leave me alone! Get away from me!"

Next, she'd be throwing something to slow our dad down or anger him even more, and then she'd be running past us again while attempting to avoid his revengeful wrath. Eventually, the odds played out against Jean because of our dad's sheer physical size and strength. He was a very big and powerful man. On-the-other-hand, Jean, although larger and stronger for her age, and oh, so brave for her size, was simply outmanned and outgunned.

Jean had been born in 1923, and no one knows for sure, but Jean used to say, when you could get ever even her to talk about our dad, "I used to fight with that old man from the time I was an infant!"

It showed from all her bruises and battle scars too. Ultimately, therefore, Jean would once again accept her *losing cause* and make her escape by racing out the front door and slamming it shut behind her. When finally protected by outdoor spaces and landscape shadows, Jean would remain hidden from view sometimes for hours on end. Slowly, at least she would recover, and then she would sneak back into the house and go to bed.

During most of those violent episodes, however, we younger ones would anguish in our rooms or hiding places somewhere in the house all curled up trying to avoid contact within their war zones. Later, as adults, we were able to recognize that as youngsters we were simply trying to avoid becoming collateral damage. Jean would have been noticeably saddened and angered even more had any of us been injured too. Our dad, however, would never have even slowed down at all to note or care about any of us being hurt. If anything, he would have just used our injuries as sustenance for stoking his fuming fires.

All-the-while, we others would be whispering to ourselves and each other pleading to God for both she and our dad to cease their ugly fighting. Of course, the very youngest ones were almost always terrified and usually in tears from the violent commotions. We older others would grab the younger ones pulling them to safety while we just stood back, kept our distances, and shook in disbelief and shock. Later, in retrospect, we would confide in each other, "At least she got out alive!"

Jean returned to school and finished high school there in Hayward, Wisconsin while living with our grandmother. I'm sure she was able to calm down somewhat from the stressful life she led at home because of her violent distasteful life struggling with our father. Her relationship with our dad affected her emotionally too. Jean never got over her hatred for our dad; however, it caused her to think more about the rest of us younger ones.

No, it was no secret that there was no-love-lost between Jean and our dad. Jean talked to us others often about getting out and going on her own. She even began forging some plans in her own mind to do just that. Some of her plans would even eventually influence some of the rest of us. Jean made-up her mind at a young age to attend college and become successful. She worked hard on various jobs and always seemed to be busy supporting herself.

Later, with Jean long gone from our family home, some of us others would even arrange to join her. Fact is, Jean and I became the closest of all us brothers and sisters. She had always been defensive of me and often took up my case against our dad and stepmother. I looked up to my big, defiant sister as a true heroin in my eyes. I wanted to be with Jean and follow her. She was strong-willed and defiant to a fault, but Jean had goals, big goals. I figured that if I were with her someway, I'd be safe, secure, and likely to become, in my own way, a success too.

Of course, once Jean was unceremoniously booted from the family-home, at that time, however, I still worried about my own welfare and status with the family household. Sure, I also worried about my absent, older sibs, but it was critically important at that time for me to focus on my *own* present state-of-conditions. I needed to prioritize and focus on dealing with any uncertainties regarding my elder siblings later.

Plus, soon after Jean's departure, we all learned that she had persisted and continued with her ambitious plans and dream of owning property somewhere. She had envisioned some place like a farm, or something, where all of us McCord kids could live out our lives together in privacy. Yet, there was still something else even more important to Jean than a farm. Most important to her than anything else, I began to realize and understand, was her own, personal *code of conduct,* a kind of *decree,* or even her *first commandment.* I mean that Jean practically swore by that *life's code* with a blood oath. Her singular and paramount rule: Never, I mean *never,* having to take orders from any man.

Yeah, she was hardcore, alright. Jean had grown up learning to defend herself by being tough, and that tough exterior sort of grew on her. She was hard. In fact, I think that after Jean had been sent away from home, it was probably there in Hayward, Wisconsin, and surely after that in Cleveland, that Jean, I suppose, developed her own personal lifestyle.

I believe that Jean had learned first-hand not to trust men, thanks to her relationship with our dad. She had learned not to like them or even have anything to do with them except when absolutely necessary. By that time in her life, it seemed, and especially having survived those years around our dad, Jean had just learned never to want or need a man in her life anymore. She became completely content and satisfied, so she said, without men trying to control her.

Oh, there are other stories on that subject of Jean and men, but not here. Honestly, I should explain that whatever hang-ups Jean had with our dad, and then with men in general, that part of her life never had any influence on any of the rest of us. Fact is, I truly remained blind-eyed ignorant of Jean's private-lifestyle.

I always figured that even despite her crude behavior and behind that rough-tough exterior, Jean still managed to become popular enough. The truth as it appeared to me was that Jean always seemed to have lots of friends. Oh, sure, they were mostly all girlfriends with a few male exceptions, but so what? I was happy for her friendships. What was to worry about? Jean was content, mostly, and that was what pleased me.

Jean, however, also remained true to her goals and dreams. She continued working as much as possible, and by the very early 1940's, she always found a decent paying job in a Cleveland factory somewhere. It was then, too, that she even started going to college during evenings after work while there in Cleveland. But another of her life's *rule-of-thumb* mantras became: W*ork hard; spend half; and save half.* She continued working, began saving her money, and planning, planning, and planning. I have to admit, though, that because of her willful and powerful self-discipline, Jean became just about the most *independent* woman, if not person, I ever met…

ROY "BO" MCCORD, JR.

Okay, so now is a good time to mention what happened to our big brother, Bo. His case was kind of similar in some ways, but still very different than Jean's too. Truth is, he was actually the first to go. I wasn't living with the family when that happened, but I was still close to him because of those earlier years when I had lived together with the whole family. And, Bo got sent away well before Jean.

He was only fourteen when he was forced out, but it was not too much longer after his departure that Jean was gone too. It was about a year and a half later, in fact, and it was an interim period wherein I had been returned to the family once again, but well after our mother had died. Bo's departure was sort of the first *clearing-out* by our dad of disobedient and argumentative kids. Or, it was a *house-cleaning* and purification process of all agitators by our stepmother.

And I am still saddened to repeat that Bo's leaving, or getting-the-boot, so-to-speak, happened while I was still completely rejected from the family nest. All my brothers and sisters had been living together at that time, but without me, in Missouri, of all places. When Jean was forced out, while I had been home for only a short period of time, was about when Bo had ultimately ended-up living in Hayward, Wisconsin. I hadn't been allowed to rejoin the family until shortly after Bo's departure, unfortunately. But before I did return home, I had actually had a personal and emotional encounter with my brother, Bo, under the darndest circumstances…

Right around then, I was about twelve years old at the time, I had been living with my aunt Kate in St. Paul, Minnesota. Like I mentioned, the rest of my immediate family had all been living together, without me, somewhere in Missouri. Through the grapevine, which consisted of my nosey aunt and her daughter's nosey and energetic gossip, I had already heard that Bo had been sent away from the family for something he had apparently done wrong. He was gone somewhere, and I worried for him already.

Well, one cold, winter night while I lay restless in my upstairs bed there in St. Paul, I heard a strange rustling noise out on the front porch. At first, it was sort of a tapping sound. I was not easily frightened, but the noise was still a little unnerving because it persisted. But, I just laid there listening and waiting for something else to happen.

Suddenly, another noise came again. More raps and louder this time. It was sort of like tapping on glass or scratching and rapping on wood. I sensed something was wrong. This wasn't typical. So, I carefully put on my robe and slippers and quietly went down the stairs watching and listening all the way. Stooping-over in a defensive and semi-crouching position, I gingerly walked across the wide living-room area to the front door in order to investigate. Seeing nothing and hearing nothing more by then, still I cautiously and ever-so-carefully opened the front door and began peering outside.

Even then, I saw little and heard nothing at first. As I stepped all the way out onto the cold, dark porch and stood by the steps leading down to the front walkway, it quickly dawned on me how freezing it was outdoors. But I listened some more and pulling my robe more tightly about me because of the bitter cold and chilled breeze, I continued watching everywhere looking about for some movement. There was nothing but the icy wind.

It was a nasty breeze that night, though, and I remember clearly how it blew right over the porch freezing my nostrils. When I inhaled and sucked-in that burning cold air, my nose, face, and body were numbed. Then when I breathed out, my freezing cold, exhaled breath was turned into smoke.

For a moment, I recall getting somewhat distracted while watching my frozen breath. Suddenly, once again out of the darkness came another noise, but this time it was speech. I heard a faint, whispered calling-out, "Sissssy-Ppppatsy, is that you?"

Well, of course, at first, I was fearfully startled, and I let out a slightly muffled scream while almost leaping out of my pajamas. I mean, it's like when you have all your senses primed, and you are ready to respond to any action with an appropriate reaction, and you still get the creeps scared out of you when something does happen. I suppose, too, that my nerves were so frigid and keen that my startled behavior must have surprised that voice too. If it had been a real prowler, I think I would have scared him away.

Nevertheless, after a brief recovery period, though, I figured out what was probably going on. There was that immediate and crazy, emotional concoction that instantly brewed in my mind. I was suddenly filled with surprise, anticipation, excitement and delight all rushing through my mind simultaneously. Only my brother, Bo, ever called me by that name, *Sissy-Patsy*. He had always used it affectionately toward me when we had lived together before our mom's passing, and I sported its remembrance like a badge of honor in my memories.

It was still so very dark outside, and who knew for sure what was really happening, so to be safe, I quickly responded by returning his call, "Just a minute! I'm going to get Aunt Kate. Wait a minute, and I'll be right back!"

I quickly jumped back inside the house closing the door gently against the fierce, outside freezing gusts of wind which kept-up their steady torment. Racing back across the rug-covered floor, I bounded upstairs two-steps at a time to Aunt Kate's bedroom. Roughly and deliberately loud, I jerked-open her door and rushed into her room calling out softly, but gravely and anxiously, "Aunt Kate! Aunt Kate! Get up! Someone is at the front door! It's my brother! It's Bo! Come on, we have to let him in."

Aunt Kate had been deep asleep and having been so rudely awakened, she wasn't easily buying into her foolish niece's announcement. "Child, it's late," she muttered, "and you were dreaming. Now go back to bed."

Oh, no, I wasn't going away. I was certain of Bo's presence and equally emphatic, "No! Aunt Kate, please, I heard him. Bo's there! It's freezing outside. You've got to come! Please!"

This bantering went back and forth for much too long. Truly, minutes passed, or maybe it was only seconds. I'm not sure, but I remained vigilant and relentless. "Aunt Kate, you've got to hurry," I continued, "I know it's Bo. I'm sure of it. Please help him."

Finally, Aunt Kate begrudgingly got up while mumbling something unintelligibly profane under her breath. Not as hastily as I desired, but even so, she then threw on a heavy robe covering her winter pajamas and stepped into her boot like slippers. Then, Aunt Kate, still mumbling words suggesting frustration, disbelief, and then shocked reactions to the coldness now so noticeable in the house, followed me downstairs to the front door and out onto the porch.

Right away we both immediately could see something, or someone, there in the shadows. Clear over at the end of the porch and curled-up on the big, front-porch swing with a small piece of carpet covering himself for shelter from the cruel cold, was my older brother, Bo. He was exhausted, looked like he was turning blue in the night's dimmed lighting and was no doubt practically freezing from the bitter cold.

With wildly chattering teeth, Bo quickly and briefly informed us of his circumstances. He had been walking for hours trying to find our address that night. By then, Bo was shaking all over. Aunt Kate recognized the danger of hyperthermia for Bo and began moving quickly.

She brought Bo inside and kept him wrapped-up with a heavy quilt that I had hurriedly fetched from the hall closet until he could be put into a warm bath to take his chill away. Then Aunt Kate gave him a cup of hot tea with molasses in it to warm his insides. Afterwards, not wishing to bother him any more with additional questioning, Aunt Kate had me retrieve some more blankets and make a bed for Bo on the front-room couch so that he could try and sleep the rest of the night away.

The next morning, we learned of Bo's status and situation. Sure enough, we found out that he was a runaway from his care home and on his way to Wisconsin. He had been walking for miles and miles during the previous, cold winter day in between countless brief rides all the way from Missouri to St. Paul, Minnesota. Bo had been forced to walk even more once he had finally gotten into city limits and then had to continue walking well into that freezing dead-of-night.

When he finally found the place, Bo explained that he had tried to awaken someone for quite a while with no luck. But finally, well, it was me who really did hear all the actual commotion and went outside to check it out. I had been right all along, after all, and Bo would likely have frozen to death on that porch swing under that dinky piece of carpet had he not been rescued.

After a warm breakfast meal, however, and some brief thanks with hugs and kisses, Bo was gone again to finish his venture. He told us he was heading for a relative's house in Wisconsin near our grandma. I hugged Bo really hard and watched him stride-off down the sidewalk. It was right after he had turned, slipped around a street corner, and had quickly disappeared, that I had a sudden and complete relapse of all my injured emotions: I wasn't allowed to be home, but by then *Bo had been completely tossed from the family, and now he was on his own way trying to survive.*

I felt a deep longing, a wanting, waving over my consciousness. I even felt a little dizzy from the mixed emotions. Oh, how I wanted to also leave just then, to run away and be with Bo. Suddenly, I had wanted once again so desperately to be with one of my very own siblings, my family.

Of course, right away I understood that my tagging-along after Bo would not work out. I knew that I could only be dead-weight for him. So, I did not pursue that sweet but fleeting desire. But Bo's leaving, after such a brief *hello/goodbye*, had left me speechless and filled with a sadness and huge void, an emptiness, inside me. Slowly that hallow, confidential feeling began filling-up with my prayers that softly and ever-so-quietly whispered their urgent cry for mercy and approval. I almost urgently wanted to be back home once again with my remaining brother and sisters, to be loved and love back…

PATRICIA "PATSY" MCCORD

Okay, so now would be a good time to fill-in some gaps, I suppose, and share some background information and explain a little bit of my own, personal history. I guess I should start by explaining that at that time back when I was growing-up with distant aunts, and mostly living elsewhere, I was not told much about my family or siblings by other relatives with whom I lived. Because of that denial of information, I was usually in a state of wonder and worry. Of course the wonder and the anxiety grew as I got older.

I did not know or understand very much of anything that was going on concerning my family members. I'm certain that my aunts who watched over me knew quite a bit of my family's current issues, and especially those that involved me directly or indirectly. Apparently, though, either they did not want to burden me with updates, or they felt as though I did not deserve to know what was going on with my family. They made me feel as though whatever they knew was *none of my business.*

I suppose I could say that because their arrangements with my parents, including my real mom, and later my stepmother, for the most part, I was just a bystander, an ignorant, little meaningless kid. Nevertheless, I did want to know everything that concerned my family, and therefore, me. I eavesdropped on many phone calls listening to one-way, whispered responses trying to learn who was calling and what any recent news may have been about. I didn't even know anyone's phone numbers. Nor was I allowed to make any long-distance calls, anyway. But, no matter what, I still had feelings, plenty of them, and I watched and listened to everything that was happening around me trying to deduce whatever I might.

Here, then, is a brief synopsis of my own emotional state at that time:

I was born in May of 1926, and I was immediately whisked away to live with a distant relative. I was returned home, well, sent to live with my family when I was five- years old. At nine, our mother died, and I was sent away again to live with a different relative. A few years later, I returned to our family under duress until the war started, at which time, I was sent away again. All those times away from my family, I had little news or information about what was happening to them. It became ever so incredibly hurtful and agonizing to my feelings of self-worth.

I suppose in self-defense I should mention, or explain, that while I was living with an aunt at about age eleven or twelve, learning about my family moving to and living in Missouri, for example, didn't come as any big surprise or hurt me that much more. Because of my unknown crimes, or whatever, I wasn't being allowed to be with them at all, ever, let alone Missouri.

Yet, I had learned through various means how during those years without me, my family had moved many times: From St. Paul, Minnesota to Sioux Falls, South Dakota; from there to Fargo, North Dakota; then back to Sioux Falls; and then on to Missouri. One more move on their part without me included with the family, more-or-less, didn't matter much to me anymore. I was becoming calloused to the hurt. However, it was still always just the same question of: "Why?" that bothered me so much.

My aunts, whom I had been forced to live with at various times, never told me anything about my family's moves or recent updates. But, I'd hear about them anyway, maybe by eaves- dropping on phone calls or slipped phrases from private conversations. I used to just get so frustrated because I never got good reasons as to why I was excluded or practically abandoned. I asked myself over-and-over again about what I had done wrong. I asked others, and I prayed for answers to my questions all the time: "What was so wrong with me?" Or, "What had I done to deserve being cast-away?" Or, even the most stressful, "Why did my dad and Edith hate me so much?" I never understood why I deserved such rejection or neglect.

As a child, when my anxiety became most alarming and hurtful, nothing or no one else ever explained anything to me either. One aunt would respond when I'd ask about it, by putting the issue back on me: "Why, Little-Patsy, don't you like living here with me? What's so bad about me?" Another aunt just left the answers, or truth, really hanging-in- the-air with her insensitive responses, "Oh, who knows, Child, but don't worry about it. It's really none of your concern. I'm your family now. Besides, I'm sure they had their reasons."

That last one was a real butt-kicker! "They had their reasons!" I just used to get so frustrated because I never got a reasonable explanation from anyone as to why I had been excluded all those times. I questioned over-and-over in my heart and mind why I was not included in family-matters. It wasn't until years later that I began to understand things a little more clearly. But, nothing or nobody explained anything to me at the time. Later in my life, even my siblings, when pressed by my incessant questioning, were hesitant in their responses, or protective, or whatever, but still never gave any decent answers to me.

Only one time, still as teenagers, did an older sister remark off-handedly to me in frustration after being so pressed by my constant, monotonous and on-going inquiries, "Oh, maybe our dad thinks you were never his child!"

"What?" I queried a bit stunned. Now that response really confused me and temporarily opened the floodgates for more anxiety-ridden questions, "What do you mean? I don't understand. Not his child? What in hell are you talking about? How is that even possible?"

Like I mentioned earlier, I was kind of a naïve child. Yet, it wasn't until after I had given birth to children of my own, and then again even after some of them were practically grown, that I began to recognize or understand the parenting situation or dilemma better. However, as a youngster, and even as a young woman, I never accepted that explanation and always challenged it in my mind.

My siblings never brought the issue up much either, at least not in front of me, except indirectly in conversations about our father's character, behavior, and his own noticeably frequent infidelities… That, or when any of them talked about our mother's burden: Her pressures from child-rearing, from being married to a mean, cruel wife and child-beating husband and his continuous and often long absences only to return so begrudgingly in his typical ill-behavior. I resented that account, though, and I held it against my dad and stepmother for the rest of their lives…

"BO" MCCORD

(Continued)

But that's enough self-pity and side-tracking about me. I was talking about what happened to our *big brother,* Bo, and how our parents, well, dad and stepmother, had managed, finally, to get rid of him. Living at home for a brief period before I had been sent-away once again after our mother's death, I did watch many awful and explosive dealings with our dad toward Bo. After I had been sent away again, and later-on in my life, when I was able to get caught-up on plenty of past and sordid, family details, I learned that once Edith had joined the family, Bo had presumably taken a definite disliking to her.

I don't think that Edith was ever deliberately mean to Bo. On the contrary, it was probably that she just represented an uncompromising ally to our cruel and mean dad. Bo probably thought, *He who is friends with my enemy is also my enemy.* Apparently too, Edith seemed quite willing to reciprocate with her own negative attitude toward Bo. The facts are likely that after having dealt for several years with Bo's continued and progressively deteriorating relationship with Edith, and especially with our dad, the two of them plotted to get rid of Bo. Encouraged and led by Edith's Catholic connections, they arranged to have Bo referred and sent to *Father Flanagan's Boys Home* across-state to the town of Myrtle, Missouri. Bo was sent there due to his *deviant and incorrigible behavior.*

Apparently, as the story goes, Bo had been accused by Edith of stealing something of hers. Shortly thereafter, Bo overheard Edith, while she was angry-as-all-get-up, talking to another person on the phone. She was claiming that she had finally had enough of Bo's insubordination and was going to have him placed in a home. Once Bo heard that eavesdropped news, supposedly, he quickly grabbed a few things, packed them into a loose bag which he slung over his shoulder and immediately ran away. No hugs and kisses. No goodbyes. He just left on-the-spot.

Well, Bo didn't get far before being caught-up-to by local police authorities. Sure enough, though, right after that, Bo was immediately placed and transferred over to *Father Flanagan's Boys Home* in Myrtle. Today, the place is still a very well-known and reputable boy's home called "Master's Ranch Christian Academy," It still receives *wayward boys*, too.

A sort of unique fact back then, however, was that not too long after Bo was sent there, the *home's* name was changed from *Father Flanagan's Boy's Home* to the more recognized and well-known *Boys Town*. The place really became popular after Bo arrived and was even the focus of a film by the same name, <u>Boys Town</u>, in 1938. The movie was a huge success and made the *home* and its priest-director even more well-known after that. Two terrific stars in the film which helped make it successful were the wonderful Mickey Rooney, as an incorrigible youth who was rescued by the great actor, Spencer Tracy, who made the priest a household name by playing *Father Flanagan*.

Sadly, our brother did not experience much character-building there. I am not suggesting that he continued with his argumentative and defensive behavior. I don't know for sure; maybe he did. Unfortunately, though, Bo was still so angry at life and at all his ill-tidings that he remained fairly obstinate. Perhaps, he never really gave the place, or Father Flanagan, much opportunity to work with him. Additionally, Father Flanagan still had a few strict rules to follow at his *Boys Home*, which were difficult for Bo to deal with. One mandate involved an absolute intolerance of alcohol.

Wouldn't you know it, after Bo had been at the home for only a few months, apparently, he got upset over some condition or requirement and rebelled. He snuck out of the boy's dormitory and climbed over the compound's outer fence and ran from the premises in the dead-of-night. Then, still only fourteen, Bo managed to hike into the local town of Myrtle, several miles away, get somebody to buy him some booze and proceed to get drunk-as-a-skunk. That night, while still staggering from his waylaid condition, Bo attempted to sneak back onto the restricted grounds, and naturally, he got caught.

Unfortunately, alcohol abuse was one rule that even the priest, Father Flanagan, would not abide by. Imagine that, a priest not tolerating alcohol. That sounds a little to me like a fish who could not tolerate water. Oh, sorry. Shame on me! But, regardless, Bo had crossed-the-line, and there was no going back. After a brief, investigative hearing, it was determined that there was no viable excuse for Bo's behavior. He had to be used as an example for others. He had to leave.

Anyway, Bo realized that he was about to be tossed out of *Father Flanagan's Boys Home* for "Non-Compliance and Unacceptable Behavior," more-or-less. But even that didn't stop Bo and make him consider and acknowledge his dire circumstances. Once he got word of his pending *expulsion*, Bo took-off again, and that time he didn't get caught. Of course, I doubt that Father Flanagan sent out much of a search-party, considering all. However, looking back, I sort of feel like you've got to give Bo some credit, though.

Still only fourteen years old, Bo managed to run, walk, and hitch-hike all the way from *Boy's Home* there in Myrtle, Missouri clear-up to St. Paul, Minnesota. That was where he and I had our brief, little *chilly interlude* with him freezing on the porch swing at my Aunt Kate's house. And then, he did go on to Hayward, Wisconsin just like he said he would. Once he arrived there, I learned, he looked-up an uncle of ours and convinced him to allow Bo to stay there and live. That was our Uncle John, who was blind, we were all told. We heard that old, blind Uncle John must have felt merciful and decided to help his nephew after he discovered Bo sleeping outside in his car for three freezing nights.

Anyway, we kids used to tease Bo afterwards that Mickey Rooney had played *him* in the movie. Who knows, maybe it was true. Rooney was of a small stature too, so Bo could sort of relate to it. That made him smile for a change, though, and that was an unusually good sign for Bo. Funny thing is, blind ol' Uncle John and his place were somehow able to do what didn't happen at our family's home or even at *Father Flanagan's Boys Home*.

Bo had a lot of emotional repairing to do, and for some God-willing, blessed, or special reason, blind Uncle John just couldn't see any of Bo's faults. He somehow looked past Bo's anger and short-comings and saw deep inside Bo some real potential with the right kind of guidance. Uncle John helped Bo simply by giving him responsibilities and encouragement.

Bo responded positively and began doing really well. Steadily, he even got mentally and physically stronger. Strong enough, I might mention here, that he went on to join the U.S. Army Air Corps, was stationed in Italy and fought during the big war for his country and against the Axis powers. More on that later.

I need to emphasize, in Bo's defense, that our dad and Bo fought, and I mean *fought*, all the time. I remember many of them when I was younger, but those arguments mostly ended-up in tears for Bo. It was mostly because of our dad's contempt for Bo's scrawny, weak, and diseased body. You see, Bo had suffered terribly as a child from rickets disease because of calcium-deprivation and remained thereafter small and weak for his age. Our dad's distain and constant scorn of Bo had forced terrible, emotional upheavals in his psyche.

Our dad continuously referred to Bo as the *runt-of-the-family* which shamed and embarrassed our brother all the time. With his small stature, diseased and bowed legs and weakened body, Bo was ridiculed all the time by our father at home and especially in public. In town, in fact, were places and occasions when our dad would poke fun and laugh at Bo the most. He liked using his son as the brunt of his humor and tasteless jokes about Bo's frail stature in order to amuse other men who were his audience. Our dad would laugh, sneer and mock Bo while Bo was in their presence. Somehow, in some demented way, our dad seemed vindicated when Bo would begin crying and run back home sobbing. Bo was just trying to escape our dad's ridicule and his equally disgusting crowd's deriding mirth.

I can still remember watching and hearing our dad teasing and mocking Bo when I was much younger. It was during that period when I had been brought back home at the age of five to live for the first time with my entire family. It was a deliriously happy time for me, but I can recall Bo crying a lot from our dad's scorning, slapping him all the time, and laughing at him. However, Bo's serious, physical abuse did not occur until later after I had been sent away again at age nine following our mother's death.

I was told later that shortly after I was gone, our dad's torment and beatings of Bo got much worse. For a very long time there at home, I heard tales told years later, that our dad would even deliberately pick-on Bo by physically shoving him around just to get him all riled-up and feisty. Then our dad would counter Bo's anger and innocent, pathetic retaliations by beating him, once again proving to himself over-and-over just how meek and frail and pitiful Bo really was.

As a result of all those years of child-abuse, Bo grew up despising our dad from a very early age. Fact is, Bo's true given name was Roy Jr., of all things, named after our dad. I suppose maybe our dad was embarrassed by little Bo as his own namesake. At an early age, though, Bo began rebelling angrily and vehemently against his given, birth-name choice preferring, and even demanding, to be called by his nickname only. We other kids at home understood his feelings. All of us except for maybe the baby, Jackie-Boy, who was too young to yet understand, sided with Bo. We others all sympathetically and protectively obliged him.

Much of Bo's violent-beating episodes, I would learn about later and after I returned to the family-fold at age thirteen. Even still, when I was young and living at home between ages of five and nine, I personally bared witness to the cruel, verbal attacks, scornful antics, and ridicule from our dad. I never understood them back then, but I remember being mostly fearful for my own predicament. I didn't dare challenge our dad or plead with him to leave Bo alone because in my own anxiety-ridden mind that could potentially mean immediate dismissal of my place there at home too. I do remember praying a lot, though, and crying for Bo's sake.

A few years later when some of us saw Bo again, he told us that he had been grateful to get booted-out of our family-household *prison* and get the opportunity to turn his life around somewhere else, even at Father Flanagan's. It took a couple more difficult turns before Bo's life began shaping-up to the better, though, and I'll talk more about that later. For right now, however, let it suffice to know that Bo finally became more emotionally stable in his life at our Uncle John's place in Wisconsin.

It was there, in fact, in Hayward, Wisconsin, where nobody knew Bo's past. He was effectively able to start-over and begin again. He ate right because Uncle John made him, and Bo's health improved too. None of us knew much about Uncle John except that he was nearly blind from macular degeneration, and he came from our mother's side of the family. Maybe he was lonely and wanted company for himself. Or, maybe he knew all about our dad's temperament, intolerance, and vile dealings with Bo. No matter, for whatever reason he just chose to rescue Bo when providence or circumstances provided an opportunity to do so. Regardless, Uncle John was nice, he helped Bo and it was a good move for our brother.

Bo went on to finish high school there. He was also able to find odd jobs around town to help earn his keep at our uncle's place. A couple years later, though, after our eldest sister Jean had been sent packing and went to live with our grandmother, who also happened to be in Hayward, Wisconsin, Bo would sort of transfer over to live with our grandmother and Jean for a while.

A bit later after Grandma had passed-away, Jean and Bo both moved-in together in Cleveland, Ohio because they had heard about plenty of good-paying jobs available there. Factories were opening-up and producing war goods that could be sent over to our European Allies. The Germs were causing a hell of a racket over there, and lots of supplies were needed by our British friends to fight them. Both Jean and Bo found decent jobs in factories and got situated there.

They even shared an apartment, and that was a catch because they both had very stubborn and independent values. Sort of like oil and water, although I would never dare to insinuate who was what. In fact, after a while, it was actually there in Cleveland where I finally got to see Bo regularly again. It had been a long time since that brief, freezing rescue of Bo that night in St. Paul at Aunt Kate's place a few years earlier. We even had a chance to sort of bond together and get to know each other…

· · · · ·

MARY "SIS" MCCORD

Finally, of course, I can't forget about that other wonderful sibling who was also absent from our home when the war started. It was our big sister, Mary, who was Brother Bo's twin, by-the-way. Both born in 1924, of course, they spent their lives arguing with each other over who came first, or who was the youngest, depending on the situation! Like her predecessors before her, though, once "Sis" *came-of-age,* so to speak, she spoke-out against our dad and Edith once-too-often or had one-too-many insubordinate arguments with them. So, *Sis* too was sent packing.

Her case was a little different, though. By that time, I suppose our dad had gotten even more inflexible with his rules against insubordination in our family's home. That power and control factor seemed to make him even more intolerant and ruthless with his punishments. We kids all talked about him a lot when we were together. That is, except for Jean and Bo. They refused to hear his name spoken. But the rest of us mostly agreed that our dad enjoyed watching us kids dive for cover when he passed to avoid a potential slap. We were walking on-eggshells around him most of the time, and he loved it.

When Sis was sent out, though, that was it! Sis Mary was ordered out of the house on a late evening literally with only a small suitcase in her hand. With a brusque, "Get out!" from our dad, he slammed the front-door closed behind her as she stepped out. The same age as Jean had been when she left home, Sis was seventeen-years old too and kicked-out for her own disciplinary *inauguration.*

Plus, to make it worse, it all happened in the dark of a moonless night. After a really heated argument with our dad, he simply exploded and commanded Sis out of the house. As I recall, it had something to do with Mary simply wanting to go out with friends and stay-out later that night than usual. Well, in a rather cruel and intolerant fashion, our dad decided to give Sis her wish, I suppose. Permanently.

Unlike Bo and Jean, however, Sis was never physically abused by our dad that much. Oh, she got her share of disciplining, as I recall, but usually only with words. Sis was always too pretty to be struck in anger. She looked so stylish and fashionable most of the time. It seemed like Sis's make-up was usually so perfect too. She honestly looked like a real fashion-magazine model or a Hollywood celebrity. Even our dad couldn't strike out at that image.

Nevertheless, words can hurt more than actions sometimes. The real cruelty that our mean father thrust upon our sweet, sister Mary were his vicious and hurtful remarks. He seemed to enjoy hurting Sis's feelings by snidely commenting about her weight-issue. Mary was a little bit large, perhaps, but still beautiful to anyone's eyes. Yet, our dad would poke fun at her whenever he chose just to watch her cringe and suffer. When he got angry, he was even more vile with his ridicule.

"Hey, what happened to you?" he would begin, "I heard you got fired from your job because you kept eating all the doughnuts served at the company meetings. Now look at you."

To make things worse, when Sis finally crossed some imaginary, critical line, she was forced to leave the house, on-the-spot. The rest of us younger kids stood by helpless as could be and crying over our dad's sudden tantrum and decision. Sis was so popular with us kids and with her own friends at school. We all just loved her to pieces and admired her looks and gumption. Yes, it was true that she did have a bit of a heated-Irish, foul mouth on her, and that was what usually got her in trouble in the first place.

In a way, for all three older kids, it was their mouths that got all of them booted. Gee, if they could only have taken their beatings and just kept quiet about it all, everything would have been just peachy! Hah! Not with McCord kids. Our dad may have been mean, cruel and insensitive, but he managed to create some strong, hard-willed, defiant, and aggressive personalities in his children who grew-up that way to oppose him effectively.

Sis, though, was sent away without any help or support from family at all. She was put out-on-the-streets that terribly darkened night and had to find her own way clear from Sioux Falls, South Dakota, in the dead-of-night I must repeat, all the way over to upstate Duluth, Minnesota. Look it up on a map! That was just crazy for a pretty, young woman to have to do at her age and so late at night. Sis made it, however, and that was where she would remain living for a short time with our aunt, Annie...

When we kids finally heard where Sis had gone, it was probably more impressionable to me than any of the others. That was because I had been raised by Aunt Annie from my birth until I was five years old. I knew sweet, Aunt Annie and her home very well. I never knew of any other family until I was old enough to recognize and appreciate visits from other aunts, more sisters of my mother. I was a relatively stable and happy child, but those visits were also the first times of being treated dismissively, like I wasn't there or wanted.

Naturally, that was also the time when I first began questioning everything with the big "Why?" Sis was going to the same place where I had once been kept away from my family. A prisoner of sorts, or a reject or some kind of misfit. Looking back, though, life with Aunt Annie was less of a punishment than it was a refuge. Regardless, I had been kept away and separated deliberately from my siblings while there. It was of no mind or concern to me, however, because I never knew anything different, at least not until I finally met all my sisters and brothers, and my Mom and even Dad...

Therefore, I was happy and relieved that Sis Mary would be there at that quaint, little farmhouse with Aunt Annie, whom I loved. She was a kind, old woman and would be supportive of Sis's needs. And to think that Sis had actually made it there safely, with only a bruised ego, no injuries and lessening degrees of stress seemed like a miracle. We kids shed some tears-of-joy for her, for sure.

Somehow, Sis had managed to remain unscathed from a number of potentially dangerous hitch-hiked car rides to and from bus stations. Fortunately, Sis was not broke. She had survived several late-night, lonely bus terminals and bus-rides paid with earnings she had saved from various jobs that she had worked after school. Of course, Sis admitted later, that she also survived and made it all the way to Aunt Annie's place having spent an exhausting amount of relentless walking.

It was there, however, at dear old Aunt Annie's home on the outskirts of Duluth, Minnesota that Sis managed to finish high school and get a decent-paying office-job in town as a secretary. It was a perfect fit for her too. Sis's beauty and style made the office look good, and Sis really liked those stylish positions of office personnel. That was also where Sis blossomed into the beautiful, articulate, and fashionably fun person that she became.

Of all *places*, too, Sister Jean came from Cleveland to join Mary there in Duluth for a visit. Of all *things*, too, the two of them up and decided to move in together and rent some living-space from a family in town where they could both work and help support each other. Apparently, that went well for a while until they both felt the urge to go to Cleveland and room together with Bo. That was a win-win-win deal. Shared rent and living expenses. Nice.

Of all my family siblings too, it would be Sis who later left Cleveland and rescued me from some unknown and undesirable placement somewhere. In fact, it wasn't too many months later, after the war had started and was already raging across both oceans, that Sis and I would be joining up. That's another fun adventure, and I'll get to it later…

Truth-be-told, though, it wasn't to be for quite some time that all we kids would be united together again. A lot of mishaps and adventures were to take place for all of us. Some crazy times occurred while only two or three of us were living or traveling together. Other wild exploits happened to some of us while completely on our own. But, I still recall fondly those memories of living with each of them. It was always special to me to be with as many of my sisters as I could, and brothers too, when possible. We were always working and struggling toward a time when we could all be reunited together once more. But it sure was a hell-of-a-ride getting there.

If I'm religiously honest about it, maybe one of the good things derived from all those chronic, Catholic church lessons during my *catechismic* (catastrophic-same difference!) up-bringing was all that agitated pressure and forced impressions pressed upon all us children of the *power of prayer*. Oh, how I believed in it. Still do. Prayer was a release of tension and stress for someone. Still is. But, for me it always meant someone to talk to anytime about anything that troubled me.

One-sided conversations, I'll grant you, but it was still a great way for me to dump stress on someone or something else. And it is nice to always have a good listener handy. No matter what I might say to God, or Jesus, or Mary, or any of the saints, I knew I was never being ignored; I was always heard. Plus, it never mattered if I just prayed a little, or if I poured-out my soul while confessing wrong-doings. Whether I was pleading for something I wanted, or not, I always felt better than I had before.

Prayer means *hope*. We pray, and it gives us *hope* that things will get better. *Praying* means *hoping*, and without *hope*, well, that's just about the end-of-the-line for any of us. So, I surely kept right on *praying*, and that kept me *hoping*. Heck, I was *full of hope*.

Oh, Lordy, I can remember all those countless and repetitive silent prayers while kneeling in church or at my bedside. I prayed nearly every night of my youth both at home and especially those years away living with relatives. I can't forget praying the Rosary either. Wow! Talk about repetitive and redundant prayer! "Our Father(s)," "Hail, Mary(s)" and "Holy Mary(s) over and over again as Penance from my Catholic Church confessional visits for my confessed sins in order to receive forgiveness and grace. And, of course, I recall my continuous barrage of personal pleadings in church on most Sundays kneeling and praying for all of us McCord kids to be reunited again… someway…somehow… someday…

However, back to that life-shattering day of December 7th, 1941, and recalling once more those of us still living at home with our dad and Edith, it was all of us youngest children. Each of my brothers and sisters were all unique with their own special interests. I had wonderful experiences with each of them at different times, and we shared some pretty, unique times together. If I'm going to tell about some of those times, I think that I should introduce the rest of the cast, so-to-speak. And really, all my family members deserve to be mentioned here.

To that end, therefore, I want to briefly share a little background of each of my other family members, those key characters in my life, I suppose. I have already talked about my older siblings, so to share a little information about each of the other, younger siblings seems only justified. Let me go down the list chronologically after me…

COLLEEN MCCORD

To be honest, the true, next sibling who came after me was our middle brother, Jerry, who had been two years younger than me. Sadly, though, he had passed-away from unusual circumstances which occurred not long after I had come back home at age five. I'll talk about Jerry later, but right now I want to mention those siblings living there in our home at the time of the beginning of WWII.

Therefore, next after Jerry would be my vivacious younger sister, Colleen, who was four years younger than me. Colleen was born in 1930 and would have been two years younger than our deceased brother, Jerry, at that time. But, by the start of the war for us, she was already a spree and cheerful eleven-year old. Talk about industrious too. That girl loved to go around the neighborhood helping out and finding ways to earn money. At first, she worked to have spending money; then she worked to help support our stepmother's income. Talk about hardworking.

Right now, I can even visualize our living-room back then again with us kids in it… Colleen was there and flopped out and spread across our living room sofa reading some movie star magazine. She was enthralled with movie stars and such and was always reading magazines about Hollywood, movies, fashion, and design. Colleen was really into it too. She knew all kinds of information about all the actors and actresses and what was going on in their lives.

She loved going to movies, too, whenever we could afford it, or we managed to sneak in some way. She was so happy watching all her favorite movie stars on the big screen. She used to get so giddy just hearing any news about who was in what new film. Colleen practically became hysterical with excitement whenever she got any used, hand-me-down magazines sent to her by our older sister, *Sis* Mary. I used to think Colleen was always a bit overdramatic, but that was probably Hollywood's influence, ha, ha! But she and Sis both shared a common bond with their mutual pleasures from the *Four M's*: Music, models, make-up, and movie stars.

By the time of this story's beginning, unfortunately, Sis was already gone and moved from Aunt Annie's in Duluth, to living with our grandma. But for Colleen and Sis, it didn't matter. They stayed close through occasional phone calls and with letters and such from the postal service. Colleen would practically start hyperventilating whenever a package of second-hand magazines arrived for her in the mail from Sis. Colleen loved and appreciated them so much. With big, wide grins of astonishment and pleasure or open-mouthed gaping at some shocking Hollywood scandal, Colleen used to eagerly devour every page ravenously from every periodical.

I still remember that when Colleen and Sis were together, they could gossip for hours-on-end about the latest news of movies and stars and starlets' lives. Colleen adored Sis, and they both seemed to shine that much more brightly whenever in contact with each other. I suppose their mutual love of all-things-Hollywood and its bonding effect just seemed to stoke each other's flames. It was nice…

LORRAINE JANNETTE "JANN" MCCORD

Next in line among our younger set was sister, Jann, short for Lorraine Jannette. Little Jannie was born in 1932, so at the war's beginning, for US involvement anyway, she would have been nine years old and in fourth grade. Jann was another reader among us remaining kids, and her love for books made us both form a common bond. She and I became really close, and I adored helping take care of her when she came home from the hospital with Mom. Colleen was a baby too, so I got to be a big help caring for both of them and bonding with them. Later, when I returned home at thirteen-years of age, we renewed the bonds we had made earlier.

I especially loved talking with Jann and helping her with schoolwork. Being older and reading more technical books for my grades helped me to share a lot of information that Jann was really interested in. With school we both shared many common interests. I enjoyed offering-up tidbits of something I had learned in school which may have embellished something she was studying. No matter. Jann was eager to listen and hear and read about anything new and special in the world. She just loved learning.

And Jann loved sharing anything that she had recently learned too. She enjoyed reading about all sorts of amazing places on Earth and about human conditions everywhere. She would become very serious whenever she had an opportunity to point out some unusual, significant, or unique feature about our planet or its inhabitants. A natural, social-sciences teacher, I think. In fact, I remember that on that very same Sunday we are now discussing, Jann had been studying a map of some sort. Yes, it was a world map, now that I recall, and that map helped us a little later on that afternoon to partly visualize what had happened. Most importantly, we used her map to find the Hawaiian Islands and try to make more sense of what was happening.

Just like me, though, Jann loved history and geography. Reading about people and places of long-ago ages and their magnificence, turmoil and contributions to social growth and learning would get her all excited. Jann was only nine, but she loved sharing little historical and geographical facts with anyone who would listen. She was always eager to point out something new and interesting to others, especially me. Yes, now that I recall, it sure *was* a world map, and she had been working on a school project about China on that horrible day in December.

We both relished looking at picture books and travelogues of faraway places and talking about seeing all of them together someday. We even promised each other that when we were both all grown-up, we would travel together too. We agreed to go with one another someday and visit some of those amazing historical sites, fascinating cities, and cultural places like the Louvre Museum in Paris, and such. Funny how life turns out because in so many ways and times, we did just that. But those are other fun, exasperating but memorable stories for another time…

JOSEPH "JACKIE-BOY" MCCORD

F inally, then, to round off our family-line, came little Jack, our baby brother. Born in 1934, he was seven years old at the war's start. What is so clear to recall of *Jackie-boy*, our nickname for him, was his noise factor. Oh, my goodness, I can remember how loud he used to be. He always liked playing with his little, wooden toy soldiers, or cowboys and Indians, or something. Jackie-boy, we always called him, used to run all over the house, and outside when weather permitted, screaming, and shouting with vivid war cries while holding up his toy airplanes high in the air bombing and blasting his imaginary enemies to Tim-Buk-To. It was that, or else he was *yaw hootin'* all over the place chasing and charging fantasy, Indian encampments and madly shooting them down with his tiny, heroic, wooden cavalry soldiers. Both were equally satisfying for that child's dreamy victories.

However, Jackie-boy seemed to just relish making violently loud noises during his fiercely imagined battles. He loved westerns too, and he ever-so-proudly enjoyed portraying and displaying his drop-dead-serious, mental infatuations with South Dakota-type cowboys. Anything heroic and boisterous and he was into it. *Fourth of July Parades* and renditions of the "Star-Spangled Banner" used to get him so excited that he always beamed with delight and joy.

Our little brother was fun to watch, sometimes, as he fiercely, courageously, and victoriously charged about the house whooping, and whopping and hollering to his glee's content. However, his noise levels were all too often exasperating, to say the least. Quietness didn't seem to be a condition that he understood or believed in. The only one who could quiet him down was our dad. One growling command and Jackie-Boy was instantly transformed into a meek, silent mouse…

I suppose that fortunately for us others, at that certain time when we youngest ones were all gathered together in our living room on that dreadful December day, young Jackie-boy surprised us all by playing mutely, for once in his life, with his little toy caricatures as he organized and arranged them in peculiar fantasy orders. Needless to say, certainly none of us girls encouraged him into acting out any more of his war-play games that particular time. That would have laid waste to our peaceful moments of relaxation and showered us instead with his typical sheer chaos leaving us in total exasperation. Little did we realize, at the time, however, that our own dad would attempt the same thing just a little later that very same day.

Like I said, though, we kids were all spread about the room. We were all quietly playing, reading, relaxing, studying, and just enjoying ourselves as we paid attention to our individual activities, all-the-while appreciating the warmth of being inside. For me, though, it was probably even more special. By then, I had still only been back at home for less than a couple years. I was still kind of a new homebody. It was a special feeling for me to be home once again and living with just the remainder of my partial family again.

That issue, my *come-and-go anxiety*, constantly forced me to examine and appreciate those special moments when I was home and sharing time with my family. It caused me to pay close attention to details and absorb every day's most modest and typical activities with gratefulness. Yet, I was always so timidly anxious dealing with family members, especially my dad and stepmother.

I was fearful of conflicts with my siblings because I would be scorned and punished by my parents, and any arguments with them likely meant immediately being vanquished. Talk about insecurity. I now know and understand that my self-doubt was because of subconscious stress that I felt most of the time. The anxiety was there even when I was relatively happy because I always remained astute and focused on conditions around me lest the pleasing status, I felt, might abruptly end…

MARIE HELMS MCCORD

Even still, that period in my life was unique and memorable for me. Only a couple years before the Pearl Harbor bombing, I had been allowed to return back home. It had been one of those special, brief stretches in my life when I was included among family members. Well, all of us younger ones had been there, anyway. Of course, there were two other absent but important family members, besides Bo and Jean and Sis, who were no longer with us either. As I mentioned earlier, one was our younger brother, Jerry; the other, however, was our beloved mother, Marie.

Our real mother, Marie, had died six years earlier in 1935 due to complications from a horrid and unprofessional abortion. At the time, abortions were considered sacrilegious, and illegal, therefore, few of our family spoke the truth about it, but rather said her passing was due to an unfortunate miscarriage. In either case, the fact remaining was that our mother bled to death, hemorrhaging from a *kitchen-table abortion*. But that's not what I'm talking about right now. The hurtful point to me was that at the tender age of nine-years old, and right after our mom's funeral while the whole family was in dreadful mourning, I was sent away again immediately.

From five-years of age on, I had already been carrying around inside me an uneasy feeling. I had already heard vague stories of having been sent to live with my aunt Annie right after my birth. That became more confounding to me as I grew. Yet, one *uneasy* sensation was that perhaps Aunt Annie had finally had enough of me and wanted to get rid of me too. The other more pleasing sensation was that possibly Mom had been the sole reason I was being brought back to the family in the first place. I can remember that once I arrived back home at age five-years, how she used to hug me so tightly all-the-time and tell me how happy she was that I was back home with her. I sure never got that welcoming from our dad…ever. He was always very stand-offish to me, like I was non-existent or unworthy of his attention.

But giving credit-where-credit-is-due, eventually, he was the one who had actually come personally to get me and bring me back. I always appreciated that fact, although my head was sort of spinning over my new circumstances. And there were plenty of new changes all around to try and absorb. To start with, by that time, my family was then living in Fargo, North Dakota. So, that was where I was taken to join them, and that is where this part of my story begins.

Of course, I cannot forget or deny how thrilled my mother and older siblings were that I had been returned too. They all lauded attention over me practically smothering me with delight. Little-*Patsy* was home. I was told by the elder siblings that they had vague recollections of my birth and of me coming home from the hospital with Mother. But, it had been such a brief period from that point until quick arrangements were made to send me away. They were happy to see me, though. No doubt, however, and my elder siblings confirmed the fact, my return had been due to Mother's endless pressure on our dad to finally come and get me from Aunt Annie's home in Minnesota and bring me back home where I belonged…

That next time I was forced out from the family was four years later right after Mom's death in 1935. It had been a relatively easy endeavor at that time, for my dad at least. A year earlier, our family had already moved back to St. Paul for another new job-assignment for our dad. With our mother's passing, my dad quickly and simply shipped me across town to our Aunt Kate's, our mother's sister, who still lived right there in St. Paul.

But here comes the kicker: If my being abruptly sent away was not sudden and shocking enough for me, without any further warnings or adieus, our dad grabbed all the other kids, minus me, of course, and moved to St. Cloud, Minnesota, about a hundred miles to the north. That's where our dad rented a new family home, set up household and hired a housekeeper/child-care person to watch over the others while he traveled away for his new airport job.

Naturally, you might imagine how my head and emotions were practically spinning out-of-control. I became practically delirious crying and trying to deal with understanding all those recent, upheaval-type changes: Mom had suddenly died for some unknown reason, without any warning and was gone; I had been immediately sent away to live with an unfriendly Aunt Kate and her mean daughter, my cousin; our dad moved himself and all my sisters and brothers up to St. Cloud supposedly because he had a new airport job, all but vanishing from me again; and then he had hired some new caretaker to watch over all the other children… all except for me.

For inexorable reasons, I had been dismissed, sent away, dropped like a bad-habit, simply gotten rid-of like a non-belonged, and never even given courteous or remotest explanations as to *why*. Talk about feeling unwanted. I had been sent away… and abandoned again… But, why?

STEPMOTHER EDITH MCCORD

However, for right now it's important to mention yet another integral member of our present family at that time. She was the last member to join our family, our stepmother, Edith, who deserves attention. Not long after that whole charade of being deposited with another aunt and then abandoned again, came the real kickers which obliterated my feelings. I was stunned yet again, and my feelings crushed once more, when I heard the next latest news: Less than six-months after my dad and siblings' disappearance, our dad managed to find another woman who would marry him. So, they married, and then the whole bunch of them moved to Sioux Falls, South Dakota without so much as a "Howdy-do, or adios, ninita (little girl)! Apparently, my dad was chasing yet another new, airport job and I wasn't considered family material.

But that new woman had agreed to take on the formidable task and challenge of accepting and raising his seven children as her own. Truth is, I heard and learned years later, that our dad had actually seriously misled her about the home front. With me gone, he had told his fiancé that there were supposedly only three little ones at home. He was probably already making plans to rid the house of the oldest ones. So, apparently, he lied.

Actually, that would have been six children because I wasn't around. Nevertheless, it was her job, however, to raise all those other new stepchildren and do so especially during his long absences away either chasing new jobs or chasing skirts. Our dad had earned quite a reputation as a womanizer. Who knew for sure? And believe me, our dad was seldom around because of his constant search for work. Over time, I developed a theory about that too. I think he was continuously forced out, relieved of duties, or fired because after a while, nobody at his jobsite could stand him due to his braggadocio behavior or contentiousness.

Anyway, later in my life while looking back and reflecting upon those circumstances, I learned to recognize and appreciate how Edith must have really been another *jewel-in-a-rock-pile.* How our dad ever found her and managed to get her to accept his child-rearing situation is beyond me. He really lucked out. Or else, he lied, married her, and then showed her the reality of the circumstances.

Considering it all, though, she must have had a good heart and one as big as all outdoors. That, or she was incredibly desperate to marry anyone under any circumstances. However, like our real mother, Edith was also a very devout Catholic, and therein lay a curious but grievous difference between them. Whereas our mother was a kind, sweet and gentle Catholic, Edith was a hard-core, old-school, harsh-speaking, and no-nonsense Catholic.

Of course, I never even got to meet Edith until I returned home again at age thirteen. My family had already been all over the map by then, but they just happened to be back in Sioux Falls, SD again by that juncture. Meeting her, though, and getting to know her the first time, felt sort of weird to me back then. We were both new to each other, but she had the upper hand on me because she had already become established as the new *homemaker.* However, supposedly reared and cut-from-similar-(Catholic textile) cloths, our mother and stepmother were from totally different *Catholic* fabrics.

Where *Mom Marie* was made from silk, *Edith* came from canvas. It was beauty, softness, shine, and close-knit comfort from one compared to hardness, coarseness, crudeness, and practicality from the other. Where Mother smiled so often for us children's benefit, was so soft-spoken yet firm while delivering her scriptural wisdoms while getting us all to do our chores and having us attend church every Sunday, *Edith* carried a perpetual frown on her face, was unbendingly strict about her church attendance demands and was harshly stern with her chronic denouncements of sinful behavior. I just presumed that they both had experienced very different catechism experiences, teachers, or priests, and nuns, no doubt. Probably their own upbringings were very different too. Who knew for sure. Go figure.

But they were both very different with how they dealt with us kids. Maybe our real Mom got us to move forward by encouraging us to follow her gentle example and by utilizing patient coaxing and encouragement. On-the-other-hand, our inexperienced, newer, and non-related stepmom only understood strict obedience for children's guidelines. Edith demanded we move forward by using her scriptural warnings punctuated with pushes and shoves. Of course, it didn't help the actual situations much either that our mom was ten feet tall, it seemed, and Edith was only about five-foot in her high-heeled boots.

Come-to-think-of-it, identifying those differences between Edith and our mother may have explained why there was so much conflict between her and us older ones. Jean, Bo, Sis, and me all had distinct and pleasing memories of our blood-mother, Marie. After her death, it was so abrupt to have Edith, a virtual stranger, suddenly thrust upon our family using her new, rough, and crude style of motherly care and attention.

It was the only way Edith knew, and yet it was so foreign and unacceptable to us. Plus, there was the obvious fact that we older brew already towered over Edith in stature. When making demands upon us, maybe it appeared awkward and highly defensive to Edith. Perhaps, the sheer necessity for her to stare straight-up at us while shaking her finger and spewing scriptural taunts was challenging and difficult to her wary being.

Maybe we older kids subconsciously sensed some sort of misguided, *heightened*, and foreboding power and superiority over that meek, smaller, weaker, and insensitive *Mom* replacement. Edith's only grasp and understanding of child-rearing for any age was through disciplinary action and demands. Her only tools or weapons to apply for childcare were her continual onslaught of Biblical admonitions and our local priest's supportive rebukes. The defiant, older kids only had to deal with those priests once-a-week during confession just prior to Sunday mass, or briefly afterwards, when they were called upon by a priest addressing our stepmother's grievances.

Those kids serious and most critical weapon against Edith, on-the-other-hand, was *ignorance*; they ignored her. Ignoring someone, in itself, is very powerful stuff. It does more damage to relationships than even verbal conflict. With *words,* we know where another stands, and we can begin resolutions to change, modify or eradicate differences. With *silence,* or *ignoring* another as though they did not exist, however, then a poor issue may only get worse.

I suppose there was some genuine solace and reward for Edith derived from her child-care efforts. They most surely would have come from her care of the youngsters: Colleen, Jann, and Jackie-Boy. They had all been so young at Mom's death that they fairly quickly and comfortably merged and adapted into an acceptance-mode of Edith. Early on, they all even began referring to her as "Mom." Sadly, the defiance to acceptance range amongst all us kids' behavior and dealings with Edith varied so much and must have seemed obvious to outsiders. Between the youngest and the oldest of us McCord brew ranged a wide berth of acceptance and tolerance to denial and rebuke...

Later as an adult, and while considering Edith's situation way back then, I realized how difficult it must have been for her. So often, incidents must have been very hurtful, challenging, and regrettable to our stepmother. Though never bonding with Edith as a youngster or even as a young adult, eventually I grew to understand, respect, and appreciate her awkward, traumatic, and challenging situations. Perhaps, Edith even saw her *mother-replacement* duties as a Godly *mission-in-life* and bore the brunt of her Christian burden with self-sacrifice and martyrdom.

Nevertheless, Edith's stout, and hard-core Catholicism helped her survive under those formidable circumstances, as did all we older, more obstinate McCord kids. Even though Edith and the youngest ones continued their mutually satisfying relationship and acceptance with Edith's role in their lives, I believe now that considering us older children, only I grew-up to truly recognize and fully appreciate Edith so much more. That would circumstantially occur years later, after I had produced my own brew of children. What's that line about *not judging another until you have walked a mile in their moccasins*?

Regrettably, however, the three oldest McCord kids were not very obliging to Edith while sharing the same household. Their defiance of her wishes was unfortunately at the root of so many problems and domestic conflicts. Edith had been unaccepted by the oldest kids and considered as a trespasser and an unknown, both unfit and an unworthy quantity. It had been bad enough having the old man constantly badgering and yelling and viciously smacking everyone around demanding respect with unflinching obedience. It was another thing having a new "mother" telling us what to do and all-the-time warning us of damnation's consequences if we disobeyed or misbehaved.

For a couple years there in Sioux Falls, South Dakota, where I had awkwardly returned home again with my family at age thirteen, I had my first experiences of Edith's care. During the brief period preceding that foreboding December 7th, I had observed a constant state-of-war within our own household. The range of acceptance of Edith and unquestioning obedience to her will from us McCord kids varied from zero to 100 percent. That fact was also very obvious amongst us children too.

It was understandable how the youngest three, Colleen, Jann and Jackie-boy had succumbed years earlier to acceptance of our stepmother. Afterall, they were the neediest of us kids and most wanting of a motherhood role in their lives. We older children, however, always referred to our stepmom only by her first name, Edith. That was it. She was considered little more than just an interloper, a stranger, in fact. The younger ones were content and happy to call her *Mom*; they always did what Edith told them to do without provocation, dispute, or arguments.

Ha! That was hardly the same result from us older, defiant ones. Certainly, disapproval showed from us elder children. But like I mentioned before, the all-out rebellion was not from me, though. I was too unsure of myself and scared to disobey. By that time of my re-arrival, Bo was already gone because of his disobedience. Jean and Sis were constantly battling with Edith and our dad over chores or wants and needs or anything and everything.

As a result, they both had received continual castigation, and Jean often received severe punishment from our dad. Both were constantly on slippery slopes for their defiant and argumentative behavior. In time, as I explained earlier, they also, one-after-the-other, were forced-out of our home once they came of age… *Coming of age* probably meant to our dad, "Old enough to walk on their own!"

But, there you have it. That's some background information telling about all the family members who were active-participants on-and-off, anyway. Well, that is except for me… and our dad, of course…

ON THE FARM

Duluth, Minnesota

So, now, if it's my turn for a telling, then it just becomes a bit more complicated and sensitive, I suppose. Heck, what can I say? I was kind of a weird case. I never understood much of my feelings or actions during my growing-up years. It seemed like I was always in a state-of-anxiety, upset over something or confused about myself most of the time.

For one thing, I was *stuck-in-the-middle* of us kids' line and having been a late-arrival to the family-mix, I became sort of wishy-washy and overly concerned about family matters. I loved being back home, but I feared the worst for myself for most occasions most of the time. If I didn't know what was happening, I worried. If I didn't understand, even worse. I continuously challenged my awareness with the same question: What was *this* activity, or situation or circumstance going to mean, or what might it do, to me?

I began feeling like a *throw-away ragdoll* that didn't belong to anybody in particular, but everyone could just sort of toss it around from time-to-time and entertain themselves with it for a while. When they became bored with the doll, they just left it alone, tossed it into a corner somewhere or left it for someone else to deal with. Nobody, however, ever considered where or with which person that scrawny ragdoll preferred to be.

I mean, I grew-up from infancy to childhood with Aunt Annie thinking that with her was where I was supposed to be. It was all I knew. Then suddenly, a big, giant man showed up all alone at our farmhouse and took me away with him. I mean I was kind of scared but excited, at the same time, to hear that I was finally going to meet all my brothers and sisters and my own actual, for real *Mother*. *Outside family* were people that I had only just recently begun thinking and wondering about, but it was still a significant period as I could remember. And, apparently, those *other* family members were all excited and anxious and waiting to see me too, so I was told.

I was darn curious, however, and so right away, the *anxieties* began developing. I wondered about what was happening and why. Who was this man whom Aunt Annie had introduced to me as *the man who would take me home with him to meet my mother and other family members?*

"Patricia, dear," I still remember Aunt Annie beginning, "I have some exciting news for you! Remember how I told you about your mother, and all your brothers and sisters and how they lived far, far away? Well, this man is going to take you back to his home, and you are going to go and live with him, and your mom and all your brothers and sisters. Go pack your things!"

Auntie's voice sounded gentle and kindly, yet firm but reassuring. I think I even sensed a little bit of a quiver in her voice. She sounded happy, but sad, at the same time.

Anyway, I was confounded and utterly confused. I thought to myself, "Huh? What do you mean? Why am I going anywhere? I don't want to go. Aren't you coming too, Auntie? What do you mean '*Go away* and live somewhere else...' What's a family?"

Lots of questions began bursting inside my head. I was so bewildered from everything happening so fast that I just sort of kept quiet, let the surge of questions continue to swell and build-up in my mind and just went along with things having full trust in Aunt Annie's judgement. Afterall, Aunt Annie was everything to me; she was my breakfast, lunch, and dinner, and security blanket. She was the one who tucked-me-in each night. I never knew anybody else. But, whatever was happening to me now must be alright because Aunt Annie said it was. She had always taken care of me before, and I had never known anything better or different...

You see, I had been sent away at birth, and naturally, never knew or understood anything from my past. It was just me and Aunt Annie together up there in her little farmhouse just on the outskirts of our small town of Duluth, Minnesota. It was all I knew. Everything that I did had evolved around her: Playing with my rag dolls that she had given me; helping Aunt Annie cook our meals and clean our house; running outside to play in the front yard and showing-off to Aunt Annie all my skills of tree-climbing; and sometimes, even exploring the inside of the big old, dilapidated barn out back when Aunt Annie sent me to collect chicken eggs from the coop.

Right next to the old, beat-up, worn, red-painted barn and leaning up against its dark stained and weathered-board siding was our chicken coop. Aunt Annie kept quite a few chickens in there too. For as long as I could remember, it had been my job to take care of them. I recall really enjoying that part of my childhood with Aunt Annie. Those chickens were my job and my responsibility. I had to go out there and clean-up and change their water container with fresh, clean water from the old, hand-pump. Then I had to throw all the chickens enclosed in the penned-up coop fresh chicken-scratch for food and finally, gather-up all the fresh eggs I could find for our meals.

I also had to rake and scrape-up all the poop that those filthy chickens spread everywhere all the time. That was a nasty job, but I did it. I just remember often thinking how disgusting it was that chickens would eat, sleep, lay eggs, and poop in the very same areas. Yuck! At least they had nice, soft straw-beds raised-up above the crappy ground for them to sleep-in and lay their eggs.

Of course, old Gizzard ruled the roost. He was the one-and-only rooster that Aunt Annie kept around. He was the absolute king, and he let everybody know it every single morning just as daybreak came. Old Gizzard spent every day just clucking and pecking and harassing the females while he dug and scratched for some wayward, missing seeds he might discover.

We would have a few male chicks once in a while too. Aunt Annie saw to it that some hens were allowed to keep their eggs and just sit on them all-the-time. After any eggs hatched and there were a bunch of chicks, it was fun to watch them all grow-up bigger. However, once any were big enough to be recognized as male roosters, well then, they just disappeared.

Old Gizzard was the one who really singled them out from the females. He would start attacking some of the young chickens for no good reason.

Aunt Annie would say right then and there that there would be no fighting in her coop. Right away, Auntie decided, and the young roosters were removed.

I remember Aunt Annie explaining to me what really happened to those young roosters, and then the day that she finally showed me:

ROOSTER ROASTING 101

First thing was starting to boil a big pot of water. While the water was heating-up, Aunt Annie put on a pair of flexible, water-proof gloves and then took a blanket along with her inside the chicken-coop. She'd sort of scare and separate one of the young males into a corner of the coop. Then she'd toss the blanket over the top of it. Carefully scooping-up the blanket, she would have trapped a young rooster in her arms. Next, she would reach underneath the blanket and grab the young rooster-in-making by its legs.

Next stage was Auntie hauling the bird-by its legs over to a big, 'ol smooth-cut piece of log stump laying on its face with an ax buried in it. If she hadn't done so already while walking the bird to the log, Aunt Annie would then swing the chicken round-and-round several times in small arcs through the air to make the bird dizzy and motionless. Then, without any fanfare at all, and very quickly to boot, Aunt Annie would lay the rooster's upper-body, neck, and head straightaway on that log stump, chopping-block. Holding the chicken there firmly with her left hand, Auntie would grab the ax with her other hand, and with a swift, dead-on aim, she chopped that bird's head right off its neck.

For the next minute, or so, it was kind of hilarious once Aunt Annie let go of the chicken's legs. She would sort of toss that headless bird away from us and let it bounce on the ground. Then that crazy chicken- which didn't even know it was dead yet- would run, and flop, and twist, and turn all around the backyard crashing into anything in its path. I swore that it looked like that headless chicken was running all over the place in search of its lost skull. Finally, though, it would finish and lie still mostly motionless except for a little bit of quivering.

Then came the final stage of preparing that chicken. Aunt Annie went back inside the house and retrieved the big pot of heating water, which had by then gained just the right temperature: pretty hot, but not nearly boiling. She carried the pot outside and set it down right on the very same "killing-block." Aunt Annie's next step, and a very unceremonious one, was fetching the dead chicken and plopping it straight-away into the hot pot of water. She then began using a stick or something to hold the chicken down under the water letting the bird soak while the water absorbed through its feathers.

Finally, Aunt Annie would grab the bird's legs again using the pair of gloves she had initially put-on, lift it from the pan of hot water and shake the water from it. Then, while Auntie held the bird so the feathers lay toward her, she would rapidly start plucking away, and the feathers were removed easily and with little trouble.

Last came the cleaning-up part. Auntie would rinse the chicken, gut it, clean it, and then cut it all-up into appropriate pieces, or leave it whole. And finally, boiled, baked, or fried, dinner was served. Or, my favorite was, roasted cockerel!

That was my whole life: The farm and once every week or so, a short trip into town for basics shopping. That was it. On those go-to-town occasions, Aunt Annie would load me up into her old, beat-up, rusted-out, black-Ford truck, and we'd putter all the way into town spitting smoke and fumes out the tailpipes and bouncing along the pot-holed road which led up to the main highway into town. Yes, those are fond memories of times with Aunt Annie that were special for me. They formed a strong bond between us.

I never forgot her, and it was always doing those little things with her like entertaining occasional guests and visiting and shopping sprees into town that made her even more special to me. It was like she was my conduit to the outside-world, and I let everybody I met know about it. It was always a big deal to go into town with Aunt Annie for me. I have to chuckle just recalling how I loved sticking half my body out the truck's passenger window and watch whatever was coming at us with the strong breeze blowing on my face. Such childish fun!

We would drive into the outskirts of Duluth to the big grocery-hardware store off the main highway, and not too far away, and do Auntie's shopping for basic staples. I remember getting all excited each and every time seeing and watching all those curious people in the stores. Some even became familiar to me, but that didn't matter. I was fearless and loved talking to others and making friends with anybody and everybody, no matter who.

I'd see somebody inside the grocery/hardware store and walk right up to them without warning and begin mingling. I'd start announcing things about myself, and I guess initiating the first type of net-working: Making new contacts, I suppose.

"Hi, my name is Patricia," I'd start off, "and I am helping my auntie go shopping for food and stuff. I'm her big helper. What's your name? What are you getting? Have you got any nieces too? I'm five-years old, and I'm gonna go to school real soon."

Typical precocious child, but certainly fearless and friendly. I imagine that I caused a few folks to be delightfully overwhelmed with my curiosities, questions, and precocity. Honestly, I don't really remember much about their answers, but I do recall getting excited going into town, nevertheless, to see any new or unusual sights or people. At an early age, therefore, I believe I began developing my personality into a real *people-type* character. Since all I knew was Aunt Annie and the farm, well, just about anything or anyone else could get my attention and excitement all captivated and bursting with curiosity.

To be honest, though, there were a couple of visitors from time-to-time to the farm that I recall meeting that were more unpleasant and awkward than they were exciting. Oh, I was curious as all get-up at first about them too, but they were the most confounding types and left me more confused than clear.

The first time I remember visitors coming, I was introduced to them as Aunt Mary, Aunt Liz and Aunt Kate who had all came visiting for overnight all from the big city of St. Paul. I retained a few vague memories each visit until I was fairly clear on who they all were. They were all very friendly and hugged and kissed Aunt Annie also calling her, "Auntie," rather than by name. I believe that they were likely some of the ones that Auntie used to talk to regularly on the house phone. I was told also that they were my mother's sisters too. That sounded important, I supposed, so I was always extra congenial to them.

When it came to me, though, they were all kind of stand-offish. "Hello child," they'd say. "How do you do, little girl?"

Well, usually that was all it would take for me to go into a minute-by-minute description of whatever was on my mind at the time including a wide-assortment of questions regarding them too.

"I do real good," I'd begin with a quick start. "I'm four (and on another, later occasion, five), and I like climbing trees. And I help Auntie a lot,… and I'm a big girl,… and I'm going to go to school real soon…" I think I might have talked non-stop if they didn't shut me up. New faces to practice my *networking skills* on, I suppose.

And I had plenty of questions for them too when they came visiting. 'Who are you? What's your name? Where do you live? Do you go to the same store we do for milk and stuff? St. Paul? Where's that? Have you seen our chickens before? Wanna go see them now? Wanna climb our tree with me?"

I suppose that I may have seemed a bit overbearing at that age. Or, maybe folks just thought of me as just a tad bit overwhelming. But I had questions, lots of them, for anybody who'd stand there and listen, and I loved company of newfound friends.

I got to know our mailman too when he occasionally stopped to deliver a letter or a package. He was an elderly and friendly man named Mr. Fletcher. He was nice whenever he brought something to my auntie. I used to always greet him outside, if weather permitted, and ask him the same kind of questions each time with persistence and a continuously inquisitive mind.

"Hey, hello there, Mr. Fletcher," I almost always started off. "Where're you going? What you got with you today? Want to watch me climb that tree? I can get up there real fast. Can I go along with you if my auntie says it's okay? I can help you carry stuff and give it away for you."

He'd usually just laugh and shake his head while teasing, "My-my-my, young lady. You sure do have a lot of questions! You gonna grow-up and be a cop someday, or work for the government? Or, maybe an adventurer to learn all sorts of new things. I think you should work in a library, maybe, where you can find answers to anything."

Well, I didn't know what he meant at that age, of course. I mean, what was a *library* to an unschooled five-year old? But Mr. Fletcher was always very friendly, and fact is, he was probably the first person I was going to miss after I was gone. Well, I mean after Aunt Annie, of course. *He* was the first person *outside*, that is, that I would miss on a daily basis. That point surely included those nieces of my auntie: Kate, Liz, and Mary. They were all sort of uppity to me, though, and never paid me much attention. It was like I had *cooties,* or something, to them.

I'd stare at them, and they'd just swoosh me away like a fly. "Okay, child, now go away and let the big people visit," was how they'd get rid of me. "We have important things to share with each other, and it's not for your ears."

Well, I had important things to do too, like climbing trees. And so, I did, but with a little hurt inside and disappointment and confusion. Who were they really, and why were they here?

Later on, four years, to be exact, I would get to know all of them much more closely and especially one of them, my aunt Kate, who still lived in St. Paul, Minnesota. I grew to realize, years later, that the whole swarm of them, except Aunt Annie, were nothing but a bunch of dawdling gossipers who thrilled at sharing secrets with co-conspirators, but never with the one who was the subject of their nosey chattering.

Those attitudes between us really discouraged any real bonding for any of us. Sure, I was always civil toward any of them, of course. I was even polite and courteous, during brief, future meetings, but my relationships with any of them never went much further than that. But way back at that farm in Duluth when I can remember being four or five-years of age and living with the only real person in my life, my otherwise mother, Aunt Annie, I never developed many feelings for anyone else, let alone those other aunts. Besides, I had only met or seen any of them a few times each in my whole life, anyway, that I can recall.

Even still, their seemingly rude visits to Aunt Annie's farm back then were a little perplexing for a friendly, outgoing five-year old child. For one thing, no matter what, I was still always excited at new visitors coming to our home. It was always a pleasing chance to talk to someone new. I loved hearing about anything and everything about them and about wherever they came.

Those aunts' visits, however, were quite a twist in my experiences, you might imagine, compared with other folks in town, or nice old Mr. Fletcher. All of Aunt Annie's *nieces*, in turn, practically snuffed me out of their way while appearing, well, kind of annoyed with me. All my questions, more than anything, apparently, really bothered them. They'd respond with comments like, "What? Well, I never... That's nice, child. Why don't you go and play outside while I talk to my aunt, your *caretaker?*" ...

Caretaker? What's a *caretaker*? Yeah, so whatever. Aunt Annie did *take care* of me, so I supposed that was just another name for *my auntie*.

Anyway, back to the strangest visit of all: A man who had arrived just so he could take me away from everything I knew and cherished... just like that!

Maybe you can imagine a small child who had lived a fairly secure and sheltered existence for the first part of her life suddenly being introduced to a stranger who was about to take her away from all she held near and dear. Traumatic, you think? Not so, however. It was like I mentioned earlier: I had complete faith and trust in Aunt Annie. She would never do me any harm, nor let anyone else do so either.

That man, who had been introduced to me as just another person, must be someone who would be good to me, I figured. Plus, I was supposed to be going somewhere where I actually had a whole bunch of brothers and sisters waiting to meet me. That sounded fun. And the really curious part was the chance to meet the person who was my actual mother. Her name was Marie, I had learned, and she loved me very much, I was told...

PATSY, COME HOME

Fargo, North Dakota

The next part of my life began as a blur. So many new experiences to have, new people to meet and especially meeting the one who held me the most and told me over and over how much she had missed me and loved me. Wow! You might imagine just how overwhelmed and semi-delirious I became with joy. I had heard talk, of course, of my mother, but how does a four or five-year old compute such a thing and make any sense of it? On top of that amazing, loving rush I received from my mother, I was darn near suffocated by the crushing hugs and tug-o-war with my body that my siblings had with me. They all wanted to hold me, especially the older ones who just seemed like they were about to bust-open with joy and excitement.

The youngest one at that time was Colleen, and she was only one-year old. Naturally, having a real live infant to hold and play with was absolutely enthralling. After all, she was *my baby sister!* Plus, I had a baby brother too! His name was Jerry, and he was three and seemed just as excited as the others. In fact, he and I were close enough in age that we could sort of easily bond to each other.

We got along famously, and he followed me around almost constantly from dawn to bedtime. I suppose that because I wasn't that much bigger than him, he could relate better to me too. With my older brother and sisters always smiling at me, Jerry constantly following beside me like a shadow and with little, baby Colleen to hold and cuddle, well, you can imagine that I was in *seventh heaven* and feeling so much *belonging* that it made me dizzy with happiness.

How could I not feel truly blessed? It was a really nice welcoming. I was the central showpiece, the honored one, and I was welcomed back home with many loving, open arms with hugs and kisses all around. That is, with the exception of that tall, quiet, and strange man who had picked me up from Aunt Annie's. After that, he sort of dropped-out of the picture, and I was seldom to ever have any visual contact, let alone verbal or physical, with him.

Of course, there was our mother, Marie, who showered me with love and kisses and any extra attention she could offer. Plus, there was the talk and excitement that Mother was pregnant and going to have yet another child soon. Wasn't that supposed to be exciting? At that age, I couldn't understand any of the inner-dealings of family-issues or dilemmas.

I do remember clearly that although Mom smiled at me a lot, she always looked very tired. In fact, if she ever had a slight break from little Colleen's baby care or from kitchen duties preparing meals, I noticed how she would fall asleep on the couch, or on the kitchen table or even sitting-upright in any chair. Mother worked very hard all the time, and mostly all by herself…

HAND'S OFF

I guess this is a good segue to talk about that big, man who had come to the farm and picked me up to bring home to my family. Roy McCord was his name, and from the very beginning, I seldom heard any reference to him as "my father" or "Father" or "Dad" or "Daddy." Occasionally, I heard the others, especially the younger ones calling him "Daddy," but hardly ever from others. I sensed some deep-rooted tension already on-hand right away. It would take a while before I would learn to recognize the real stress and issues relating to him.

It was true that he had *brought me home* to my original family, but the relationship fairly well ended there. There were no hugs and squeezes or kisses from him. On the contrary, he remained quite aloof from me, and I seemed all but unrecognizable to him. Whenever he was present, I would watch him with a strange curiosity and interest. Then I would hear the younger others calling him Daddy, and I felt strong desires to reference him the same way. Yet, when I did, there was recognition by the others of whom I spoke, but there was never an inkling of awareness from him.

And, of course, our initial meeting and journey together was a real clash of excitement and confusion. In fairly short order, I had been packed-up and delivered unto that giant stranger. I had climbed into his shiny, new car and sat obediently and practically silently all the way from Duluth to St. Paul, where another incredible surprise occurred. But first, you have to relate to the fact of me, Miss Walkie-Talkie, being silent for 100 miles of travel. Absolutely unheard of! This man, whom I had the eerie sense of maybe actually being my *father* was very odd to me.

For one thing, Aunt Annie *was* my *family*. Yeah, sure, I had met her nieces, my aunts, whom I was told were also my real mother's sisters too, but that was all just a clash of vagueness and disorientation. There had been a few, irregular references to *mother* and *father* that I had caught in my aunts' conversations, but they were all still mostly oblivious to my mental grasp at the time.

And then this huge, silent man took me in his big car and drove me away from my entire previous life. *Silent* was the right word, too. I mean he never spoke but a couple of words all the way to our first destination. For the longest time, he just sat there and quietly drove his car while looking straight ahead most of the way. Actually, I did get one response from him when I tried modeling my behavior after him. He liked fidgeting with a machine in the car that made noises when he turned some dials. We never heard anything but mostly scratchy sounds, but he kept right on twisting and turning those dials intent on getting some plausible sounds. Nothing, though.

Of course, curiosity got the best of me. I was impressed with the noisemaker even if that's all that ever did come out of it. So, once when *the man* stopped his doodling with the dials, I reached over and attempted twisting them too. But I was cut short. "Don't touch those!" he ordered. "Keep your hands off!"

"Ooops! "Yes, Sir," was my instant reply, and I recognized, although did not understand, the barrier between us.

But, I was a natural talker and couldn't keep my mouth shut for too long, or else I'd bust! So, naturally, I tried to engage him in conversation in the beginning, but to no avail. I mean, I was full of wonder and excitement and curiosity and needed to know what was happening. So, I had to try and encourage him to speak, and I did so with some of my best openers:

"Where are we going? Are we there yet? How long will it be?" were the first, obvious standards of mine for breaking into conversation. But, they didn't work. Just stern silence.

Like they say, "(His) silence was deafening!" When you are ignored, that tends to shut you up pretty fast. I remember just thinking to myself, "Well, this man is different, alright."

My frustration finally did hit its peak, though, and showed its awkward side after I couldn't hardly take his *quietness* anymore. I suddenly quizzically blurted out, "Who are you?"

I got put in my place real quick too when he all but grumbled out, "I'm taking you to see your mother. Now be quiet because I'm thinking." So much for discourse.

I remember stopping at a gas station like Aunt Annie used to have to do from time to time for her truck, and that was about the first time I heard him say anything to me on his own. "Do you need to go to the bathroom?" he gruffly asked.

There was my opening, "Yes, Sir, I do, Sir. I'll hurry too, Sir. Can I get some candy like Aunt Annie lets me?" Oh, sure, give me an inch, and I'll take…

"Just go and do your business," he responded, "and get back in the car. Hurry-up!"

That was it! I did my business, got back in the car, he paid the gas attendant, and we were off again to complete the first stage of our journey to my new home.

But who would have guessed that I was in for my first, well, actually second, real surprise. The first one, we were already in the process of doing: Going to a new home. The next one really shocked me, though.

Once we arrived at the huge city of St. Paul, I was all but dumbstruck by all the cars and so much traffic and gigantic buildings everywhere. Lots of people were walking all over the place going in-and-out of all kinds of stores or businesses or houses. It was just an incredible sight for a little farm girl to see for the first time. Before long, the big man beside me driving pulled his car in front of a large, white, two-story house with windows all around and a big front porch on it with a swing and chairs to sit on. It was white, mostly made of wood but it had some bricks all around the bottom of it too. There was a white, picket fence all along the front and sides of the house with a gate right in the middle which, when opened, led up a short walkway to steps leading up onto the porch and the house's front door..

Well, next came a couple of quick surprises. First, was while we were just climbing out of the car, the front door flung wide-open to the inside. Then a screen door burst-open, and a little boy came running out practically falling-over himself bounding down the stairs.

"Daddy!" he yelled, and he charged toward us. Then the big man opened the gate and put his hand on the boys head calming him.

"Jerry," he began, "This is Patricia, your sister. We are taking her back to our house. Go get your things. We have to leave very soon. We are going to fly in an airplane."

Oh, my God, my head began swirling in confusion trying to adjust and adapt to this new situation. *Jerry* and *sister* meant that he was my *brother*? And the little boy said, "*Daddy*?" Did that mean that he was *my daddy too*, after all? That would explain a lot.

But then there was *Airplane*? *Flying*? You've got to be kidding! Too much! My sensation chart was showing overload.

Suddenly, one of Aunt Annie's nieces, whom I had met before at the farm, walked out casually to greet us also. It was the one called: Aunt Kate, the one who did not like talking to me very much. Right behind her, a young lady showed-up too, who was leaning on the doorframe watching me.

"Hello, Roy," I heard her begin. "I see you got the little child. Care for a cup of coffee, or something?"

"No, thanks," *my dad* replied, "We've got to go, or I could be too late for the flight to Fargo. Jerry, go get your jacket and stuff."

"Hello, Child. Do you remember me?" Aunt Kate addressed me. Then she added, "So what do you think of your little half-brother? That young lady up on the porch is my daughter. She is your cousin, Rosalie."

No movement came from the cousin on the porch, just stiffened staring. But no matter because I was still in a state-of-shock. Little did I know that in a few years I would get to know them both all too well. At that moment, however, all I could manage was simple responses, "Hey. Hi. Yeah! Wow!"

No frills, no thrills, no hugs, or kisses. Howdy-doodie. See you later. That fast, and we were packed-up again, back in the car and driving away. But now was a little different because the new, little *brother* of mine just couldn't take his eyes-off me or keep his hands-off me either. We had both gotten into the back seat, and little Jerry snuggled right-up to me like I was his long, lost family. Come to think of it, I was, wasn't I. Anyway, he was thrilled to meet me, and after the sheer shock of our brief introduction, I easily began warming-up to him too.

Jerry was sweet, excitable, and very loving. We made instant friends, and a special bond began developing. With Jerry practically climbing into my lap the whole rest of the way, we talked up a storm about all sorts of silly, children's stuff and curiosities. Before long, our *dad* had dropped-off the car to some people and we were taken over to this giant place with all kinds of enormous airplanes scattered around on it.

I remember being in awe of the airport, and with Jerry clinging to my hand, we followed our dad around inside a big building and then to a stair that led-up inside one of those big planes. Before I knew it, we were off-and-running, and soon after, we were flying way-up high over the clouds and the land below. Talk about a day's adventure! But it never matched what was yet to come.

REUNION

Fargo, North Dakota

Then, suddenly, I was with my new, real, full, and complete family. The overwhelming feeling slowly and steadily declined, and I gradually began to find a comfortable place and feeling within this new home. We were sort of crowded in that brick house in Fargo, North Dakota. Our dad, my new dad, worked at the very airport that he, Jerry and I had flown into. He had something to do with airport-security and radios, I was informed. Our dad talked on a radio to everybody who worked at that airport to keep everyone in touch with each other. He wore a uniform with a hat and all and he had a badge to identify himself.

Like I said, our home was a bit crowded, but I didn't care one bit. There were a total of eight of us living in that relatively modest, brick house: Parents, two boys and four girls. Baby Colleen was in the parents' room, big brother Bo and Jerry were in another room, and I was put in the room with my older sisters, Jean, and Mary. I was so excited that I just ran around *like a chicken with its head cut-off*, doing whatever I was told by whomever said so. I had so many questions for all of them that I exhausted myself just learning new things about my family, and my new home and the locality.

Of course, the instant, yet still developing, bond between our mother and me was genuine and very loving and special. I remember how pleased I was every Sunday on our way to church services in our neighborhood. Mother would push a carriage with Colleen in it and always let me walk along beside her while Jerry was on the other side. That continued until I began asserting my assuredness and started advancing my borders. That too was when I began bonding strongly with my older sisters, Jean, and

Mary. They were both happy to include me in their group, and I felt extra-special being included.

It didn't take long, either, before I noticed an uncomfortable relationship between Jean and Bo with our dad. Jean was already sassing our dad, and he was not very nice with his comments to her. Our father would pick on Bo a lot, too, and make him cry. Jean would become defensive for Bo and get mad as all hell and calling-out our dad for it.

I suppose looking-back on things back then, those was the beginnings of the *family wars* that I am now recalling more clearly. I have thought a lot about them over-the-years, and that is why I am sharing those memories now. We kids laughed and played together really well. Fact is, Mother and we kids all got along famously, but when it came to any interaction with our dad, the joy sort of collapsed.

Our dad worked a lot at the airport, we were told. Many times he was already gone in the morning before we kids were up for breakfast, and he didn't come home until very late at night. That was when we kids could hear our parents arguing and fighting in the other room. That went on until our mom finally came into the front room with us kids and grabbed-up baby Colleen from where we were playing with her and waddled down the hallway in tears to their bedroom for the night. Sometimes, our dad just stayed there in the kitchen alone for a while before going to bed himself. Other times, he would get really angry and just leave the house slamming the front door shut behind him and not returning again until the next night or the next or...

Usually, it was Jean who made sure the rest of us kids got ready for bed and then got prepared for the next day's activities which was typically school. I think, too, that Jean must have learned to argue with our dad from her experiences listening-in on our parents arguing and fighting. Jean was already nine-years old at that time and big for her age. She was very smart too, and she was extremely protective of all us kids and especially from our dad.

Like I mentioned before, our dad liked to pick-on poor, little Bo and make him cry. Jean would jump right in there over and over again screaming at our dad, *"Leave him alone, you mean man!"*

Of course, that was just a perfect excuse for our dad to immediately change his focus and coarse and begin yelling at Jean while pushing, shoving, and slapping her around. Oh, yes, I remember those wars sadly, very well. Wish I didn't.

Trying to capsulate much of what occurred during those next four years at home with my family is like trying to squeeze the history of the world into a comic book. All you can do is touch upon any super highlights, both good and bad, and those occasions which left serious impressions upon your mind and indelible memories ingrained upon your soul. It was a time of incredible joy and devastating sadness; thrills and chills; bliss and agony.

How would I describe those rapid-fire, life-changing years? I suppose by just throwing the whole grab-bag out there and try to explain and define each at a time. Sure, those years had some happy moments. I was continually carried along by the loving warmth I felt from the other members of my family with the obvious exception of our father. For the next whole chapter of my life, I was forced to deal with him as though I did not exist. True, he didn't have much interaction with any of the other McCord children either, except for those vicious arguments and fighting with Jean and little Bo. But those obvious disconnections on his part might as well have been stones thrown at my heart.

At least he was decent enough with the younger children. Regardless of our dad's rudeness or meanness to some or coldness and disparity toward we others, Jerry worshiped the ground he walked on. He was always excited whenever our dad appeared and was constantly looking and waiting for that special hug he might receive from him. Our mother, on the other hand, tried desperately to make-up for his negligence. She was always making excuses for our dad too.

"Oh, children, don't bother your father right now," she would defend. "He's been working so hard, and he is tired. Let him rest, or eat his dinner, or do his work, or blah, blah, blah. He needs to be left alone."

Right. Well, actually we all learned, and the elder kids already knew, that when he was left alone, that was when there was noticeably general peace in the house. Although I was truly bothered by our dad's dismissiveness toward us children, I learned to accept that fate. He did not care to know me much at all, so, so-be-it. I just developed a behavior pattern concerning him of *slow-and-steady*. Neither did I expect joys of warmth and inclusion from him, nor sorrows of exclusion.

I just learned to carry-on. Always fearful of his chronic and increasing levels of anger and violence toward our mother and especially Jean and Bo, I learned to practice keeping my distance from him. I would not allow myself to become saddened or remorseful from his negativity; nor would I become excitable and pleased by his unusually irregular fits of decency and happiness. I was a nobody to him, so I learned to make it clear that he was not high on my list of significant persons either.

Other than that, our family-life moved right on along while living there in the Fargo, South Dakota until the worst events that anyone might imagine occurred to us. An important and immediate highlight of the period, however, developed and was directly connected to the loving connection my older brother, Bo, had toward me. All my life, until that time, I was always known as Patricia. That was my name. What would you otherwise expect? But leave it to my brother, Bo, and that all changed in a heartbeat. Right away to him, I was *Little, Sissy-Patsy*. No more formal *Patricia* nonsense. I was inaugurated into the family then. I was a full-fledged member, with an official nickname, and accordingly, must be distinguished by my own appropriate nomenclature.

Well, after a while, and a couple of serious growth spurts, the *Little* portion necessitated being dropped. The other siblings liked the shortened version of plain and simple *Patsy*, so that caught on and stuck permanently for the rest of my life. Because Bo had invented the nickname, he was the last to let go of the *Sissy* part, but it never mattered to me. I was overjoyed any time I ever heard any of them call me by my new special name. I was *Patsy*, and that suited me just fine. It stuck to me like glue, and it was all I knew or cared to know of myself after that loving and welcoming inauguration…

KINDERGARTEN DAZE

I suppose that *name games* are relevant to speak of because it certainly had an effect on my future schooling. To begin with, I might mention that my second thrilling moment occurred right after coming home. It was the beginning of school, and I was five-years old. That meant that I got to start school. I was then officially registered and enrolled in Kindergarten.

All of us oldest kids were attending the local Catholic, private school. Our mother would not have allowed it any other way. I think I mentioned before how serious Catholicism was to her. It was in a nice way too. I remember actually enjoying going to church with my mother. It probably impacted my life so much with her influence, that I made all my own children attend Catholic Mass services on a regular basis into adulthood, and even had my two oldest boys become *altar boys*. But making any of them attend Catholic School was another subject. I had few memories of pleasant times while attending Catholic school.

Right from the very beginning of kindergarten, I was treated like some sort of deviant and continuously corrected for my apparent obvious shortcomings. To say that the nuns or sisters who ran Catholic School classrooms were strict would be like saying, "Niagara is a waterfall," or "The Mississippi is a river." *Strict* was not the appropriate word to describe their classroom control. It was more like *harsh, severe, cruel, vindictive, malicious,* and *spiteful*. I never understood whether the sisters and nuns in classrooms simply liked an elite few students in the class, or whether, in actuality, they hated them all. Or, they hated their own lives and dealing with us ignorant little devils was undeserved and vicious penalties in their lives.

Either way, those nuns and sisters sure seemed to find new and creative ways to punish me. I was probably one of the most excited students to just be there in the first place too. I mean, I was proud to be a *student* and absolutely elated to go to school with my older sisters and brother. Mother was as happy as I was for me to be in school. Jean emphasized all the time how important education was for success in life. It was an honor to attend school. But, unfortunately, the teachers did not see it that way. It seemed to me in later years like I was more of a curse to them than any dutiful student. They were simply uncompromising in their negative behavior and attitude toward me.

The simplest of examples I might offer was their official, introductory welcoming into the classroom using their strategy called, the *Name Game*. Once we kindergarten students had been assigned our desks, given our nametags to pin on our blouses or shirts and provided our basic pencil/paper supplies, Sister-teacher wanted us all to learn and memorize everybody's names in class. So, there I sat upright, hands folded on my desk and watching and waiting for any instructions to follow. The teacher went row by row and desk by desk asking each child to identify themselves to the other students.

"Young man, what is your name? the Sister inquired.

The boy quickly responded proudly, "My name is Robert!"

"Very good, Robert," Sister awarded, and then on to the next, "What is your name, young lady?

"My name is Suzanne," answered the child.

"Very good, Suzanne," replied Sister. And it went on and on like this throughout the whole classroom. There was Robert, Suzanne, Thomas, Julia, and on and on until finally, Sister arrived at my desk.

"And what is your name, young lady?" Sister asked.

I was so emboldened and proud that I loudly burst forth. "My name is Patsy!" I proclaimed.

Well, Sister just instantly bolted upright as if she'd just been kicked in the kazoo, and she abruptly quizzed again, "No, Child, that is not right. Now, what is your name?"

I have to admit, that at first, I thought that this was still some kind of a fun and hospitable game we were playing. Right then, I just imagined that it was my silly turn, and I was center stage playing the *game*. So, I playfully countered again, "My name is Patsy McCord!"

Then quickly, it turned ugly. The sister snatched my left hand, held it up and commanded, "Look at your name tag. What does it say?"

Well, I bent my head over spiritly playing along, but of course, I couldn't read upside-down. Heck, I couldn't read at all, but I just continued the puzzling game by underlining the words on my nametag with my right-hand index-finger and vehemently pronouncing once again, maybe even with a slight touch of arrogance that time, "Why, Teacher, it says, "My name is *Patsy*!"

There was uproarious laughter in the classroom. I looked all around grinning-up a storm at my success thus far playing Sister's *name game.* Unfortunately, Sister was not laughing. In fact, she was not smiling even. Immediately, she jarred her head upright, and demanded, "Quiet, all of you. Be silent!" Instantly, there was a deep hush in the classroom.

I guess that had done it! The teacher now had her first opportunity to set down rules and standards of behavior. In her right hand, Sister was holding and carrying a rather large ruler. I figured it was probably a tool used for precise measurements or to aim and point-out various objects or words during our lessons. I was not prepared for what happened next, however.

While still holding my left hand-up high, and with the ruler raised in her right hand, Sister swiftly and harshly began swatting my knuckles one letter-after-the-other stating, "Your name is: *P-(whack!) A-(whack!) T-R-I C-I-A, Patricia!*" Then, with a final note of added emphasis, she finished her spelling lesson with one last smack across all my knuckles and a resounding, "Not Patsy!" she angrily declared.

Foolish me. In the beginning, and after the first letter, "P," with its nasty-ruler swat, I still considered it a game with unusual outcomes. But, by the third and fourth letters, "T," and "R," I realized this was no game. I was really being punished. I tried to control my emotions and handle the swatting courageously, but it just hurt too much. I was so shocked by the pain, and then so saddened with my disgrace, that tears began freely flowing down my face.

Embarrassment, shame, and confusion all merged their humiliating emotions combining to collectively rob me of any dignity. So, I certainly let out a few non-rebel yells, "Ouch! Ow! Ohhh!" until Sister's climactic last smack with her painful and punishing ruler.

But Sister wasn't through yet. Her violent lesson had not been completed. She angrily demanded one more time, "Young lady, what is your name?"

I was upset and still slightly sobbing, but I prepared my answer carefully and dutifully. After all, game or no game, there were rules: So, I exclaimed meekly yet defiantly, "My name is Patricia ***"PATSY"*** McCord!"

Let's just sort of leave that story and move on with one final observation: *For me and Catholic School, it was all-uphill after that!* The nuns never took to me after that. Oh, I was a good enough student and wanted to do well, but they were not partial to me in any way, shape, or form. For some reason, I was unworthy in their eyes. No matter how much obedience, or studiousness or active and willing participation I showed, I was contemptible and undeserving in their eyes.

Unfortunately, that sort of characterization continued throughout my Catholic School upbringing. Wherever we went, Mother, and Edith later, always placed us kids in Catholic Schools because of their stringent faith and belief in religious training in school. For whatever reasons, those classroom teacher nuns and sisters just didn't take to me, and I grew to be ever more disengaged with their attitudes, standards, and beliefs. I simply always did the best I could in school and just tried to please myself after that earliest of all lessons and not worry about them much anymore.

In fact, a rather satisfying sidenote, however, occurred during periods that I attended regular, public schools, after I was no longer living with my family. During several years in St. Paul while attending fourth grade through seventh grade, and a couple years later in my tenth grade, sophomore year, I did exceptionally well in school. In fact, during my tenth-grade year, I had been forced to enroll myself in a Duluth, Minnesota high school in order to seemingly maintain apparent normalcy and regularity. For that fleeting period of about one full semester, though, I got straight A's from all my teachers and subjects. I was *normal* after all, no matter what the nuns thought. And my name was *Patsy*!

Yes, I suppose that school didn't get-off to such a good start for me, but that didn't mean those years were all miserable. On the contrary, in spite of the Catholic Schools, and their nuns and sisters as teachers, I studied hard and tried to stay focused on whatever subjects I was given. After all, I had some very bright older sisters and a brother who constantly set the bar high for me to try and reach.

Jean was always very smart and could easily handle whatever studies she had. Bo was very sharp too, but he had a lot of issues at school because he held a poor attitude. He was angry or upset so much of the time that he just kept to himself a lot at school and at home. He developed a pretty bad and spiteful mouth, and as a result, was not too popular with other students. Plus, he still maintained a weakened and frail frame. Between that and our father's ridicule, he became very shy of others except to fight with other boys who taunted him..

Sis Mary had no problems, though, but it was more like she just didn't care that much either. She usually had her head inside her artsy, fashion, glamour, and Hollywood Stars magazines whenever possible. She was very popular at school, and she always had a lot of friends hanging around her, especially boys. That aspect of her life was much more important to Sis than studying and homework. But she did okay in school, and she never got into any trouble, unlike Jean and Bo. They both managed several fights each year, and poor Mom was called in for student reviews and teacher/Principal meetings all too often…

JERROLD "JERRY" MCCORD

Unfortunately, if I set the subject of school aside for the time being, I now feel a necessity to explain about the first really dreadful and tragic happening for our dysfunctional, emotionally bruised family. Of all things, the story actually begins on a positive note, for a change, and involved an actual, initial family treat from our dad who had arranged it for us kids. In the back yard of our home there in Fargo, North Dakota, our dad had a friend come over and build a series of cages arranged up-high on a long platform-stand for us kids. There were six pens, one for each of us children: Jean, Bo, Sis, me, Jerry, and Colleen.

Incidentally, the newest addition to the family had arrived two years earlier in 1932. Little Jann was the family's newest child, and still much too young for that new experiment, so she had been excused from the *treat*. The rest of us were beside ourselves with anticipation, curiosity, and thrills. We all anxiously, restlessly and filled-to-the-brim with excitement awaited for what lay ahead. What in heaven's name were these cages for. What possibly could be in store for us?

Shortly after the cages or pens were completed, our curiosity and enthusiasm peaked just in time for one afternoon that fall, when the answers to our dilemma arrived. The six of us kids all received our very own fully-grown rabbits. We all got our rabbit pets to play with, to feed and water and to take care of and watch over. Our father was emphatic about those points as he warned, "You all had better take good care of your pets because if you don't, we shall eat yours first!"

Yikes! "Yours first!" was foreboding, but we all knew it could mean any of us or all of us. So, we put the future out of our minds and focused on the absolute here-and-now. Our rabbits were handed to us one-by-one by age from our dad, with a begrudging Jean accepting the first one reluctantly.

Then we were told to place them in their cages in the same order, Jean on one end all the way down to Colleen on the other far end. We were all thrilled and in joyful bliss as we proceeded to cart our little rabbits all around the yard careful not to let any of them get away.

Yeah, sure! Almost immediately, those frightened rabbits began shoving and pushing roughly with their powerful hind feet while struggling to get away from their handlers. More than once, some rabbits managed to kick and leap-out of our startled and scratched arms. Then whomever was available would help the scared, runaway rabbit be cornered and caught again and returned to its rightful owner's arms or hurriedly dumbed-back inside its pen. Colleen was only two-years old, of course, so she had the most trouble, but once her bunny was placed in her cage, she was elatedly on cloud nine.

Every day after school, all of us played with and hung on to our rabbits for dear life. Each of us struggled holding them all the while receiving our share of kicks, scratches, and claw marks. But those funny bunnies were ours, and we named them, played with them and they remained ours forever, so we believed. As days went by, we all responsibly visited our little bunnies before going to school each day and then dutifully again once we arrived home.

We cleaned underneath their messy cages too. I was the most experienced in that category, so I emphatically glorified my experienced role from my chicken-tender days. I boastfully showed them all about changing their bowls with fresh water. We gave them their rabbit-pellet food and snacks like carrots and lettuce. We took dutiful care of them.

We each also carefully and controllably took our pets out of their pens as well we could. We all played with them even though those large rabbits were strong and played so rough while trying constantly to escape their captor's grasps. And we each gave them illustrious and comical names which brought uproarious laughter to all of us.

We loved our bunnies and played daily with them joyously. Hands down, though, Jerry was the most watchful and attentive owner of us all. He adored his pet. Several weeks passed, and we were all content with our added pet responsibilities and enjoyed the pleasure received from their ownership. Life was blissful. Unfortunately, Little-Jerry was the first one of us kids to get sick…

His rabbit was caged right next to mine, so I easily noticed Jerry's rabbit-cage being empty so much of the time. It was because Jerry loved taking his rabbit from its pen and holding it contentedly in his arms somewhere for hours at a time. Unfortunately, one morning before we older ones rushed off for school, Jerry arose with us and went outside to visit and play with his rabbit. A minute later, we all heard his screams and wailing.

When we got to him, we could see that Jerry's little bunny was laying there lifeless in his arms. Jerry was rocking the bunny harshly trying to shake it back to life. He was cuddling it closely in his arms, kissing it's face and mouth while pleading for its reawakening and resuscitation. But, of course, it was to no avail. The rabbit had curiously just up-and-died.

It had only been quite a few weeks after receiving our pets, however, when Jerry's rabbit had died. He was so grievously disappointed afterwards that when we others all-in-turn offered-up our own pets as replacement gifts for his loss, Jerry refused and chose rather to sit alone and sulk while mourning his loss. Several days later, however, Jerry began complaining of severe stomach pains. He began feeling nauseous and started vomiting harshly and continuously. His throat was inflamed, and his lymph glands were swollen, but he grievously complained about terrible pains in his stomach.

In another day or two, the rest of us McCord kids all, one-by-one, began complaining of sore throats too. Both Big Brother *Bo* and his twin, *Sis* Mary, and Colleen were the next to come down really sick shortly after Jerry. By the next day or after that, Jean, and I both fell to the rapidly expanding illness. Very soon thereafter, our home was turned into a virtual hospital ward.

Jean, Bo, and I were placed into the parent's bedroom because we three could fit in our parent's big bed. Mary and Colleen, who were obviously the worst afflicted after Jerry, were spread out upon the living-room couch and made as comfortable as possible. Jerry, who continued deteriorating more each day, was left placed alone in his and Bo's third bedroom. Our mother wanted him there so that she could sit and care for Jerry while he required attention, or she could sleep beside him in the other bed while he slept.

Our parents, who managed to avoid contamination, kept our unharmed Baby Jann away from the rest of us when they took over the other the remaining girls' bedroom. Our dad managed to stay at work for extra-particularly long shifts, so the burden of nursing care was fully thrust upon our mother. We know that under the circumstances, she did everything that she could. But, in only a few days, Jerry was really struggling with his pains and terrible symptoms. Mary and two-year old Colleen continued rapidly failing too. Our mother became horribly alarmed and demanded that Jerry, Mary, and Colleen be admitted to Fargo Hospital's Emergency Ward.

The three of them were immediately admitted to the hospital; however, the severity of Jerry's case kept him permanently in Emergency. In a couple more days, both Mary and Colleen were discharged to return home, and we readjusted the sleeping places to accommodate them. As days passed, all of us at home began showing strong, positive signs of recovery. Yet, we all remained very concerned over Jerry's well-being.

That was when we had the opportunity to learn about and understand what had happened to all of us. What had caused this terrible rash of illnesses? Finally the diagnosis came, and it was both astonishing and agonizing. Those of us at home, including our two sickest sisters and poor, little Jerry were all suffering from streptococcus.

It turned out that Jerry's pet, his very own, little rabbit, had mysteriously come down with the strep disease. We never learned why or how. Perhaps, it had been bitten by a diseased animal before or during our ownership, but the disease had eventually killed it. Jerry had likely contracted the disease from all his kissing and cuddling of his sick and then dead animal. That also explained why Jerry had likely developed the worst case of strep of all. His was streptococcus which had advanced to his stomach. That stage of illness was extremely dangerous and very potentially mortal.

Fortunately, under twenty-four-hour care, the rest of us all began showing steady improvement. We had all only suffered severe sore throats, and Sis Mary and Colleen had been afflicted the worse. We would all recover completely., however. Sadly, however, my little, *shadow* brother, Jerry's case rapidly deteriorated. It took only one week more for the terrible, streptococcus abdominal sickness to claim our brother's life. It was rare to occur, but in a few cases of the sickness, it attacks the stomach of typically young boys, and the diseased bacteria destroyed Jerry's body from deep inside.

Shortly thereafter, the rest of us kids including Mary and Colleen had all recovered and were fully well again. Our loss of Jerry, though, devastated our family. Only a few weeks earlier, we kids had all been gleefully holding our pet rabbits and playing fully to the end of a child's delight. Little did we know at the time that one of those rabbits, Jerry's bunny, had become strep infected. The scratches Jerry received from his infected rabbit and/or his doleful kisses given after its death caused his mortal illness. His contagion had likely been passed-on and spread to us kids which caused all our strep sickness. Jerry's little, beloved-pet rabbit had, ultimately, died from the disease, and had taken his life and him from us...

Jerry's death caused a great sadness overwhelming our family. In actuality, only our newest family addition, Lorraine Jannette "Jann," helped us regain our ground by forcing us to focus on her newest life and thus place our tragic, great loss of Jerry behind us. Yet, the hurt and emptiness Jerry left behind still took its toll regardless. Our home filled with sadness and gloom clear-up until the end of the school year. Also, it seemed naturally obvious that Jerry's passing had been the single, strongest motive for us to leave our home in Fargo, South Dakota and move away,... far away.

So, the entire family, absent Jerry, moved once again. It was certainly a saddened event, but nevertheless, unusually both curious and interesting to me. With all the family's previous moves around the country, this was the first move where I was included. I was terribly hurt with Jerry's passing. He had been my little shadow, but by then I was also ever so grateful to be included with the others in that next move and adventure. That time, it was going to be clear back to Minnesota again.

I believe that because of our mother's saddened and anxiety-ridden coaxing, our dad had arranged for a new work assignment at his previous worksite, the St. Paul-Minneapolis Airport. Once again, he would rejoin their Radio and Communications Airport Security team. That summer of 1932, we left behind us Fargo, North Dakota and with it the *great sadness* of Jerry's loss. We moved as an entire family all the way back to St. Paul, the actual city of my birth...

NEW HOME, NEW START

St. Paul, Minnesota

Now returned back to St. Paul, our family was able to develop closer ties to our mother's other sisters. For whatever reason, our mom was fairly close to Aunt Kate. Oh, I remembered that aunt quite well, and her stand-offish daughter, Rosalie. We all saw them on a fairly regular, visitation basis. Even Aunt Annie came all the way down from Duluth on a bus to visit with us. It was wonderful seeing her again. Our Mom needed their visits too for moral support, I imagine.

Little Jann was by then barely over a year old. She was just becoming a toddler when the latest surprising news was announced: Mother was pregnant again. We saw her belly begin protruding, but there was very little fanfare or teasing or joy that came with Mom's pregnancy that time. Nothing had changed much in her relationship experienced with our dad either, or with our, for that matter. He still worked long, long hours at the airport and was often gone overnight, or sometimes for several nights. We never really quite knew for sure when he might arrive back home.

Not that it bothered any of us kids much. It was like the song goes, "Peace in the Valley" during his absences. When home, he was willing to get into a fight with any of us who might get in his way, antagonize, or challenge him. And, yes, I remember almost all of those fights during that period. Dad would pick on Bo and make fun of his scrawniness, and then he would fight like hell with Jean when she defended Bo. He and Mom argued so often over his absences and tardiness that she was in a constant state of anxiety and sorrow. When he was home, if our dad was not yelling at our mother over marital issues, then he was yelling at us kids and warning us to stay out of his way.

Attending school improved somewhat. At least I was not treated like I had some communicable disease or something. I got adjusted to the new school and it went okay. Then, a new year came, 1934, and another new baby. Wouldn't you know it? It was another boy. Not one to replace Jerry. That could never happen, but a new, little character for all of us to tease and play and care for. Of course, Baby Jann was just about two-years old by then, Colleen was about four-years old, and I was going on eight-years old. Another baby meant that much more effort and struggle for our mom. But, newborns babies are supposed to bring brand new smiles into a home.

Okay, I imagine that you may be guessing where this story is going. So, I think I'll cut to the chase of another, yet tangential and totally different episode weaving through our family's worn-out, tension-laced fabric. Actually, it is a story which was relatively shocking to our family, and to the whole darn country at the time, for that matter. I'm going to tell about that now and just touch on it a bit, so I can move on to the really sad state-of-affairs for our family. Our family had already suffered, but that was only practice for what was to come.

In the meantime, let me talk briefly about the difficult case of our dad. I'll start with a brief accounting of another side-story and then go on to discuss his merits or demerits more in full. But, first: Our dad's *near-death* experience and its effects on our family...

BAD DAD "ROY"

As mentioned earlier, our dad worked at many different larger airports. He was their radio and communications expert taking all calls regarding security-dispatches and alarms. One time on a nightshift in late 1934 at the Minneapolis-St. Paul Airport, our dad got called out to investigate a disturbance, and it almost cost him his life. He got shot-up many times really badly and almost died from his injuries. The story was in all the newspapers, and he became somewhat of a celebrity because of surviving that ordeal.

The really bad part was that our dad spent a couple months in the hospital, and we were practically destitute for income. The Airport people did help us somewhat as did our mom's sisters. And, actually, all things considered, especially including our dad's temporary hospital stay, a soothing and pleasing calm was enjoyed at our home. We all knew, however, that his absence was only small relief, and like they say, "It was the *calm-before-the-storm!*"

After our dad finally returned home from the hospital, he was like another huge burden on our mom. By then, she had to manage all of us kids and get us bigger ones on our ways to school. Plus, she had the littlest ones, Colleen, Jann and her infant, Jackie-Boy, needing attention all the time. Our dad was very demanding and wanted all sorts of things done for him, brought to him and he wanted everything immediately and on-the-spot.

None of us kids wanted to do much for him because we were too afraid of injuries to ourselves if we got too close to him. So, usually, it meant that our mom would have to drop whatever she was doing and go check on our dad's needs whenever he started yelling. Believe me, he yelled a lot, and we kids didn't get too close because he hit a lot, too. Poor Mom.

Now I suppose I can talk about our real *family torn* and truly becoming unraveled from its inner struggles and dysfunction. Eventually, our dad healed enough, and he went back to work. His old boss even gave him his same old job assignment again. This time, however, our dad was instructed to ONLY stay with his radio equipment and NO MORE running around the grounds looking for trouble. That was well enough, but what happened next typically should have been wonderful new news but was not well received at all.

It was 1935, and our mother was pregnant again. Happy? Hardly. How in the world could that happen, you might ask. Personally, I had no idea. The *family stork was going to make another visit* was all I may have known. But like I have suggested, our dad was a formidable man. And he was very demanding. On top of all that, once the news was out, we could hear our dad yelling at our mother like never before. That time, I got it and understood better. He was accusing our mother of having cheated on him… again. Our dad was a constant barrage of vicious, bitter, verbal attacks usually followed by thrown objects smashed against countertops, walls, furniture, or even at us sometimes. Poor Mom.

However, it would not be for many years before we kids would learn how much our mother was so incredibly disappointed and traumatized with stress and depression. Our dad gave very little support, if any, to her. He did no child-rearing at all except to yell and holler and order us kids to do things usually for him. He didn't mind smacking any of us that he could catch either, for whatever reason or none at all.

Fact is, if any of us bigger kids got too close to him, he liked to laugh and loudly pronounce after smacking one of us upside our head, "There, that was for what you did, and I didn't catch you! Ha! Ha! Ha!"

Honestly, our dad brought far more stress into the house when he was there. Mom had three children that needed constant attention, four that required basic care and needs met and a demanding husband whenever he was around. There were too many mouths to feed by then, and you could only add so much water to the soup. On top of all that, our mother was a devout Catholic, and during sermons, it seemed that the priests were always preaching about sin and salvation and the needs and glory of the church to grow in numbers.

Talking about extra stress, I'll bet I forgot to mention another reason why my family moved so much. For one thing, our dad's knowledge and skill usually were in high demand. Airports needed what he could do. So, usually, our dad never had much problem finding a new job. It only meant that he along with, and sometimes without, the family had to move far distances away. That *usefulness* came in very handy for our dad because he was terrible about paying rent for our homes. He would typically drag a landlord on-and-on with phony promises until the tension between them was extreme. Then, often without any warning to his wife and family, they would all be told to pack-up their gear because they were moving.

Another dent in his character was with the Catholic schools that we kids all attended. Our dad was a non-practicing Catholic, but he talked a good line of ardent, faith-based promises for us kids' registration and the ensuing monthly fees. And, of course, he never paid them. It got more than embarrassing for all us kids going to school.

In time, we all were trying to avoid at all costs being singled-out by one of the nuns or priests at the schools. Inevitably, they would vehemently quiz us about our father's intentions for payment of late fees. If cornered, we kids had all agreed to just stand there and look stupid while shrugging our shoulders and confessing sheer ignorance.

When serious pleading came from one of the staffs, we would let our lips quiver a bit and then passively testify, "I don't know, *Sister*." Or, "I don't know nothin', *Father*. Nobody never told me nothin."

That went on until the excuses from our dad just collapsed, and the school authorities were about to take serious action. Lo-and-behold, that would also be another time and different excuse for our dad to arrive home all hurriedly and excitedly announcing, "Guess what, everyone? Grab your shit 'cause we gotta git!" Or, words to that effect, anyway.

Well, I'm exaggerating a bit there, but you get the idea. Along with all of our dad's other less-than-charming qualities, he was also a lying, cheating, skinflint, con man. Of course, I wasn't with the family most of those times, but I heard all the stories. However, I was one of us kids who was often questioned by the nuns and priests about our dad's payment intentions. And I'll tell you that I did not appreciate having to stand there before another Catholic Inquisition with my thumb up-my-butt, acting dumb as can be and my tongue hanging-out while my head bobbed in discord and confusion…

However, for right now it's important for me to mention a little more regarding our natural mother's plight. Her death had been so tragic others might believe unnecessary. Our mother was weak, she as a criminal and she was a mortal sinner. Who can go inside the mind of someone so desperate that they would need to choose some path so unrecognized and illegal and against all church rules? Perhaps, only others who had followed the same path in their lives. Who knows for sure?

I have heard that statistically here in America in 2014, nearly twenty per cent of pregnancies were terminated. And that did not include miscarriages, forced or otherwise. But here is some additional information about our mother, and you can decide for yourselves.

ABORTION

Getting back to our mom's predicament, though, I need to explain differences in frames-of-reference at that time for all of us. You must realize that none of us kids had any idea, understanding or grasp of our mother's dilemma nor the agonizing challenges which faced her. Perhaps, there is no one can even relate to the depth of her anxiety and stress when her decision is explained. Ultimately, our Gospel-breathing, thoroughbred-Catholic mother chose to go against her Catholic Christian faith's strict guidance and rules against abortion, and in her mind, even God's *commanded will*, so-to-speak.

Our dad, *her husband*, was no help at all and no one she could lean on. Besides, he was gone so much of the time and usually on very long shifts, or company travel or whatever he was in the mood to do. Thus, he provided nominal, if any, moral, physical, or fiscal support. Years later, as adults we learned from our aunts that his negligence, more than anything else, persuaded our mom to make the dreadful decision and arrangements for herself, and all by herself.

Apparently, at the time, and without any of her sisters' knowledge of what was about to happen, our mother furtively took measures along with one of her sisters to cover for her. Using some lame excuse, our mom asked Aunt Kate to help her by watching the little ones at home while she ran some important errands. Once on her own during that desperately lonely and sad morning, our mom secretly sought out the address of a *criminal* doctor to do her bidding.

In 1934, abortions were illegal in Minnesota and mostly anywhere. Besides breaking civil law, in her mind our mother was violating Catholic and Christian law, so she faced damnation for her decision anyway. What was the difference? Potential jail if she were caught and eternal damnation at her life's end. Even with all that staggering legal and religious pressure upon her, our mother chose to avoid any more of her personal and obviously painful continued *hell-on-earth* with her ongoing pregnancies. Somehow, she had come upon a name and a place, and she visited some sneaky, illegal, back-office, alley-way hack to do the *kitchen table,* miserable job for her.

Who knows what really may have transpired that afternoon. None of us would ever know the full truth. But, obviously, it was a *lost cause* from the very beginning. The abortion, apparently, had been successful. Unfortunately, the so-called *hack*-doctor had used some crude instrument such as a coat-hanger to serve his distasteful but demanded and significantly paid-for task. As a result, Mother began hemorrhaging.

Years later, we learned that Mother had barely regained consciousness from the abysmal affair. At least, rather than releasing her to just return home, the *phony physician* wrestled-up an inkling of decency. Once he recognized his bloody disaster and its ensuing life-threatening danger, the *failed physician* did arrange to have our mom to taken to Emergency for immediate attention and care.

Unfortunately, too much time had lapsed between the beginning of the procedure until the time Mom was dealt with in Emergency at the hospital. She had lost far too much blood by then, and there was little that the hospital doctors could do to help her. Our mother died that October day on a hospital operating table. Her stress and depression had ultimately resulted in costing two lives.

How do you explain something like that to anyone? How is it possible to define the limits of one's shredded emotions? Of course, we McCord children were simply stunned and devastated. We older ones had left for school that morning happy as might be expected. We returned home after school with no more mother! How? What? Why? Everybody was crying and asking each other the same unanswerable questions especially, "Why? Why? Why?"

Later, as adults, I guess that we learned to accept, if not appreciate or understand, our mother's plight. We even gave her sisters, our aunts, some reasonable credit for covering-up for their sister. They all were likely ashamed and embarrassed at the time, but they managed to come up with a reasonably plausible explanation: *Our mother had experienced a miscarriage, and the accidental and unstoppable hemorrhaging which followed cost our mother her life.*

It was more lies and deceit to save more pain and hurt from us kids, or more likely less shame and embarrassment for them. *Miscarriages* were considered *natural* and acceptably tragic; *abortions,* on the other hand, were illegal and considered *abysmal* and unforgiveable. We were told that *our mom had sadly bled to death,* end-of-story. That was the explanation back then. Later, after we children were all adults and learned the truth regarding her *failed abortion,* it was still the same result: *Our mother had bled to death...*

You decide...

CONFESSIONAL

I am thinking that right now might be a pretty good time to confess my sins. If people would kindly act as my *Confessor Priest*, then I should be able to make something of this effort and get this wrongful and shameful memory off my non-exonerated shoulders, be given my modest *penan*ce, and be forgiven for my iniquities:

"Forgive me, *Father* (Readers), for I have sinned… It's been sixty-years, or way more, since my last *Confession*. These are my sins: Blah, blah, blah."

Come to think of it, that's really pretty easy, isn't it? All those evil, criminal, and sinful acts performed by countless Catholics, and all they have to do is just the same thing as I just muttered, but in a *Confessional Booth,* inside a Catholic Church and with an ordained priest. Dump a lot off one's shoulders, receive a little redundant penance from a Rosery (like: *Our Father* and *Hail Mary* and *Holy Mary*), and "Voila!" One is *free as can be*; free *to sin ag'in*. It's *Simple Simon* stuff for wayward, and regular sinners, yet, "Wow!" What a *Power Play* it is for priests. Do ya wanna go to heaven? Just beg a priest, "Forgive me, Father!"

Oh, I suppose I'm just feeling bad about myself or sorry for all my sins or unexcused wrong-doings, or nasty thoughts right about now after so much reflection on my past and my relationship with my mother. So, I just sort of jumped onto a wild tangent to clear my head. Sorry, if I misled you. I don't need a priest, or you, no offense, to step in-between my God and me in order to have my sins forgiven and hell-bound directions revoked.

No, I left the Catholic Church a long time ago and chose to *simplify* my life even more. Now, I just go straight to the *Main One* (Himself, Herself, Person), *Itself.* Believe me, God knows what I'm talking about, too. Oh, sure, I've already done the *Confessional* thing before… lots of times. And I have prayed to God by myself directly for forgiveness, guidance and support all the rest of my life. I never knew what else to do.

Now, I'm willing to put my heart and soul on a sacrificial-block, more or less, by *confessing* my shortcomings to you and try to seek your understanding and forgiveness.

Alright. Okay. Here it goes, and…

Please forgive me, for I have sinned:

"I was only nine years old. Incredibly, I had been brought back home to live with my entire family a little over four years before, so far. I was absolutely ecstatic about being home with everyone and especially my mother. I adored her, and I know that she loved me too because she told me so, over-and-over whenever I was near her.

Talk about feeling good, safe, secure, and happy! She made me feel over- joyed with her abundance of shared love. I prayed all the time to give thanks for my blessings. I also prayed for a lot of other things too like "fixing my dad," and rescuing my sad, big brother, Bo, and helping my angry, Big Sister Jean. But giving thanks for returning me be back to my mom was primary and extra-special.

That is why afterwards, I felt so ashamed of myself once Mom was gone. Of course, just like my siblings, maybe even more, I cried like a baby at her passing. I didn't understand all the details, but I recognized enough to realize that she was gone from me forever except in my memories (my mind) and in my prayers (my soul). I should have gone on and on with my tell-tale sobbing and bereavement and mourning. I loved her so much. Now, I would never see her again…ever! I would miss her even more evermore. She was my rock, my conduit to my entire family.

*But what did I do almost simultaneously to the news of my mother's passing, her **death**? My shameless, self-serving, warning-signals began frantically beeping inside my brain… My nearly spontaneous stress indicators started leaping-off my emotional chart. Anxiety filled my mind with its horrid motives: Oh, my God! Mom you are gone! What's going to happen to me?*

> *You were my bridge to security and love and belongingness. You were my liaison, my connection, to faith, and hope and family. You were my conduit to joy and happiness and fulfillment. You were the one who brought me back. You were the one who never wanted me to leave in the first place. Now you are gone! What in God's name is going to happen to me?*
>
> *I was shocked and stupefied by news of my mother's death. Also, like every- one else, I was filled with sadness and dread. But in those brief, conflicting moments, my dormant, anxiety-ridden mind instantly emerged again and immediately discarded all distressing facts of my mother's passing and focused, instead on my own miserable, selfish needs.*
>
> *I began silently crying, "Who could, or would, look out for me now?"*
>
> *In more expressive terms, I had allowed my mother's, most-revered station, her special place way-up-there on us kids' tip-top of our Pinnacle of Light and Love... to instantly collapse and plummet to earth, while I ran around frantically* **like-a-chicken-with-its-head-cut-off** *trying desperately to determine my own immediate future and selfish salvation.*
>
> **Shame on me! Please forgive me!**

Thank you. I needed that! I have wanted for a long time to share that grievous period of my life. You must appreciate that for any child, that sort of agony and ordeal is truly like riding on some sort of powerful, *anxiety-train* combined with a lop-sided, *Merry-Go-Round*, spinning round-and-round, in loops-and-twists, making left-turns-and-right-turns, up-and-down, and faster-and-faster, all at the same time. All you can think of is, "Please *stop*! I'm getting sick! Let me off! I want to get off! *NOW*!"

Granted, I didn't talk like that when I was just nine-years old. Heck, I didn't even think like that. But maybe you can get a better idea of a poor, previously abandoned child who had learned enough to know and understand from where she once came. Then later, after she had finally been righteously reunited and celebrated with her loving matriarch, along with an adoring throng of siblings and had dwelled amongst them lovingly, she suffers again by suddenly losing her single, one-and-only safety-link, her unique and special conduit to that precious and previous life.

All fears, stress, worries, apprehension, distrust, and anxiety that had finally, steadily, and *almost* completely been dispatched to some secret, hidden place in her mind… were then breaking-out and were back again in full-crisis mode! Everything, all my ills, was still right there in the forefront of her mind just waiting to spring-out and consume my happiness…

For all means-and-purposes, those phantom apprehensions from my brief, previous years had all but been *practically* eliminated. To aid in my welcoming and comfort, my fears had been steadily weakened, shut-off, closed-down, and stored-away from interfering with my joy. Those growing, glorious, desired, and precious pleasures of my placement among my family were solidifying. And my immediate burst of family acceptance had been due primarily to the efforts of my dear, sweet, and then, suddenly, departed mother.

There-and-then, and all too easily, I *simply* and quickly began recognizing those awful faces of otherwise, previously hidden, but bleakly harbored feelings. I instantly realized that all my ill-feelings had only been provisionally absent, never vanquished and just away on a vague, temporary basis. I had been snatched up four years earlier from a simple, ordinary, modestly happy, and accepted existence and *replaced* among strong and stout branches of my family's tree. It had happened but by my mother's gracious love and grace of God. Yet, all along I had only been welcomed and included because I desperately and gingerly clung onto a fleeting and relative, motherly *visa*.

There-and-then, facing anguishing and corporal truth of my mother's demise, those torturous and punishing anxieties reared their ugly, terrorizing heads once more. They came crashing-out from their cages and burst forth from their provisional, holding-cells engulfing and swallowing me whole again. Afterwards and once more, with no say, pleading or input, I was spewed out once again. That next time, however, my existence would be cast out upon a hurtful, barely accepting, resentful, unforgiving, and lonely wasteland.

CINDERELLA COMPLEX

St. Paul, Minnesota

Okay, you have guessed or interpreted my outcome from Mother's absence already. I suppose that I have painted a fairly bleak picture of my tenuous sitting-on the good ol' family-tree. For some predetermined, but misunderstood reasons, the branch I proudly sat upon broke. Or, perhaps, more bluntly and directly, I was pushed, shoved and knocked-off.

Wouldn't you know it, not even a day passed after my loving mother's funeral and memorial service, that I was crudely instructed to gather *all* my belongings and prepare to leave our home's premises. I was immediately being sent away from the services with none other than my less-than-dear Aunt Kate and her daughter, Cousin Rosalie, a wretched, unwelcoming, and despicable person by anyone's standards.

Less than a few minutes were obliged for me to stuff all my worldly belongings into a crude bag while I cried desperately with meager attempts to offer my goodbyes and hugs to all my brothers and sisters. Once again, we McCord children were being torn apart, and those tears and wailings of ours were enough to sail a ship away.

Inside Aunt Kate's car, my face smeared bluntly against the passenger's and rear-window's cold glass, I desperately wiped its steaming surface clean trying to keep my distancing images intact. I bawled like a baby watching my vanishing siblings and brief, previous life disappear into the background. I could tell that my hurt and disarray were not merely confined to my own heart. My brothers and sisters shared pain and anguish with me.

While holding baby Jackie-Boy in her arms, Jean, Bo, Mary, Colleen, and even little Jann stood crowded together as a group on the street waving frantically and all crying profusely at my sudden departure. Between sobs, I begged and pleaded with my aunt for an explanation as to why I had been singled-out and was being sent away. Her silence only harshly confused my sentiments.

During the brief drive from our house to Aunt Kate's home across town, it was Cousin Rosalie who rudely and crudely proposed an explanation.

"You're leaving because he doesn't want you there," my crude cousin began. "You're not part of *his* family anymore…and never were!" she cruelly and heartlessly announced.

I was both shocked and disturbed at the same time. "What are you talking about?" I queried in my mind. I was too surprised by Rosalie's remark to respond verbally. "'Not part of *his* family, anymore!'" I cried to myself, "What are you trying to say?"

Aunt Kate quickly jumped into the one-way conversation, "Child, you are still *my niece*, so you are *now part of my family*."

By then, I had found my voice and parried, "No! I want to go home! I want to be with my sisters and brothers! Take me back!"

"Well, you're not gonna," blurted out my cousin. "You have no choice."

"But, I don't want to go with you. I want to go back home!" I defensively exclaimed.

By then, I can vaguely recall her words and only imagine what Aunt Kate must have been thinking, but she was obviously in no mood to listen to my wailing. I remember those strange words when Aunt Kate attempted to close our debate.

Confusing me more than ever, she spoke out threateningly, "Well, you have no say, Child. Thank your lucky stars you have me to take care of you. Your mother was my *sister!* Be grateful you are not being placed in an *orphanage* somewhere. Then you'd really be sorry!"

"I had no say, you say?" I considered.

Alright, I supposed that I could understand that much and deal with it. But, be *thankful* and *grateful*? I don't think so. Why should I? And placed in an *orphanage*? What was she talking about? And what did she mean by *orphanage*? The only thing I could relate to *orphanage* about was the newspaper comic strip of *Little Orphan Annie* and her dog, Sandy.

It had always been fun and entertaining to read about her adventures and mishaps especially after she started living with "Daddy" Warbucks. "But what would that ever have to do with me," I pondered.

That, however, was the beginning of another multi-year absence from my family. I ended-up living with Aunt Kate from the middle of 4th grade until I was in the middle of eighth grade. As you may guess, I was not too well received by either Aunt Kate or her daughter, Rosalie. Those years passed slowly and despondently. I was unhappy and disheartened most of the time. Aunt Kate was never mean to me. It was just that she was never nice to me either.

My memories recall that she provided for me adequately but, perhaps, begrudgingly so. I remember several occasions hearing her talk on the phone, probably to my other aunts, her sisters. She tended to whisper a lot, but I could hear certain negativity in her words when she spoke about "no good" and "louse" and "no support" and "Schools cost money. Doesn't he know that?" or "Does he think money grows on trees?" After a phone conversation, and she saw me walk by, I often got similar remarks, "Child, you just don't know how lucky you are to be living here."

At that age, I didn't know or understand what she meant by such statements. All I knew was that I wanted to be with my brothers and sisters, not be there with her and her mean daughter. As time passed, I caught hearsay and tidbits from phone calls that suggested things were not going well at home, but it was difficult for me to digest the entire situation under my circumstances. Yet, my confusion was only to be confounded and compounded even more in relatively short terms when I heard the most recent gossip regarding my dad and my family.

I just ignored Aunt Kate and Rosalie's explanations for my dad's sudden departure. What did they know? They didn't even like him. I'm pretty sure Aunt Kate was upset, though, because my dad never came by to visit, or tell her anything and, apparently, never gave her any money for my care. But he probably owed everybody. Take a number and get-in-line. That was his way.

However, maybe he got a new job or wanted a change of scenery. Maybe he got fired because everybody at work got tired of listening to his "Creepy" stories. Or, maybe he owed too much money to the school my brother and sisters had been attending there in St. Paul. That was sure a possibility. Or, probably, the best reason was that he owed rent for the place where they were presently living. He wasn't very good about paying people what he owed them.

Anyway, my whole family was gone from me again, and my heart was broken again. Then, shortly thereafter, I heard from another of Aunt Kate's countless telephone conversations that, apparently, my dad had hired a live-in housekeeper for a new home he had rented quite a way away to take care of things and watch over all the kids. He had gotten a new job again, but this time it was far away, so he was going to be gone for long stretches at a time. My God go figure. First, our mom is gone, and then our dad ditches everyone.

I have to admit, though, that the *new* house was probably a lot quieter after that; however, I would never know. I had been left out, not included in the loop, unconsidered, and discontinued. At least part of my prayers had been answered, though. If our dad was gone, then Jean and Bo would be better-off for a while, anyway. And maybe our dad was going somewhere so he could be "fixed." We, or rather, *they* would have to wait and see. I, on the other hand, would just have to continue and do life on my own, more-or-less.

Aunt Kate had put me into another Catholic School, St. Luke's, because maybe she knew that my mother would have wanted that for me. Anyway, I did okay. I know I was always envious of all the other kids with their moms and dads always coming to school to visit their teachers, or see what was going on, or dropping them all off at school and then picking them up again afterwards.

Aunt Kate could not or would not ever do that for me. She was busy enough with her own daughter and household chores, so I understood. St. Luke's was only a short distance away, a mile or so, so I could walk it easily in the rain or shine. And for sure, I never caused any problems at school, so she was never ordered to come to school about me.

I just *carried-on,* and did my duties, and did my chores, and kept my mouth shut, for the most part. My school grades were okay, nothing spectacular. Perhaps, that was because I daydreamed a lot, and none of my classes seemed spectacularly interesting to me. I think I missed Jean's encouragement and emphasis on the importance of education. Whatever. Time passed, and my life just went on by.

Then, another bombshell came down crashing upon my head. I could tell it was a big deal by all the noise my aunt and cousin made, "Why, I never! Who does he think he is? How could that possibly have happened?"

I guess I was glad to hear their exclamations and questions because when I finally sorted out the news, those were the same reactions and questions I had. "Why? Who? How?" I freaked out in my mind.

Our dad had met somebody new and had married her! He had brought her back to his home and practically dumped her off on the kids and took-off again on a long-distance job somewhere. "Is that for honest," I remember thinking, "or was it just a joke?"

I mean, I couldn't get over that one. "How could that have happened? Do people really do that kind of thing?" I pondered.

The funny part of it, I suppose, was looking back on that situation and event later, when I reconsidered that I could have been asking about either of them! My dad *or* his new bride. Who loses a wife, or a husband for that matter, after *fifteen years of marriage* and then gets *remarried* so soon and quickly afterwards? And who would up-and-marry a man so fast, so soon, after he had just become a widower? Plus, why would somebody marry someone else so quickly who had a full house of children still living there? I mean, I was ten years old by then, and I could not even comprehend its explanation.

Wouldn't you know it, though, but a few months later, I got the opportunity to meet my actual, new stepmother. True, I didn't live with her, or them, but being married to my dad still made her my stepmother too, like it or not. Anyway, a surprise was in store for me, as it turned out. Grandmother Agnus on my mother's side of the family, arrived from Cleveland, Ohio to visit her other daughters, including Aunt Kate.

Fact was, I learned later was that she was my aunt Annie's sister. Therefore, that made her my mother's mother. Anyway, she had decided that the following morning of her visit there with Aunt Kate, she would continue on in her travels and take me with her to visit my dad, his new wife, Edith, and all my brothers and sisters.

I remember leaping for joy, I got so excited. I was allowed to miss school the next day with appropriate explanations and permissions and leave with my grandmother for the day's visit. As it turned out, it wasn't even that far away. It was south of St. Paul and straight-on down the Mississippi River.

We arrived there in Redwing, MN one early afternoon that winter of 1936. My dad was gone at work, of course, but I remember meeting Edith for the first time.

It was sort of awkward, at first, but I knew my place and manners. So, it was all, "Yes, Mam," and "No, Mam," and "Thank you, or no thank you, Mam." The honest to God truth, though? My first impression of Edith was about how short she was! I mean, I am no Amazon, myself, by-any-stretch-of-the-imagination, but at ten-and-a-half-years old? It seemed like I was already a foot taller than she was! The *heightened* sensation was almost overwhelming, and I really struggled maintaining my composure with my Yes'ms and No'ms to keep from busting out laughing. I mean that *I really looked down upon her!* Literally.

But the exciting part was that immediately upon arrival, I got to see my little sister, Jann, and my baby brother, Jackie-boy. My whole family, plus Edith, all lived together in a decent enough house in a nice enough neighborhood that was part of some newer home development there in Redwing, MN. After we arrived, I got to run-up to the front door and knock to let them know we were there. I remember feeling a little bit awkward because I was really knocking on a door asking for permission to enter my family's house. It was kind of weird. Surreal, I think they say today.

But, oh, sure, Little Jann remembered me really well, and Jackie-boy jumped-up wanting me to hold him and seemed all excited. Maybe Jackie-Boy was just feeding-off all the excitement, but I really think he remembered me too. Anyway, we hugged and hugged, and it made me very happy to be with them both. They were living in a big house too, as I recall, because there were lots of bedrooms for everyone. I carried Jackie-boy, who was already a toddler but wanted me to hold him, while Little Jann held my hand and led me all around while Edith showed Grandma and me about the house.

There were bedrooms for Bo and Jackie-Boy, another for Jean and Mary, still another for Colleen and Jann, and a final one for my dad and Edith. Plus, they had a nice, big kitchen for Edith to probably spend most of her life in, and a fairly large living room with a great big radio up against a wall. That was hand's off, though, I heard. Only their dad, I mean *our dad*, could touch the dials on it to make it work.

After a reasonable visit, however, I asked permission for what I really had come to do. I was almost beside myself anxiously waiting for an opportunity to see my older brother and sisters. Colleen was in school too, so I would even be able to see her too. So, after an appropriate time of manners greeting Edith and my little sibs, I asked for directions to their school. It was a little further away, I learned, but no matter. There were easy directions, and I could walk there in no time.

So, off I went, with a promise to Jann for a quick return and a giant smile upon my face. What I best recall, however, from that brief and excited visit with my siblings once students were dismissed from school for the day, was how frozen my hands were by the time I arrived at their school. They all knew I was coming, so they were already looking for me while I waited to greet them. It was crazy exciting, but I was afraid my hands were going to break apart while holding and squeezing each of them. Exciting, but crazy cold, I remember.

We all had a wonderful visit, and I got to catch-up on all the news regarding all of them. Jean still argued a lot with our dad, but at school, she was the science class star. She told me that all the teachers were amazed with her abilities. Bo was still being picked-on by our dad a lot and emphasized how he never wanted to be called *Roy* again. He was doing alright at school but liked to focus on art projects and be left alone most of the time.

Sis was *Sis*. I remember how beautiful and glamorous she looked. I think she was preparing for a life as a movie star celebrity, or as a model or something. Colleen was so happy to see me too, but already I could tell how she and Sis had become so close, though. Right after our quick hellos, Colleen walked along right next to Sis trying to find any new news in one of Sis Mary's Hollywood magazines.

It was a nice visit that day. Short, but worthwhile. I was so happy to catch-up visiting with all of them and hearing their news. I was really appreciative of the chance that Grandma Agnus had given me. It was important too because, as it turned out, I was not to see any of them again for nearly three more years. Eventually, I was to first have a surprised and short encounter with Bo, but his brief visit a few years later provided important impetus I required to force another needed and necessary reunion.

So, what do I say now? I went back home. Well, to Aunt Kate's house, anyway, and began carrying-on again, just like always. I got up... and did my chores like cleaning my room and the kitchen after breakfast… went to school… came home… did my major chores like cleaning the bathrooms… sweeping… mopping… dusting… and whatever else was required of me.

I helped set the table for dinner and assist Aunt Kate with anything else and then cleaned-up the kitchen right after dinner. Then it was time for me to do any of my homework and studying. When time allowed, I loved to read adventure stories and mystery novels that I got from the school library and anything about traveling to far-away places. That was thrilling to me. To be anywhere else than where I was…

Did you notice or wonder about Rosalie all that time? Gee, what was she doing while I was cleaning-up her house? She was quite a bit older than me at that time. Probably like about eighteen or nineteen. She had already graduated from high school and was out and about looking for a job or just playing around with all her friends all the time. When she was at home, though, she loved to boss me around even more than her mom.

"Patricia, you need to sweep the hallway," Rosalie loved to begin, "and don't forget to sweep in my room too. Just stay out of my things, or there will be hell-to-pay!"

Or, often she would love to order and boast at the same time, "Patricia, set the table for four tonight. My boyfriend is coming over for dinner. And just leave him alone afterwards because we'll be visiting and don't want to be bothered by a child."

Yes, she was a Prima Donna, and her mother just let her rule the roost. Whatever (Rosa) wants, (Rosa) gets. That was about the actual circumstances. Lo and behold, Rosalie wanted a baby, we supposed. So, she and her boyfriend got together and made one, so to speak. That wasn't enough, though, for our bossy, inconsiderate, and sex-hand-out, little runaround.

Oh, no! Work was scarce in those days except for people who had a really good skill or trade. Rosalie's baby's daddy, and future husband, was like most of the knock-arounds, or knock-er-ups: unemployed and out-of-work. So, our little vamp, scamp or tramp demanded of her mother to let her would-be fiancé move into the house with the rest of us.

Rosalie had to have her husband-to-be be right there with her while she was pregnant and preparing to bring a new child into the world. The only catch was that Aunt Kate, the Grandmother-to-be, was going to have to do all the work and preparations. Rosalie was slightly *above all-that,* of course. Besides, I was around to do much of the cleaning-up, and the two lovebirds would be so busy, anyway, trying to think-up appropriate names for their little demon.

Of course, I immediately offered up my choice of a name for *it* when it arrived. In my mind, I snidely exclaimed, "Hey, I know what to name it! Call *it*, "Asshole," after yourselves!"

Oh, I wouldn't have dared! She would have beaten me up for sure, and then cried for her mommy to kick me while I was down. Let's face it. There was no love lost between me and my cousin. Cousin-smousin! She was a whiner, a complainer, a do-nothing, a cry-baby, and an all-around mean, nasty and bullyish-bitch. Hmmm, come to think of it. Yes, sounds like an *Asshole* to me!

Anyway, what's all this nasty reflection and character-assassination have to do with anything? Alright, sorry for my brief diversion and absence of sophistication. The whole melodramatic tangent, however, led to the ultimate, climatic episode which would send me on a relatively new path. It would be one that would build my character, strengthen my resolve, and give me the confidence that I could do anything if I set my mind to it.

Well, anyway, that was my life back then: *The Ugly Duckling* story. I just had to mind my manners, do my chores, go to school, and try to keep my mouth shut. Honestly, though, I couldn't wait for it to end. But during the interim, there were several incidents that occurred involving me and my *other* family that kept most of us on our feet. Time passed, and sometimes, it seemed like I just passed-on through it obliviously. I think I began becoming desensitized or insensitive to whatever any new news was.

And yet, leave it to my dad. It never ceased to amaze me that still after so much passing time, I'd get surprised at something he pulled. Occasionally, once-in-a-great-while, I'd hear something or see something that would absolutely, and at least temporarily, shake-up my whole world. Honestly, I have to admit that my dad still managed to pull-off some of the most exasperating, harmful, and shocking stunts. He just had a way of suddenly surprising everyone when they least expected it.

It would always go something like this: Oh, but wait, folks! That's not all! There's more! To be sure, there had not even been a "Hello!" or, a "Howdy Doodie!" when my dad had married Edith. Nor was there any kind of a "Welcome-To-Your-New-Home" celebration!" Nope. He hadn't even provided a decent wedding reception with invitations to meet all the family. No, none of that happened.

We had always heard anything and everything second-hand, that some way regarded his whereabouts and life. It was usually well after-the-fact, at that. And if all that hadn't have been enough, right after his shocking news, of moving to Redwing and then re-marrying, we heard another spontaneous, real stunner.

Once again, yes, one-more-time, but this time it was with our dad's new bride included, he had packed-up all the kids and everything else he could jam into his car and trailer, and he moved…again. Once again, also, there was not so much as a phone call or card advising me or Aunt Kate of his intentions. No, sir! They (he) had just packed-up and moved all the way back to Sioux Falls, South Dakota once again. Good bye to us! Good luck to them! And good riddance to all!

After that, I pretty well lost track of my dad, my family and Edith. I told myself not to care anymore. Just concentrate on my own life and let him just do whatever he was going to do. Just forget about what you had no control-over. Focus on school like Jean emphasized, and one day, I would be able to find all of them again, except for my dad or Edith. I didn't care about them anymore. But, one day, I would find and get all my sisters and brothers together again someday, some way.

Of course, I still listened and heard things and stored all the pertinent or relevant tidbits of information away in my mind. For instance, a year or so later, I forget now, I heard something about them all moving back our way but to Missouri, for some reason. That, of course, was where Edith had apparently, had her final, falling-out with Brother Bo and had him sent to Father Flanagan's Home for Boys (*Boy's Town*).

And now you remember the story about how Brother Bo ran away from there, walked, hitch-hiked, and nearly froze-to-death finding me and us at Aunt Kate's house. I already explained how Bo, at age fourteen, then left for Ohio and began the courageous effort to reassemble his character and become somebody that he and the rest of us could be proud of. And I hinted that that was also an incident that started my gears turning frantically. I wanted to go home, but there was not a chance, yet, that anything like that was going to happen. I just had to wait, carry-on, and take my opportunity when I had the chance.

Soon after that, even more upsetting news arrived. By then, however, I was just noting it without much obvious, outward expression or signs of frustration. Regardless of my feelings, though, our dad had packed-up everyone and everything yet once again and left Missouri that time not long after dumping Bo off at Father Flanagan's *Boy's Town*. Naturally, he didn't bother taking me along with them even though he had room for another person now.

Plus, he didn't even have the courtesy to call-up and say, "Hi, and by-the-way, good-bye!" How ruthless and cold he seemed. Honest-to-God, I was really getting angered besides hurt and saddened anymore. I was truly beginning to recognize and understand that he really did not care about me anymore, or ever. Regardless, I had begun reaching my fill of him and his actions. Oh, but who was I kidding? I would jump at any chance to return home to my family if I could…

It was actually only a little over a year later when that *opportunity* came. Unfortunately, it did not come as any decent prospect came. On the contrary, it came full-force and right-in-the-face when I was least expecting it. And wouldn't you know it, on top of everything else that was going on, it had to involve everybody in the whole darn house. I could never get a decent, little chance to make something positive happen for myself the *easy way.*

I had to get the whole household and all the cops in the local precinct all screaming, "Holy Schomlie! Find her and lock her up!" Everyone was on the lookouts to find me first!

Alright, so let me explain. To look back and describe it all now, however, honest-to-God, it seems almost laughable. Mostly innocent, I tell you. I didn't mean for a darn thing to happen, But darned if it didn't!

You see, by that time in our home, or rather, Aunt Kate's home, we had a full household. There was Aunt Kate, Rosalie, and me for sure. But now there were two more appendages to the *Aunt Kate Consortium-of-Influence*: A brand, new *dependent baby* and a brand new, *dependent husband* and *dependent father* to the *dependent baby*. When I was home, I worked pretty darn hard all of the time just trying to help Aunt Kate keep up with all the necessary goings on.

Regardless, the *happily married* and *dependent couple,* their obviously *dependent baby* and I had to *depend* almost completely on Aunt Kate for anything and everything. Honestly, I do not know how she managed, or did it. All I know is that she did, and I grew to really appreciate her efforts, even if she never did accept me completely as a whole person.

Leave it to me, however, I could always accidentally, or inadvertently, find an innocent way to unintentionally knock a hornet's nest off its tree branch or stir up a den of rattlesnakes and then run for cover leaving all the hullabaloo scrambling behind me. Anyway, that's sort of what happened to me with my next episode of: "Cinderella loses a shoe!" The only difference between us, me, and Cinderella, was that I never got a gown or a big party or a "Fairy God Mother!" Nope, all I got was a lost shoe, that's it! And I ended up running down the street half-way bare-footed.

Anyway, here's how *the-beginning-of-the-end…* of that chapter in my life began:

ROLLING STONE

First off, my dad had again managed to rile-up affairs again, so much as he could, without necessarily trying that hard. But trouble just always seemed to find him or follow him and keep him on his toes. I always liked and understood that phrase, "A rolling stone gathers no moss" because that was our dad. He never stayed put long enough to gain any *moss*, whatsoever. But, the word for him and my family was that once Bo was out of the family portrait, he had found another means, or excuse or reason to pull-up-stakes again. So, like I mentioned just before, for whatever reason, excuse or circumstance, my dad pulled-up states and headed back to Sioux Falls.

I suppose that he must have left a reasonable impression on the airport-security team so that they welcomed him back again. Like I have said, he was actually pretty good at what he did. Radio-communication experts or security and communications-experienced people could usually find work wherever they went. So, that probably took care of the job-end of matters. As far as household rent was concerned, or school registration costs and monthly fees that were likely due mattered, well, that was a different story. Those situations were typically just a loaded-up trailer and car-ride in-the-dead-of-night away from being resolved. At least, on his end, it was…

⚭

I've often considered that my dad's sole contribution to American society was not his child-rearing skills, hah; nor his specialized airport-communications and radio expertise. No, in actuality, it was no doubt the long-lasting and consistent record he developed of running-away from any and all creditors. New city? Brand new start. Just don't return to the same school for the children, or, perhaps, the same employer, or for sure the same landlord. No, sirree. New places meant new faces. There was never any "going back!" Always forward, more, or less.

Therefore, because of his unique talent, ability, or habit of running-out on any creditors he ever managed to develop, society had to change in order to deal with such scoundrels. That was how, "Background Checks" came into existence, I imagined. Singlehandedly, my dad managed to bring all the employers of the country together on one focused aim: *"Find out who you're dealing with before you hire them! Learn about their past employers. Get references!"*

The same thing held true for landlords. They all organized and developed *Home Owners' Rental Codes* and *Renters' Histories*. Any new potential renters had to bring references from previous landlord(s) for a specified amount of time back. That way, any new, potential landlords could review rental histories of their potential, wannabe renters and make-up their collective minds over any risks involved.

Finally, schools all got on board with that concept, especially the Catholic churches. School and Attendance Records were organized into folders which began following all minor children around everywhere they went. Join a new school? You had to identify the previous school with the Records Clerk. Their job was to contact the previously attended school and have the students' records mailed to the new school. Piece of cake!

What an extraordinary improvement came as a result of all that organizing. And it was all probably due to the immense lack-of-effort and dead-of night resolve on my dad's part. Wow! He should be famous!

Anyway, in time, telephone communications and then computer internet and email just drove those kinds of people into beggar's dust. Just like his eventual hobby of being a ham-radio enthusiast was wiped-out for its legitimacy by cell phones, Facebook, Instagram, Linked-In, and all those other internet, social-networking communications, and instant-gratification services. Eventually, other cheaters like my dad lost their ability to go almost anywhere, find a new job, get a nice home to rent, or find another decent, Catholic school to send their kids. Their dirty deeds and bad habits were shut down and ended mercilessly.

Well, I got ahead of myself for a moment because that didn't happen for a long time. Actually, in the meantime, our dad just continued paving-the-way for all those future, frustrated, mandatory, and necessity's-needs inventions. Everybody improved their record-keeping methods, background-information gathering and multiple, personal-history reporting to make their own jobs and livelihoods more efficient and profitable.

And they all should have offered thanks, indirectly, for all those previously lost-out dealings with none other than Roy "Leave-'em-hangin'" McCord. I confess that there may be some (similar fools) who agreed that my dad was simply just a man-of-vision and far-ahead-of-his-time...

REJECTED AGAIN

But, getting back to me and my problems once more, that last move of my dad really irked me. Then, on-top-of-that, Brother Bo stole by in the deep darkness and freeze of midnight. Those two events really started me reflecting sadly about my family again. No matter, those incidents just managed to get my resolve up and running and turn up the flame for my tea-kettle water to heat-up. But, it would be two other near future and unrelated events or incidents which would torment me to tears and ultimately, the latter event would close this chapter of my life.

The first of these soon-to-be coming attractions would be a disheartening and cruel decision denying me a perfect opportunity for a highly desired reunion with my older brother, Bo, and sister, Jean. The second quasi-violent incident would involve my bratty, bitchy cousin, and her child. The first action got my body's blood to start boiling; however, the second spontaneous incident got my kettle to blow like Yellowstone's *Old Faithful* and burn-off steam like nobody's business. Let me explain…

As mentioned before, my presence in Aunt Kate's household was clearly understood. I *understood* that I was the last one to receive any consideration. I was there but by the grace of Aunt Kate and as a favor to my underserving father and as an honorary favor to my dearly- departed mother, Aunt Kate's sister. As long as I knew my place, performed my responsible duties to help pay-my-way and kept out-of-the-way as much as possible, I would continue to be welcome.

Change any of those conditions in any way, shape or form or deny, defy, or refuse any of their additional demands or requests, and my tenuous place among that charitable household would result in immediate tension and potential revocation of all services. That was when I usually began daydreaming, thinking about and do mental, comparative studies of my cousin Rosalie's situation versus mine. She had everything. I had nothing. She would get more. I would get less. Those were the undeniable and unchangeable rules.

Then, an unexpected event took place. Remember my Grandmother Agnus, the one who had taken me a couple years earlier to Redwing, OH to see my siblings and meet my, well, my sibling's anyway, new stepmother, Edith? Well, suddenly, and without much warning, she died. She was Aunt Kate's mother and Aunt Annie's sister and the other more obscure aunts, and our mother's mom too. The family all immediately stressed at the tragic and surprising news. Although, deeply saddened by my grandmother's sudden demise, I was still particularly concerned over other factors.

I had previously learned through my aunt and her daughter's grapevine, and from multiple attempts of successful eavesdropping, that my big brother, Bo, had left Uncle's John's home and had joined Sister Jean across town in Hayward, Ohio to live with Grandmother Agnus in her home. Then, Grandma's sudden death had changed everything. Now, right after the funeral and memorial services, the decision had already been determined that the home would be sold, and proceeds divided among the remaining three daughters as inheritors.

Jean and Bo would have to go. They were going to be allowed to remain there until the home was properly marketed for sale. It meant, however, that there likely would only be a brief opportunity at the funeral services to see them both together again at the same time. They would have to leave, and no plans had been made for that yet. It was going to be a one-and-only chance to see them.

Right away, Aunt Kate told everyone to prepare for the long drive to Hayward, Ohio. She began making immediate plans for the venture and to gather-up all necessary legal paperwork, memorabilia pictures for the memorial services and travel belongings for the expected, one-week venture. I had just celebrated my thirteenth birthday a few weeks earlier, and now school was out for the summer.

That alone had been enough to energize me and get me excited for a festive summer. Plus, I had come a long ways with my studies. Because of so much turmoil in my life previously, I had been held back a grade in between fourth and fifth. By then, however, I had regained my proper level and had even advanced to the front of our class. Going to Hayward, Ohio was sort of like a reward to me for having done well.

The teachers and the priests at school all admired and respected Aunt Kate. They were all more than happy to send supportive notes home about my advances, merits, and endeavors. What a difference paying those required registration fees meant, huh? Who would have thought? Anyway, I was happy with school. I would be entering the eighth grade and final year before high school.

And, it was summertime, and that was pleasing in itself. On top of that, although due to sad but necessary circumstances, I would get to travel to Hayward, Ohio to see my beloved, admired and respected sister Jean. Plus, I would get another chance in less than one year's time to see Bo once again. I was very hyped-up and excited for those immediate, future-family visits and potential possibilities. Who knew what might come of such a visit? I pondered breathlessly.

Then, the next morning arrived, and some other obscure, distant relative, an uncle of some sort, pulled-up outside our house with his large car. Right away, everyone hurriedly began carrying their belongings out to his car for loading. Now then, here came the kicker and the boiling-point both joined together at the hip. Something came-up, and I was beaten before I even began fighting...

Almost immediately, the new, and obscure, car-owner *uncle* raised his hand way-up high exclaiming, "Whoa there, everyone! The trunk is already stuffed completely full of my things and some of yours. Now you are all wanting the rest of you to go, four more adults *and* a child, *plus me* because *I am* the one driving this beast, *and* the rest of your belongings, and have it all go together inside my car? I don't think so. Either some of your belongings have got to go, or somebody does. Either way, make-up your minds."

I'll tell you, it took all but a flash of consideration and a snap of my aunt Kate's fingers to resolve the matter. Without further thought, Aunt Kate turned to me and flatly stated, "I am sorry, Patricia, but there is not enough room for you to go. Take your belongings back into the house. We shall be back in a week. There are plenty of provisions inside for you to get by. There is also a little extra cash I always keep inside the cookie jar for any small but necessary emergencies. Just don't spend it all on bubble gum!" She actually grinned at her self-amused, token joke.

Of course, I argued back immediately and profusely. I cried out loudly in meager protestations, "George doesn't need to go. He's nobody to the family." I meant that in more ways than one. Then I continued laboring my argument, "He doesn't need to see anybody. He never ever knew Grandma Agnus. If he stays, then I can go!"

Naturally, Rosalie had to quickly jump into the debate to defend her worthless husband's attendance. She snidely quipped, "Well, he's more a part of this family than you are. At least he knows where he came from. And nobody cares if you are there or not, either. So shut-up and get your stuff out of this car now!"

I told you she was bossy and a real bitch. I wanted to punch her right in the face, but Aunt Kate came to her rescue. "Now stop that arguing, Patricia," she refereed. "Everybody wants to meet Rosalie's husband and their new baby. It's very important that they be there to represent my family."

"But, Aunt Kate!"

"No, Child, it's too bad, but that is just the way it is. Now, remove your things, and take them back inside."

"But!" But, I did not even get in the last word.

As I dutifully dragged my suitcase from the rear seat, I deliberately let it bash into Cousin Rosalie's legs. I never apologized at all but felt only slightly comforted by the blow to her leg and dignity.

It was actually Rosalie, however, who got in the *last words* when at first, she gritted her teeth growling at my suitcase bashing, because then, she tore my heart-out when she smirked, "And good-riddance to fatherless trash!"

I watched from the top of the entry stairs and front porch as they all drove-off happily and contentedly leaving me in their rear-view mirror and exhaust fumes. I was so saddened and remorseful. Loneliness and a longing to be returned to my family once again rose-up flooding my brain. With scrambled thoughts, my mind rambled over several varying possibilities: Just leave the house and run away, maybe even to Hayward, Ohio. Wouldn't that be a great joke on them if I were already there to greet them! Oh, yes! Hilarious!

Or, a more vengeful and frightening proposal: I'd burn the house down to the ground, and that is what they would have to find upon their return.

Except, I would be there with *all my* saved, personal belongings beside me and a broken, empty cookie jar laying just close enough to be seen. And my mouth would be casually chomping-away on an enormous mouthful of bubble-gum. Ah, sweet revenge!

If I planned it exactly right, I could be using the remainder of the cookie-jar funds to have a well-planned, taxicab waiting for me. I could sourly say to all, "Ooops! Whatever happened? Sorry! But time to go. Good riddance!"

Oh, yes, in those days, I did have an active and sometimes brutal imagination. But who wouldn't after all the unimaginable dismissals I had received from home, and schools and from relatives. All those interminable rejections. To hell with the whole lot of them. Come-hell-or-high-water, I was going to figure out a way to get out of there. I did not belong there. It was *not* my home. I did not want to be there, anymore. I wanted to go home to whomever was still left. I just had to figure out a way…

YULETIDE FEVER

Little did I know or realize that I did not have to wait too much longer for an opportune opportunity. Several months later, all the required ingredients fell into place. I was about to make a mud-pie disaster, but I didn't know how to serve it all-up. I would learn quickly, however, as a unique turn-of-events exploded upon my watch, and I was forced to take significant and life-changing actions to deal with it all.

"Deck the halls with balls of holly. Fa la la la la la la la laaaaa!"

Anyhow, like I complained before, at that household, I was the unofficial housemaid. I took care of just about everything I was supposed to do, and I helped Aunt Kate with anything else that she needed or required. In a relatively short course-of-time, Prima Donna had their little baby. Like everyone else, I had to confess, he was a cute, little rascal. He reminded me in many ways of my time with Jann as a little baby and then our tiny, baby brother, Jackie-Boy. I suppose that's only because Rosalie's baby was small too, and cute and cuddly like all babies usually are. But therein ended any other similarities.

For one thing, I practically did everything else around that house that required cleaning or preparing. However, I absolutely, hands-down, zero arguments, no questions asked, was ***not*** going to get trapped into caring for that baby. Whenever the slightest inkling of resistance came-up regarding my position, I simply said, "No way! Not my baby. Not my business." Case was closed. I had my own rules, and they were permanent and unalterable.

In fact, even before the baby came, I began exercising my independence a little by finally going so far as to say, "Cousin Rosalie, your bedroom is yours and your husband's. You two can clean it yourselves. I am not. She would get indignant as all get out, but I didn't care. After all, I figured, what were they going to do? Send me to an orphanage? (By that time, I had learned a little about those). I said to myself, "Please! Do it! Go ahead! Do me a favor. I'll love it!"

Well, that wasn't going to happen realistically. We all knew it, but just the thought was empowering to me. I was gaining self-confidence and mental fortitude. I could, and did, learn to deal with Rosalie. I had just realized that with her type, I had to be absolutely firm. I needed to draw a line-in-the-sand and call her on the first inch of trespassing, if ever or whenever she stepped across. I had to admit, too, she reacted properly and appropriately to that sort of firm-stand practice.

Of course, it wasn't long at all before the *Dudley Duo* attempted to spring on me for babysitting. Still, I had to be strong and continue with my firmness. "Sorry," I'd lie, "but I have a lot of really important homework to do, and there is *just no way!*"

In my mind, I was preparing for an argumentative follow-up on Rosalie's part. If needed, I'd energetically respond, "Oh, no, sorry again. My nights are all just filled-to-the-brim until school's out…No, wait! Until graduation… from college! Sorry!"

That was my imagination running rampant, but it helped me pass the time. Usually, she'd just give me the big *"Harrumphs"* show, throw back her shoulders, toss her head way-up, and stomp away, indignant as all get-up, like she had a broom-handle stuck-up her Yazoo. Probably did! Like the one I refused to use to sweep-out her and Georgie's bedroom!

But just moments later, right after that fizzled-out scene, I'd hear her calling, "Mom! Patricia's being mean again and won't watch Junior. Will you please take him so me and George can go to the movies… again? We really need to go. Please?"

Naturally, Aunt Kate was a dutiful grandma and a spoiling mother. So, Rosalie always got her way, and they left Little Georgie into Grandma's capable willing and caring hands and were gone in less than two shakes.

If it was a chess match, though, I wasn't that good a player. I'd take a pawn by refusing to do something to help my cousin. But then it would usually backfire because I'd lose a night! Get it? A *night*, not a *knight*! Alright. Joke's over. In fact, the joke's on me because *I would lose* a big chunk of my *night*.

Aunt Kate would then get psychologically even with me. She did so by finding some massive chore for me to do keeping me occupied and away from my studies anyway. Jobs like cleaning the stove or peeling potatoes or churning milk to make butter for the next day's meals. Like I said, earlier, I felt like Cinderella without any of the amenities.

My cousin and her husband would often take-off and be gone under those same circumstances, too. Soon thereafter, the little toddler would be upstairs playing with Aunt Kate, or was at least being managed, and I would be downstairs, usually in the kitchen, completing some *off-the-wall chore* like… *cleaning the walls*! Nice pun, right? Anyway, I tried to keep a level head about it all and stay relatively happy as possible under my conditions. Besides, my private, personal time allowed me the extreme privilege of some unique, creative time to help pass my drudgeries away.

I would think about my situation and fill my chore-time up with verse and rhyme and song to please my mood. In fact, I made up a cute little limerick that used to just tickle me pink while confusing everyone else when I hummed it out loud and sang the verse in my head to myself. Let me give you an example that I used to love to hum and sing all the time around the house. I especially loved to *hum* this special tune right in front of my cousin, Rosalie, and her *broke-most-of-time* husband, George. They all used to ask me why I was humming so much day-in-and-day-out, and I'd simply reply, "Because some songs just make me happy!"

Here is my very own, personally created favorite. But, hold onto your horses because this may go big-time!

GEORGIE PORGIE

> Georgie Porgie
> Loved his pudding and pie,
> And he kissed all the girls
> 'Til he made them all cry.
> Then he found another
> Who would never deny,
> And now they got a baby
> Who makes them both cry!

Oh, I was so proud of myself! I just kept on humming that song every evening in my cousin and George's presence, and they would just look at me like I was weird, or something. But, I was laughing my *proverbial arse*-off!

However, the moment of truth was drawing near. I could tell. It was like something I could almost smell-in-the-air, but I couldn't tell from which direction it was coming. And I didn't know when, or where or what would happen either. I was just getting sort of antsy and pretty sure something unusual would occur that was going to *blow* that *proverbial steam-lid off!*

And who would have thought that my darling, toddler second-cousin, or whatever, little Mini-Georgie, would become the star culprit and cause of our steamy explosion? Oh, yes, he surely would, but I need to set the stage first for emphasis. Let me begin by explaining that Little Georgie was even more spoiled than his miserable mom. "Whatever Georgie wants... Georgie... had better get fast, or he would start screaming his bloody, little head off!"

Oh, how often I used to say exhaustively to myself, "Oh, come on, Cousin. Just five minutes alone! Please, that's all I need with him! I can fix *all* your troubles that fast. I promise!"

Of course, you might recognize my dilemma, though, can you? If I dealt with Georgie, then I'd be allowing Rosalie to *cross my line in the sand!* After that, I'd be a goner. No more game with rules. I'd have lost even before I made my next move. So, nope, no way, Jose. Spoiled, or not, little Mini-Georgie was to remain all their problem and none of my own...

But here comes the big catch: *Catch 22*, at that; Medusa's Head; a cracked-mirror of bad luck; *any bodies stepping-over-the-line!* That damned line had two sides to it. They could not step-over onto my side, nor could *I ever step-over* onto their side *either*! And so, what did I go and do? *Right!* *I* stepped-over the line onto their side big-time, and my goose got cooked!

It was Christmas time, and noel merriment was spread across the community. Not necessary to mention, but it was Winter, and snow was everywhere too. It covered all the rooftops, any sections of sidewalks left unattended by home owners or renters. Snow smoothly layered itself over all the lawns up and down our street. The neighborhood traffic had dug trenches through the snow- covered streets for other cars to follow-in their pathways as they passed. It was still so cold outside that all the places compacted by foot or roadway traffic had been crushed and hardened into ice and made slippery-as-hell.

Now that sounds like an oxymoron, doesn't it, sort of like *colder-than-hell*!

Oh, so sorry, got side-tracked there… Anyway, it was freezing cold outside. You get the picture, and I was happy as heaven that it was a holiday period with no school. I had a reprieve, except on Sundays for Mass services, from trudging over all those dangerous snow-packed sidewalks and across those treacherous neighborhood streets. Plus, it was so cold outside that any breeze at all in the air would freeze your nostrils as you breathed. You really had to protect yourself if you ever ventured-forth outside into that frozen wasteland.

If they dared, someone had better be dressed properly to weather the weather, so to speak. There was an understood *dress code* everywhere for this time of inclement weather. It always minimally included the following instructions and items: Dress in layers; use many thin, warm layers of appropriate clothing rather than a few thick layers; wear winter socks and insulated boots if you could; use a good quality coat, or a parka, or jacket, or something; wear a base-layer of clothing and then another warm layer over that; wear a nice warm hat that pulled-down over your ears; an added scarf to protect your neckline from the freezing chill would be well advised; and, of course; and finally, of course, anyone braving the outdoors for business or pleasure had better have on thick, warm and decent gloves for their hands and fingers.

Those finger digits were usually the first to go, break-down and give-in to the frigid coldness. Typically, toes were next. Take your gloves off, though, for any reason or purpose to play, do some sort of business activity or wrestle with some necessary task requiring exposed fingers, and the coldness could be merciless. I actually loved the wintery snowfalls, but only from a distance. Like from inside a nice, toasty living room watching it through frosted-over, steam-covered windows. Yeah, that, or in the movies or postcards, but *not* in it, actually. It was always enough for me just to pass through it to get somewhere else necessary and warm.

Anyway, I was happy as a lark to be inside our warm and cozy bungalow, rather than outside suffering from that freezing tempest. I only had to spread the front-room curtains aside and peek outside to appreciate my place on earth. That bitter, subzero white avalanche had overwhelmed and entrapped our entire region forcing nearly everybody indoors to escape certain chilling harm. I was gleefully humming away with Christmas tunes I recalled, and occasionally I would toss into the mixed set a few flippant exercises and variations of my favorite *Georgie Porgie* limerick. I was content as what might be expected under my circumstances.

Then, everything, my whole world, suddenly collapsed in a matter of rapidly paced time-bomb minutes…

CHRISTMAS CRUNCH

I had been all alone and by myself busy and nosey and curious about many of the gifts that were all beautifully wrapped and placed under our cheerfully decorated Christmas tree. I had even gone to somewhat selfish extents to separate my gifts from others and stack them together for my joyful review and pleasure. I was pleasantly occupied and happy…

Suddenly, and like out-of-nowhere, I spotted Little Georgie-Porgie, Jr. come into the front room and casually sauntered over next to me to watch what was going-on and perhaps participate. He was a big three-year old by then with a decent grasp of Christmas, meaning he understood about getting gifts. Then, without so much as a warning or a "Watch this!" that little monster unbuttoned his coveralls, pulled-out his tiny whizzer and began peeing all over *my* duly organized and separated gifts. *Mine*!

At first, I couldn't believe my eyes or ears. That little, Dudley spin-off effectively had his back to me once he joined me by the Christmas tree. I was sort of ignoring him still engrossed in my own imagination and thoughts of what fun and surprise lay ahead for me inside all those pretty wrappings. Then, the unique sounds and then vision became obvious and unmistakable. I could hear the peeing stream as it flowed out and over my presents. I could hear the splashing and spraying of his pee as it engulfed and drenched all my gifts. I could hear his childish giddiness and joyful laughter and snickering as he *drowned all my Christmas offerings*.

Then, I understood and could clearly see his deliberate weaving and oscillating and stretching his little, monstrous body as he attempted to submerge my entire gift arrangement with his vengeful pee. Only seconds had passed since that filthy, little upstart began his mischievous and ornery, urinary exercise, yet I still had barely enough time to react.

And react I absolutely did. Releasing an angry and most ungodly shriek of my own, something definitely meant to terrorize little children during Halloween, not at Christmastime, I leapt to my feet, and in one full sweep, knocked that little brat far backwards and entirely-off his feet. His uncontrolled peeing spree continued, though, with its wild spray was now raining down over himself, me, other nearby gifts, and the floor around us.

Shocked by my reaction, though, instantly Georgie, Jr., himself, recovered from my own surprise attack, and let out his own grievous scream. Although my deliberately raging, punch-push had obviously and likely mortified the entire neighborhood of potential child endangerment, I was just beginning. Once I fully took hold of him and grasped his nasty, smelly, self-drenched little body frame into my hands, I proceeded with my previously mental behavior-training mode. I flipped him over onto his stomach and over my extended leg and began wailing-away upon his spoiled, rotten behind while lacking all mercy.

I am certain that multiple spews of unencumbered profanity, not fit for a child's ears, came wrathfully cascading from my super-antagonized mouth. Yet, none of it interfered with my punishing, walloping actions. In fact, my expletives probably added timing, rhythm, dimension, and emphasis to each delivered whack. I was on a roll and just getting started. I had taken that spoiled-rotten child's absolutely necessary, behavioral-training needs completely into my own hands now. I was going to give him the lesson-of-a-lifetime. One that he finally, and so deservedly, needed in order to avoid his clearly approaching, juvenile delinquent-life's sake.

Unfortunately, however, or maybe not, Georgie Jr.'s initial defensive screams were enough to awaken the dead, and he continued with his howling and gasping and choking sobs as I masterfully persisted with my untethered punishment. Obviously and naturally, though, his almost unnatural bellowing drew attention from his mother, Rosalie. Honestly, I believe that she may have rounded the corner, from the stairwell leading to the bedrooms above, and stepped into the living-room just in time to watch me knock Georgie Jr. down in the first place. Perhaps, she may have even mistaken my initial action as playful roughness teasing her rough-and-tumble little son, and future dud, just like his father.

However, there was no mistaking my next actions once I thrust that child over onto his belly across my leg and began mercilessly pounding on his backside. My cousin, Rosalie, the little brat's astonished mother, screamed out loud then, in anguished terror. With fear, anger, and revenge in her eyes, immediately, she charged across the room in split-second timing and grabbed her child from my torturous hands. After practically flinging her screaming, horrified child across the room to a point of safety, Rosalie suddenly turned and, in a crazed attack-mode, viciously charged me with her untrained, and almost silly, counter measures.

Granted, Rosalie was well into her early twenties by then, and arguably bigger and stronger than me, and she was an angry, defensive mother. However, I was still big for my age at thirteen-and-a-half-years, had oodles of self-defense training from my siblings and parental observations and was outdoorsy and tough as they came when it involved defensive struggles. Unlike my softened cousin who had been given everything all her life, I had grown tough being forced to earn anything for myself the hard way. To my natural advantage too, I quickly noted that even protective mothers had to know some offensive and protective skills or else when necessary, they could be extremely disadvantaged.

That factor was abundantly obvious in this case. My cousin's miserably spoiled lifestyle had taught her nothing about protecting herself from harm's way or how to protect her own child. Rosalie's wild, miscalculated swinging-arms and easily countered clawing and grappling was no match for my trained, refined, skilled, and extremely effective blocking guards. Then, quickly converting from a very adequate defensive mode, I countered with my own fully geared-up and aggressive offensive focus. I instantly charged her with cleanly-aimed and direct face and body shots using my tightened, hardened, and swift fists like mini-sledgehammers.

Like the saying goes: "She never knew what hit her!" or, "She never saw it coming!" I was all over that witch like hornets on a hambone. A couple more faintly reactive, but helplessly thwarted swings on her part, and my cousin's defensive mechanisms completely disintegrated. That phase ushered in my next revenge cycle where I elected to continue, and get even, you might say. Rosalie's past four years of bullying, mean-tempered behavior, and cruel words toward me were now about to receive their due cost.

I was so fast, so direct and explicit in my actions that Cousin Rosalie could not even speak. She was speechless! Her shocked, wide-opened, and almost bulging eyes could barely, blankly stare as I fixated on punches to her face, exactly measured strikes to her throat and a flurry of furious blows to her arms and chest, Rosalie was completely disabled. She was void of any further offensive or even defensive actions or effort. She was like a rag doll that I could have my way and will with. Ultimately, she barely managed to turn, while gasping for air, and crawl away as I closed-out the encounter with a final, couple of well-placed boots to her large, protruding butt.

Rosalie then gathered-up enough resistance to drag and force her body into full retreat managing to exhaustedly crawl-away and stumble to the stairwell. I noted immediately that while she had managed to escape my wrath, she had actually crawled-away and completely and irresponsibly forgot about her now, unprotected child. Instead, she proceeded staggering-up the stairs to her bedroom while seeking her mother's attention with overly dramatic pants, "Muutherr! Muutherrr, help me! She's trrryinnng to kkkill meee and Georrgie, Juniorrr...! Heelllp!"

Ooops! A moment came for me to reflect on that recent melee. I knew that I had gone and done it that time. There would be no forgiveness, not for any attack against Aunt Kate's beloved, perfect angel. Nor would there be any excuses accepted for the unintended but deliberate and ruthless persecution of her darling, and beautifully budding grandchild. No, there was no hope for me now, and there was no turning back. I would likely not even have an opportunity for an *orphanage option*. No, on the contrary, there would be no saving's grace for me. I knew and understood that disingenuous family, and I recognized my place among it... at the deepest bottom. The only placement from them that I could look forward to was jail.

Did I mention that Aunt Kate was a fairly respected member of the neighborhood, our community, and our local Catholic Church. She offered volunteer-time and personal-action services to the East St. Paul Community Actions Committee, leadership and time to the St. Luke's Catholic Women's League, and she was a faithful and generous donor to all three of those organizations. She was liked, admired, and revered among her peers. One word from her, and I was likely liable for the electric chair... or maybe even a firing squad!

HOME FOR THE HOLIDAZE

My new unfortunate position would be clearly understood. A minimum, four-year invitation and protracted stay to remain with Aunt Kate had come to a miserable end, I knew. I thought for a moment more and recognized one lucky factor in my favor. My half-cousin-in-law, Georgie-Porgie, Sr. had fortunately been gone for the afternoon. Supposedly, he was off looking for a job, but we all knew that he was most likely just out drinking with his fellow duds. Had he been home, however, the outcome would most likely have ended quite severely different for me.

There had been no love lost between him and me. Except for a couple of off-center remarks and somewhat suggestive comments that he had made toward me on a few occasions, we seldom had any other words for each other. He knew I did not like or respect him, and he disliked me for that fact. Under those previous circumstances and conditions, my behavior, and actions that day toward his little boy would have been all he needed to become brutally hurtful to me. Most likely, I would have ended-up in a hospital and then sent to jail immediately following my discharge.

No, the answer to my immediate crisis was clear: *Get Out of Dodge!* I needed to *get out fast and as far away as I could manage.* There would never come moments for reflection, consideration, and thoughtful dialog regarding the incident. I had been a *semi-slave* at the bottom of the ladder of respectability and countenance. I was an *ugly duckling* with no chance for any remarkable transformation. I was a shoeless Cinderella with no fairy-godmother. And I had reached the end-of-the-line. All I could hope to do was get out immediately with the clothes on my back.

Leaping-up from my kneeling position, my unplanned and spontaneous reactions told me to shove my boots on immediately. Swiftly completing that time-consuming activity, I quickly snatched my overcoat from its hanging spot by the front door and roughly thrust it on crudely covering my shoulders. Then, in one ongoing blur of action, I flung open the front door, shoved the screen door open with my foot and held it there and then conscientiously pulled the front door behind me back to its closed position. Finally, in that last stage of blurred and crazed action, I frightenedly bolted down the steps, raced over the entrance walkway, threw open the front gate and leapt through slamming it shut behind me. Unofficially entering the outside world, I hurriedly headed for the downtown area of St. Paul.

Another fortunate discovery was a small bit of change still left-over in my overcoat's pocket. It was money meant for a possible weekend movie or some sort of entertainment. However, now it was going to be my ticket *out of Dodge!* I had plenty of money to catch the nearest city bus-line which would take me directly down town to the bus terminal and train station. I quickly considered options and determined that I would try the train station first.

I walked quickly to the nearest bus stop and stood there shivering for several minutes waiting for the next bus to come by. Naturally, I worriedly kept looking behind me or over my shoulder to see if anyone suspicious was coming my way, like a police car or something. I did not know how long it might take before Aunt Kate called authorities about me. I figured that with all of my personal belongings still there, they would not consider that I had gone far. Maybe I was even still hiding in the house, somewhere.

Any bus arriving was going to be alright. I knew most of the routes from trips I taken many times before to go into town for a movie or window shopping and such. Lots of times when I had all afternoon to myself, I liked just riding a bus all the way to the end of his route. I learned a lot about the city that way. Fortunately, I already knew that it would be easy to get to where I wanted. It didn't matter which one stopped because, no matter, I could catch it and then go downtown where I would get-off and grab a transfer to catch another bus that would take me almost directly to the Union Train Station on 4th East St.

Once there, I could make up my mind what was next, but at least I could get out of this terrible freezing weather. Both the train station and the bus station had fairly large terminals which provided temporary shelter and protection from the elements. However, I had already noticed that the bus station was smaller and somewhat limited in scope, especially for late night travelers. The train station, on-the-other-hand, was much larger and had fairly decent accommodations.

Of course, a bus did arrive shortly thereafter, and I am sure that the driver checked-me-out head-to-toe noting how I had terribly failed the *winter wardrobe dress code* for outdoors. It was true too, and I was suffering for it. My nose and neck were freezing, and my fingers were all practically numb from the awful chill in the air.

Eventually, however, I did get to the Union Station, and that was where my next big challenge and dilemma came. There was no doubt in my mind that I was not going back to Aunt Kate's. That would be a *death wish*. But where to go was the real big question? Naturally, I wanted to go and stay with Jean and Bo. I had already heard that they both had been forced out of Grandma Agnus's house and had decided to go on to Cleveland, Ohio where a lot more and better jobs were to be found. Factories were springing-up all over or converting their products to sell to the British and French who were busy fighting against the terrible, Nazi-German military.

I remembered from living at home before, that Jean had defended Bo so many times against our Dad when they were together, and Jean almost always took a serious shellacking for her protective efforts. After leaving Grandma's house together and heading to Cleveland, I had also learned that they were renting an apartment together. That was a big deal, in itself, because even with all Jean's defenses of Bo, they still never got along very well as siblings. Both of them were too riled-up from our dad, maybe, or both too stubborn in their own ways; however, they had apparently learned how to put their differences aside and live and work together for their own betterment.

I was happy for that, but it did not really help me much. I had no idea where in Cleveland they lived or how to get in touch with them. I didn't even know if they had a phone. Probably not, because lots of places like apartment buildings had to share one phone for lots of residents. In many high-rise buildings, there was one phone on each floor to be shared.

But that was no help to me. So, I really thought about and considered my other option of going back home. I really did not know what to expect, and I had not even seen my dad in several years. He had been gone when Aunt Agnus took me to visit everyone a couple years earlier. But I thought that I may have made a decent enough impression on the new stepmother, Edith. Maybe? Possibly?

It was worth a try. So, I found the public phones up against a far wall in the train station and hurried over to them. Although there were lots of people bustling and hanging around the station that time of day, either waiting for someone arriving or for their train to depart, there were still a couple of unoccupied phones. It was early evening for me and even an hour earlier at my dad's place since they were on Mountain Time, and we were Central. I knew my dad's home phone number already because I had memorized it right away after I saw it on my Aunt's message-wall. However, I had never called Sioux Falls, South Dakota before. I had never been allowed.

I remember making that first phone call, though. I lifted the receiver and dialed "O" for operator and told her the number. A moment later, the lady operator instructed me to insert a certain amount of change. I was excited and pleased too, because I had just enough left-over change to make a call. The phone rang and moments later, a voice came on the line, and momentarily, I was startled... It had to have been Edith, just stating, "Hello.."

"Hi, Edith, this is Patsy."

"Patsy? Oh, Patricia? Is this you?" Edith asked.

"Yeah, hi, it's me. Can I talk to my dad, please?"

"Well, I'm sorry, Patricia, but your father is not home. He won't be back for a couple more days. He's away at a radio-training school, or something, in Denver. Can you call back then?

"Oh, no!" I exclaimed, "I don't have any more money."

"Money? Why do you need money?"

"Oh, no. No reason. I just didn't have enough change to buy some... some, uh, bubblegum until later, that's all."

"Oh, alright, then, dear. Just call back in a couple more days. In the evening, of course, so your father can get home from his job first."

"Wait! Just a second! When he gets home, please have him call me at this number. Okay?" I read the phone number back to Edith that was taped on that machine.

"Alright, Dear, if that's what you want. Anything else?"

"No, that's all. Please make sure he calls, though. Okay? Thanks."

"Okay, Bye-bye, then," were Edith's last words.

"Bye, bye, then," was all the more I could say, and we disconnected.

I wanted to take time and talk to anyone else there too, just to say, "Hello," but I knew I had to save my change. Calls cost more money, and I knew the operator was going to come back on the line and interrupt us telling me to insert more dimes, so I changed my mind. That was when I really began worrying, though. Whatever was I supposed to do for two more days?

"Oh, hi, Aunt Kate. Mind if I just hang-around for a couple more days and then run-off again? Pleeeease?"

No, hardly not. I think the word *hang* was probably the appropriate verb, though. But what was I going to do? No doubt, Aunt Kate, or Rosalie or even *Dudley Georgie,* by now, had contacted the police and were on the lookout for me.

I could almost hear the cries and warnings on the phone after they realized that I was truly gone. "Yes, officers! She's a vicious, violent attempted murderess, and she's on the loose. Look everywhere for her. Catch her! Lock her up! She's a menace to society! And watch out! She's armed and dangerous! She stole all the long, razor-sharp butcher knives from our kitchen. She'll stab you for sure! Be careful, for God's sake!"

Nope. No going back for me. I just had to figure-out how to survive until I could at least contact my dad. It sounded like it was going to be a long wait.

The train station was at least moderately warm and viable. As long as I stayed away from those big, entrance doors or the gate-doors leading to the various trains platforms, I'd be okay. Those brutal gusts of freezing wind that blasted through any opening doors would just chill-you- to-the-bone if you were standing near them. Not knowing what to do next, I just sat down on one of the *Waiting Area* benches and tried to collect my thoughts.

Well, I'm not going to go over every detail of my ordeal, but suffice to say that it *was a long wait*…I mostly just sat there for several hours at a time, and then got up and walked around a bit and then just sat there… and. Night came, and I just curled-up on one of the seats and slept as best I could. Of course, one of the station agents came by and inquired of my status, so I just lied, naturally.

"Oh, sorry," I smiled, "I just picked-up the wrong schedule and read it. He's on a different train than I thought."

'Well, shouldn't you go back home and come back later?'

"Oh, no, it's okay. I'm fine. I'll just wait. Thanks, though."

That agent would leave, but then another would come over the next morning, and we'd have to go through the same process of questions-answers again. But, that wasn't the worst part. Usually, I sat or stretched-out on one of the chairs nearest to the Ladies' bathroom. That was because already by that next morning, I noticed that police were coming into the station. They were deliberately scanning over the entire crowd. It was obvious that they were looking for someone. Someone like me, do you think?

That's what I thought, anyway. So, as soon as I spotted one or more of them enter into the station, I leapt-up from my seat and ran like hell to the bathroom. Once inside, I quickly took-over one of the stalls, locked it from inside and then stood-up on the toilet-seat off the ground. Eventually, I would hear someone walk-in, walk around for a bit and then leave. I was pretty sure that it was a cop. So, I didn't take any chances but just stayed in there for another hour or two to make sure it was safe for me.

If I walked back-out into the main train-station from the lavatory and there was still a policeman or two hanging around looking or watching, then I quick-as-a-wink jumped-back into the bathroom and repeated the same routine once more. I actually had to go through that *routine* several more times because it seemed apparent that by the next day's evening, those police were likely looking for a young lady about my exact same age, exact same height and build and dressed exactly the same way as me. Hmmm. What a coincidence!

Anyway, I'd like to say that the time just passed so quickly, but it didn't. If it hadn't been for those occasional on-my-toes, hide-and-seek episodes, I might have collapsed with hunger and lack of sleep. Funny thing was that the train-station agents must have been informed by the police, were wise to the situation and were on the lookout for somebody *exactly* like me too. But, after a while, all I received from them were just sort of kind and basic questions.

"You okay, kid? Still waiting for your train to come-in? Your daddy still supposed to show-up?" Their questions were never insulting, mean or suspicious, either. By the second day, I actually began thinking that maybe they were all on the *watch-out* for me and not the *look-out*. Oh, sure, in a big, train-station like that there always likely to be creeps and pickpockets, and molesters hanging around too, just watching and waiting for their prey. But those same agents must have been guarding me too. Because as soon as some shiftless person approached me to offer their kind services or some candy, or food or anything, there would be an agent right there, on-the-spot and in a second.

"Get away from that young girl! She doesn't need a thing from you. Now get out before I call the cops!"

I was immediately relieved, although I was prepared to tell the creep, or whatever, to take a hike, anyway, but I really appreciated the protective interference.

"Then, one time, one agent was so kind with his follow-up after threatening and chasing some hustler away, "Don't worry, kid. I know the cops are the last ones you want to see or talk too. Here's a couple dollars. Why don't you go over to the snack bar and get something good to eat. Try their soup. It ain't bad, and it will surely help to warm-up your insides."

I remember being surprised, embarrassed and oh, so happy to have something to eat. I gratefully took the man's money, thanked him profusely and dashed-off to the lounge area and snack bar to get something to eat. I thought the agent might even be watching me, so I for sure bought some soup, plus some crackers and cheese and a soda-pop. I was starving, I felt, and that was just about one of the best meals I had ever had.

Afterwards, when I went quietly back to my chair near the bathrooms, I looked across the station to the agent who had helped me, and I smiled and nodded to thank him again in appreciation. I saw him give me a thumbs-up sign and a returned smile. I was relieved and more-or-less content.

No more cops the next day except just occasionally as they walked through the station on their standard route of surveillance. I think that I was in the clear, sort of, by then, but I still didn't take any chances. I even supposed by then, that I was probably entertainment for the ticket and service agents because once any policeman walked-in, they could quickly spot me dashing for the bathrooms again. Ha! Ha! Funny. But, I didn't mind. Today was the day, two days later that my dad should finally be home.

I waited anxiously all that day, morning, noon, and evening for a phone call from the same one that I had given the number to Edith. All day long, nothing. I started getting worried. When would he call? Please call. Then a phone rang, but it wasn't my phone. I raced over and picked-up the receiver anyway.

"Hello! Hello! Dad, is this you?" I almost frantically inquired.

"Huh?" was the response. "Is this Parson's Bakery? Oh, sorry, wrong number."

Yes, very wrong. Nothing was going right. For a while afterwards, still nothing, but I just patiently waited. Then, of all things, and with like four phones available for use, some guy comes over and takes the phone I am waiting tolerantly for to receive my call.

I quickly dashed up to the man and burst out, "Sir, please use another phone. I am waiting for a call on that one."

The fellow gave me a quick up-and-down scan with his beady eyes, and then shooed me away with a curt reply, "Beat it, kid. Can't ya see I'm busy?" He turned his back on me and continued with his call.

Ten or fifteen minutes later, he hung-up the phone, turned around and saw me in the near distance and spit out, "All yours, kid. Have at 'er!" I hated him.

I wanted to punch him right in his tiny, unblinking eyes. Instead, I just smirked him away with a snort and continued sitting where I was and watching that phone. Time passed, and still there was nothing.

Then, wouldn't you know it. Just as another policeman entered the station and looked like he was searching for the crowd again, and I went racing-off for the ladies bathroom to climb above one of the toilets once more behind a locked-stall door, I actually heard my name being broadcast over the train-station loudspeakers.

"Patricia McCord. Patricia McCord. Please go to Ticket Window Number Eight. Patricia McCord, Window Eight please."

"Oh, my God!" I thought. What do I do? Quick decision. I turned and raced for Window Eight. For some reason, the policeman wasn't even bothered by the announcement or by my sudden reactions. Must not have been listening, I supposed. But I was there at the window in no time at all.

"Yes, Sir. That's me! What is it, please?" I begged.

"I just got a call from a Roy McCord. That your dad?" he asked.

"Oh, yes, Sir! That's him. What did he say?" I pleaded.

"Just that he wants to talk to you. Come around the corner there, young lady and take this call. He's on the line, right now."

Wow! My heart was pounding! Instantly, I dashed around the corner of the window booths and ran to the man at Number Eight. He just sort of smiled and handed me the phone. He had been talking to my dad, probably.

"Hello! Dad, is it you? Really you? Dad, I want to come home. I don't want to be at Aunt Kate's, anymore. Please let me come home." I was nervous as all get-up. Sweating bullets, like they say.

His answer was sort of indirect, but also somewhat relieving. "Well, it's more like you can't go back to your aunt's house. She's got the police and everyone looking for you. How you ever managed to be at that train station, I'll never guess." At least he wasn't angry and vile. That was a start.

"Yes, Sir. Sorry, Sir," I whimpered, "There was a big misunderstanding, but I just want to come home again. Please can I, please?"

"Well, I guess that we don't have much choice," my dad continued, "The police have been watching you for two days now, and so have the train-station agents. And none of them seem to want you either. Let me talk to the Ticket-Sales man again. Wait for his instructions."

I was trembling like an earthquake was shaking underneath us, or probably more like a big, giant train was passing-by, but I practically shoved the phone back into the agent's hand and waited.

A minute later, the agent hung-up the phone, started punching some numbers on a machine of his and then smiling at me, handed me a ticket, and said, "Gate Four, young lady. Train Twenty-nine in thirty-five minutes. All aboard! Now, scoot, and go home. Good luck!"

I was dumfounded and surprised and delighted all-in-one. I probably had the biggest grin on my face that that agent had ever seen, but I gleefully snatched the ticket from his hand, turned and raced for Gate Four calling over my shoulder, "Thank you. Thank you, so much! See you!"

My tribulations there at the train station were finally over. I exhaled deeply to myself while considering that, hopefully, my difficulties in St. Paul, Minnesota and life with Aunt Kate were also over. In twenty minutes more, I was aboard Train Number Twenty-nine, seated comfortably in a booth by a nice window and waiting for my five-hour train ride to Sioux Falls, South Dakota. The next chapter of my life was about to begin…

I was in a strange mood, as I recall. I was so relieved to be gone from my aunt's house and the unhappy pressure that I always felt there. Of course, I also recognized that I wasn't winning any popularity contests there, either. But, no matter. I was going home where I wanted to be. My beautiful, older sister, Mary, or *Sis,* we called her was there to help guide me. Younger Colleen and Jann and little Jackie-Boy were there to hug and visit and play with too.

I knew that it was going to be somewhat awkward dealing with my new, stepmother, Edith, but I was gratefully up to the task. The big question on my mind, however, was why and how my dad had responded the way that he had. I mean, he had been fairly forthright and even urgent in getting me aboard the very next available train. I couldn't figure out why. All I knew was that I was ever so happy and thankful. I was returning home. The *prodigal daughter.*

I kept flashing back on those wonderful years between five and nine that I had lived with my family the first time. They had been so loving, and I had felt so loved even if there were all those issues at school and with my dad's affections, or rather, lack of. But I carried around all the fond, caring, and pleasing memories to help carry me through my present times. It's sort of a human nature thing, I believe. From all the bad times in our lives mixed-in with the good, when we are somehow taken away or removed from our otherwise *normal* existence, our minds and memories just sort of intentionally cast-off the bad ones and leave the good recollections to hang onto. That was how I wanted to remember being back home.

CONUNDRUM

Sioux Falls, South Dakota

N ow, don't get me wrong. Those few, brief years with Mother, though blessed, were still stained with sadness, pain, violence, and ultimate tragedy. They were usually all directly or indirectly due to our dad's intentions, too. Later, at thirteen-years of age, when I finally returned home once again, stepmother Edith was at the helm. Things just did not sail smoothly the same way anymore under any circumstances. It was like a dark, menacing cloud was always hovering above us ready to pour its torrential rains down upon our voyage, or parade or any potential happiness. Our home was a *pain-shelter* harboring sadness brought inside from all types of external, unfortunate, and traumatic events.

I was to learn, however, that probably the main reason my dad had even allowed me to return in the first place, was of some sort of misdialed, miscalculated, or mistaken pride he had felt for me from my fighting incident at Aunt Kate's. It seems that the dislike or non-appreciation felt toward my dad was mutual for him too. In some demented way, he was happy to hear of the ruckus that I had caused at Aunt Kate's home that Christmas of 1939.

After all, she was not his kin, and Aunt Kate never showed any liking for him. At the same time, he had little or no regard for her, either. She was a sister of my mom who lived across town and was willing to take me in under our abysmal circumstances. That was all. She was someone that he could use. But, apparently, he admired or respected my gumption. To beat hell out of a little child and then punch-out the mother? Well, that was something worthy of attention, and it was right-up-his-alley and worthy of sharing with his buddies.

On top of all that, at the same time when I snuck away from Aunt Kate's house and took a train back home again, my mind and body were changing too. Mentally and physically I was becoming really aware of my family's surroundings and its effects and impact upon me. My mind was learning and growing, and my body was maturing, forcing both into continual emotional conflict. On-one-hand, I had to continuously watch my *p*'s and *q*'s always remaining ever-mindful of my tender situation and ever-precarious standing within the family fold.

On-the-other-hand, I was thirteen-and-a-half years old and becoming a young woman already. I deserved the right to voice my opinions, and I wanted desperately to be heard. I wanted to be able to make decisions regarding my own life. Yet, I always feared speaking-up because it might have ended-up being my first and last time.

But, then again, there I was… stuck-in-the-middle. At first, regarding Edith, I was, "Yes, Mam," and "No, Mam," and I did whatever I was told by her. Of our dad, I *always* obeyed him. Obedience to him was purely out of fear. It was true too that once I had been allowed to return to the family home back from Aunt Kate's, I was so grateful. I did not want to take any chances and mess-up my opportunity. I just kept my mouth shut most of the time, watched everything going on around me and thought constantly about my tenuous placement.

I understand now that I obeyed Edith more because of her adult status and newly placed maternal position, at least to me, in our family. I suppose it was a little like being in the military: You may not like an officer, but you had to respect and salute their rank. I obeyed her also because of my joy from having even been reincluded at all, regardless of any stepmother.

After all, Edith had already been with the family for nearly four years by then and had all but earned her grasp of our family's situation. At thirteen-years of age and returning once again to my family with Edith now at the helm, I was sort of like a little, lost homeless lamb. I would have accepted any new ewe as my sheep mother, as long as I was allowed back in the same flock.

So, for those next nearly two years, I felt like I was in a real *conundrum*. I didn't hardly know our new stepmother, Edith (new to me, anyway), from a hole-in-the-wall; however, I was dolefully forced to remain stiffly respectful and compliant to her wishes and commands. I understood my tenuous place, too, but I remained ever observant and vigilant. I was ever mindful of where I was, but I also carefully persisted in gaining more trusted ground or security.

I watched all the interaction between the younger siblings with Edith and those more cavalier attitudes of Mary toward Edith. Also, I had heard about the recent past's nearly daily array of arguments between Jean and Edith. I noted where Jean's defiance and disobedience nearly always resulted in physical, violent, and vicious fights with our dad.

I had seen first-hand so many of the terrible, often bloody, battles which physically occurred between our dad and Jean when I had been younger from five to nine-years of age. Our dad would start-out talking loudly and then move on to shouting in Jean's face. Jean just glared at him and shouted right back. Then, our dad would begin shoving Jean backwards, and that was when she began punching and kicking back. Jean's physical defiance was all it took after that for our dad to start swinging and go for lethal blows. His rage became so intense that he quickly turned violently aggressive and seemed to frantically obsess on catching and hurting Jean..

Jean was always big for her age, and she even had a tough-guy image about her developed from the time when she was fairly young. She seemed to have a mean streak of her own too, but she was never any match for our dad, of course, in any real altercations. She would scream and holler back at him challenging every threat he made. Jean was never afraid to kick and punch our dad back when the physical stuff began.

But she was never any real threat to him. Jean's fight with mostly self-defensive postures. Thus, ultimately, when struggles wore on, Jean would wear-out and then run-for-cover out the front door. Later that night, she would sneak back in staying out-of-sight until our dad was usually gone the next morning. Fortunately, our dad never attacked or injured Jean while in her sleep. Perhaps, in his mind, every day was war, but sleeping time was a sort of armistice.

That is what I remembered, at least, from years earlier while all of us kids were there at home. To be honest, though, those altercations and arguments between Jean and our dad, and Bo as an even younger child and our dad, were what I clearly remember and easily recall from that earlier period. By the time I returned back to the family-home that Christmas in 1939, my brother, Bo, and Jean were both already gone from the house. Bo had already been gone for nearly three years, and Jean had been forced to leave not long after her seventeenth birthday but before I arrived that Christmas.

From tales I heard from others, though, They both had some God-awful battles with our dad. For sure, though, Bo always came out on the short end. I was told that when he finally left home for *Flanagan's Boys Home,* he was bruised and battered from head-to-toe. Like I mentioned once before, at least Jean had walked away alive and on-her-own two feet.

Sis Mary would argue with Edith too, and very often those disputes would carry over to our dad too. She would continue arguing with him too, but in no way to the same degree as Jean or even Bo. Sis was an arguer but no fighter. She was always so occupied with her looks, and she was strikingly pretty. But, not that kind of *striking.* Her fights usually always ended-up with her in tears and wailing about any indignations and running off to her room to sulk.

Jean, on-the-other-hand, and for inexplicable reasons, always stayed and fought. Even during that gleeful period for me at five years of age, when I was brought back home until nine-years of age before our mother's passing, I can still clearly remember Jean arguing and complaining about just about everything with our dad. She never argued with our mother, Marie, though. Never. Jean adored her just like all the rest of us. I suppose that Jean and our dad just did not ever like each other for various reasons. Like oil and water, I suppose. Just like with Bo, and his accused shortcomings of meekness and weakness but feistiness, Jean had her aspects that our father detested. It was obvious from his words and actions too.

Jean was a real tough kid, I tell you. She would give our dad lip every time he said something uncouth, or mean or unnecessary to her, or to any of us. She was really defensive about all us brothers and sisters, and especially Bo, while he was still at home. It's the darned truth, too, that Jean took so many beatings from our dad over her defenses of our scrawny and vulnerable little-*big* brother.

But even for that relatively short stint I had living at home again from thirteen-years old to fifteen, and after Bo and Jean were both already gone, I still observed all sorts of contention in our home between my older sister,

Mary, and our dad. It seemed like Sis argued with both Edith and him all the time. Sometimes, it seemed like it was, over the smallest things, too. Jean had been the one to return our dad's fiery rhetoric with her own. Sis would mostly just complain a lot about nothing much in particular. I think she was just practicing for adulthood.

By the war's start, however, to set the stage more accurately and review once again our home's *occupancy study* in December of 1941, Bo was seventeen years old by then and had been sent away from home already for over three-years. Jean was nineteen and had been forced out two years earlier, in fact. Sis was Bo's twin, so she was seventeen also, and she had already been tossed-out months before the war had even begun.

So, the point that I am trying to make is that all my elder siblings were already gone. That left me as the newly awarded leader-of-the-pack, so to speak. As mild mannered and nervous as I was around my dad, nevertheless, slowly, and steadily I matured. In time, even I began testing Edith's rules by entering into that all-too-typical, teenagers' *defiant-zone*.

RELIGIOUS TOIL

Good examples from my earliest stages of rebelliousness occurred within education and religious circles. Since we kids were all mandatory attendees to the local, private St. Michael's Catholic School, dramatic exhibitions of my rebel tendencies could be found being nurtured there on a regular basis. Our school, and its adjacent, closely associated Catholic Church, were both co-conspirators toward my ill-being. So, naturally, they both became entities to which I dispassionately attended on a regularly required basis.

I have plenty more to complain about regarding those subjects later on; however, for right now, a brief synopsis may explain much:

> Nuns and sisters, who taught my classes at St. Joseph's Parochial (High School) Academy in Sioux falls, South Dakota, made life almost unbearable for me from eighth grade well into my sophomore year. As a result, I preferred avoiding and not associating with their kind outside of school. In my experience and judgement, all nuns and sisters severely lacked patience and understanding. Their cruel and painful punishments in classrooms toward children, in general, and me in particular, naturally made me wish to elude them. Thus, even evading church attendance at all costs seemed worthwhile.
>
> It was just like the feelings I recalled from attending Kindergarten, up-to and into fourth grade, in Fargo, North Dakota. I was still some sort of incorrigible, black sheep with whom which they contemptuously dealt. But I learned to survive

their prejudicial behavior only by mere endurance of their on-going, serious reservations toward me.

I had been unhappy enough dealing with those bigots during kindergarten and beyond at St. Michael's. Then, years later, it seemed like I had been sent to practically Fargo's twin, sister-city of Sioux Falls. I had been registered into yet another Catholic School for eighth grade, and almost immediately, the stress I had felt as a small child recommenced once again, but with exponential magnification.

Couple that practically blasphemous attitude, learned at such an early age, with Edith's endless barrage of *eternal-damnation* warnings, well, defying church attendance became the simplest means to strike back. Just saying, *"No, I won't go!"* would send shockwaves shattering Edith's fanatic, zealot's code. At the same time, it would piss-off the nuns, and sisters and priests with my absences. It got so that I considered my *absences* gleefully like they was nailing *two birds with one-stone*! No, *bunches of birds*, by golly! When I was absent, I was expressing all my internal, deep-seated frustrations, disappointments and anger toward church, catechism and the whole bunch of nuns and sisters at school.

Plus, it was an indirect means for me to protest my anxiety-ridden and lowly stance within my family. Oh, sure, earlier in my life, there were factors or conditions which made me feel really good like being able to play with my siblings and being around my mother who always shared her love. Yet, there were other things that made me sort of feel sorry for myself. Heck, back then, when I was alone somewhere, I even complained out loud to myself about life-in-general and the lousy hand I had been dealt. Well, if life was a card game, I suppose.

Yet, whenever I did get around my mom or siblings, I was a Royal Flush, maintaining the simile. I always felt appreciated and loved, like a real winner. They made my life more acceptable, and I felt more grateful. Mother was kind and loving almost all the time, yet she always seemed to have an air about her of despair. But she would hug us kids and tell us she loved us for no other reason than that: *Just because...* Wow! That was powerful. You're loved... *unconditionally,* just because for no other reason than *just because* you were born. I mean, that feeling really made you feel *alive*! Pure joy!

But then again, later, after Mother was gone and I had become an adolescent, I had my moments… moments of sadness. I believe now that my melancholy was caused by the difference between having gone back home with Mother, and later, for different reasons, having returned once again with Edith there and without much fanfare at all. It was Christmas time, and there were traditional Christmas festivities which were all mostly surrounding church attendance. And oh sure, the younger sibs were all happy to see me again, but it was noticeably different to me.

I was now the *elder,* the ranking child. Yet, I had returned home again somewhat unannounced and years after Edith had been brought in to takeover all the child-rearing and household responsibilities. She was the home-boss now. It was like my homelife had been divided into two categories: *Pre-Edith* (with Mom) and *Post-Mom* with *Edith* there.

I had immediately noticed that Edith's strict, Catholic, religious dogma and rigorous adherence to her merciless, damnation messages brought tons of new stress into our home. I had learned earlier that Jean and Bo had both early-on defied and denied Edith their courtship and following. They both always went to school; they loved it. Well, Jean did, anyway. But, they both refused church attendance completely and unequivocally.

Again, it's all third-party, second-hand information and after-the-fact descriptions of what may, or may not, have occurred at home every single Sunday. I was told many variations of family-life there, but it sounded like some stories may have carried an ounce or more of truth. As one story goes, though, first both Jean and Bo used to link their arms together, and then Jean on her own, both asserting defiant, personal protestations and self-conceived, fashionable testaments declaring, "Hell, no! I won't go. I don't believe in all that (church) nonsense!"

I am certain that at first, Edith was stunned to her very core. She was likely embarrassed and ashamed of her own, self-assigned parental failures. Because of both Jean and Bo, Edith may have possibly considered herself as some sort of miserably failing parent and, therefore, a disappointing and unforgiveable sinner to God. I am pretty sure that her own, priest-*confessional* time was likely consumed with beseeching tones of self-doubt. No doubt, Jean, and Bo's insolent, if not delinquent, behavior, and disavowals of Edith's devout religious connections, cast deep shadows of subconscious resentment on her own attitudes toward them.

Eventually, it even seems obvious that her bitterness toward them became most certainly cause for emotional detachments with both of them. Her willingness to see both of them gone grew proportionally to their relationship's developing faults. Soon, thereafter, her privately absolved wishes were made obvious and apparent to our dad. That is perhaps why Bo's sudden departure from Edith's tribulations, and Jean's exit about a year later, *apparently* made space for my return. Who can say, for sure.

Then, it became my turn as the newest, potentially burgeoning example of deviant, delinquent and sacrilegious behavior. Just like vanquished Brother Bo, I mentally argued that I would rather *freeze outside* than burn inside this *hellish household*. And shortly after that epiphany, just like our wonderfully strong, protective and castaway-sister, Jean, I wanted to model my own personal rebellion after her cause. Finally, and most recently, our exiled Sis Mary before me made me want to prepare and join all their prestigious, rebellious ranks.

I too considered refusing instructions for us kids to *prepare for church*. My willingness and preparedness (for church) became especially challenged and tested during our horrible winters in Sioux Falls. In fact, you might say that my *get-up-and-go* was directly proportional to weather conditions outside: During summer times with no school, or nuns or sisters to speak of or contend with, Sunday Morning Mass on a bright, cheery, and already warming day made church and catechism afterwards relatively tolerable, almost cheery. However, when it was so bitterly, ass-freezing cold outside, still dark as sin and ever-so-early in those frozen, winter mornings, well, I just quietly moaned and groaned and dragged-my-feet tediously all the while attempting to slow and ease the inevitable process of interminable pain.

Finally, and ultimately in full-rebelliousness mode, I, *Patsy-do-goodie*, determined to find resolve in refusing Edith's, "Prepare for church!" command. So, I dug down deep inside my bowels to the very depths and roots of all my anxieties... and... ah, shoot! No,... I *balked, I chicken-out* and I *prepared for church*.

Well, I told you I was sort of feeble and *wishey-washy*. It was because I was always ever mindful of what had already happened to my older siblings. Remember? All of them had already been vanquished. I could be next! I was constantly afraid of something similar happening to me at any time or place and for any reason. So, yes, I chickened out. That was me: All words, no action! Hah! I should say, *"All thoughts, and no words or action!"*

But, it was true: I was anxious, or over-anxious, or anxiety ridden. Yet, isn't it so true that most teenagers have naïve ways of constantly *casting-their-fates-into-the-wind*? I was no exception, just perhaps to a lesser degree. Therefore, even with my shallowness, timidity, or plain and simple cowardice, I had started to slightly test those defiant waters. Serious but sincere *obedience struggles* began developing inside my head. I was in *constant-conflict* over appropriate responses to Edith's demands, and especially ones about church attendance.

I didn't like going to church anymore, so I began emphatically announcing my distaste and opposition. Well, alright, I may have just mumbled some slight antipathy under-my-breath, or whispered it to myself, while I slovenly trudged along with all the other foot-traffic over the freshly packed, icy snow on our way to St. Joseph's Sunday Morning Mass.

At least I looked discouraged! But the big point for me was that at least I was thinking about rebuttal! That was a lot for me back then. In my mind, I always faced my dad's disapproval, his scorn and Edith's potential influence on him. Let's face it! It takes *a lot of courage* for a coward to be brave!

Well, okay, so sure, maybe I only just sort of stuck my big toe in the water, that's all. But even with all that freezing snow around us, the water was scalding hot! And that was a bunch for me. At the time, I was also teased by others as well. My oldest-younger siblings called me little, *Patsy-goodie-two-shoes*, too. Challenging anything at all during my probationary placements at school or at home with my family seemed to me, or probably would to anyone else who knew my circumstances or had a brain in their head, like a death-defying act- of-war.

Speaking of war and my worst-of-days' story, though, like I mentioned before, by that fateful time in December of '41, I was fifteen years old. I was a young lady already. In my mind, I had now begun determining aspects of my own life. Regardless of my position (at the bottom, or not) on that painfully imagined rung of our *family's placement ladder*, there were some things that I definitely did not like, disliked, or even hated. I mean, I was even reading American history in my social studies class about revolutions and our own forefathers' defiance of their king, for God's sake!

I wanted everybody to know about my displeasures: 1) I did not enjoy those mean nuns and sisters at school or the church's difficult and disciplined, catechism lessons; 2) for sure I did not enjoy feeling like I was considered *last place* all the time with family matters; 3) and finally, I despised always being subjected to Edith's eternal reprimands and dreary caveats:

A graceless and tortured afterlife awaits (me) should I back-step even once, and surely, it would be shame I'd feel in this present-life when filled with ill-repute.

Why, it's no wonder that I used to fantasize about *shaming myself with ill-repute* all the time! It sounded dangerous, thrilling, fun, and disobedient. How good could that be? Gee, I could even be just like my big brother and sisters. I could get thrown-out, run-away, go find them, be with them, wherever that was, and live happily ever-after.

Oh, alright, yes. I only *imagined* my endless supply of rebellious retorts and mighty, mental displays of deviant defiance. But my thoughts were running rampant, and I fantasized all kinds of retaliations against their rules-of-obeisance. Well, true again, I did only imagine them, but by goodness, at least I did get myself all worked-up and upset! That was something, at least, for me, anyway.

In fact, I think that it was way back then that I began developing my somewhat cavalier, wavy and casual-like take on religious upbringings and theological messaging, in the first place. I liked the part about God and Jesus loving me, and it was really nice to talk to them and ask for favors. And, wow, did I ask for a lot! But, I adamantly despised Edith's and our church's "angry God" portends: *Walk a straight line or Burn in Hellfire's Everlasting Damnation Forever!*

Dear God in Heaven, how in His good name could He be a loving God, a fantastic God, a joyous, fulfilling God, and yet be so merciless to us little wishy washers?

I mean, I honestly and truly tried to be good and never hurt anybody, so why would a merciful God want to punish me for some little indiscretions? I almost always did as I was told, even by our stepmother, Edith. But sometimes, I would just get distracted and forgetful. (Heck, I'm not much better today, either!) I really preferred my mother's interpretation of God as a wise and gentle and supportive God, not Edith's agonizing, frightening and darkness-filled fear of God…

Wow! I guess I got a lot off my chest with all that ranting and raving. But since that childhood period, I've changed my views about a lot of things. Maybe I've still hung on to a few of the same old attitudes too, though, and even some of the quasi-sacrilegious ones. But looking back now, I should note that our stepmother, Edith, was truly an integral part of our children's growth and progress. Maybe for a small, unrelated, and inexperienced woman dealing with a bunch of hungry, growing, and rebellious teenagers, discipline, and hard-core religion, Catholic or otherwise, were her only tools or weapons, she believed.

Perhaps, at that early-age time, I wasn't too fond of her. I had returned back home, true, but to a new house and a new person and forced to adapt to her ways even in my excited and anxious state. Plus, this *Edith* was to be obeyed also at all times and at all costs, I learned. Since then, however, I have learned to appreciate the unmistakably valuable role she played in our early lives and childhood development.

Fact is, it's sort of satisfying that this portion of my storytelling has actually become a personal tribute to that woman. It's sort of my very own testimonial, if you will, and a long overdue offering of thanks, appreciation, and a memorial commentary for Edith:

"If you are listening, *Mother* Edith, then please accept my apologies. I am truly sorry for any hardships I may have caused you. Please forgive all the tumultuous aggravation you no doubt suffered while helping to raise us *hellions*. I am grateful that you ever even dared to try and deal with us McCord kids. I am truly appreciative of the good help that you did perform for us. You were a good woman, in deed, and indeed truly deserved your blessed afterlife. *Amen.*"

Of course, I have to add, "Even if you are up there, we know you are likely without our dad because Heaven knows he is probably somewhere else… and likely begging for an ice-cold glass of water!" Oh, shame on me… Let's move on…

Anyway, now you have heard a little about my family members way back then, and hopefully, gained a little insight into our family's early *hysteria!* Getting back to the topic-at-hand, though, that miserable Sunday's cursed day of mass destruction gets right to the point right away…

I remember, we kids were all together in the living-room, Edith was in the adjoining kitchen preparing that evening's dinner. It was mostly quiet, and I was mostly content and happy with the moment at hand. However, you must remember that by that time in my life, I had already learned all too well that things can change very quickly…

BOMBS AWAY!

So, okay, are you still with me? Once again, I am *still* there in the living room with all my younger sibs. The day is Sunday afternoon, December 7, 1941… As mentioned, we kids were scattered all about the room and busy doing our own things. *Right then*, just while I was fairly absorbed with my English homework reading assignment and feeling all warm, cozy and peaceful inside, suddenly came a loud commotion from down below in the basement.

In a long-running howling cry, our father, Roy McCord, came bounding up the stairs screaming hysterically, "Pearl Harbor is being attacked!… Pearl Harbor is being attacked! It's being attacked by the Japanese! We're being bombed by the Japs! Pearl Harbor! Pearl Harbor! It's being bombed!"

Our dad rounded the corner of our hallway and then froze. He just stood there in front of us kids and staring at us like trying to find his bearings. "Where am I?" he may have been asking himself. "Who are these strangers looking back at me?" "What am I doing?" were questions overwhelming his confused mind.

Momentarily, he was speechless like a giant madman with open-mouthed shock and dumbfounded astonishment pouring out his eyes. He continued rearing there almost swaying with nausea and imbalance while limply flailing his arms in the air attempting to communicate without words. Our dad just stood there while gesturing with up-and-down movements from his loosely waving and outstretched arms. Then his hands would abruptly pummel downward almost striking the floor like something falling out of the sky and crashing onto the earth.

As he frantically continued signaling to his young audience, he turned and sought out each of our own confused faces seeking some forms of acknowledgement and understanding. I think he believed that if his words weren't reaching us, then maybe his game-of-charades waving his arms about might instill clarity, understanding or at least fear in us kids.

Not so. Not even a wink of appreciation came from most of us. To us, our dad was just being maniacal again, but in a different way this time. It was like he was really agitated and frustrated yet more confused than anything. His more typical blood-red, huge, violent glare wasn't there, and he was lost-for-words.

That, in itself, was very uncharacteristic. When our dad was usually angry, a constant bombardment of multi-syllable, shocking and horrifying curse words poured from his mouth in a tirade of raging threats. But, this time our dad was not cursing. He seemed so shocked and temporarily mentally displaced that he was actually speechless.

Oh, we kids were stunned by his actions, though. He usually always made us anxious, but this time we were all mostly just confused by his movements, words, or lack of and his physical features. But this particular time, it was his weird actions and mostly silence that concerned us... Something wasn't right, so the safest action was to just sit there, stare and wait for something else to give. And that's just what all we kids did. He wanted our attention and surely got it. But we were all dazed too, so we just silently stared back at the confusion in his face.

Getting no empathy or sympathy from any of us kids, but rather just blank faces or quizzical stares, our dad turned swiftly on his heels and bolted for the front door. Grabbing the doorknob and forcefully jerking the door wide-open with a jarring yank, a sudden rush of cold air burst past him and into our living room. Instantly, we all sensed the face-freezing coldness slapping our faces and rushing underneath our warm overclothes. The bone-jarring chill immediately replaced the comfortable warmth we had been experiencing. Instantly, I recognized the axiom: *chilled-to-the-bone*.

It took longer for our dad to readjust and react from his already stunned behavior. The cold air continued to rush past him, over him and through him seeking to fill the enormous void it had discovered in our previously toasty, cozy home. Yet, our dad just continued standing there solid as a block-of-ice in that open doorway allowing the freezing elements to continue charging inside our home. And he, just staring outside and still bewildered, stood there behaving as though he too had, himself, been smitten from the painful cold and had been frozen solid.

Fortunately, after seemingly ages, that same constant rush of cold air was enough to snap him out of his seeming trance. Finally, our dad appeared to regain his awareness and reacted to the bitter cold blasting against his face. Fortunately, it had shaken him back to reality. However, our dad still managed to shock the rest of us with his next move.

Quickly and without even a backward glance to any of us, our dad huffed-and-puffed expanding his huge chest, reached around the door to the coat rack and practically ripping it from the wall, he yanked his own overcoat from it. He flung the heavy coat around himself and inserted his arms in one-swift motion. Then he pulled the coat tightly around his neck, quickly buttoned it and pulled the front door behind him, slamming it loudly shut-again as he now alone faced the burning cold, dark-gray outdoors.

Once the door had been closed again and the sudden, deep-freeze began melting away, my alertness was regained, and curiosity took over. I dropped my book, leapt-up from my prone position and bounded over to the couch forcing Colleen to quickly move aside for me. I know she was curious too as to what was happening, so she willingly followed suit and merged with my actions. Simultaneously, we pulled the front-window curtains wide-apart and stared, almost gawking with astonishment, as we watched our father's next moves.

Driven by his crazy weird message, or by the nearly unbearable freezing conditions outside in the freezing weather, our dad practically leapt off the porch and moved as swiftly as he could over the ice-covered walkway and straight out into the middle of our neighborhood street. Once there, and standing directly in front of our house, our dad once again began his bizarre charade antics, but combined them with his crazy, frantic, and alarming speech.

Nearly shrieking, he began bellowing out his insane message over-and-over for all the neighborhood to hear, "Everyone! Pearl Harbor is under attack! It's being bombed! Yes, bombed by the Japs, I tell you. Pearl Harbor is being bombed right now! Do you hear me? Bombed!..."

Our father's seeming hysteria continued to shock and confuse us kids. But for me, our dad's bizarre behavior, while briefly dazing us kids for a few seconds, quickly brought on a swath of recollections and a past-reality for me. Memories rapidly filled my mind and then rapidly began pushing, shoving, and rushing together filling all the space in the living-room and replacing the cold air that had spread about. Then, regaining my composure, I leapt from the couch and front-window and rushed to the front door rechecking to make certain it was fully closed. But with that angry, bitter-cold wind dispersing, thoughts began racing through my mind trying to make sense of what was happening.

I did not like sudden change. Anything remotely similar to it gave me goosebumps of anxiety. This seemed different, though, yet it still gave me another kind of chill, one of foreboding. I didn't know what was happening, and I hated that feeling. And all that while, all I could do was still watch our dad outside in the street through the small, door-glass window while he ranted and raved.

I could hear his almost frantic but persistent screaming outside on that frozen, ice-packed street in that awful cold. His actions made my mind whirl. Eventually, I began considering potential outcomes of his bizarre and unusual behavior. Ultimately, I wanted to figure-out just how this incident was then going to affect me…

BRAGGART

To our father's acclaim, however, at one brief time during the mid-1930s, our dad was an honest-to-goodness real, local celebrity. It was a period of time when I had been allowed to live with our family, so I recall the occurrence first hand and remember it well. It was while our family was still living in St. Paul, Minnesota and was due to a somewhat notorious but noteworthy incident that had happened which had involved him. Dad loved to talk about that *incident* too, and he even carried proof around with him.

When repeating his story and my dad felt need for confirmation, flair, or emphasis, he would reach inside his inner, front-coat pocket where he inevitably kept a big, front-page newspaper story from the January 16, 1934, Minneapolis Star Tribune. Right there was a well-defined picture of the shotgun and machine-gun blasted vehicle he had been in, and it even had a big picture of him too.

I suppose Dad mostly carried it around just in case someone was skeptical of his bragging. Anyway, no matter, all the fellas at the local barbershop and other favorite, town folk centers knew his story very well too. That was probably due to the endless number of times they had all been forced to listen to our dad's countless, immodest accountings and versions. He loved talking anyway, usually about himself, so his *shoot-up* storytelling was a common repetition.

All too often, we kids would be tagging along while our dad visited someplace, and inevitably, some tongue-in-cheek prodding would come from a local jokester taunting our dad. It was that or one of the local patrons would provoke him by sarcastically questioning him, "Hey, Roy, I heard a story 'bout you. Is it true that once a few years back you tried to rob some gangster, or something like that?"

Well, that kind of teasing or lack of deference was all it would take for our dad to shake the questioner-off with a broad wave of his hand disagreeing loudly and boldly, "No, you got it all wrong! Let me tell you exactly what happened, and you gotta hear this because it involved none other than Alvin *Creepy* Karpis, himself!"

That, of course, was all it would take for a few, near-by townspeople to start sneaking away, or smile, grin, yawn, or shake their heads and settle-in for another lengthy, energetic, and boastful soliloquy from my dad.

One more time, he would be retelling yet another version about his near-death experience at the hands of that highly publicized and infamous gangster. And I have to hand it to him, fact is, it was a darn good story. Heck, our dad, for whatever it was worth, deserved to brag a little. After all, the incident did turn out to be life-changing for him and, therefore, all us kids too. We McCord children knew for a fact, and all too well, that he was never the same afterwards...

HEROIC INJURIES

A nyway, as the story goes, while investigating a suspicious incident in the winter of 1934 in St. Paul, Minnesota, our dad, Roy McCord, had been shot nearly to death by gangsters. At that time, he was working as a radio-operator for a security-service company assigned to the St. Paul Airport. As I mentioned earlier, our father was really good with radio-equipment and knew a lot about communications at that time. His job was to maintain communications contact with all security placed throughout the airport. Our dad checked-in with all of the security guards on a timely schedule and passed on any special, required instructions he was told. In return, the guards would all contact him about any needs, or special instructions or to pass on any unusual news.

Of course, when the *incident* happened, it was in early-January, on a graveyard-shift well past 1:00 A.M. in the dead-of-night. So, it was freezing, and all the streets were icy and slippery. Dad's shift had started-off as a typical, quiet, and slow evening in the St. Paul Airport Security Control Center where the lead-duty guard had his office, and our dad had his communications-station with all his radio equipment. That was when a call had come into the Control Center from a nervous homeowner in the vicinity who reported that some very suspicious prowlers had been lurking around the area. Since all airport grounds and surrounding areas were part of the surveillance and protection responsibilities of the security-department personnel, it was a natural request for them to review that particular *prowler* matter, deal with it and report back any findings.

In his frequent retellings of the incident, our dad always enjoyed recalling, for the benefit of all his guest listeners, that he had been pretty bored with that particularly slow night. He had even been spending time chatting longer than necessary with all the guards on duty who were spread all over the airport grounds and throughout the main terminal. Supposedly, our dad was just *unofficially* chatting to pass time easier. He liked to note that he was also simultaneously twisting and turning all the knobs on his radio equipment to achieve different signal variations to amuse himself.

Dad remembered, so he said, that he even heard the ominous phone call ringing in the Security Control Center Main Office and watched through the office window as his boss, Sgt. Harvey Bristol, listened to the call attentively and jotted down some notes. When Harvey, who was the night-shift supervisor, briskly set the phone back into its cradle, turned and rose swiftly from his chair and hurriedly grabbed his heavy coat and warm hat on the way-out his office door, Dad figured something important was on the brink. Hurriedly, the boss stepped into the main communications-center and called out to his second-in-command, Cpl. Charley "CC" Connors, to quickly join him. He then headed straight for the exit door and the car lot.

Dad said that he'd never forget watching his supervisor's sudden, second-thought and then turning to our dad and offering his cheerful request to him: "Hey, Roy, it's slower than snails round here. Why don't you come along and give us another set of eyes for our lookout? Seems some prowlers are on-the-loose in the residential zone, and we got to try and find them and chase them away, or something. Wanna have some fun? Would you like to come along and help us?"

Of course, Dad couldn't refuse his boss. It was certainly quiet and with little to do that night, and they would all still have their portable radios for any necessary radio-contact with any other, airport-security agents. And, naturally, Dad did not want to seem nervous or scared about chasing a couple of neighborhood thieves Of course, he accepted with his casual tease:

"Sure, I'll tag along. Somebody's got to protect you guys from these juvenile delinquents! I'll hold them down while you guys frisk 'em, beat 'em-up, and we'll split-up whatever goods they've got between us!"

Dad said he remembered getting mixed-reactions from his two cohorts about his slight: A sort of shrugged chuckle from his boss, Harvey, and a slight, snickering-sign of contempt from Cpl. Charley, who didn't seem to appreciate Dad's remarks. But, my dad just smiled, nodded and got-up right away. Then, grabbing his own coat and hat, he too joined the others heading for the building's Exit door.

His boss, Harvey, seemed just a little anxious and maybe even glad to finally get out for a bit-of-action. It was true, according to my dad, that it had been very slow all week and boring as opera, especially the past several days. So, just a tad bit over-excited, the boss quickly announced, "Alright, I'm driving; let's take my car."

A few steps out from the Control Center's self-locking, metal door and into the freezing, cold-night air, Sgt. Harvey was already walking swiftly in front while heading for his Security Center Patrol Car. It was a sleek looking, black, 1932 Ford Model B, Tudor Sedan. It had all the official Airport Security Insignia and Security Center identification on the top and bottom of the doors with large illustrations of an authoritative badge in the center of the writing.

Hurriedly, Sgt. Harvey called back over his shoulder to Charley and my dad, "Okay, Charley, you take the back seat. You can watch both sides of the neighborhoods and behind us too just in case someone jumps-out after we pass. Roy (my dad), you take the front passenger-side, and give us eyes to the right-side neighborhood yards and streets. I'll watch the frontal areas and both sides too."

My dad said that he remembered just being relieved to quickly get into the patrol car and out of that cold, chilling-to-the-bone night air. He even added that part of him was sort of excited about the change of pace and the new role for him. He said that he was hoping for a little excitement to help get his blood circulating to warm him up; however, the other part of his thinking was wishing this little escapade would end soon so that he could get back to his cozy, comfortable, warm, friendly, and safe radio-equipment. He was very comfortable there with his electronics, but not so much in this new environment and role.

But, like my dad enjoyed emphasizing, "I had agreed to go, and an opportunity to stretch my legs would do me good, I thought."

A moment later, all three men, dressed for cold weather, hurried to the boss's Patrol Car. Naturally, of course, all three happened to be dressed in full, airport security-guard regalia, which included uniforms with all the appropriate badges and insignia patches. The only real difference between their security garb was that my dad's uniform did not have any rank insignia on it because he was not official security-personnel, but rather Communications Management.

Carefully, but hurriedly, though, the three agents swiftly moved over the icy, frozen parking lot grounds to the Supervisor's parking space. My dad says he was already shaking with cold while waiting for his boss to unlock his car door, lift his seat forward allowing Charley to climb into the rear seat, then shove his seat back into place, and reach-over to unlock the other door for my dad. Once unlocked, Dad says, he ripped-open the door frantically and scrambled into the vehicle slamming the door shut behind him.

A moment later, Sgt. Harvey climbed in, himself, and started the car engine. The Ford reliably and instantly gave a grunt and roared to life. Letting the engine warm-up for a minute to calm its idle, Boss Harvey slipped the gearshift into place and began steering the car out of the Control Center parking lot and on toward the Airport Exit area and then turning into an adjacent, residential neighborhood of the St. Paul Airport.

The three of them were already on modest alert as Harvey self-assuredly eased the car over the icy-covered thoroughfare and exited into the housing district toward the specified area in question. It was then that he affirmably but casually barked out his second set of surveillance instructions: "Both of you stay alert. Watch out for anything unusual: Broken or open gates, broken or open windows, unusual flashlight movements inside any houses, and that kind of stuff. Anybody outside in this cold of night has got to be suspicious too. It's probably nothing at all, but at least we can say we looked."

After the instructions were given, slowly and carefully, and one-by-one, the lookout security team surveyed the surrounding areas as the C.C. Patrol Car moved through the residential area blocks. They continued cruising all the way-up one residential street to its natural dead-end, turned left to drive-up to the next parallel street and begin their watchful endeavors back-down, but this time in the opposite direction throughout the entire, residential-neighborhood streets.

All-the-while, throughout their endeavor, each C.C. Night Security Agent had his eyes more than casually focused on any surrounding homes and their yards. They were all cautiously watching for anything unusual. Naturally, my dad emphasizes at that point in the story that his eyes were glued to the houses and their respective yards straining to see anything unsettling. Would you guess that it didn't take long for them all to become "unsettled."

Anyway, as one of our dad's many, slightly varied versions goes, this is what may have happened: All-of-a-sudden, just as their Airport Security Patrol Car slowly passed one otherwise quiet intersection, my dad says he was the first to notice something. He had always regularly boasted in his storytelling that by that time during that brutally cold night, he had already begun searching every-which-way in order to better assist the other two agents.

Regardless of his memory or not, or who saw what first, my dad says that once he spotted the suspicious activity, he cried out loudly, "Stop the car!"

Apparently, there was another car about two blocks away, up the street and on their right-side, Dad recounted. Ever-so-slowly, it was cruising down an intersecting, residential street and coming right towards them just as their patrol car passed by. Sgt. Harvey, hearing my dad's commanding outburst, slammed on the brakes bringing their car to a sudden, jolting halt. Then, having both others spotted the other, dark sedan too, they all observed while the suspicious other car slowly crawled-up the intersecting street toward them and with its headlights off.

That, in itself, was way too suspicious, so Driver Sgt. Harvey quickly reacted even further. He put their patrol car in reverse and backed it up to the center of the intersection, where the suspicious car was approaching, and stopped. Their Patrol Car was all but blocking that perpendicular, cross-street traffic by then. And by then, my dad recounted, the suspiciously approaching vehicle was only merely a block away.

By that time, all three agents were staring wide-eyed in the same direction at the other unlit, dark car. Almost in unison they all cried out in mixed chorus, "Look up there! Look at that black car! It's lights are out! Why is it driving so slowly? That's gotta be them! Those are our prowlers, alright!"

Suddenly, things picked-up rapidly right after their first sighting. No doubt, the suspicious car's driver had also spotted their patrol car, and it, too, had instantly stopped in its tracks. That was probably so that its occupants could observe my dad's patrol car and decide what to do. Almost immediately, the suspects made their decision. As they watched the patrol car quickly stop, back-up a bit and block the prowler's eventual, intersecting way, they must have realized for sure that they had been seen and were being watched. So, they quickly made their move. They chose to make a fast get-away!

All hell broke loose! The prowlers' car was no longer suspicious. By then it was the Patrol Car Security Agents' targeted suspect vehicle. Only a block away and staring right down at the patrol car's left, passenger-side, suddenly the *get-away* car's actions surprised my dad and his security guard cohorts. Unexpectedly, the suspects' car's engine revved-up roaring loudly. Then, with ice and smoke spewing from its rear-tires, the getaway-car madly and wildly spun its tires there for several seconds on the icy street attempting to grab some traction.

Suddenly, their car lurched forward with a scream and a jolt and burst into its next approaching intersection. With its two right tires practically lifting-up from the ground, the nearly half, air-born car was screeching and skidding on its two left tires as it rushed to make an ear-piercing, screaming, steaming, and smoking left-turn in that intersection one block down and heading away in the opposite direction of the Patrol Car. Continuing its raucous emissions of ice and smoke and death-chilled roars, the car raced-off up the other parallel street and going away from my dad's car.

It was an obvious attempted getaway. My dad says he remembers hollering out, "They're making a run for it! Let's go get those bastards!"

Sgt Harvey immediately chose to follow the other fast-moving getaway vehicle. He quickly attached his single, white beacon, police light to its attached holder on the car's roof and flicked it on. He then mercilessly shoved the stick-shift into 1st gear, popped the clutch and spun the steering-wheel full-swing to make a reverse-direction turn. The patrol car's rear tires also spewed ice as the car lurched forward beginning its wide, sharp-circular turn. Harvey ground the gas pedal into the floor of their patrol car even more, and the car spun-round and then righted itself and lurched-up the parallel street. Their car jerked forward, roared and they were in full, race-mode pursuit.

Sometimes, my dad suggested that they were all hooting and hollering and determined to give chase after the other car. Other times, he mentioned that they were all drop-dead serious about their task-at-hand and totally silent and focused on their chase. I suppose my dad just sort of felt the crowd and reacted with any tidbits which energized his audience. But, he always had his newspaper photograph to pull out and offer as evidence of their chase at an appropriate time, or if the crowd was beginning to shake their heads in disbelief.

Their own '32 Ford, Airport Security Patrol Car, which was only a four-cylinder, still had some guts to it. Being on residential streets anyway and having familiarity with the street layout, gave them an advantage they also considered. As Sgt. Harvey raced up-and-down through its gears depending on speeding-up and slowing-down and for any needed quick turns, their car took its acceleration commands and leapt onward accelerating rapidly and forcing its own tires to spin and grasp for traction at each turn or take-off.

Yes, they were actually racing-down parallel streets to each other while the Patrol Car remained in hot-pursuit catching-up with the getaway-speeders. At that point, of course, neither my dad nor the Security Agents knew who or what was going on. All they understood was that this car they were chasing was likely their suspected prowlers, and tonight the security patrol had spotted their car.

"Too bad for them," my dad stated, and the other two agents agreed. "Foolish, drunken teenagers, would-be burglars or whoever and whatever makes no difference anymore. Those punks inside that runaway, getaway car are trying to escape capture and the law. We'll get 'em!"

The situation soon became obvious, however. My dad says that to himself, Sgt. Harvey Bristol and Cpl. Charley Connors, the getaway car was rapidly accelerating more and gaining ground on them. The suspects were succeeding with their getaway, escape attempt. As the Security Patrol car raced-up each parallel street and through each respective intersection to the Getaways, the Agents could tell that the other car was steadily pulling ahead of them and leaving the patrol car lacking further behind. But Sgt. Harvey seemed determined to capture his prey, though. So, attempting to begin catching-up again, he floored the gas-pedal and made it an all-or-nothing, breakneck chase.

My dad tells everyone that by that time, it was a hell of a chase. Both he and Cpl. Charlie clutched tightly ahold of whatever they could grab for stability. They all set themselves up for a wild, high-speed race in the dead-of-night through that otherwise, quiet sleeping neighborhood of St. Paul. Sure enough, with the patrol car's engine groaning, and Harvey's adept driving-skill, their Ford sped-up even faster. For a few brief seconds, as intersection-after-intersection rushed by their own speeding Patrol Car, it even appeared that my dad and the Security Agents were actually gaining ground on the getaway car. Wow! Were they in for a surprise!

Suddenly, at the very next intersection both cars entered, the security agents saw no taillights of any black, getaway sedan racing through their intersection on their own parallel street. Instead, a black car, of still the same description, had made a screeching sharp, right turn and was now coming straight toward our dad's street. Somewhat confused, Harvey slammed on the brakes and brought their own car to a screeching sliding stop. All three were baffled and spoke to themselves under their breaths, "Why would that other car turn and come directly into the agents' lap for an obvious and easy capture?" It didn't make sense at first.

Nevertheless, counting his good fortune, anyway, Harvey finished their sliding-stop and then eased forward carefully swerving their St. Paul Airport Security Patrol Car over to the left side of the street to a clear spot and came to another sudden stop. All they could do was just silently wait and watch for the getaway car's next move. Would it race on past and continue heading away from them again? Would they force Harvey's patrol car to turn around, thus losing valuable time in the chase? Did those *getaways* have any plan at all? Seconds later, they became baffled even more.

The black, sedan getaway-car, another Ford, by-the-way, came screeching, and peeling straight into the exact same intersection as behind the CC Patrol Car. The three agents then stared perplexed, and in disbelief, as the getaway car then proceeded to lean ever-so-hard on its two left tires again tilting the vehicle into another sharp, almost air-born right-angle, left-turn as the car rounded the corner. The so-called getaway car had shockingly turned and made a rapid and crazed left-turn and began roaring, and squealing, and peeling, and racing again. This time, however, it went right on up the same street as my dad and the agents were paused on in their patrol car.

As the getaway car then raced on past my dad's CC Patrol Car, tires still spinning wildly grasping for traction, the occupants were laughing and howling-out their open windows while their car's blaring horn blasted away with long torrents of abusive honking. My dad now acknowledges that he and the other agents then recognized that the suspects were actually deliberately taunting the Airport Security Agents. Plus, it became obvious to them too, that coincidentally, the other car, just like them, also had three occupants inside. In fact, my dad even said he believes that he saw the driver with his car door-window rolled down laughing out-loud and flipping-off the security car agents as they sped by the Airport Control Center Security Patrol Car.

Still baffled there inside my dad's CC Patrol Car, he and the other two security agents were simply sitting there and shaking her heads in disbelief. Sgt. Harvey Bristol, himself just a bit shocked, still managed to blurt out, "What in hell is going on? Do they want to play or something? Oh, these guys are really somethin'. Are they gonna get it!"

Well, the three agents had been sitting there in their car briefly while waiting for whatever action might occur, but they sure had not expected that *action*. Spit-right-in-the-face of the law? Reacting instantly, though, Harvey, really angry by now, shoved down the car's clutch, manually forced the gearshift back into 1st gear once again and he forced their Ford Security Car to peel-out onto the residential street from his stopping point. Now, directly behind the getaway car, Harvey floored the accelerator pedal into high-speed mode and then smoothly flipped through the other two gears to get maximum effect and speed.

My dad always liked to interject at this point of the story that he too felt just like his boss, their driver, Sgt. Harvey Bristol, "Those *getaway* creeps wanted to race? Well, look-out 'cause here we came!"

Both cars were now squealing and peeling and roaring down a residential street in the pitch-dark middle of a freezing night with only their car lights shining the way. The single, white beacon light attached to the roof of the CC Patrol Car was little more than a courtesy notice for any pedestrians by warning and advising them of some emergency. Although it was less than effective lighting, nevertheless, it was still glaring at the getaway car too. It definitely identified who was who by the attached light beam coming from the security car rooftop. It was obvious to tell which car was being chased, the bad guys, and which car was doing the chasing, the lit-up good guys.

Airport Security Patrol Sgt. Harvey was a good driver too, according to my dad; he was well-trained for pursuits. He stayed right-up with the other car and had his roof-light glaring down-upon the getaway car clear on down the long residential street. It was strange to my dad, though, he'd say, because it almost seemed like the getaway car was not trying to actually go their fastest and *get away*. It even appeared that the agents inside their slower patrol car with its little four-cylinder engine was actually gaining on that other bigger, faster getaway car. That was curious to them too because all three agents agreed that the getaway car was a brand new, '34 Model 18, Ford's newest model with the specially built V-8 engine and much faster than their own car.

Regardless, the CC Airport Security agents stayed right with the getaway car. They both had already left the residential area and were on a wider street going through part of the city's, small-business district by then. Larger, brick and mortar buildings were lining the street and providing little cover for the getaway car. The agents even figured that the getaways might likely crash into another vehicle or truck or something right in front of them. In fact, it seemed like a strong possibility because the getaway driver was wildly weaving and swerving all over the street. My dad repeated that it was like its driver was still taunting them!

Then, once again the unthinkable occurred, and the CC Security Agents were not mentally prepared to understand what was happening. The getaway car suddenly slammed on it brakes and abruptly came to a screeching, skidding, and sliding stop. The car even slid slightly sideways as its rear-end began fish-tailing a bit, but then it stopped right in the middle-of-the- street blocking the way forward. "What in hell? Were they finally giving-up?" my dad said he wondered.

Sgt. Harvey Bristol didn't have a clue as to what was happening with the other car either, but his reactions and professionalism demanded that he not take any hazardous chances. Who knew what was going on? So, he swiftly applied his own car brakes and brought the Security Patrol vehicle to a halting stop about fifty yards behind and to the left of the now stopped getaway sedan. Puzzled as all get out, the three agents, including my dad, just sat there still as church mice, and waited. They had no idea what was going-on nor why. What were these creeps trying to do? What did they want?

With no clue for what to expect, nor any idea of what was about to happen, my dad and the other agents started considering their situation and their options. They had already determined that the driver and other occupants of their car were most likely the reported prowlers. Those criminals had been caught red-handed sneaking around the residential neighborhood. They also knew there were three occupants, and all of them had been desperately trying to escape. Thus, the chase.

Then again, maybe it was just a car with three boozing teenagers out having some midnight fun on a Saturday night. Stupid, young punk kids. Whatever the explanation, though, the agents were dismayed and confounded as to why the other car had come to such a sudden stop. Maybe the driver was sick and just needed a moment to barf and clear his stomach.

Sadly, and unfortunately, it was going to turn out to be a violently poor decision to chase after those prowlers' in their speeding getaway car. By then, both cars were closed-in together on that freezing, middle-of-the-winter night on an early Sunday morning escapade. My dad, Sgt. Harvey and Cpl. Charlie had gone beyond their typical, airport duties providing basic security and communications. On that ultimately ominous night, they had chosen to find, follow and then chase after that other suspicious car. It was one night that at least my dad would live to regret, even if he did now occasionally try to brag about it.

Little did my dad, or his security guard co-workers, realize that night who was inside that speeding, black Ford, getaway sedan. Had they known, those poor, inexperienced, out-maneuvered, and out-gunned airport-security cops, and our even poorer, radio-cop father, may have wisely retreated and radioed the real St. Paul City Police for guidance or back-up. That, or they could have gotten-to-hell-away. I suppose though, sometimes, people just get caught-up in a moment, or they get carried away with their own, self-assumed duties, power, self-righteousness, or whatever. Oh, if they had only known.

No matter their reasoning or intent, it truly was very unfortunate that they didn't understand or appreciate the situation they were in. It was also too bad that they hadn't recognized or known of the occupants inside that speeding getaway suspect sedan. Sometimes, our *reactive minds* act faster than our *considerate ones*. They had no business following that getaway car clear-out of their jurisdiction, anyway. And, for God's sake, not chasing those brutes, anyway.

As ill-fate turned-out, the key character inside that getaway car was none other than the horrible, ill-famed, and notorious Alvin (Ray) "Creepy" Karpis, himself. Joining him inside that gangster's car were a couple other thugs from his dangerous gang of killers. In that dark, evil moment, my dad and his security patrol co-workers were just sitting there curiously waiting for what was to happen. They just watched, waited, and wondered. Karpis, on-the-other-hand, the evil leader, was cruelly and pleasingly plotting their next move.

Alvin Ray Karpis, known for his sinister-looking, *creepy* smile, was already on the FBI's #1 Most-Wanted, Dead-or-Alive fugitive-list in America. His famous face was plastered on every U.S. Post-Office wall in every little town and big city across the country. His poster was right up there on those P.O. walls next to another famous, violent criminal of that period, John Dillinger, whose own profile image was later to become the FBI's, and even present-day target range, bulls-eye targets for shooting practice.

However, at that time, in 1933 and 1934, Karpis and his thugs were even more notorious than the infamous John Dillinger and his band of bank-robbin' outlaws. Fact is that Dillinger was killed about five months after my dad's incident with Karpis. Plus, Alvin "Creepy" Karpis committed violent crimes for almost two years after Dillinger's death. It was said that FBI Director J. Edgar Hoover, himself, got so criticized and hyped-up over Karpis's arrest that he actually got personally involved in Karpis's capture down in New Orleans, Louisiana in 1936.

I'm telling you, Karpis was a bad man, a violent killer with no conscience. He was a real *creep*. Yeah, he and his whole gang were all bad and dangerous and all killers by their own reputations. Today, all we can imagine on that fateful night with the getaway sedan stopped there and parked directly ahead of my dad and the two security agents, was that Karpis and his two other thug, gang members were inside that getaway sedan plotting what to do next.

Later, after everyone had been able to determine just what must have happened, it became cruelly obvious that those *creeps* were not about to go away without a fight or without making a statement. Their nasty, sinister prowling plans earlier probably meant that they were looking for a temporary hideout place to lay-low. Or, they really were scoping out residences to simply rob and burglarize. In any case, in their minds they believed, their activity had been interrupted by some hokey-pokey, local St. Paul Police, and they were going to make those coppers feel their wrath.

Maybe Karpis even got a little nervous, or just plain nasty, when he and his other criminal cohorts saw the approaching black car with all the official markings on it. To top it all off, my father and the other security agents inside it were actually chasing after their vehicle. Something like that in Karpis's warped mind could not be tolerated. No sleezy coppers were ever gonna take him-in so easily. His plans were always for swift and violent reactions with total annihilation of his opposition.

Shortly after both cars had been parked diagonally across that St. Paul city street from each other, and lying momentarily motionless for only a few seconds, all-of-a-sudden, all hell broke out! Both of the getaway car's doors were abruptly flung-open. Simultaneously, two gang members stepped-out from their black, shadowy sedan. Karpis climbed out from the passenger-side and swiftly walked back around to the rear of their car. He was wielding a machine-gun at his hip, and it was poised and raised and aimed at the St. Paul Airport Security Control Center Patrol Car. Another gang member burst out from Karpis's side from the backseat. He briskly caught up with Karpis, and then momentarily, the two stood there side-by-side facing the patrol car.

Swiftly and methodically then, they both began walking right along beside each other straight toward the Security Patrol Car. The second gunman was holding a shotgun firmly grasped in his hands, shouldered and ready-to-fire. Both gangsters pointed their weapons directly at the would-be cop car with my dad and the other two, airport-security agents inside.

According to my dad, everything was a blur after that and happened so fast. After jumping out of their vehicle and joining each other to its rear, the gangsters were already so close that there was little the Airport Security Guards could do to react. They were trapped. My dad and his co-workers must have been in a state-of-shock and bewilderment while staring at those two approaching gunmen. What could they do? There wasn't even enough reaction time to put the car in reverse and try to outdistance the killers with the guns.

Walking steps-by-steps, precisely and directly toward the patrol car facing them, and without any hesitation whatsoever, the two killers both opened-fire simultaneously on the vehicle. Rapidly, steadily, mercilessly, and side-by-side the two killers continued walking toward our dad's car with both their weapons blazing away. My dad and his airport-security, co-workers were by now scrambling for their lives inside the CC Patrol Car desperately seeking protection from the torrent of bullets and shotgun blasts which had begun literally rocking their security car to-and-fro from the smashing and penetrating bullets. Shattering glass was spraying all over them.

The two killers just calmly, progressively, and calculatingly continued with their attack. They increased their shooting incessantly with an endless array of gun shots. They continued blasting and riddling the security-vehicle with screaming hails of gunfire. Shotgun blast-after-blast sprayed hell upon the unsuspecting patrol-car in violent unison with the cruel barrage of Thompson, machine-gun terror. The shooters went on endlessly with their brazen attack and totally overwhelmed the car's occupants with glass-shattering and pounding firepower.

They blasted out the front-windshield and closed windows of the car's passenger-side. Bullet-path studies, afterward, suggested that Karpis likely even raised his Thompson high up in the air and fired down in an angle into the patrol car. The helpless patrol car's occupants were frozen with fear from the bullets smashing into their car. All they could do was press themselves ever lower to the car's floor and wait for that one, single shot which might make everything in their brain go dark. Death, itself, was right outside their door. All the while the festive killers were said to have been grinning and laughing madly throughout the onslaught.

In fact, later, according to some actual nearby eyewitnesses, a few local folks had alarmingly peeked-out their homes or business windows to check on all the commotion and uproar curiously and anxiously. It was later reported that they had even seen a man with a shotgun quickly run straight-up to the assailed car. It was noted from witnesses that systematically the shotgun killer peered inside the shattered, front passenger-door window while jerking his head in all directions likely scanning the car's gruesome contents for affirmation of their slaughter.

Clearly satisfied with his grisly review, the shotgun-killer, now holding his weapon across his waist with both hands, then turned and hurriedly ran back to their gangsters' getaway sedan. Karpis had already retreated to their car, and then with both assailants back inside, the third occupant, who was the vehicle's driver, immediately had the black sedan, racing away. The killers' car had been sitting there and idling waiting with the getaway-driver inside preparing his escape. The car's engine revved-up one more time, it was said by onlookers that night, and menacingly, it swiftly swerved back onto the main street fishtailing as it sped-away.

No doubt their gangster car was filled that night with vile laughter by an excited and triumphant Karpis as it zoomed away from that ghastly scene. They had left the attacked, patrol-car wrecked and ravaged with machine-gun bullet-holes, shotgun blasts, shattered and destroyed glass throughout, and the security car's occupants in utter paralyzed, bloody, and agonized shock.

Photos from the local, Minneapolis Star Tribune newspaper the following day showed the horrible condition of the attacked, security-patrol vehicle that our dad and his co-security workers had been in: Dozens of bullet holes had penetrated the car's body; shotgun blasts pummeled my dad's passenger-side's exterior; side-door windows and front and rear windshields had been shattered.

Broken glass was splattered everywhere around the vehicle and across the near-by grounds and had ripped itself into the brick and mortar walled buildings next to the car. The agents were stunned, in states-of-shock, and two of them were badly injured. The driver had been wounded and severely hurt. Our dad had apparently taken the brunt of most of the blasts and bullets. He was horribly battered and left nearly lifeless. All three had been left for dead.

Somehow, miraculously, once Security Patrol Agent Cpl. Charles Connors, in the backseat of the patrol car, recognized what was coming, he had quick-wittedly ducked down and dropped all the way down to the floor even before the gunfire began. Fortunately, his quick-thinking avoided any injury whatsoever from all the machine-gun shots, shotgun blasts and spraying, shattered glass. He even remained deadly silent and still in the attack's aftermath, while the shotgun-killer assailant ran over and peeked into the severely damaged and bullet-riddled vehicle. The assailant had turned from his carnage review and quickly left leaving the silent and hidden, backseat passenger, security-agent unharmed. But he sure must have been rightfully stunned and shaken by his encounter with Karpis and his gang. The fact that he lived was amazing and having been uninjured was surely a miracle.

The St. Paul Airport-Security Agent and Supervisor, Sgt. Harvey Bristal, the CC Patrol Car's driver, had also instinctively ducked down and turned his body away from the oncoming flood of bullets and shotgun blasts. Even still, he was shot and injured in his upper-right shoulder area during the barrage. Painfully wounded, he had slumped over into the driver's side door opening in agony and shock. Fearful and pained, he too laid there motionless, also wisely playing-dead. The shotgun-assailant must have believed that the driver had been killed. There was blood all over his upper torso clothing and coat, and the patrol car's horrific display of a blood-splattered and bullet-riddled interior looked so gruesome that it too, must have apparently, satisfied the killer.

Sgt. Harvey Bristol, however, did survive, and after minimal care at the local hospital, managed to regain his health and good condition. The prowler search had been his mission, and it had been his choice to give chase after the speeding-car, even beyond his jurisdiction. He was fortunate to have suffered only minor injuries. He too, however, would have a lifetime memory and story from his purple-heart accounting of the shocking and infamous, Alvin "Creepy" Karpis incident.

My dad, unfortunately, took the full brunt of the attack with his whole body. When the shooting began, he too impulsively twisted his body away from the onslaught of firepower. He was in the front-passenger's seat, but he threw himself over and down toward the driver's side which also actually served as additional cover for the driver. Smartly, though, my dad lowered his head as far down as possible and just crunched-up his body to take the bullet and shotgun blasts' barrage. Unfortunately, there was no way to protect his body from bullet-after-bullet hitting on my dad's unprotected right-side. More bullets plunged menacingly into his back shoving him even further down and up-against the driver. A continuum of more shotgun blasts and more Thompson Machine-Gun bullet sprays sliced and grazed his head with deadly aim while ripping, tearing, and penetrating most of his exposed, upper torso.

My dad was likely unconscious from blood loss splattered all over his head, coat, and pants. He was no doubt bleeding profusely when the shotgun shooter ran over to the car's passenger-side, blasted-out window to review and check-on the carnage of their gang's cruel victory. Obviously, my dad's slumped-over, heavily bloodied body appeared as though he were dead too. It was his blatant appearance of death that likely saved my dad's life. Obviously, the shotgun-killer had been satisfied with what he saw because, according to eyewitnesses as described earlier, he then quickly turned and ran back to their own car for their escape.

It was probably hard to imagine from any onlookers how anyone might have survived the vicious attack. The car was virtually destroyed. Newspaper stories included ugly, vile photographs of the assailed patrol car to add imagery to the headlines. The story made all the papers, especially the <u>Star Tribune</u>, and my dad and the other security-patrol agents earned their well-deserved times of fame.

Like I said earlier, it was a big story back then, and our dad was considered a hero just because he survived that evil altercation with Alvin Karpis, himself. Honestly, though, I have-to-hand-it-to-him, he did deserve some credit too. That incident had occurred while the three security agents had put themselves in danger during their line-of-duty. Even though he was a communications-man and unarmed, my dad had volunteered to go-along with his co-workers and friends as an investigative-lookout.

As a result for actually going along, he had been forced onto the frontlines of a vicious, warzone, criminal-assault. Even if our dad hadn't been a hero in the true sense of the word, he still deserved some serious credit just for having lived. He survived to talk, or even deservedly brag about the whole incident. So what if he embellished a few points here and there? He had a right to brag. Not too many Karpis victims ever survived to brag about it.

Those gangsters, including Karpis, had shot and hit our father eight times with their bombardment of machine-gun bullets and shotgun blasts. He had been shot by bullets all over his upper body with most of the gunshots in his back. It was truly amazing that he had even lived through it at all. After the shooting and lengthy stay in Emergency Care, our dad spent many weeks in the St. Paul Hospital slowly recovering. Then he spent many months after that at home in bed. Many more months followed with him on crutches once he could get out of bed. It seemed to everyone else that for a very, very long time he was in recovery.

Years later, after his own capture by none other than the FBI's own famous Director, J. Edgar Hoover, Karpis even wrote of the incident in his own, personal autobiography. Karpis easily recalled the incident although he wasn't too clear about the exact date or even sure of the location. He wrote, however, that at that time, he had really believed it was the local police chasing after him and his boys. The car had looked *police-like* and official, and its passengers were all wearing *cop-like* uniforms. Of course, he also validated his recollection because, after all, he was being chased. So, it all made sense to him.

Years later, in his own tell-all autobiography, it would have been difficult for that filthy murderer to recall for sure all his shootings. So many chases and so many shoot-outs had occurred, I guess, that Karpis, *The Killer,* just couldn't keep 'em all straight. I suppose it was hard after a while to remember every detail of so many shenanigans. Although, Karpis figured in his mind, according to recollections in his book, that he actually did mistake that airport security-car for coppers, and he thought for sure that he had left the driver and passengers fall or dead.

As Karpis described later in his *tell-all* interviews in prison, he even grunted when he heard about survivors and sounded a little bit disappointed, "No, I don't actually remember the exact area or even the year, but I do recall shooting-up that car. For sure, we mistook it for the local police with all its insignia and stuff on the doors. But, it was late at night and real dark, and after we were done, I surely thought we had killed 'em all!"

Yeah, I guess my poor 'ol dad was fortunate at that. I remember how it seemed like forever, though, after that incident that our father complained of pains so much of the time. Fact is that his complaints went on for as long as I remember being near him after that. For that reason, too, he probably just didn't want us kids around bothering him at all. He liked staying by himself a lot more after that. That pain and injury issue limiting his range of movement, along with his familiarity with radio-communications from his work, I supposed, is what started his interest in fooling around with his ham-radio equipment.

Our dad's poor health had not only affected his disposition, but it had also harmed his ability to get new, good jobs too. Although the St. Paul, airport-operations people were decent enough and had lauded credit on our father offering his job back once he recovered, he still became very restless. Once an acceptable period had passed for his healing, our dad actually did even return to his previous job at the same St. Paul Airport doing his exact same radio-operations and communications work again.

However, it didn't matter much because he didn't stay there very long afterwards. I'm not sure if it was relentless pain and discomfort from sitting at his radio-set desk so much of the time or being reminded over-and-over of the agonizing incident by watching his now healthy co-workers and noting how he had suffered so much worse from the shooting. Or, maybe he got tired of being pushed aside or taking second fiddle to the other two co-workers in recalling and retelling that awful night to others. Regardless, fact is, he didn't stay there or anywhere else, for that matter, for very long periods of time. I suppose that he may have even become very agitated with his painful condition and needed to continually move-on from one job to find another.

Also, that usually meant that, sometimes, our dad had to travel far-away to get work. He never fully recovered nor was ever fully-well after that. Health problems just seemed to plague him all the time. Often, he would just quit a job without notice complaining that the work simply caused more pain to his injured areas and back. In fact, a lot of times, he would just pack-up and leave us at home with our stepmother. He would go-off to seek some new employment elsewhere, almost always with an airport and most often somewhere distant.

Truth-be-told, although we McCord children grew-up to recognize the hardships and difficulties there must have been on our dad, under his circumstances, and stepmother, we kids were not all that unhappy with his absences. My four sisters and oldest brother and I often talked amongst ourselves about the harmful effects of that Karpis shooting and the toll it may have had on our dad. We all agreed that the shooting incident and its associated injuries to our dad might have been the very things that made him so mean to all of us kids. But we knew there was more to it than just that.

Sadly, there were plenty of other recollections from my older brother and sisters, and younger sisters too, about our father's *meanness* far before the Karpis incident.. Many of those recollected memories were of terrible, violent issues with our dad long before that evil time as night security communications specialist and long before ol' *Creepy* Karpis ever got to him. But those are other stories still to be told. Just not here and yet.

During the "creepy" period, for a while anyway, us kids sort of gave-up, gave-in and accepted our father's own meanness, temper and behavior. We were willing to give him a little leeway. We agreed amongst ourselves to accept the explanation that after the incident, and mostly to our misfortune anyway, our terrible relationship with our dad was because he just couldn't help himself from all the pain and such. Is there such a thing as *unconditional love* of children for their parents? I suppose that deep down we children really want to love our mothers and fathers. It takes a great deal of *conditions* to overwhelm and affect that caring.

PEARL HARBOR

However, our dad's incident with "Creepy" Karpis had been nearly eight years earlier. Our family, with me in it finally, was now living in a quiet neighborhood of Sioux Falls, South Dakota. Folks hardly gave our father any mind any more, let alone credit for his supposed heroic past. Our pa's new, serious hobby with ham-radio communications was all the recent rage to him. Now the neighbors and town folk just barely acknowledged his somewhat eccentric, braggadocio behavior concerning all his world-wide, prized, ham-radio contacts. They paid even less heed to his previous era of heroics.

Nearly everybody in our town, it seemed, had heard our dad's stories before from countless telling's. The crowds had all long-ago tired of giving him all his practically narcissistic demand for attention and respect. Maybe that was why he demanded so much submissiveness from us kids and hardly ever tolerated any childish silliness. Perhaps, our father was getting such little acknowledgement outside his home too from neighbors or anyone else that he demanded ultimate subservience and platitudes of obedience from all of us family-members inside his house. Truth be told, ours was not a loving-family atmosphere at home. At least, it was not while he was home.

So, it was of little consequence and no surprise to anyone, on that freezing cold, godawful and fateful afternoon of December 7, 1941, that our neighborhood barely even noticed or paid any mind to our dad standing and turning and flailing his arms in the middle-of-the-street while screaming crazy antics about bombs and bullets. For all they knew or cared, perhaps, it was just another wild exaggeration of our father's personal vendetta against the Karpis gang for his personal pain and injuries. Our father had been deemed by locals as somewhat eccentric.

Our dad's frantic, almost hysterical screams of "Jap attack! Pearl Harbor is getting bombed! The Japs are coming!" and on-and-on with his panic-stricken cries were hardly taken seriously by anyone. Yet, for those few, remaining daylight hours, on that otherwise calm afternoon, there was no exception for our neighbors' disbelief, indifference, or genuine apathy. None of them seemed concerned or paid our dad any attention. A few window blinds were briefly stretched-open, including ours, for peeking eyes to assess the outside disturbance. Maybe even a couple front doors were narrowly pried open with heads peeking out here-or-there to quickly assess the source of the commotion before being slammed shut again to the freezing draft and with complete indifference.

We children and family members were also only mildly different from all the others too. I remember looking up from my school books when I first heard our dad hollering. I laid there staring wide-mouthed at his crazed look and cringing from his apparent almost hysterical screams. Initially, I must admit that my heart began racing, and I was filling with a worried and stressful apprehension. What in heaven's name was going on? Once more, just briefly, but still evident, I became fearful of my own status. It seemed all the time to me that my own personal, psychological health depended directly and respectively on my dad's own present condition and state-of-mind.

Then, I just watched as our mad-man father dashed outside into that freezing torrent of ice and snow and wind. Like I said before, after he ran outside, and I had checked the front door again for its closure, his continued aberrant behavior was still enough to warrant even my reaction. Climbing onto the couch for a moment and leaning over to peek outside our frosted-over windows, I curiously wanted to see what he was doing.

Well, simply put, his wild, ear-piercing, and frantic lamentations just persisted. He continued shouting and flailing his arms above himself like a mad man possessed, all-the-while twisting about in his own frozen tracks in all four directions, probably seeking a crowd. And he was doing it all *right there* in the middle of our deserted, snow-frozen, and ice-covered street, I tell you. He continued his antics for several more minutes, I guess. Eventually, with absolutely no on-lookers or curious neighbors yet confronting or questioning him, our dad finally gave up and came back inside. He had been rewarded with absolutely no audience at all that afternoon for his outlandish warnings.

Although seeming much longer, after a while, even I lost curiosity and returned to my books. My own temporary state-of-anxiety began relaxing. Then, in a few more minutes, our dad rushed back into the house shaking his head, mumbling perversely and profanely to himself and disappeared once again below. It seemed like he was vanquishing and exiling himself back into his private, central-intelligence domain of a basement. I guessed that the momentary excitement was over, and so I, too, just shrugged and quietly resumed my studies.

Those stressful minutes were finally over for the time being. Once again, I felt a brief *return to calm* seeping inside of me. My temporary spell of apprehension began easing, and those clear and awful recent memories of abandonment and distraught feelings once more temporarily faded having returned to vague, but quickly available storage vaults, in the back of my mind. I was able to relax again with my studies and focus once more on my English assignment reviewing Shakespeare's Hamlet and whether he was *to be or not to be,* after all.

But even that didn't last for too long, and wow! I sure was wrong. Little did any of us realize that just earlier, our dad had been correct all along, and the whole world was about to flip upside-down. Soon, none of our lives or scant family recollections were ever to be the same again. The world was changing, changing fast and drastically. My life would take another tailspin of dramatic adjustments again, and so would those lives of all my sisters and brothers too. The war conditions this time would tear us all apart from each other, and we would all, ultimately, be shipped, sent, and spread across many states, and even the world.

Remorsefully, I acknowledged to myself that my special, yet brief, trial-period of stability and internal comfort, having been returned to my partial family, was not destined to be, after all. If democracy and civilization, themselves, were then on trial for their sheer existence, so was meager little me, and all of us, McCord-family children. Soon, we all would be dealing again with more of our very own, internally private wars.

Having spent vastly more time away from my family than any of the others, and feeling by far the most affected by separations, I pledged to myself and God Almighty to lead our family's reunification cause. I felt so strongly that we McCord clan siblings must all be back together for our own safety, security, and well-being. Who could know, or even grasp, the coming war's looming potential, or devastation and effects on everyone involved? Who among us could remotely guess what directions, or meanings or purposes might arise from its consequences and effects on our nation, let alone on we measly, minor characters on its world class stage of plays?

My family, we McCord siblings, would desperately come to appreciate the nuance: *Strength in numbers*. We needed it for the very nature and spirit of our beings and lives. We would have to find, or I would, some valiant, effective, and victorious plans and means to return us all back together… where we belonged… to live in peace and where we could remain forever…

CHANGE IN THE AIR

St. Paul, Minnesota

Hours later, following our dad's wild testimonial in our street, he was still in his basement devoted and intensely tied to his ham-radio equipment. Steadily outside, though, a stream of neighbors began leaving their houses to join and speculate with others right there in the same area where Dad had been screaming and carrying-on earlier. Everyone else was finally becoming aware of the actual bombing-attack facts from their own reliable sources and news outlets from their household radios. My father's hysterical bellowing on that very street in our neighborhood had been reprieved, although for very little, if any, credit offered him.

The newly broadcast news created its own paradigm of bewilderment, fear, anxiety, and stress. The worried conversations quickly engulfed everyone's attention consuming all their clarity and refilling it with immediate and shocking thoughts. Each newly arrived crowd member offered some most recent tidbit of information just heard and offered-up to the growing hysteria which was understandably building. Confusion and fear were the most prominent looks overwhelming the crowd's strained and staring faces.

Soon, the entire neighborhood was pouring out into their residential streets with shock and dismay in their eyes. Frightened looks and desperate talk filled the street, and you could hear panic in their cries. I remember even seeing terrified faces with anxious eyes darting back-and-forth crisscrossing the evening sky desperately on lookout for any potential, attacking, Japanese fighter planes. Our home, our community and the entire nation were literally and figuratively stunned.

War was imminent. It had truly become the beginning of incredible changes for everyone and especially for me, I had already imagined and assumed. As a member of the family household who had just most recently rejoined everyone after years of multiple separations, it was easy for me to feel like my bubble could burst anytime. I felt awkward, uneasy, and fearful of some dreadful act which would send me away again. In my anxious mind-set, I imagined that the word "insecure" would have my picture next to it in a dictionary illustrating its meaning.

And my emotional state was now *feeling* almost prophetic because soon our lives would be torn apart by strict, difficult, and sacrificial demands of fiscal and emotional natures put on families everywhere. Nearly everyone's life would be changed, modified, and transfixed by enormous militaristic-transitioning circumstances caused by the war. The fever and fervor of all-out war, its attrition and insatiable demands were to bring immediate changes to all of us in our town. At our schools in classes with our teachers, the sisters, and nuns, would tell us students that changes were happening to the whole, entire world.

We were not advised by the nuns, but rather practically ordered, to pray for help from God. Somehow, that demand coming from the school's nuns was hardly reassuring. It was like an airplane pilot asking his passengers to pray for a safe landing.

"Uh, oh! This doesn't sound good at all, at least not good for me," I reflected as all that talk about war, and fighting, and sacrifice, and upcoming and necessary changes were unnerving for my already fragile psychic, to say the least.

There would be no going-back again. In fact, the world would never be the same again, either. Everyone was to be affected, and it would be *the beginning of new beginnings* for us all. Fresh starts were not just offered, they were required or demanded, if not inspired. Changing lives and lifestyles began taking shape almost immediately. And like I had long expected; my head was already poised on the chopping-block.

"Hold still, Dearie," I imagined. "This will only take a moment, and then you can run crazy all-over-the-place!" I wondered how long I had to live… there. Last arrived, first gone.

Curiously though, in truth and actuality, I was already somewhat agreeable to leaving home that next time. Too much family tension going-on.

At least, by then, I had mustered-up enough confidence in my own self with survival abilities that the threat of being dislodged or sent packing again was no longer a *threat* to me. With little choice, anyway, I would accept my most certain adjustments with an open-mind and necessary brevity.

"Go ahead. Bring it on! I dare you. I can deal with it," were inner-signals providing me with strength and preparedness for any potential or expected "Notice of Visitation Cancellation!"

Our nation's ensuing involvement of the USA in the war indirectly ripped apart our family, as it did to so many others too. But it had not actually or directly caused any immediate family displacements. With the exception of the draft, and so many young men leaving their families to fight Japs in the Pacific War or Germans and Italians in Europe and Africa, it actually took months before the war-effects really hit our home. Nevertheless, the war brought with it a static, a tension, which filled-the-air everywhere.

Unfortunately, there had been a *war* going on in my family's household for years already. Initially, that big, outside world conflict had minimal immediate damaging effects on my family members. We heard about its stages and status. We watched as progressively growing local, city-wide, state-wide, and national reactions steadily developed until they were at a feverish pace. Yet, at home was a totally different kind of war. It was us kids against our father. The older you were, or the more you sassed him, the worse the battles were that raged-on, and the worse were the lickings that we kids took.

Thus, some *family-war effects*, which preceded the big war's outbreak, were our family's early-on break-ups. The eldest siblings, Jean, and Bo, had already been forced to leave home several years earlier. By late 1941, they were by then living together and working in Cleveland, Ohio. Sis Mary had been gone since early 1940, and she was living in upstate Duluth, Minnesota finishing school and also working.

By the war's start, they were all at least stable, working and relatively self-sufficient. For them, the stability they all had earned and deserved came from their home-training in *the school of hard-knocks*. None of them had been forced to leave home and make it on their own without having first survived countless, cruel bruises, brutality, and uncompromising lessons of emotional and physical duress.

But perhaps that was a more common way during those *depressing* years for many: "Spare the rod and spoil the child." Well, I can assure you of one thing: There was no *sparing* of any rods, and none of us kids ever got *spoiled,* not by our father, anyway. So, once the elders came of quasi-semi, close legal age, they were ordered out of the house. Period. No offerings of assistance or financial aid, no suggestions, or recommendations for quarters in which to live. No transportation was offered to get anyone to anywhere. Although, in-all-fairness, Bo was dropped-off at the care home.

Mostly, however, it was just, "Get out now!" demands of our father. Bo was sent away first, then Jean was expelled and, finally, Sis was sent packing without a bag.

Fortunately and eventually, Jean and Bo had hooked-up in 1940 joining each other in Hayward, Wisconsin where first Jean, and then Bo, had been decently taken-in by our caring and understanding Grandma Agnus. Both then found part-time work to help subsidize their stay, and reenrolled in school, Bo finishing high school and Jean beginning college. They became stable and even prospered somewhat during the interim. Later, due to Grandma Agnus passing-away, both were forced to leave school, travel to Cleveland on their own and go to work in armament factories in order to support themselves and the country's rising war-efforts supporting its allies.

Also, it's important here for me to note that going to work in those *war* or *military-* support manufacturing plants actually made Jean our family's first *"Rosie the Riveter."* Bo, on-the-other-hand, finished high school, and then he went to work in the munitions industry, both by age seventeen. However, in 1942, Bo would soon, thereafter, enlist in the army-air corps following his next birthday at the ripe old age of eighteen.

Sis Mary had already been gone from home for over a year. Having already turned eighteen years of age, she had been given blessings and encouragement to leave Duluth, Minnesota, and Aunt Annie and join-up with Jean and Bo in Cleveland. Jean and Mary had made an agreement where Mary would work and let Jean go to college, and the next year they would switch roles. It seemed like a nice plan… as far as plans go.

Eventually, I smelled change-in-the-air and knew, somehow, or maybe even just understood, that it would soon be my turn to go. By then, it was mid-1942, school was out for the summer, and I was already sixteen years of age.

ON MY OWN ACCORD

B ut regarding me, by then? Oh, yes, I could tell. I really could smell change, and something stunk. By then, through proxy, I had become the oldest child in the house, and had been for a notable period of time. However, that meant it must be my turn to leave coming up very soon. Talk about feeling like you were *walking-on-eggshells*? Only, I felt like mine were *razor blades*! Something was going to happen to *cut-me-off* from my family and break-up my own *unhappy* arrangement.

By that time for me, however, leaving again had become almost preferential. I was ready to take my inevitable place on the *chopping-block* and subsequent uncomfortable discharge from the premises. Alright, so be it. It would turn-out to be my joyous and pleasing opportunity to join my sisters and brothers with all their future dream-building.

There at home, things weren't good, but they weren't necessarily bad, either. My spirits weren't high, but they weren't really low either. I had finished the school year, and by then even the school sisters had been easing-off with their discriminating non-preferences toward me. I had learned how disarming smiles could be. It was difficult for them to maintain negativity toward me when all I ever responded toward them was with so much Christian-like *smiling*. Like I said, very disarming.

Even Edith had become manageable. I had finally learned how to satisfy her most basic wishes with least amount of subjugation. Granted, I always continued abiding by her strict demands of church attendance, but that was small penance (pun intended) for what I gained. Given that offering, Edith more-or-less left me alone to do whatever else I wished. Maybe, she had tired, herself, from all those years of previous screaming, and yelling, and fighting, and violence. That was not my modus-operando, and she may have noticed and appreciated it, awarding me with silence and solitaire. Besides, what worked magic and wonders with Edith was just to have minimal conversation but toss into the innocent banter a few "Amens!" and "Lord be praised!" quips. I believed that her sense-of-fellowship was very calming to her.

My dad never changed his ways, however. Maybe he had eased himself from the continual verbal attacks and physical violence because the elder renegades were gone, and partially due to my own cowardness. Yet, it was also due to us remaining kids always giving him his demanded space and privacy. No love lost, you might say, on either side.

Although never violent to me as of yet, he still always remained completely oblivious to my needs, wants or even sheer presence. I was there, but I hardly existed to him. I had, for most part, always been and continued to be a non-person in the household. I had absolutely never received even a mere inkling of affection from him. As a result, neither did he from me. Lose-lose situation.

So, yes, I would probably be leaving fairly soon too, but this time I did not mind. Besides, being the oldest child still at home, I was sixteen and ready to spread-my-wings. There had already been enough negativity in the house so that being-away from home was actually much more preferred. One by one, my older sisters and brother had been ordered out or encouraged forcefully to leave. I saw it coming, and I welcomed it, more-or-less, as just a matter of time for me...

Then, wouldn't you know it? Lo-and-behold! Suddenly, and without warning, my dear, sweet, loving, (Unghhh, NOT!) Cousin Rosalie called our house in Sioux Falls to speak to me personally, of all people. Taking the phone, I prepared for a belated, vicious, and vile attack on my past, criminal behavior. Well, hardly was that the case. Instead, Rosalie was sweet, kind, friendly, and distressed. After basic and courteous greetings, she began begging me to come back to St. Paul, stay with her family and help care for her ill mother, Aunt Kate. Gee, I was actually being welcomed somewhere. What a delightful change, for a change.

That time, I excitedly agreed to go. I mean, I had known, or at least sensed, that there was *something-in-the-air*. Something was going to happen to me, but this circumstance had definitely surprised me a bit. Being welcomed, asked, no pleaded with, to return was kind of nice. At home, I needed space and distance between myself and my father. The tension was like they say, "Thick enough to cut with a knife," and unfortunately, fantasies about knives began consuming too much of my mental activity.

Yes, I would go, and I would almost gratefully help provide care and attention to my ailing aunt. It was only right, too, because she had been the one who had taken me-in after Mother died. She had been fairly decent to me back then, even though she most definitely favored her daughter, Rosalie, and treated her like a princess. I would be lying if I denied that back then, deep down inside of me, I hadn't felt substantial feelings of envy or jealousy. I'm sure that I did. In fact, I know I did because I used to fantasize what it would feel like if my own father had treated me that way.

Oh, how heart wrenching. But the reality back then was how my aunt and cousin left me feeling like an ugly stepsister all the time. That had hurt my feelings at the time, but I had grown past all that since then. It was going to be different that next time, and I remember so willingly accepting the move. My *change in the air* was suddenly both forgiveness and compassion for my aunt and cousin's prior behavior and an opportunity to escape from my present state of mediocrity, parental loneliness, and sadness at home.

So, once again, I would be separating from my sisters and brothers; however, it was mostly understood that it was only to be for those present-summer months. After all, I was going to be a junior that coming September at school's start, and school was supposed to be a priority among us McCord brew. War activity was growing almost daily it seemed, and much would be needed for the war-cause.

If I remained at home, I could easily find some way to assist the *cause* with a job in town, but it was not necessary. I'd be away from my siblings, but I would be doing a different sort of generous service to my cousin and Aunt Kate. Furthermore, our dad was likely going to have to travel further for a decent job to cover his stripped-down family's needs even still. I rationalized that I had to go because there was no way that I could, should or would remain, anyway.

Yet, I still remember feeling anxious and bothered because of leaving. I know it was because of the fact that twice before in my life, I had been handed-off to distant relatives who had provided room-and-board and care for me because I was somehow that tainted, unwanted- one. My second abandoning I never understood and never wanted. Mom had died, and right away, I was sent-off and not allowed to return home until years later after I had practically forced and begged my own return.

That first time, of course, I have no recollection. I had been *handed-away* right at birth to my Aunt Annie who raised me until I was five-years old. I *never* ever got a reasonable explanation as to why. Plus, I was the only child not allowed to be with the entire family. It was a period for which I have never fully learned to understand, forget, or quite forgive. So, needless-to-say, although I was very agreeable to leaving that next in time in Summer 1942, I still felt odd about it.

However, that next time was not going to be just like either of the preceding hand-offs. It was not going to be against-my-will. I would go because it pleased me to go, and even under those new, wartime circumstances, I had a lot to say about it. Of course, had I refused to go, then shame and all-hell might have broken out anyway, and I easily could have been sent away, regardless. But this time there was something I could do about it, myself.

The decision was at least partly mine to make. Besides, I would be closer to my older siblings, and I could more easily stay in-touch with them. Somehow, being nearer to them made me feel a little more secure with my future surroundings.

Although I figured that I was not likely to enjoy the atmosphere during my stay with Aunt Kate, her condition was worsening, and the rising circumstances of the war demanded attrition. The war was still hardly in full swing from my observation, as of yet. It was true that the newspapers listed every day the names of any local, city boys and men who had enlisted, or were drafted. Soon after that, the same newspapers started listing names of any killed-in-action or wounded. Everybody was fully well aware of both war fronts and heard, read, and then shared news about any latest movements, battles, or losses, including KIA's.

The Pacific War was against the aggressive, Japanese expansionists who wanted to conquer and control all of Asia and the Pacific Islands. We wanted to exact revenge for Pearl Harbor, and we wanted to curtail Japan's own enormous expansionist-ideals. We wanted to quell their expansionism especially where Japan interfered with our own Asian area, economic growth plans and influence peddling.

The other European/Soviet-Union/African war was against Hitler and Mussolini because they both wanted to conquer and control all the rest of the world and divvy it-up between themselves. Our own US historical ties had so much direct linkage to so many of those countries Hitler despised, opposed, and was attempting to subjugate. So, we had taken aim against him. It was a little awkward, at first, because Germany and Italy had been our friends. But how might I paraphrase that ancient quip? *The enemy of my friends is my enemy...*

Together, Germany and Italy had joined with Japan to form the Axis Powers. They were attacking the rest of the world which had been resting peacefully until then. We, the USA, were both caught-off-guard and caught-in-the-middle. Finally, President Roosevelt, and other friendly European leaders understood that those Axis Powers would be willing to attack the USA right here at home, try to defeat and conquer us and then share all the rewards.

It had taken a while, but we had finally merged with those remaining unconquered, but retreating, European nations plus the Soviet Union to form the Allied Powers. At first, the war conflict seemed like defensive posturing. It was *us against them*, and we had a lot to do to even get prepared for war. However, our country was obviously up-to-the-task. Every day you could see another business start-up or convert to doing something for the war cause.

In the big cities, whole factories were converting from social and personal-needs products to *guns and butter* for the war fronts in Europe and the Pacific. On the waterfronts, they were busy building ships. In the interior, they were building airplanes, tanks, military vehicles, bombs, and bullets. Everywhere else, they were manufacturing foodstuffs, medicines, personal-effect items, and clothing to support both fronts, and all the soldiers, sailors, marines, air boys, and coast guard.

At my age, however, and considering my own situation, I was not overwhelmed, at first, by our dramatically growing national needs. On the contrary, in my mind I analyzed and assessed my own predicament and slowly came to similar conclusions about myself. Just like our nation then had its precise enemies, I saw a parallel for myself: It was *me against them*, with *them* being my father, stepmother and any other relatives or entities which agreed to support any separations of my brothers and sisters.

With little trust extended toward my parent/adult-perpetrators, I had only my siblings' love and trust to believe-in and focus my togetherness-ambitions toward. Nevertheless, there was a war going-on which was getting bigger every day and requiring sacrifices. In a small way, I also rationalized that my departure from home this time was my own *sacrifice* of sorts. Thus, I returned to my Aunt Kate's home in St. Paul, Minnesota, where I once again began a new stage, a new chapter in my life. It was one in which I had garnished-up control of my own well-being and my own destiny. More-or-less, I was now in charge of… the-rest-of-my-life…

SPREADING WINGS

St. Paul, Minnesota

In all honesty, returning to Aunt Kate's was not any anxiety-ridden experience for me at all. I had previously lived with her and her daughter, Cousin Rosalie, before, and I knew their home and the neighborhood surroundings very well. Although I would not be completely happy there, the upside was that the place, and the people, would not feel foreign or unknown to me. The sad, if not tragic, part was that Aunt Kate was not well. She was family, and family were supposed to do anything to lend a helping-hand to their kin.

When a family-member went down, the rest were supposed to *circle-the-wagons*. I had matured over the past two years, and by then, I looked at Aunt Kate in a different and better way. When our mother had died, Aunt Kate *circled-the wagons*, so-to-speak. She did what she could for our mother's sake by taking-in Mom's reject. I suppose that my grudge back then had been, "Why me? I already had a turn been cast-off to some circled wagons. Who's turn is next? Not mine!"

So, of course I agreed to go and leave immediately. This time, however, I would go, and I would even be grateful.

Unfortunately, my own father was likely the only exception to that *helping-hand* rule. "What's in it for me?" was his proverbial motto. Or else, he would consider, "How will this new *arrangement* benefit *me*?" He was fast on *asking* for favors but very slow on *offering* much. For me to get-out-of-his-hair and away from the dinner table, though, were obvious double-duty benefits for him.

To me, however, leaving was not earth-shattering at all. Although I would miss my younger sisters and little brother, I was going to stay focused until we all could be together again, without parental restraints, and as soon as possible. "All us kids reunited, on our own and away from our father," was the simple, basic dream of a sixteen-year-old girl. Gee whiz, how pathetic and sad, but true.

Anyway, the move back to St. Paul for that summer of 1942 in order to assist Cousin Rosalie with caring for her mom, Aunt Kate, was uneventful, in itself. As soon as I arrived, I was greeted matter-of-factly and quickly shown to my same old room that I had stayed-in a few years before. I was provided all the basic essentials to accommodate myself and then explained the house rules: Me: Cleaning, washing, shopping, cooking, and bathing and dressing Aunt Kate; Rosalie: Go to her job at the clothing factory. How interesting. It was almost the same schedule that I had before except Aunt Kate took care of herself back then, and Rosalie was in school back then. Like I said before, "I was just the ugly step-sister."

I supposed that they recalled my earlier stay when I had gotten mad at them both and run-away going back to my dearly missed family. Therefore, they probably weren't going to take any chances this time. My schedule for that summer was pretty much seven-days-a-week, with time to myself when the household slept. Rosalie had a job and was gone a lot, so I was expected to carry-the-load caring for Aunt Kate.

Giving praise for righteousness, even jerk-off Georgie-Porgie got a job in a munitions plant outside of town. Both Rosalie and he used to ride to work together each morning and return home in the evening too. Georgie-Jr. was in school, so I did not have to deal with him except to *deal with him*. Actually, he was kind of sweet and decent toward me. Go figure? Of course, they all seemed to appreciate my efforts and sacrifice, as long as I kept putting-in the *effort and sacrificing*. It was okay with me, though. Sort of a lesser-of-two-evils choice, and being with them was much more acceptable than being back at home, or less evil…

Have you ever had a summer that before you even knew it, it was over? I guess I became so involved in my duties and responsibilities, there was no time to even wonder about much else. September was right-around-the-bend, school registration was approaching and my agreement to stay and help Aunt Kate and Rosalie was obvious and apparently coming-to-an-end on two counts: first, the end-of-summer was our unwritten and verbal, contractual agreement for ending my care-assignment of Aunt Kate; secondly, from the first day I arrived for my chores, I could see that Aunt Kate was not long for this world.

She had already been diagnosed with cancer. It had begun on her face and had rapidly spread to all parts of her body. Mostly, all I could do was feed her soft foods, give her sponge baths, and help change her bed-ware attire. Her medicines and doctor's visits were mostly to ease her pain and allow her to rest more comfortably. She was going-fast, and we all knew that it would not be long before her end. But, wouldn't you know, she became so dependent on me that I still just spent most of my spare-time visiting and talking with Aunt Kate. We actually got much closer by summer's end.

Regardless of all the good vibes I may have been feeling at that time, they were all being countered by growing anxiety and stress from the looming decision of returning back to home. Granted, my obligation and need was nearly fulfilled there with Aunt Kate and Rosalie's family. Now, it was time to face the fact of returning home to another pathetic and stressful existence. My God, what an absurd transition I was going through at that time. It was time for me to leave Aunt Kate and my summer assignment, but I did not want to return home. Life was strange.

For so many years of my life, I had felt miserably rejected, usually alone in my mind and separated from my real family, my siblings. Now, I had the opportunity, after a brief hiatus, to return back to that once craved family-unit that I had so wanted, and so desperately needed, to be considered as a full-fledged member. And now, here I was, having incredibly emotional, turn-around second thoughts of going back home.

What sort of transition or *metamorphosis* was that? No, for sure I was not becoming any *butterfly*. Yet, I was no *worm* anymore, either. I guess I just thought of being years-ahead-of-my-time: I was sixteen, and I had just spent a whole, entire summer slaving-away while caretaking for my dying aunt and her entire household. I did not deserve returning to a second-rate existence where I needed to worry about everything I ever said or did and receive little if anything in return for my presence. After all, I was an adult now. Well, sort of. Almost. At least I deserved being treated better.

Yet, I knew better. That was not going to happen back at home with my father. Jean, Bo, and Mary were all already gone because of him. They were all living their lives already on their own. My dad and Edith were carrying-on with the younger siblings: Colleen at 10 yrs., Jann at 8 and Jackie-Boy at 6. I was already gone from home, again, and I wanted the same independence as my elder siblings. I wanted freedom from my *home-instilled* dreariness and self-doubt.

Besides, who was I kidding? When I thought about it, I seriously doubted if there would be any real resistance from home, from my dad anyway. Although I understood that he was taking distant jobs, and was absent so much of the time, I likely would have only had to deal with Edith mostly. That, in itself, was also encouragement to stay away. So, I was making-up my mind almost as fast this time as I had before when I decided to return to Aunt Kate's house: *I was not going back home*.

So, the moment came when I determined to deliver my message. Naturally, Aunt Kate was both displeased and feeling responsible, but we both knew that she could never forcibly object. I kindly kept trying to explain to her, "It isn't you. It's me. It's just time. I must leave."

With my aunt's progressively declining illness, and her and my progressive bonding since I was caring for her, I finally got a full explanation of my father's ill-attraction toward me from Aunt Kate. Apparently, my mother had attempted to explain the discrepancy to her, and by then, Aunt Kate felt willing to finally share her understanding with me since her own day's-were-numbered, so-to-speak. She had nothing-to-lose by finally becoming honest with me.

As Aunt Kate's explanation went, my father was modestly happy with Jean's birth and then the twins, Bo, and Mary, twelve months later. But the idea of my birth coming another year and eight months later was too overwhelming for him to accept. Apparently, he had been away on another distant job somewhere, and it left feasibly credible room for the possibility of a secret sexual rendezvous somewhere for our unfaithful mother.

I mean, he wasn't a drunk, but he was Irish, and that was just as bad. Jealousy ran in his veins to points of crisis. If you have ever seen pictures of my mother, then you know how absolutely stunning she was, pregnant or not. The problem is that our father managed to keep her pregnant and barefoot for twelve years straight. On top of that, it was common knowledge that our dad was out cavorting all-over-the-country at whim. The typical joke at the time was that he was either away looking-for-new-jobs, or new blow jobs. Like I said, he was Irish.

Anyway, Aunt Kate told me that my dad came home after a long-time away at a new *job* and found my mother pregnant again. That time, however, for some Irish-screwball reason, he did not believe that he was the *instigator*. It was more than his miscalculating mind could handle. Being Irish, to him, my birth the following May, was a revulsion of all he believed in: A wife's fidelity, and… and…well, that was about all, except for his Irish Pub *Barstool Commandment* that the Irish "…were here to *propagate the world* so that they might rule it. Unfortunately, God had invented whiskey, and that was their downfall!" Happy St. Patrick's Day!

Whatever, that nonsensical excuse of a story did not matter to me. I did not believe it in a St. Paul second, and the decision for me to leave was assisted, ultimately, yet indirectly, by Aunt Kate. She passed-away quietly in her sleep late that August. My obligation was truly completed. On-the-other-hand, I had to explain my decision to my parents. I wasn't sure, for sure, but I certainly suspected that there were not going to be any issues.

At first, my dad and Edith objected. Naturally, on-the-outside that was their responsibility to *object*. Of course, they hesitated regarding my continued absence because it was their parental responsibility and duty to do so. After all, I still was only sixteen years of age. However, after a brief conversation, they both easily succumbed and accepted my extremely vague plan.

I have to admit, too, that my plan at-that-time was at best *sketchy*. But I was deliberately leaving out any details or specifics about any contact or visitations or joining-up with either of my older sisters, or Bo. I just mentioned something general about perhaps going back-up to Duluth to see Aunt Annie again. I needed to return to school, and that was most important to me. Regardless, however, while speaking to Edith, and then my dad, I was still uncharacteristically adamant about not returning home again.

Furthermore, I could then boast, I was somewhat pleased with myself at my stance or self-defense. Neither my dad nor Edith were prepared for a defiant and obstinate *Patsy*. By the way, that was now my official, family nickname, I kind of liked it, and so it stayed. Nevertheless, I guess that I had prepared myself for some potentially heated argument rather than a discussion coming from my dad or Edith. Honestly, neither my dad nor Edith had likely expected any opposition, let alone a fight, coming from little ol' me.

I'm pretty certain, too, that my determined attitude and stubborn behavior quickly changed my dad's behavior and decision from one of faked or phony rebuttals and denials to one of absolute good riddance. By that point in my life, I pretty well had my dad pegged: He simply could not stand anyone, especially his children, who were different: Unusual and cut from the unordinary; weak or disfigured; or those who embarrassed him as shameful liabilities. Combine any of those conditions with obstinate, challenging, or insubordinate behavior, and you had a scornful, nasty, and potentially violent enemy.

Nevertheless, I remember assuring my dad and Edith, however, that I would be fine, and that they had nothing to worry about. I was also pretty sure they weren't going to worry, anyway.

PART TWO
Independence

SISTERHOOD

Of course, there were two other influences which had recently transpired, and both were encouraging and weighed-in on my decision to leave home and be on my own. The first factor, and most critical, was my focus on being with, or at least finding, my older siblings. The younger ones were still at home, and Edith dutifully cared for them, I was sure. They were, thus, not out of the equation but required minimal concern at that time. My older sisters and brother were all already, independently living on their own. Therefore, I needed to be with, or near them, in some fashion. My only other necessary influential conditions were school. I was going into my third year of high school, and I wanted to continue my education just like my older siblings had.

Right away, the first of many blessings fell into my proverbial lap: Sis Mary answered my call. We had finally spoken on the phone, and after I had probably exhausted her with my recent history and present dilemma, she had amiably agreed to a basic plan I suggested. All she did was add to it and modify it somewhat. Sis would leave her job in Cleveland, Ohio, and her work-study arrangement with Sister Jean in order to return back to Duluth, Minnesota to attend a special college program there for training teachers. She would pick-me-up right there in St. Paul, Minnesota, and the two of us would go to school in Duluth. It was Jean's turn to go to work that next year, anyway, so Jean and Bo had agreed to help support Sis and me in Duluth.

I had explained my situation fully to Sis, and she knew my mind. Money was scarce, but she would travel by bus to St. Paul to meet me. Once there, the two of us would then hitch-hike up to Duluth and find shelter somewhere together. Perhaps, she suggested we might even get lucky and get the same attic-space that she and Jean had previously rented. Either there or somewhere else, we would settle in, and I would enroll in a Duluth public school while Mary sought out her teacher's program. We would be set, and we would get by. Jean and Bo had both promised to send us support money each month for expenses. All seemed well enough.

The only unfortunate note was the timing of everything. Sis had actually already called and arranged for our *attic-rental* in Duluth. Both the Duluth high school and Sis's college program were to start immediately, so we both had to get up there right away to register. Then, unexpectedly, Sis's bus from Cleveland arrived in St. Paul with her on it one day early. I was forced to make the instant decision to give my regards and goodbyes to all and dash away to meet-up with Sis Mary.

It was unfortunate because two days later was the planned funeral service for Aunt Kate. I would miss that memorial service. I had hoped Aunt Kate's family all understood my situation. I had truly fulfilled my obligation. In all actuality, I was free to leave then.

So, lickity-split, I had my basic wardrobe and personal effects all jammed inside my soft- covered bag with a belt strapped tightly around to hold it together. After somewhat curt goodbyes called-back over my shoulder, I walked swiftly, yet eerily, with bag-in-hand up to and around that same corner heading for the local bus-stop. A feeling of Deja vu had dawned over me. It was a sense that I was sort of repeating what had happened once before, two-and-a-half-years earlier. To be precise, it was when I had run away from Aunt Kate's. This time, however, I was leaving, yet all was relatively well. The big difference was that this time I was leaving on-my-own and at least partially in-control of my own destiny.

Everything around me seemed high-lighted with detail. The colors everywhere all seemed more vibrant, and the city noises and sounds were all accented with pronounced effects. I arrived at the bus-station right on time, and my sister's bus arrived shortly thereafter. It is difficult to describe how precious that meeting was. It was so significant to me. My big sister had come to rescue me. We were finally together again and off for our first real adventure together. Sis was my heroin, and I was certain that we would blaze a very special trail together.

So, after Sis collected both her stylish suitcases, large suitcases, I might add, the two of us made our getaway. Leaving the bus terminal and the city wasn't much of an effort, so it seemed. We both talked incessantly, eager to hear each other's catchups on family-gossip tidbits and other general information. We had so much catching-up to do. It was wonderful listening to Sis talk and share about everything from comments about Jean, Bo, and our dysfunctional family, to workplace highlights, to details of dates with guys and boyfriends, to Hollywood movies and stars, to New York and fashion, to the war, and the enormous changes and growth our country was going through. She was like a walking-talking set of encyclopedias. I loved listening to her.

And how Sis could make me laugh. Fact is, she made everyone laugh because she was so bright and sharp-wittedly candid. Without maliciousness, Sis would just call things as she saw them, and usually she would delight everyone around her with her comments. Needless to say, she was very popular with her girlfriends and definitely with the boys. As we walked-on up the main boulevard heading for the highway north to Duluth, she teasingly reminisced about some relationships that she had enjoyed there in Sioux Falls, and then in Duluth and finally those in Cleveland.

For Cleveland, she seemed to have plenty to say and laugh about. She enjoyed talking about boys and men. Right away, I remembered the night that she had been kicked-out of home because she had wanted to stay out late on a date. But that was Sister Mary. For all I knew, she didn't even remember that awful and traumatic night. Sis was so joyful and easy-going. I recall on that trip to Duluth, as we hiked on-up the road, how she made me laugh so. She would coyly remark how in recent times she had just started to *love* men in uniforms... She would giggle and then add that it was especially nice to say goodbye to our soldier boys who were designated to go overseas and fight in the big war.

"I mean, it's a really fun, pleasurable and rewarding job," she teasingly laughed, "but somebody has to do it!"

That was Sis, and time passed easily and comfortably. Catching our first ride and then a second all the rest of the way to Duluth was easy too. Sis had already practiced using her thumb on this very same highway over previous times first going to Aunt Annie's, and then from-time-to-time, as she needed rides to and from Duluth to elsewhere. Obviously, none of us had cars. Besides, gasoline and tires were all *rationed* and were expensive and difficult to come by. Hitch-hiking seemed pretty easy, and rides weren't too hard to come by.

There we were, two young ladies hitch-hiking together up Highway 35 on our way to, well, mostly new sights, new sounds, and new experiences. I was proud, happy, and excited all at-the-same-time. Sis had grown-up so polished and well-traveled, so-to-speak, and I was so proud to be with her just then. I was also happy that, even partially on my own, I had arranged to be back with my family. I was only a sibling, but I was overjoyed with familial love. Plus, I was absolutely thrilled to be out on an adventure where every rock-turned was a new one, and every sight was a splendid new marking-point for our journey together.

I remember arriving in Duluth in the late afternoon, still with plenty of sunshine ahead of us. Sis easily remembered the home and family which offered us the same lodging as she and Jean had used previously that year. It was actually little more than a converted-attic space with partially slanted walls due to the roofline; however, it had two beds and shelving for our clothes and things. Very sparse, but it was all our own. Once we had eaten a meal and had flopped down for the night, we talked about our plans to register for school the next day. Our first day and first adventure together had resulted in being a complete, happy success.

The very next morning, we caught a city bus and went into downtown and then to Denfeld High School for me to register. They were busy with late registrations, so they easily took-down my information with few questions asked, and all went well. It went fairly rapidly, and I was quickly signed-up and ready to start my Junior Year. My classes were the typical subjects, and I had no problems with scheduling.

Unfortunately, it wasn't quite as easy for Sis. Her college program for future teachers was all but filled-up. We had arrived very late for registration matters, especially for college classes. She still signed-up for a couple classes that at least got the program started. Right after that, as we left the college registration building, I'll never forget how she grinned away and started laughing.

I so clearly remember her huge, red-lipstick smile and comment, "At least now, under the circumstances, I shall have more time available to find a really good job and then start checking-out the real scenery."

Right away, we were both giggling together like school girls. I knew she was talking about the *boys scene*, of course.

Things went on fairly well after that for quite a while, in fact. Sis did find a very nice office job downtown, and she was delighted with the location, its ambience and atmosphere and her pay, which she thought was very reasonable and with opportunities for advancement. Plus, she had no problem dealing with all the fellows who would eventually end-up walking past the office outside on the city sidewalk only to stop and peer inside the big, office-window for a glance at Sis. She said that her boss was tickled over the scene at first, but after-a-while, he became annoyed. Although Sis had the guys crawling all over the place after that, she still told me that she had simply given all of them a request.

Sister Mary, smiling coquettishly, simply but sternly informed her would-be suiters, "If you ever want to see me again, then you will stay away from the office windows and wait for me at a prearranged place. If you don't, and you disrespect me, we are through!"

Sis told her boss, too, what she had said and done. He was very impressed, she told me, and there was right-away a significant behavioral change in the town's male population. Sis just had a way about her. She was so witty and attractive, yet so cool, calm, and collected under-fire, she could have her way with just about anyone. As it turned out, I needed her smile, wit, and smooth talking not long into my own semester of school...

TRUANCY REPORTS

A ll seemed relatively stable for the first few months. Then, as the winter holiday season approached, I began suspecting that I was being watched. School authorities started asking little questions of me as I passed between classes in the school hallways. With relatively basic and minimal information on my registration forms, the record's clerk began becoming somewhat leery and suspicious.

The clerk would usually begin somewhat off-handedly, "Where did you say you are living?" Or, digging deeper, "Can we see or talk to your aunt?"

I would toss-off her inquiries very casually, "Out-of-town with my sick aunt. No, she is really ill and can't take visitors or make trips. I do everything for her," I lied.

Of course, when such questions started, I began getting a little nervous. Other staff would stop me in the cafeteria, hallways and school grounds asking more, but similar, personal questions about my background and present living-conditions. It got so I was often taking long ways around certain buildings just to get to my next classes in order to avoid their *Spanish Inquisition*.

It even made me shudder a bit when I was reminded of hiding-out in the train-station and standing atop toilet seats to avoid police encounters. I began wondering if maybe everybody here knew everything about me too and were just trying to taunt me into a confession. A lot of the staff were all asking the same questions, though, so I figured that they were all together and ganging-up on me.

You see, in order to cover for ourselves, Mary had used our aunt Annie's address for my home residence. Technically, I was still a minor being taken care of by another minor, my sister. Therefore, we didn't want anybody sneaking around where we really, and illegally, were staying. I supposed that the school officials were curious about how I somehow managed to travel to school each day, and then I'd return home again from such a long distance away.

Aunt Annie's farmhouse was about forty miles outside of town, and that was a lot back then. Still is to me. Nobody ever dropped-me-off or picked-me-up either. I was always seen walking toward or coming from downtown because Sis's office-job was our rendezvous point. Anyway, Denfeld school personnel were all getting suspicious of my so-called living arrangements.

Regardless, that first semester ended, and the second one began with me re-registering again for some more new classes. The school authorities were happy with my grades, performance, and attendance; however, that sort of threw-off their concerns. I seemed well and happy and was prospering. What else could they say? Oh, yeah, but where did I live and really with whom?

Some more curious and quizzical minds approached, and I began feeling like I could cut the drama in-the-air with a knife. But, a couple more months passed, although illegitimately, and school officials began demanding even more of my background information. Then, wouldn't you know it, I heard later on, that somebody on the staff, the Dean or Vice-Principal probably, drove all the way out to the southern Duluth countryside and straight to Aunt Annie's home inquiring about me.

I could only imagine, "Huh? What? You don't say? Well, I never...!"

Poor Aunt Annie was really strung-out over a barrel. She would have helped me anyway possible, but she would never lie for me. I understood.

With their new information on-hand, the school principal had the authority he required. The vice-principal and the truant officer both must have figured that they had a big payday coming. Because of my age and suspicious home-address, it seemed like they were going to detain me for investigation of being a serious runaway. Apparently, they were intent on locating me and holding me for questioning to determine appropriate actions.

Mary and I both felt like the bottom was about to fall out from under us. If I were caught-up-with, there would likely be only one solution: I was still underage with no legal or official home for which to return, so I would become a *Ward-of-the-State,* and I would be sentenced to a reform school somewhere until graduation or my eighteenth birthday. That definitely wasn't going to work for either of us.

In actuality, Sis and I did not even realize how serious the matter had become. It was already April, and Spring had sprung. The weather was fairly nice even if the tension at school was getting pretty bad. Good grades and smiles were just not cutting-it much anymore. That was when the VP and Dean had actually driven out to visit my aunt, and I didn't know about it until my US History teacher advised me.

It was a really decent piece of information and good fortune that arrived conveniently one early evening at our *attic-home*. It came just in-the-nick-of-time, too. In fact, it actually came in-person from one of my very kind, considerate and concerned teachers. Mrs. Sanders was my US History teacher, and she had always shown a fondness for me in class. I think that after having learned so much about me from all our class conversations about my multi-state, bouncing around and multi-family experiences, she may have sympathized and appreciated my *semi-worldliness*, or *stateliness*. Yes, that was it, "stateliness." I was a *stately* student!

Regardless, that day's homework-assignment, however, went way outside the realm of typical, classroom behavior and responsibilities. I was to learn later that day that Mrs. Snyder had actually followed me all the way home on that certain, conspicuous day. She had wanted to determine and confirm my true address and then deliver a woeful, but timely, warning.

As always, after school that particular day, I had gone to wait for Sis to get-off work. Then the two of us took our typical walk back to our residence. Shortly after arriving, we both let ourselves into the empty household and went upstairs, as usual, to our little attic-room and were changing clothes, chatting about the day's activities, and just relaxing. We always could hear any house ruckus or noises below, though, so we were both a bit startled and surprised when a knock suddenly came at the front-door practically only minutes after we had casually walked-in ourselves.

I was the one who actually dashed down our narrow stairs to answer the door. Upon opening it gayly, at first, I became started and surprised at our visitor. Then I became a little bit confused and even embarrassed. However, upon immediately recognizing our door guest as none other than my U.S. History teacher from school, Mrs. Snyder began quickly trying to reassure and calm my concerns.

In a very kind manner, she began advising me *not to worry*, and then she asked nicely if she could speak with my parent or aunt. Naturally, the thought crossed my mind, "This is it: My secret has been found out, I have been caught red-handed. Now I am probably going to jail.

What was I to do? By that time, Sis had stepped-up to the door, and I introduced her to my teacher. They both smiled and greeted one another, and that was when something, though, told me to trust Mrs. Snyder for several reasons: She had always been nice to me in our US History class; obviously, she had secretly and quietly waited and followed-me all that distance from school to Sis's office and then to there, our *secret* home, on her own; then, without asking, Mrs. Snyder simply stepped-inside, calmly closed the door behind her and began speaking with kindness, yet earnest urgency.

Both Sis and I listened fervently as Mrs. Snyder spoke hurriedly, but matter-of-factly of my unfortunate situation at school and of impending danger for me. Oddly, the dominant sense I remember feeling, at that moment of her visit and speech, was a strong bond-of-trust that sort of washed over me from her kind and heartwarming smile and gentle, trusting eyes.

Just now, I remember how my imagination began running rampant on me again. I momentarily began reflecting upon an existing, social rule-of-thumb which suggested: "Successful people in life all have wonderful smiles." If that was true, then Mrs. Snyder was very successful. If not, however, and I had been misguided by some aberrant social ruse, then I quickly mirrored those same thoughts and considered their exact-opposite clone: A story about *The Happy Executioner,* or something. I was either saved from drowning, or dead-in-the-water.

Did he, the *Hangman*, always have such pleasing smiles too, as he *flipped-the-switches, swung-his-axes, pulled-his-levers,* or *fired-his-rifles*? Some people found intense pleasure in helping others and smiled so nicely throughout their actions; some others, on-the-other-hand, could grin gleefully as they happily tortured their victims.

On an imaginary roll, I remember flashing-back and considering my past life. Right then, while under Mrs. Snyder's ample smiling gaze, how quickly I segued into pondering whether my dad had smiled all-those-whiles as he divvied-out his discipline. It was a sudden and brief flashback, and I was momentarily filled with morose sadness.

Then I shook my mindless wandering and returned to my present tense and its task-on-hand. Glancing again at Mrs. Snyder, while flashing back to my past's moments of insecurity, and then back again to those present actions, all I could do was return my teacher's smile. After fully interpreting Mrs. Snyder's message of imminent danger, I turned to face my sister and quickly deferred to her wiser good judgement. For a moment, Sis too was hesitant while thinking and considering our options.

After cordial smiles from my teacher, Mrs. Snyder got right to the point of her visit. We were informed that the school's truancy authorities were seeking me as a potential run-away. The law was onto us. School officials and the Truancy Office were planning to detain me the very next day at school by apprehending and removing me from none-other than Mrs. Snyder's US History class.

I remember her most kind and defiant words, "Come hell or high-water, it isn't going to happen on my watch!" Mrs. Snyder was not going to allow them to use her classroom as a trap to capture me.

Of course, I was so appreciative of my teacher's kind warning and generous, if not extraordinary, effort to assist and protect me. I recall thanking Mrs. Snyder profusely, hugging her and telling her that we would fix everything. I would be just fine. She was not to worry anymore…

FREIGHTER LATER

The next morning, Sis quit her job and collected her severance pay under *family-emergency* conditions. She simply stopped attending her evening college classes, and I never even bothered returning to Denfeld High School. We were pretty sure that authorities were set to trap and catch me once I showed-up for classes, and we were not about to give them the privilege nor excitement.

I even smiled to myself imagining Mrs. Snyder there in her classroom along with all her other students as well as the school's Principal, Vice Principal, Dean of Students, and even the local Truant Officer. After the longest while, they all would finally leave with frustration and embarrassment written all over their faces. They had been the ones ousted, bettered, tricked, and defeated. And Mrs. Snyder? Why, she'd just be standing there with the biggest, heartiest grin all over her face.

Sis Mary was grateful for how her boss, having heard about our phony conditions, had willingly, but sadly, paid-up all of her due salary plus a small tip as a fond farewell bonus. He even promised her job back if she were able to return soon. Sis and I both knew that was unlikely to be the case, though. *Never Go Back!* seemed to be our new motto. Nevertheless, with a somewhat excited jaunt and cheery gait to our step, by the time that my classes had already started that morning, Sis and I had already caught a city bus heading to the Duluth City Harbor.

We really didn't have much idea of what we were doing, but we both knew that authorities would most likely be looking out for us at typical departure points like bus or train stations. Even seeing us on a road trying to thumb-down rides was risky. Both of us had heard and agreed that many of those freighters in the Duluth Harbor on Lake Superior were going to depart and head for other destinations like Detroit, Michigan and

Cleveland, Ohio. That, in itself, was encouraging and promising because of who lived in Cleveland. Jean and Bo! All we had to do was pull-off a crazy-ride on a giant freighter and take an easy shortcut on its shipping-line, and *Voila!* we would be with Jean and Bo in hardly anytime at all.

With steel for nerves and brass for confidence, Sis and I just amiably sauntered up to what looked like some sort of ticket counter or registry of something, and we met a man-in- charge or harbor agent working there. Sis did most of the talking and all of the smiling, and we simply explained our dire straits to an obviously sympathetic person. Our explanation was clear and filled with reasonable emphasis on certain points.

"We have been both shocked and surprised," Sister Mary began, "at our recent, immediate turn of misfortune," (one might argue that was true). "Our mother passed away," (also true), "and our father is nowhere to be found," (oh, okay, maybe wishful thinking there). "We have found ourselves nearly penniless," (well, true, we had no *pennies*, per se, but we weren't broke either), or we must get to Cleveland to see our brother before he gets shipped overseas." (Okay, we did fudge that one quite-a-bit, but we did, in fact, *want to go to Cleveland and see our brother*.)

Oh, Sis had gone on so beautifully with her spur-of-the-moment oratory and so eloquently and dramatically too. And all the while, she continued showing-off those big, pearly-white teeth of hers and that magnificent heart-melting smile. I mostly just stood there beside her looking lost and forlorn, nodding or shaking my head to emphasize key points and wringing my hands together like we had reached the-end-of-line.

We both laughed about it together later-on in the afternoon, while hanging-over a ship's handrails, watching the huge Lake Superior go scooting past and seeing Duluth become fainter as it disappear behind us. While chuckling to a point of almost gagging over our concocted brassiness, we even agreed that maybe we had a future in show-business together. How about a fun, vaudeville act? We even considered naming ourselves for extra-special effect: *Mary's Patsy!*

No matter, we had spoken to the harbor agent, and he had been as kind as all get-up. It had been as easy as a walk-in-the-park. The agent really felt sorry for our believable story, too. The passage fare was normally ten dollars per person, but he signed-off the paperwork and said that it was all covered. There was room for us, anyway. The agent told us that *under the circumstances,* he could arrange for us two Boarding Fares as passengers on the Gallant Two, a medium-sized, rusty old freighter that was tied up to the docks and was presently being checked, cited, and ticketed for travel.

Its full journey was less than a ten-day round-trip which made the entire Great Lakes circuit from Duluth, MN to Buffalo, NY and back again. It was leaving shortly after we were ticketed two passages that very afternoon too. I remember how excited we got asking for permission to board the vessel, as instructed, and how we were literally jumping up-and-down after giddily running-up the gangplank and stepping aboard our getaway vessel. We were feeling good about our good fortune, so far.

That freighter would take us through *Lake Superior* and then pass through the *Straights of Sault Ste. Marie* into *Lake Huron*. After that, it had another long haul through *Lake Huron*, down a small canal at Port Huron, Michigan and then dump into *Lake Erie*. Once it arrived in *Lake Erie*, the Gallant Two was going to have a minimum of fifteen to twenty hours docking in Detroit. There, it had to unload some materials and goods and then load-up new merchandise, after which it would continue its journey all the way to Cleveland for another lengthy layover.

That was our destination, so we didn't really care about the last part of the Gallant Two's voyage. It was interesting to me, though. So, for future-reference more than anything, I learned about the rest of its journey. After that Cleveland layover, then GT went up to Buffalo, New York. Once in Buffalo, the deck hands would begin transferring the entire cargo from GT's holds to enormous, awaiting canal barges laying there in the *Erie Canal*. Canal crews would coordinate and load-up all that cargo and then make their end-runs all the way to Albany, New York. But, alas, for the Gallant Two, its destiny was to load-up again there in Buffalo and reverse its voyage all the way back to Duluth, eventually.

Sis Mary and I just stayed put in the small passenger quarters they always kept arranged, for travelers and stragglers like us, and we waited. It was a very small and sparsely furnished rectangular room. The entry doorway had a larger peephole window in it, and that served as the only visual contact provided. The inner compartment walls were all noticeably bare and whitewashed, with only a few initials, lovers hearts and a couple silly slogans like, "Kilroy Was Here," or "Warning: Gallant One sunk!" People and their pencils. I swear!

Sometimes, it became a little monotonous and boring when we couldn't see anything because of fog or darkness, but we were comfortable enough and very grateful. Some crew brought us food from their galley from time-to-time, and we were treated very nicely by everybody. Nobody ever bothered us, and there was never a need being two nervous, young, pretty women all by themselves on a big ship with an all-male crew.

I think that if Sis had gotten her way, however, she would have been making rounds flirting with all the crew-hands. She probably imagined that she was in a potential heaven. But her great personality and huge, gorgeous smile had gotten us a long way so far. I suppose, too, that by that time in Spring 1943, freighters were becoming a fairly common passage for many folks to get around.

There was a war going-on, after all, and *seeing the unusual* was fairly common. What really registered in my mind, and what I really took into consideration, was the value, fun and usefulness of these freighter rides. For me, eventually, the Gallant Two would become just the first of dozens of fantastic boat-rides and cruises all over the world. But, those are for other stories. That first boat ride is still very special to me.

Sis and I were getting very anxious to get off that boat, however, and get to our destination, Cleveland. At one point, we determined that we needed a map. Sis stepped outside our quarters, and in less than two-shakes, a crew-hand, whom she had smiled upon, breathlessly returned with one for her. Oh, Sis was so mushy with her appreciation.

Perhaps unfortunately for Sis, anyway, after studying the map, we agreed to make a small change. Once in Detroit, we decided that we would get-off the Gallant Two there and catch a city bus which most likely came near-by. Using transfers, if necessary, we would ride them all the way to the end-of-the-line on the city's outskirts. Back on a main highway, we would then hitch-hike straight south to Flint, Michigan and then keep on going south to almost Toledo. That would be where we would then turn east and hitch rides straight across on a major thoroughfare to Cleveland.

Like I just mentioned a bit ago, people everywhere were either becoming very aware of hardships and difficult circumstances for many others, or they were desensitized to unusual sights by that time. The war was in full-swing across both major oceans, and people were flocking together here-and-there all the time to manage and deal with complicated situations or assist others who were down-and-out on their luck. Soldiers and sailors were hitch-hiking all over the country in order to save money to visit their loved ones, or else they were already broke and were desperately trying to get back to their military stations or posts. A couple of ladies with suitcases hitch-hiking cross-country over the highway? Unusual? Yeah, maybe. But, heck, war was unusual too, and people saw lots of strange things and encountered many oddities throughout wartime's challenging and sometimes brutal duration and along its forsaking paths.

But, holy-schmolie, peaches and pie, and my, oh, my! We did that whole trip lickety-split without hardly any issues to complain about. We had said our kind goodbyes when leaving the ship in Detroit. We caught a bus, as figured, and then got another with a transfer that took us to our highway destination. We were two young ladies with a plan, and we followed it.

We rested when we needed to rest, we ate when we got hungry, and we just did it. We hitch-hiked all the way from Toledo to Cleveland, on Ohio State Route 2 (SR 2) and went clear to where our sister Jean was still living and working. We had kept in touch before with Jean, and we had kept her abreast of our status. After we got dropped-off in Cleveland by a very nice couple who were, themselves, traveling clear to Philadelphia, Pennsylvania, we called Jean again, so that she would be expecting us.

ELDER SIBLINGS TOGETHER

Cleveland, Ohio

J ean had given us some basic directions to get to where she was waiting for us. After a little time on a couple of buses and asking questions and directions from bus drivers, we eventually found the very location she spoke about. We were really thrilled because, just like her word, Sister Jean was there and waiting for us. Talk about craziness, or strange and unusual sightings, onlookers must have thought the three of us had gone coocoo.

We all jumped up and down and hugged each other laughing excitedly. Even Jean, who I remembered as being very somber and reserved in her mannerisms, temporarily behaved loudly and wildly. We had made it, and we were all finally together. Even Sis and I congratulated each other again and hugged and kissed having safely completed our multi-layered journey all the way from Duluth, Minnesota to Columbus, Ohio.

Jean was prepared for us, too. Earlier, she had prepared our first meal together in years, and it was truly a celebration for us. Then, she proceeded to give us the run-down and details of current events. Jean informed us that she had found a decent enough, but low-paying job. She was already established and working in an armaments factory, It was called, *The Cleveland Tank Plant*, and they were assembling tanks, mini-portable cannons, and a variety of other warfare products.

Jean was working with an entire crew, including several other women, on an assembly-line. Once we started noticing some unique advertising posters, Sis and I recognized ads posted about town soliciting women to go to work in the factories because there was such a shortage of male workers. So many young and middle-aged men had been drafted or volunteered to go off and fight. But recall, what I mentioned earlier? An original *Rosie*. My sister, Jean, was a *Rosie-the-Riveter.* Needless to say, I was very proud of her.

Other news came along, too. Jean had estranged herself from most of the family when she left, but she still had ties to Grandma Agnus's daughters, our own deceased mother's sisters, and some other kin. They all knew that Jean was, how do you say it, *different.* Yes, and she had a rough-tough outer exterior that you really didn't want to cross. But, some of our mother's sisters from St. Paul, MN and Hayward, WI like Aunt Liz and Aunt Mary had learned to understand Jean's history and accept her occasional, crude behavior. Besides, we all had allies with them if for no other fact than none of them ever liked their rotten, braggart brother-in-law, our father.

I hadn't touched bases with home or my cousin, Rosalie, for several months by that time and was somewhat out-of-touch with recent goings-on. Jean filled us in with what she had heard from our aunts' phone calls. All in all, it was like nothing we wouldn't have expected, and our dad was continuing with his chronic foul moods, rotten behavior, and occasional, long absences. The story was that while our dad was at home, everybody ate pretty good. When he was gone, however, the family ate very skimpily. Colleen was twelve years old, and we were told that she was finding odd jobs around town to earn money to give to Edith for food.

We sisters talked together for hours and hours after we were reunited. It was obvious right from the start, that Jean was the leader of our pack. Looking back, I pretty well suppose that Jean also thought that she was the brains too, and therefore the planner and our supreme *chief-in-charge.* A few times, we even teased her mockingly by referring to her as, "Ike." How did we know that she would whole-heartedly approve of our teased endowment offered her as *Supreme Commander*? Good ol' Five-Star General Dwight D. Eisenhower was doing a bang-up job over there in Europe against Hitler's armies and his menacing Nazis. So, any positive comparisons to *Big Ike* were soundly accepted, appreciated, and agreed with by Jean.

No matter what, though, Jean was the oldest, most experienced and, no question, the smartest. Both Sis and I accepted that notion, so we would offer our own candid remarks, but then pretty much do as Jean told us to do. It was okay, however, because she wanted just as badly as us to get our other, younger siblings back where they belonged, with us. We made a vow, there in Cleveland, that we would do everything in our power to collect-up Colleen, Jann, and Jackie-Boy. Our common vision was to arrange for all of us to be together and live supportively, even communally. How about that? The first *hippie compound*, and there weren't even any hippies yet, back then!

We all recognized how difficult that *promise* was going to be to make happen, but we were up to the task. We just needed the right opportunities. We would do it in time and at the right time. Then, wouldn't you know it? Right when we had collectively made our staunch promises to reconnect us McCord kids all back together, we heard some new and startling news come from our brother Bo. He had his own apartment a few miles away, and it was easy for us to get together.

It was wonderful seeing him again there in Cleveland. Mary was ecstatic to finally see her twin again. He looked so much bigger, stronger, healthier, and handsomer. He was no longer the little-big brother from years past. We had a very nice reunion, and we even shared some more forgettable episodes of our past lives with our father. Bo, actually, made some derogatory comments and then refused to discuss him anymore. That was something that Bo and Jean did see eye-to-eye on and extremely closely. They both agreed vehemently that they would be happiest if neither of them ever heard our dad's name mentioned again for the rest of their own lives. Sis and I understood, and sort of acknowledged the strain and kept the topic aside.

Then Jean and Sis went off together to do something, and Brother Bo and I had some very special, quality-time together. When alone, Bo confided in me some facts or details about himself and Jean. I had noticed that they were civil to each other but hardly friendly. It was a fact that he and Jean had been roommates for several prior months there in Cleveland, but they had recently split-up.

However, Bo was fairly candid. He said that after just so long, he could not take Jean's bossiness any more. Apparently, they just did not get along very well, and Bo became frustrated with her need for power and control over him. I thought about it and could see his point: Two stubborn, angry individuals having survived similar past cruelties, yet whose viewpoints were far separated, and neither wanted to take orders from the other. Bo also said that their differences never came to blows with actual physical fighting involved. However, he added that he sensed something like that might occur, and he did not want any part of it. So, he left.

The other issue Brother Bo spoke about was Jean's lifestyle and how it just did not suit his own. Like he had learned, understood, and accepted, Jean was *different*, but he did not appreciate Jean throwing her lifestyle in his face and admitted that her behavior had really gotten him upset. He said that it got so bad that Jean would bring so many different lady friends into their apartment, but all of them were very stand-offish to Bo and usually had little to say to him or anything to do with him. After only a short while since becoming roommates, when one of Jean's friends showed-up, Bo said that he would simply grab his coat and go out for long evenings away.

After a while, Bo said that Jean's visitors situation really bothered him, and he would bring it up with her. Inevitably, they would always get into terrible screaming matches. He noted that he even began reflecting back on his relationship with our dad, and that would really bother him. After all those years, what had happened? He had rid himself of our father's selfish, vile behavior only to regain the same hardline, angry tones from our sister, Jean.

Plus, I remember both of us laughing when he chuckled and admitted also, that he did not want to get into a physical altercation with Jean because, no doubt, she would beat hell-out-of-him! That is what ultimately drove Bo to find and keep his very own apartment far away from Jean's rule and influence. He was much happier, he believed, more or less, but Bo was still angry inside and still driven to make something of himself, in spite of our father.

That was when I heard and spread the surprising news. My brother Bo had actually chosen me, his *Sissy-Patsy*, to be his messenger to everyone else in the family. And so, I did. Bo had enlisted in the United States Army Air Corp. He would be leaving in a few days for the St. Petersburg Training Center in St. Petersburg, Florida.

After bootcamp training, Bo was to receive advanced, specialized training in aircraft maintenance and flight engineering. He had been advised that eventually, after all his training was completed, in another six-months, or so, Bo was going to be sent overseas to one of the several

Army Air Corps fields in Southern Italy or Sicily. That was where he would be participating in a variety of bombing missions over Italy and, hopefully, over Germany, before too long.

So much for getting the entire family all together again. Goodbye, Brother Bo. Thanks a lot, World War II, and especially thanks to you, you filthy, rotten Adolf. Drop a bomb on his head for us, Brother Bo. While Jean just sort of stood there sullenly, Sis and I hugged Bo and wished him safe-keeping and to stay in touch with us as best he could. We would be praying for his safe return and hoping that one day soon he would join the rest of us for our idealized family reunions.

Things were relatively calm for a change after that. After a couple days, Sis Mary shocked both me, and then Jean later, when she went into town on the bus line and returned that very early afternoon announcing that she had gotten a really nice job in a textile factory that made blankets and other bedding and pillows and even branching out into uniforms and clothing gear for our Armed forces. When I asked her about her new job, I inquired as to how she thought she might like working on an assembly-line?

Sis just looked at me, somewhat surprised for a moment. Then that fantastic smile spread its wings and carried us all up to a pleasing space. We all just knew that she was going to have something very special or funny to add. She had our full attention too.

Sister Mary simply announced without the slightest hesitation, "Are you kidding? Me and machines? Hardly. It might damage my nails! No, I got a really cushy job as secretary to the second-in-charge in the plant's Administration Office. For some reason, the Assistant Director saw me inquiring at the Personnel Desk and asking about employment. He walked over and checked out my application personally. He really seemed to like me and thought my resume was perfect for the position. What else can I say?"

We were astonished, but we really shouldn't have been. I still asked incredulously, "You mean you just walked into the building, and you got hired for a top secretarial job?"

"Yes, that's just what happened," Sis continued smiling. "On top of that, the Assistant Director walked me aside to show me my new desk near his office, and he wants to talk to me about my future with the company."

"Sis, we're so proud of you! You're amazing! How in the world do you do it? Just give them a piece of paper and then smile?" I laughed while asking.

"Well, yes, sort of except that he also asked me if I'd like to out for dinner with him and talk about my future on Friday night."

"You're kidding?" I asked all wide-eyed. "What did you say!"

"Why, I said, 'Absolutely not!'" Sis pronounced indignantly and then added, "I'm busy then, but Saturday would be just fine!" Then her gigantic smile overwhelmed everyone again.

Jean kind of scoffed and walked away, but Sis and I had a terrific laugh together.

No matter, Sis getting work so fast was a good thing, and I was happy for her. All the pieces were beginning to fall into some sort of order. We all kept hoping that our dreams would be answered, but we also knew that there were plenty more pieces to fit into the puzzle. There was still a lot to be done to make it happen.

Our goals now evolved around our younger siblings. We needed to plan, work, and prepare for somehow getting Colleen, Jann, and Jackie-Boy with us wherever we were and away from that diabolical, maniac father of ours. We had all been through some very precarious developments thus far. There had been difficult times getting to where we were, but we were dealing with it. And now, finally, we older ones were on our own, and it was nice to have a little bit of stability in all our lives, for a change.

SEARCH FOR WORK

One thing was for sure. There was bountiful work to be found within Cleveland for all sorts of crafts and jobs. Just about anybody who wanted work could find some. The war was in full-swing, and assembly-lines were cranking out ammunition and artillery shells endlessly. Munitions work was everywhere, and support efforts were abundant. Wars are always terribly expensive and simply required all kinds of support. Soldiers overseas in the trenches and sailors on the seas all needed the same general kinds of things as back home: Food, clothes, shelter, transportation. Plus, they needed medicine, personal effects and contact from home. Factories were pouring out all sorts of those goods, and Red Cross, USO, churches, and private individuals were trying their best to support our troops.

Here at home it meant that with the slightest bit of effort, anyone with a little ambition could find work easily and right away. If you had skills, then you could practically write-your-own-ticket. Unfortunately, I was still only sixteen going on seventeen years old, so I was limited in what types of jobs I could find. The minimum age was eighteen for any of the better paying, factory jobs. It was late January in a very cold wintertime of 1943, but springtime felt like it was fast approaching. I was anxious to get busy and do something productive.

One unfortunate aspect of my circumstances was that I had been forced to drop-out of high school because of my Denfeld High School issue. Because of any potential warrants that may have been put on me by my dad after he was notified, I would most likely have become a ward of the court or state and taken from Sis Mary. I was probably just put down in the books as another drop-out statistic. Besides, I wasn't too popular with the school management personnel. They don't like being shown-up or embarrassed.

The frustrating flip side of the school issue, however, was the fact that I couldn't even attempt enrolling in a Cleveland high school somewhere. There would be way too many questions asked and verification of grades and attendance records required. Since it was still barely in the beginning of a school semester, any new local, high-school registrars would need records from Denfeld High if I were to try and enroll in order to complete that semester. Too many questions asked could mean trouble. It was a sure bet that our dad would not allow Sis or Jean to be my legal guardians. He would rather have seen me go to some sort of Reform School for incorrigible runaways. Therefore, for the time being, anyway, school was not an option.

On the bright side, though, was the possibility that I could go to work and help support myself and the household. Jean had already begun talking about and explaining *her* dreams for all of us, and it meant towing-the-line when and where she was involved. I didn't have a job yet, so I was sort of out of that equation, thus far, but I understood Jean's plans. She envisioned all of us together and living on a farm somewhere. A working farm, or just a place to hang-our-hats, it didn't matter. That was what she had wanted for us McCord sibling clan.

When it came to Sis Mary, I could tell her brain was running ninety miles an hour… With her broad, ingenuous smile present, I could almost hear her thoughts.

"Farm, Jean, huh?" Sis smiled and continued thinking, "Good for you, but I'll tell you one thing. I'm not working on a farm. No scraping-up chicken shit or milking cows at dawn and dusk for me. I may live on a farm, but I'll be driving into town in my slick-looking car and working in a nice office somewhere. I am meant for style, glamour, and sophistication; not dirt, cow-shit, and a farmer's vocabulary. Sorry, but bright lights are what I want to see, not cow manure and being stuck in the country."

I just knew that she couldn't imagine any potential male suiters for her driving up to our farm in their beat-up, rusted-out, pick-up trucks and then wading through some filthy pigsty or cornfield trying to find her to seek an evening's date.

"Not tonight, Henry," my mind's imagination carried-on for Sis's benefit, "I gots lots mo' corn t' pick an' git it into the house wheres I kin shuck it, grind it-up and make us some cornmeal fer tomorra's breakfast. Maybe next month after harvest…"

Between Sis's smile and my imagination, I could make myself chuckle a lot of the time.

Oh, a farm was truly a grand idea, but it certainly had its weak points for some of us. Mary had been on the farm with Aunt Annie for a short time after she had left home until Jean came over from Cleveland. Then Jean and Sis had stayed in Duluth in that attic apartment for a short while before both finally went back to Cleveland for their work-study arrangement. As for me, I had already lived on a farm with Aunt Annie. I had loved it back then. Jean's farm idea made perfect sense to me. It was like completing a whole circle-cycle: I began on a farm, and I would end-up on a farm. Nice.

Previously, Jean had been going to college, but she and Mary had that arrangement. When they were both living in Cleveland before, the agreement was that Mary would work and support them both, while Jean went to college. After one year, they would switch, and Mary would go to college while Jean worked and supported them. That was their state-of-affairs situation, anyway, when Mary had left Cleveland and stopped in St. Paul to pick me up when the two of us both ventured to Duluth together for school. Sis Mary's plan was to enroll in that Duluth special teacher's college, while Jean remained in Cleveland and would begin working in a factory.

Anyway, by that new time, the situation had changed rather dramatically. Now Jean and Sis were going to both be working, and I would be unemployed and out-of-school. They would be providing for my upkeep and paying for my welfare and expenses. That was the first time in my life that I felt like I might not be *paying-my-own-way* or *earning-my-own-keep*. Somehow, I had not minded the arrangement that much in Duluth. All I did there was help around the house and assist with meal preparation and cleaning-up. Mary's income and some occasional, and very minimal-support money from Jean and Bo got us by well enough.

Even still, things were different. Everybody needed to pull-their-own-weight and find work, if possible, to support our household. Plus, it was imperative to some, well one, anyway, Jean, to begin diligent and significant savings for her pie-in-the-sky farm. We all should have known, or guessed, that finding a job was not going to be difficult for Sis. In hardly no time at all, she made-the-rounds and visited her old friends where she heard about various office-type job-openings around town. Right away, practically that first day she went out looking, Sis found a job and was hired on-the-spot. She was going to be earning decent money too.

Sister Mary's smile was infectious, I tell you. I swear, when she beamed, she could probably convince somebody into quitting their job just so she could have it. Sis was always very friendly, and everybody liked her. She was funny and clever and fun to be around. And she sure knew how to enjoy herself. Fact is, we never got to see much of Sis there in Cleveland. She worked all day, and then she would get invited on dates and to parties and movies and all kinds of entertainment. She liked her job, but it was obvious that she loved her socializing and nightlife even more. I was happy for her.

For me, however, it would be a little more difficult to find a job. I had never worked for anybody before except caring for a household or a sick person. I really had minimal experience doing anything except caring for Aunt Kate and babysitting my younger siblings. It was important, nevertheless, that I find some work somewhere and help pay my way. I considered that Jean might even be pleased if I suggested that all of my most likely meager earnings get put into "our" *farm account*. Anyway, I wanted a job, would be seventeen in a couple months or so, and there were supposed to be lots of jobs out there for anyone who looked to find one. I was ready to look.

With best intentions in my mind then, early one morning soon thereafter, I left our apartment right after Jean and Mary had gone-off to their jobs. I was seeking to find my own kind of work, whatever that was. I was looking for something that I might be qualified to do considering my age and lack-of-experience. Anything would really be okay to me as long as I could do the work and earn some income. So, who would have guessed that in no time, on that particularly fateful day, I was wandering-up the street toward downtown district, searching and looking for anything that might pop-up and be interesting?

It didn't take that long either to find something interesting. With all that advertising of so many jobs available in the factories, many folks had left their previous jobs for higher-paying factory ones. Lo and behold, just a few blocks from our apartment on the way downtown, I spotted something. There was a business that was advertising that they were looking to hire someone. I had only been walking for a few blocks when crossed at an intersection and passed-by a gas-station. It was right next door to a big department store that everyone knew very well.

I saw a "Help Wanted" sign hanging on the gas-station office door. Immediately, I considered my options: The gas-station was close by; it was pretty greasy and dirty, so I knew I could make it look better; probably, I would be pumping-gas for everyone, and that couldn't be hard to learn or do; the pay might not be much, but it would sure beat nothing. Could my job *search* be over that soon? It would become the very first place in my life that I had ever tried to get a job.

I was a little bit anxious and excited about talking to some stranger for work. So, I just took a deep breath, *pulled a 'Mary'* by smiling big as I could and went straight toward the office. Like I mentioned, my first job-hunt outing was going to be with a company everyone recognized. I was actually going to try and find employment with Sears and Roebuck. The job offered was for the Sears gas-station which was even attached to S&R's big department store building.

That particular station was right on a busy intersection. As mentioned, the station itself, was connected directly to the large Sears building. It had a gas service island out front with access on both sides and two gas pumps for service. The service-station office was built right up against the Sears building's wall, and directly connected to it was a large garage area big enough for lots of tools, equipment, storage, and two cars for servicing. One of the car zones, the far-right one, had a large, narrow pit in it. Cars could drove over that hole and be serviced from underneath for oil changes and such.

In those days, besides huge catalog sales and large department stores, Sears and Roebuck also operated and ran a series of local, gasoline stations which they always located right beside their big stores. During the war years, Sears was bigtime into selling gas. I supposed that they were trying to branch-out, or something. Anyway, the work looked promising, the location was great for me, and the pay would be adequate, I was sure, but actually, I didn't even care that much. It was a job. So, I walked-in...

SEARS & ROEBUCK GAS-STATION

First Job

Anyway, once I went inside that gas-station office, I walked over to another doorway and asked a man who was inside the adjacent garage about the *Help Wanted* sign. I guessed that he must have been the owner or manager because once he heard my voice, he paused and turned from whatever he was doing. Then with both his hands on his hips he looked me up-and-down from where he was standing and began asking a few, general questions. I answered back honestly and energetically. Then I smiled, and I promised to work hard. Then I smiled some more, and I promised never to miss work.

I suppose he liked me because after that quick interview, Mr. Smith gave me the job starting that very next day. He did turn-out to be the owner, and liked being called, "Smitty" because that was the nametag sewn onto his work shirt, In one quick effort, I was already on a payroll and working for Sears and Roebuck Company. Well, sort of, but not really. Mr. Smith, *Smitty*, owned the business, but he had a special arrangement with S&R to run and operate the station. He paid S&R a portion of his profits as a lease payment.

No matter what, I had a job and would be earning a living. I would be able to pay my own way and not be a burden. I remember feeling proud and satisfied and giddy all over. I was so very excited that I ran all the way back home to tell my sisters all about it that evening. I even had dinner already for them when they arrived, so I could share my news at the table.

Naturally, they were both very pleased. Any money coming in helped. Jean was already doing arithmetic figuring-out expenses and shared amounts from each of us. I was just happy to contribute at all. I remember too, that right after Sis congratulated me, she was already getting changed for a movie-date that evening. That was something else she enjoyed. She told us that when she went out and had good times, the boys almost always paid for it. She was happy for me too, though. Jean was pleased with me too, but she always frowned at Sister Mary with one of her *life-lesson jewels:* "Two much play gets in your way!"

Sis would just laugh-out-loud and call back over her shoulder as she dashed out the door for some hot date somewhere, "Not enough play... makes life boring as hell!"

Before I go on telling more about our adventures, I think that now would be a good time to provide some necessary background information. Things were different back then. To some they might have even seemed a little harsh. It was wartime, though, and things were tough all over. People just learned to do what they had to do in order to survive. But, what I'm talking about is how this brand-new job for me turned out to be a whole lot more than I ever imagined. How could I ever imagine that just pumping-gas" at a friendly, local gas-station could be very dangerous? My comments about being a "nice" girl might explain a little.

However, the simple idea I had of just pumping-gas for-a-living turned out to be frightfully more dangerous than I ever imagined. Let me explain. A little background is necessary to show how "pumping gas" was dangerous, at least for me. Let me first say that you have to understand that I was a good girl. I was a very nice person. Oh, sure, I had given some nuns and sisters a bit of trouble, and my dad and stepmother a teeny tiny bit too, but that was different. I mean that I was a very sweet young lady, but I was also very naïve. Maybe too nice.

Anyway, here's the background:

By 1943, "Rationing" was going-on in full-force in Cleveland and, of course, all over the country. Necessities were hard to get. The US government was demanding from its citizens at home everything we could muster-up in terms of the war-effort to throw at the enemy. That meant that all the factories pumped-out bombs-and-bullets, war munitions like there was no tomorrow. Aircraft manufacturing plants were pushing- out all sorts of airplanes from fighter-jets to bombers. Many other plants were also developing and making all sorts of materials for the war-cause including food products, essential clothing and uniforms, bedding, and personal items like soap, candy, chocolate, and cigarettes.

It meant that everything within reason went to the war-cause. It meant that we here at home had to do without and sacrifice our daily desires and wants and needs. Oh, we might get some of it, but we would not get that much. It all started beginning in 1941 right after Pearl Harbor's bombing. The Japs had already conquered much of Southeast Asia including Malaya and Java which cut-off almost all of our rubber imports to make tires. So, the government passed laws controlling purchases of car tires.

> That apparently worked so well that fairly soon plenty of things were controlled and *rationed* by the end of 1943. Typical everyday things that most of us have always taken for granted were identified and controlled by over 8,000 government-appointed, rationing boards. Those boards were set-up all around the country for people to go to and receive required purchasing stamps for all those listed products.
>
> I'll tell you that the list of *rationed* products controlled by those boards with their little War Ration Stamp Books really got down to basic things that we all usually take for granted. The list seemed endless with products including all of the following and a lot more: Tires, gasoline, engine oil products, typewriters, bicycles, footwear (like boots and shoes), silk and nylon products, wood and coal, fuel oil, meat, shortening, cheese, butter and margarine, canned, bottled, and frozen, processed foods, canned milk and on and on including jams and jellies. Can you believe it? Jams and jellies! War was hell, but by God, our soldiers were going to get to butter their toast and put jelly on it too!

For any of those special necessities, people at home could only purchase them by offering-up adequate and appropriate government provided stamps from their assigned War Ration Book. When you wanted or needed something on the "rationing" list, then you gave your appropriate stamps to the business proprietor. In fact, the first thing for purchasing those *rationed* things was coughing-up the required stamp or stamps. No stamps, no buy.

> Just about everyone did whatever they could to beg, borrow or whatever to get extra stamps in order to buy more of whatever it was that they wanted from rationing stations or stores. People pleaded with friends and others for their stamps for purchases. Sometimes, it got dicey. People would get turned down or rejected for additional stamps from others. Most businesses dealing with *rationed* items would refuse pleaders or beggars because the word would get-out fast to others wanting more who would then rush to those "easy-touch" places to *beg for more*.
>
> Businesses, themselves, were only issued specific numbers or pounds or gallons of restricted items to be exactly covered by the correct number of stamps. People got upset. Others got greedy. Still others, didn't care at all. They would just take whatever they wanted, whenever they wanted and wherever they wanted. It could be dangerous.

So, this whole *rationing* background and my own *niceness* should help explain about that situation of my first job. I wanted that job because it looked fairly easy and interesting, and I believed that I could handle it. Being a gas-station attendant seemed fairly simple to do, so it was appealing.

I thought to myself, "How difficult could pumping-gas be? Piece-of-cake! Easy-peasy, pumpkin-and-pie!" What I didn't know and had to learn the hard way later-on, would make me cry.

ROBIN HOODLUM

I started the very next afternoon. I was going to be on the second-shift, or swing-shift. I was to start at three P.M. and work until ten P.M. Another daytime employee was there, but he was in a hurry to leave, so I didn't meet him except to nod hello/goodbye. *Smitty* was there, though, and right-away, he began showing-me-the-ropes.

My directions were very simple: When a new customer came in, I was to ask how much gas they wanted, and then I was to crank the lever on the pump to clear the dial and pour gas into the customer's tank or gas can. Next, I would receive from the customer the correct number of *ration* stamps from their War Ration Book and money for the gas purchase. Then, I was to put everything into the cash register-till. Also, I was to return any due change to the customer, if necessary. To top-off our service, I would clean the cars' windshields too, if they asked, but that was about it. Our mechanic in the garage would handle all repair inquiries.

That first day, Mr. Smith or Smitty, stayed for my whole shift. After a couple of customers came in, he started letting me to the work on my own while he stood back, watched, and chatted with his buddy in the garage until that man, the garage mechanic went home. All went well, and the two of us got along very well with me talking about myself and my sisters and him talking about the war and Cleveland and such.

At closing-time, Mr. Smith showed me how to clear the pumps and lock them up, put the money and stamps from the register away in the floor safe and close-up the office. It went very well and before I knew it, I was on my way home. Mr. Smith even offered to give me a ride home, but I reassured him that I was so close it was not even necessary. The day had gone very well.

That very next day that I came to work, *Smitty* was not there, but I got to greet and learn a little more about another member of the station's staff. His name was Mr. Beauregard Jefferson, and he was the gas-station's garage mechanic. He told me to call him "Beau," though, and I introduced myself as Patsy. At first, he said, "That's okay, Miss, but I'll just call you 'Miss McCord.'" He must have been a southern gentleman who was big on manners.

I quickly responded, "Okay, then, you are 'Mr. Jefferson' to me."

He looked me over for a moment, and then chuckling, he said, "Alright, then, 'Ms. Patsy,' it is!"

"Nice to meet you, 'Mr. Beau!'" I laughed along with him, and we both got along really well after that.

Right after that, in fact, I learned about other aspects of the job. Beau said that he would usually be too busy working underneath cars or on their engines to help much, but I could always call on him if needed. He told me about Smitty's other gas-station down by the waterfront. That place was a much rougher location, and it was common to have issues come up daily which required our boss, Mr. Smith, to attend. He assured me that I was going to stay right there at the Sear's Station because the other place was nowhere for a lady. I thanked him and reassured Mr. Beau that I would work very hard and be very honest. He smiled at me, and I think we both hit-it-off really well.

At first, the work seemed fairly simple. People came in to get gas for their car. Often times, I filled-up gas cans, too, that they brought-in to take home and store-up for themselves or anybody else, I supposed. I never knew for sure because it didn't matter as long as they had the proper stamps from their War Ration Book and money for their purchase.

I pumped gas into car-after-car and made all the appropriate transactions. If they needed repairs or mechanical help, I would sent them inside to see Smitty, or Mr. Beau, the mechanic-on-duty, when either were there. Usually, when one of them was there, though, they would be working in the garage on a car repair. If either had a chance, and saw that I was really busy, though, they came over and helped me out until things calmed down again.

Usually, however, Smitty or Beau were gone mostly when I was on duty. Smitty, the owner, was usually over at the harbor station dealing with more difficult traffic. Often times, he would come over and visit me in the late afternoon when he was going home. Sometimes, he even stayed later to help out. Mr. Beau was very seldom there in the late afternoon or evening because his shift would have ended, and usually he always left a couple hours after I got there.

Then one day early on, I showed up even a little earlier, so I had the chance to meet the other daytime employee, Joey. Right after that, Joey liked to stay longer and hang around with me and visit. Sometimes, he even took care of some customers while I was busy with another. Very nice of him, it began.

I was friendly and got along well with everyone else too. Give the customers gas, then take their stamps and money. Put it all in the till, hand back any change, and go on to service the next customer. When things got a little slow, that was when I took time to clean-up around the station. Both Smitty and Mr. Beau noticed the effort too, and they both appreciated it.

I remember when I first started cleaning the place up a little. Smitty teased me, and said something like, "That's what this dump needed. A lady's touch.!"

I laughed right back at him and countered, "No, just a mop!"

Then Mr. Beau jumped-in chuckling and panned very seriously, "A what? Now, I know what a wrench is, and I've seen a screwdriver before, but a *mop*? Never heard of it!"

"It shows!" I'd laugh and then get back to cleaning the office smiling all the while. I liked my job. I was a good employee, and both Smitty and Mr. Beau liked my attitude and effort...

Slowly and steadily, though, things started changing. Joey, who worked the dayshift from 6:30 AM to 3:00 PM, before me, started telling me what to do once I showed-up for my shift. I was to be there from 3:00 PM until closing at 9:30 PM, so I could clean-up and be gone by 10:00 PM. Thus, our shifts never overlapped unless Joey was real busy with a customer when I arrived, and I had to jump right-in with another customer which I always did when I got there a bit early.

Once I got to the station and started working, though, Joey just loved telling me what to do. He started acting like he was my boss and would tell me to take certain cars as customers while he took others. He would tell me to empty trash cans and such even when they didn't need it. I let him because I was new, and he had been there a while before me. Plus, I didn't want to have any problems with anybody. I liked my job, and I wanted to keep it that way.

Eventually, though, Joey was telling me a day-ahead-of-time that he would need an hour or so off during an afternoon. He would play boss and tell me to come-in early the next day and help cover for him. Joey even said that Smitty or Beau didn't even need to know because it was just a switch & cover between us friends. He said they wouldn't notice anyway, because they were always busy with car engines, or else they were both gone. As long as the pumps, the *yard*, we called it, was managed, they didn't care, so Joey said.

I didn't know any better because it was my first job, after all. So, I almost always agreed. Besides, I never really had anything else to do, anyway. Joey said that he'd cover by helping me on my shift to make up any difference. I didn't mind, and he had been there longer than me, so he had seniority, I assumed. Mostly, though, he worked the dayshift, and I came-on in the later afternoon and worked until closing time. I was content mostly because I was just glad to have a job, and Joey was nice enough to me.

As time passed, I began to notice that Joey was staying a little later after his dayshift ended just so he could chat with me, supposedly. That was when Mr. Beau had already left for the day, and Smitty was probably busy at his other station by the waterfront. In fact, Joey liked staying and visiting with me especially after the mechanic and the owner were both gone for the day. Occasionally, Smitty would be back-and-forth between stations, but usually he was gone in the afternoons and evenings.

That was always when Joey would stick around and start talking to me more often. I figured it was because no one else was around, so nobody was around watching him or us. Anyway, like I said, Joey seemed to like me and was very friendly at first. But that was when Joey started telling me things, and I was sort of his captive audience. Oh, did I mention that he was really cute, too? What was a blushing young girl to do?

At first, Joey just started talking badly about our boss and our mechanic. He told me that Smitty was actually some sort of gangster and worked for bigtime criminals. Then he added that Beau was hiding-out here, too, under Smitty's watch and care at that gas-station because he was *Wanted* by the police for a shooting in Toledo, Ohio. I have to say that Joey's revelations bothered me a lot, but I needed the job, so I continued on working. Plus, Smitty and Mr. Beau were always very nice to me, and polite and encouraging. Bad or not, I did like them, but Joey continued telling me more things about the owner and his mechanic sidekick.

Joey told me on another occasion that most of the time, Smitty was filling-up his storage tanks with stolen, illegal gas which had been smuggled into the country from Canada. He said that the gas we sold was totally illegal. However, he assured me that I had nothing to worry about because police and the authorities never worried about employees. The police knew that staff were always innocent and clean. I was relieved a little.

I should say, "I was relieved for a little *while*." Clear definitions of good and bad, right, and wrong started getting really muddled in my young, naïve, and inexperienced mind. I began to feel really conflicted. Unfortunately, things just got even more muddled, murky, and gray. My situation was no longer feeling comfortable for me. I did my job, but I began developing those same old, queasy, nervous anxieties whenever I was pumping that *stolen* gas into somebody's car. Gee, if the customers only knew, what would they think? Or do?

That was when the first actual *incident* occurred. Everybody was gone except for me at the beginning of my shift in the late afternoon. Shortly afterwards, Joey showed-up smiling and was especially nice to me helping-out and cleaning-up. That was part of my job. I cleaned-up the office and in the garage sometimes because Smitty and Beau were both messy and left the place dirty and greasy by the time I came to work.

Anyway, a customer arrived carrying two gas cans with him. I went to help him, but Joey just said, "That's okay, Patsy. I got this. You can go back to what you were doing."

I was somewhat uncomfortable, though, because it was actually my shift, my job, and my responsibility. But as I returned to my garage cleaning, I watched to see what went on with Joey and the customer. When Joey finished filling the man's two gas cans, the customer just took them and walked away. No stamps, no money, no nothing. I didn't understand, so I approached Joey about it.

"Hey, Joey," I asked matter-of-factly, "Why didn't that man give you his stamps and money for the gas?

At first, Joey just stammered, "Uh, uh, well, you see, he didn't have any with him."

"Why not, Joey? I was told to never give gas without gas stamps first and then the money," I queried.

"Uh, well, that was a poor fellow who was really down-and-out. I filled-up his cans, and then he told me he didn't have any stamps or money. I felt sorry for the bugger, and I just wanted to help him and his family," was Joey's innocent response.

Still, I followed-up, "Okay, Joey, but this is my shift, and I was told not to give out any gas without coupon stamps and cash." I started feeling a little uneasy. "You do what you want on your shift, but not on mine."

"Yeah," Joey persisted, "But sometimes, we just have to help out the poor." And he continued on a mini crusade, "Remember, Patsy, that all this gas is stolen anyway. It's like we're just giving it back to people for free. We're kind of like small-time *Robin Hoods!*"

I paused to consider his analogy. I sort of liked it, but I still felt a bit dissatisfied and uncomfortable. I went back to cleaning, while Joey just fiddled around with scribbling something into a notebook of his. All was quiet for a while, and then another customer arrived in his big, nice fancy car. As I approached the customer, Joey started to wave me off. I refused.

"This is my shift, Joey, and I want to help *my* customers," I emphatically declared. "If you want to help, you finish sweeping the garage, I insisted. Then I finalized my argument, "I'll do the gas!"

Joey was a little taken-aback, but he sort of slumbered-away. The customer, who had watched our little interaction, stared at Joey, and seemed a bit miffed as he frowned at me, but climbing out of his car, he brusquely directed, "Yeah, Chicky, put ten gallons in it for me."

Straightaway, I nicely demanded, "I need your Ration Book, please, and one dollar and fifty cents, please." (How about those days, huh? Gas was fifteen cents a gallon back then!)

For a moment, the man just stared at me, and then he looked over to Joey with a questioning face, "Hey, what's going on here? I thought you said things were okay, Joey?"

Joey was sheepishly half-staring at the man and half at the ground while shrugging his shoulders, and then he motioned for me to come over to him. I did, and then Joey started talking nonstop.

He began pleading, "Look, Patsy, remember what I said about the *Robin Hoods*? Well, this poor guy needs some help too. He's a real friend to me. Can't you help him a little for me? He only wants ten gallons of gas, and he'll for sure pay me back tomorrow when it's my shift. Won't you help this poor guy out?"

I didn't like being put-on–the-spot like that, but I gave-in with a nod of approval stating, "Okay, Joey, I will this time, but he's going to pay you back, and you are going to pay the station back tomorrow, right?"

"Yeah, sure he will," Joey affirmed, "I promise." Then, Joey glanced over at the customer and added his go-ahead with a salvaging nod and a circled-forefinger and thumb, *OK* sign. "It's fine," Joey quipped. "She's good. We'll square things up tomorrow, right?" he added. Right then, I could have sworn I saw Joey toss a wink at the customer.

As I began filling the customer's gas tank, I listened intently to the man and Joey's conversation. I watched, too, as the customer nodded toward Joey but shook his head a little while shrugging, "Boy, I don't know about you, Joey. I thought we was pals, you know?"

Suddenly, Joey acted a little unnerved, "Yeah, yeah, we are," he stammered, "Sure we are." Then he emphatically finished with, "No, no, really, it's fine, Mr. Carnauba. Really, she's okay. She's just new, and she'll come around. I swear."

I watched as that customer, *Mr. Carnauba*, nodded approvingly while lightly shaking his palms-up spread hands, "Okay, then, Joey. That's a good boy. This means a lot to *The Boss*." Mr. Carnauba finished by tapping his temple and advising, "He'll appreciate the favor. I'll let him know."

As I replaced the gas cap to the car tank and the nozzle back to the pump, I still reemphasized to Mr. Carnauba, "Okay, Sir, there you go then, and you'll clear this-up with Joey tomorrow, right?"

The customer climbed back into his car, started the engine and looked over at me quizzically, "Huh? Uh, oh yeah, sure thing, Chicky. Tomorrow. Right!" Mr. Carnauba rolled-up his car window, and as he pulled away, I saw his shoulders sort of rising and falling rapidly, and I was certain that he was chuckling to himself. Real funny.

I was upset, and I didn't like that man at all. He called me, *Chicky*. The nerve of that guy. So, I walked straight over to Joey, who had sort of cowered-back inside the garage, and I confronted him.

"Joey," I sternly inquired, "Who was that man? I thought you said he was your friend. And what did he mean by '*The Boss* will appreciate it?' Did he mean our Mr. Smith, the owner here? What's going on, Joey? I don't like that guy. He laughed at me!"

Joey started rapidly pushing-air with his hands and tried to calm me down, "Whoa, wait a minute. Slow down. It's all fine now. No, not our *boss* here. It's a different boss. A bigtime, powerful man. And I was just trying to do him a favor, but you got in the way," Joey connived.

"Well," I began defending myself, "That man looked like he had a lot of dough on him, and he could have afforded paying for that gas."

"Yeah, but you see," Joey concocted, "He, uh, he didn't have any stamps. Yeah, that's it! He didn't bring his ration-book, and I just wanted to do him a favor, so he would do one for me."

I was too quick with my debating response for Joey, though, "How did you know he didn't have any gas-stamps? I was the one helping him."

Good ol' smooth-talking Joey was fast to counter, "I, uh, saw him yesterday, and we arranged for him to get some gas here today." Joey was shaking his head, "Okay, then? Any more questions?"

"Yes," I thought to myself, "About a dozen or more," but I didn't continue except to announce, "Okay, Joey, but you do that sort of dealing on your shift, not mine."

By then, Joey seemed just a bit perturbed when he responded, "Look, Patsy, that man…"

Quickly, I interjected, "You mean *Mr. Carnaubaaaaa*, your *friend*?"

"Yes, that man, my friend," Joey was clinching his teeth as he continue, "He is a very important man. You don't mess around with him. I was doing him a big plus, so he'd remember me and help me get a better job."

"Oh, I thought you were just doing him a favor until he paid tomorrow with cash and stamps?" I squeaked as I put my little dig into his arguments. "Whatever happened to *Robin Hood*," I mocked.

Joey was really on the defensive by now, "Look, that man is a really dangerous fella. He was just trying to get some of the gas back that was stolen from him. I just helped him out a little, so he would help me. That's all."

Oh, now I was a little confused and getting frustrated and angry. I was climbing into a very argumentative mood and wanted to challenge Joey.

I began blurting out, "If it was gas stolen from him, why didn't he just take it all and have the police here, too? If he's so *b a d* and had gas *stolen* from him, then why doesn't he use his own gas? What's going on, Joey?"

Joey was definitely flustered, but he continued, "Because he just needed some gas right now, and he didn't have any gas-stamps! Wow! Get off my back, why don'cha?"

Oh, no, I wasn't done yet, so I continued arguing, "You said, 'Yesterday, you made *arrangements*.' So, why today, here-and-now and on my shift? Why not yours?"

Joey was actually a pretty good thinker under pressure, though. He was fairly quick with more answers, so he next retorted, "Because he didn't have any stamps, and his boss and our boss don't get along at all. So, just do your job, and I'll do mine and let me deal with those people. Got it?"

No, I did not get it at all, and I wasn't just going to leave it alone. I was actually getting pretty mad at Joey for having started all this *wheelin'-dealin'* on my shift. His story and excuses were getting wider and deeper and full of more holes than a hobo's socks the more that he talked. Plus, he wasn't even supposed to be here in the first place. I decided to try and go-for-closure with Joey and finish that debate.

I complained adamantly, "I don't want to get involved, Joey. You just do your shift and let me do mine all by myself. Or else, let's switch, and you do this shift, and I'll do yours in the morning during the dayshift. Okay? We can arrange it with Smitty. He won't mind."

But Joey still would not relent, "I got another job at night already, so I can't give-up my day-shift. Plus, I'm supposed to be here watching Mr. Smith for my other boss? If I do good, then he's gonna get me a real good job with his organization."

"You mean you're a *spy* against our boss, Mr. Smith?" I questioned him now completely flabbergasted.

"I told you that Smith is bad news. He's a real gangster who steals gas, and I'm just giving gas. I mean, *we're* just helping others out when they need help. Okay?"

I was nowhere near satisfied, so I tried to be polite but firm, "Look, Joey, you have been nice to me, but I don't want to choose sides. I got a job from *Mr. Smith*, and he has been good to me. I just want to do my job and then go home. I don't want to cause any trouble, and I don't want to get into any, either. Do you understand?"

As the hours passed, things did not improve. In fact, they really began deteriorating. I soon learned that Joey did not understand my feelings at all, or else he just didn't care. I started keeping my distance from him and just tried to do my job on my own. Other cars continued to come in, and I began getting really conflicted.

Pretty soon, Joey had arranged a relationship between us: When he didn't recognize who the person or car was, Joey would wave at me to do the business transaction and pump the gas and collect the necessary stamps and money. If he knew the driver, or the guy walking-in with gas cans in his hands, then he would wave-me-off and do the business, himself. But, I never saw Joey ever take any gas-ration stamps, or cash for that matter. Just once-in-a-while, I noticed Joey writing things down in his notebook. I became very concerned.

That first, weird, gas-give-away shift ended, and Joey was still there until I closed-up the shop. He had a couple of brief but friendly words for me as I started my walk home, "Hey, Patsy, don't worry. It was fine today, and you done real good. Nobody knows nothing."

Well, I thought I knew everything by then, and I didn't like it one bit. I just said curtly, "Yeah, sure, Joey. Whatever you say. Goodnight." I left promptly without turning around.

The next day, I showed-up for my shift again, and I noticed that only Joey was there. He quickly responded to my arrival, "Well, look who's here? It's Robin Hood!"

"Ha! Ha! Funny! Where's Beau?" was all I could muster.

"Ahh, Beau went with Mr. Smith to the other station," Joey answered. "They are probably making arrangements to get some more stolen gas,"

He had a smirk on his face, though, and while he just grinned and watched me, I ignored him as I was going about my typical, work-routine. However, Joey just had to continue with what I considered badgering, though.

He began, "Look, yesterday was a tough day. Let's call it, a learning-lesson. Some people need gas who can't get it, so we help them. Others pay for their gas with stamps and cash. It'll be fine. No problems."

I was still very stern and emphatic, "Joey, I don't know any of those people, and they are not friends of mine. If you want to give them all free gas, then you do it, but I don't like doing it on my shift. And I'm not giving free gas to anyone whether you are here or gone."

"Hey," Joey soothed, "That's alright. I'll be here to help, and you don't have to worry about a thing. You give gas and take stamps and cash from your customers, and I'll give gas to my people who deserve it."

I was mad, "What happened to your other job? Why are you still here? *Your people* don't *deserve* free gas! If this gas was stolen by Mr. Smith, then it's just one thief stealing from another, and I don't like it at all!"

Joey reached out to me, "Whoa, Little Lady. Calm down! Everything's fine. I'm spreading the word to all the *poor folks* to wait until they see me here and not to bother you. You'll be okay. Trust me."

Boy, those were dangerous words. Trust him, he asked. No, I did not think so. Not anymore. I trusted my sisters, and I trusted God, and still in a strange way, I trusted my boss, Smitty. I did not trust Joey anymore, or just about everyone else who came into the station and especially all the ones who were *Joey's friends*. I only wanted to keep my distance from Joey from then on.

But, Joey had other plans, I suppose. Eventually, he approached me with his renewed offer, "Patsy, I gotta go into town for some business tonight, so I might not be back until later, if at all. You know the game, right? If they ask for me, then they're my friends, and I'm just helping them out. So, give them gas. Got it?"

"No!" I yelled, "I don't *got* it, and I don't *like* it either. I don't want to give *anybody* free gas or any gas without stamps and cash. Those are your deals, your friends and not mine."

By then, I remember Joey starting to feel all pushed-out-of-shape. He began acting like he was being persecuted. First, he started walking around in circles and shaking his hands with his favorite palms-up motion. Next, he outstretched his arms reaching toward me like he was welcoming me into his flock. Then Joey fell silent for a moment. Now I think that at that very moment he was trying to determine his next very important words and movements. Finally, he decided to fall back on his original, smooth-talking, and Joey tried to waylay my support with his noxious words.

"Patsy, I'm so sorry to make you feel uncomfortable," he began. "This was not the way it was supposed to be," Joey confided.

I relented a little, "Well, I just don't like to be pushed-around or used." All the time I watched his reactions.

In a kind and soothing voice, Joey persisted, "Hey, there's no problems here, Patsy. We just take gas from a crook, and we give it to the good guys. That's all. You understand, don't you?"

Well, I didn't, but it was a really weird situation to me. My own boss, Mr. Smith, was nice to me and so was his mechanic, Beau. It was hard for me to picture either of them as big-time criminals because they were always so kind to the people that they helped at the gas pumps, in the office or in the garage. I used to watch them with their customers, and they were always very polite and acted like real gentlemen. I just couldn't picture Mr. Smith or Mr. Jefferson as crooks or gas thieves. But, then again, Joey was so charming, and I wanted to believe him because he seemed to want me to be his friend. Why would Joey lie to me, anyway? He was a nice person.

I had gotten myself into quite a predicament. I liked my job and Mr. Smith, but I also liked Joey too, even though he continued each afternoon and evening on my shift giving gas away free to his *poor* friends. I suppose that I just sort of psyched myself into believing and accepting Joey for his position.

I sort of rationalized, therefore, that if what Joey said was true, and Mr. Smith and Mr. Jefferson were getting their gas free, or at least cheap, because it was stolen, then maybe Joey giving away some gas wasn't too bad. Plus, I considered that Joey wasn't really hurting anybody. He was actually helping people, his friends, I imagined. That was what Joey kept telling me, anyway.

So, the days passed, and so did my shifts at work. Joey was still there a lot of the time to *help* me out with his *poor* customers. But after a while, he started hanging around a lot less. He told me that he was getting plenty of new work from his new boss, The Big Boss, so he couldn't stick around during the evenings much.

I had plenty of occasions when *Joey's* friends showed up asking for him, or some who just pleaded with me. But, when he was gone, I always told them to come-back the next morning and talk to the boss. Or, I said something like, "Sorry, Joey's not here." Then, one day Joey offered me his next step in a *proposition*.

Joey developed nerve to ask me straight out, "Hey, look here, Cutie. Sometimes, I can't hang around this place with you on account of me having important stuff to do elsewhere. So, you would be doing me a personal favor to help them poor people who come in to the station and ask for me. If they know my name, that means they are my friends. Just help them out a little and give them some gas… for me. How about it?"

He was the one now, the bigshot, doing *them* a big favor. Yeah, right. Only Joey wanted me to be the one pumping gas for them, *not* taking stamps or money, and taking all the risk. Joey, Joey, cute little Joey. He had a lot of nerve, that's what he had! He was giving-away free gas on *my shift*, and now he wanted *me* to step-in and do *his* favors for *him*. Oh, boy, that was not going to happen.

I made it very clear to him right then. I would *never* give his *poor friends* any *free gas*. If anybody asked me for *free gas* or told me they were his *friends*, I would refuse them, but I would tell them that they could come back and see Joey the next morning. That didn't stop Joey from hanging around the service-station during my shift once-in-a-while and continue helping-out his friends. It was not long before Joey's *arrangement* really started spoiling for me. In fact, it began stinking to high heaven.

I think that Joey must have told some of his cronies to test me. The very first night Joey was not at the station during my shift was the first time some of his *poor friends* came by and asked me for gas. What a coincidence! At first, they asked to see Joey, but I believe they already knew he was gone. When I told them that, they tried pleading with me and begging me for gasoline handouts.

Some were young and sporty-looking people, and others were low-down and really scruffy, nasty people. Some characters looked similar to that first, bad-news fellow who made Joey act so nervous, that creep, *Mr. Carnauba*. A couple of them even tried a bribe, but I wasn't game. I just told them to talk to Joey, or the owner, Mr. Smith. That sent them away. Of course, there were others who were drunk and just needed some gas to get across town to some big party they were supposed to be attending. "Sure, I understand," I'd say, but "Sorry, come back tomorrow and see Joey." By then, Joey and all his *poor friends* were making me sick.

Actually, Joey's name ended up making it easier for me because I turned most of them away by politely saying, "Come see Joey here in the morning, but I can't help you tonight."

Other times, if I thought I recognized the same person again, or not, I would often say for special effect, "I am so sorry, but I can't help you today. However, if you come back tomorrow, the owner will be here, and he will surely help you." That usually sent them driving-away in a hurry while mumbling or cursing-out-loud.

Some of them really persisted, though, until once-in-a-while they would get really belligerent and even threaten me. I just quickly said that I would tell Joey all about them. Usually, they just laughed at me and sped away. But those incidents began making me sick and nervous.

One time even, some fancy-dressed character in his really nice and new, Buick Special Convertible Coupe cruised up to the gas pumps and started looking around. It was past sundown and starting to get a little dark. I walked over to help him, and he asks me, "Where's Joey?"

"He's not here," I told him and began assuming he was one of Joey's *friends*.

Right away, this fellow attests to me something like this, "Hey, well, Joey is a real stand-up-guy. I'm sure he would like you to give me ten gallons of gas *on-the-house*."

Like always before with everybody else, I refused him and told him to come back the next day and see Joey.

The guy started getting very belligerent with me, "Look, little Gas-Girl, you need to get with the program. You acting so highbrow and stuff could get you into a lot of trouble. You could even get yourself hurt. Understand? I'm gonna have some serious words with your chum, Joey."

I had a bit of a smart-mouthed when pressured and perhaps had too careless a retort for him, "He's *not* my *chum*, and don't worry, Mister, I'm going to have some *serious* words with Joey myself… and with my boss who's supposed to be here any minute now to help me close-up tonight."

That last part was a lie, of course. I always closed-down the station on my own. But, I wanted to suggest that assistance would be there right away, and that he had better not try anything funny. But, the jerk just stared at me for a moment and then sort of smirked and began shaking his head. With a laugh he just snorted, "Yeah, sure," and he quickly drove his car out the station and was gone. I didn't like that guy at all, and Joey's *friends* were really pressing their luck with me. That last customer, or not, really caused my stomach nerves to churn.

Every day, I kept getting more and more upset at him for his *arrangements*, and I did not like it at all when his so-called friends came by while Joey was gone and still tried to pressure me for gas. I kept telling them that I couldn't but for them to go see Joey the next morning. Leave me alone was all I wanted. I kept asking Joey to switch shifts with me because I was not comfortable with him giving away free gas to his *friends*. Joey's line about stealing from crooks, like Mr. Smith, and giving to the needy just started wearing-off and didn't seem plausible.

The people who paid me with cash and stamps were always very nice to me and always had kind words for me. Joey's friends, on-the-other-hand, just stopped-in, whenever they felt like it, it seemed, and announced their friendship to Joey. Reluctantly, I'd wave at Joey to come talk to his friends, and then I'd walk away from their dealings completely. I felt uneasy even being around them. I wanted no part of them or Joey's *Robin Hood* nonsense. Maybe they were poor, or broke or had no stamps, but it wasn't my place to give-away something that wasn't mine.

I would sometimes watch Joey and his cronies from the office. Or, if I were helping a legitimate customer, I could see them talking to Joey. Much of the time, they just sat or stood there and waited while Joey pumped gas for them into their cars or cans. Once they got their fill-ups, they just drove-off or walked away without even a "Hello!" or a "How de do, and thanks to you."

Actually, they didn't even look very nice to me. Most of them seemed very sullen and shifty. Not my kind of friends. They were Joey's pals. If he gave them free gas, that was his problem. Plus, God forbid that Mr. Smith or Beau noticed what was going-on. They would both surely be angry…

CONVOLUTED

Of, course, I should have expected the worst happening. That situation just could not go on for much longer. Naturally, it was not too long before the inevitable had to happen. It occurred on Joey's shift too because that was when the big, gas-delivery truck arrived to fill-up the station's tanks one afternoon. Joey told me all about it in private after I came to work. Mr. Smith and Beau were both talking in the office and doing some figuring, I supposed.

Joey saw me approaching the yard, started running toward me yelling something about getting robbed. Then he caught up to me real fast, panting and acting very anxious as he quickly pulled me aside. Calling-out loudly and directly into my face but with very precise words, Joe quietly and quickly explained what was happening, "The boss (Mr. Smith) says that we got robbed. That's the deal, got it? We got robbed! Don't say nothing more. Understand?"

Oh, yes, I understood. I was young and inexperienced, but I was not stupid. Obviously, to me by then, and at that very moment, I realized how foolish and naïve I had been. All the gas we, or rather Joey, had been giving-away for free to all his needy friends, or poor acquaintances or future-job prospects was now unaccountable. The service-station, office-register till plus the funds inside the safe did not have the funds to cover the morning's refill by the delivery man. Either money and stamps or gas was missing. There wasn't enough cash to cover the new storage-tank, refill-purchase expenses.

I didn't fully understand how it all worked, but I was starting to get a picture of what had happened: Every night at closing, I would take all the cash from the register-till and put it into Mr. Smith's safe underneath the counter. That was one of the first things I did when closing the station.

Then I finished all the rest of my chores and locked-up the office and the big garage door. The gas pumps all had locks on them too, and that was actually the very first thing I did, lock all the pumps.

That was in case somebody, or one of Joey's *friends*, came by late, and I could say, "Sorry, we're all locked-up for the night. I can't open the pumps now. It's too late. Sorry. Come back tomorrow… and see Joey."

Lots of times, I would get dirty looks, pleading stares or curious studies, but I held my ground. Occasionally, I had to add, "Well, I'm real sorry, but come in early tomorrow and talk to Joey, or my boss. They might be able to help you then."

Anyway, apparently, as far as I gathered from Joey's brief explanation, the gas-delivery, truck-driver had arrived during the dayshift and had taken his measuring tool and checked the station tanks. The tanks were obviously low, as might be expected, so he filled-them back up, did his calculations and gave Mr. Smith a bill for the amount due.

That's when Joey explained to me that Mr. Smith went into the office, opened the safe, gathered out the money inside with the paper records, and counted out what was due for the deliveryman. Joey said that Mr. Smith started getting real panicky. He added up the money again. Then he looked into the safe again. He looked at all the gas-ration stamps collected, and throughout the whole endeavor, Mr. Smith just kept his head down low while shaking it back and forth.

Joey told me later that Mr. Smith had then called for Mr. Jefferson to come in, and they talked between themselves. Then Mr. Jefferson took a turn at counting the money. Joey also told me that Mr. Smith was acting really concerned, but he finally took what money and stamps was there and added more cash from his own wallet and paid-off the delivery-driver.

Mr. Smith and Mr. Jefferson were actually in the office talking when I arrived. That was when I had spotted Joey over near the back of our service-station. Joey had shown me before that the gasoline storage tanks for the service-station were located there. Joey explained that the gasoline-truck driver had just pumped those tanks full of gas again.

That early afternoon, right when I first arrived, I saw Joey bent over studying the tank-openings, and he had been busy doing something earnestly. Once he spotted me walking onto the service-station yard, he dropped whatever he was doing and rushed-over to me. I was startled a little by his anxiousness, but he hurriedly began calling-out loudly, "The boss says that we got robbed! Got it? Robbed!"

As Joey continued rapid-fire explanations of what was going-on, I started getting very nervous. Oh, I was in a real conundrum, alright. Either gas was missing, or cash and stamps were. I closed-up shop almost every night, so I was the last one to check the register and lock the safe and the gas pumps. I was pretty sure that, at least on my shift, Joey had never been inside the register or the safe, and he sure as heck never took any money from *his* customers. Maybe Joey was stealing money from the till during his dayshift, but I doubted it. Mr. Smith was usually in the office doing paperwork, and Mr. Jefferson was almost always nearby in the garage.

However, I did know where a lot of the gas was going, and I didn't know what to do or say. I was becoming afraid of what might happen. Maybe I was going to be accused of robbing the till or the safe, or both. But then, the unexpected happened. I was not ready for what came next.

As expected, however, Mr. Smith called me into the office. I walked in meekly with my hands folded together and feeling flushed with probably a terribly guilty look on my face. Mr. Smith was still doing some counting and figuring while I just stood there frozen-like and waiting for him to speak. I could hear a drum-roll rapping-off its measures in my mind. Was this the end... of me?

Finally, he looked-up at me from his office-chair and explained what was happening. He smiled reassuringly at me and spoke, "Miss Patsy (he liked calling me that), a terrible thing has happened at this station. Now, I'm not blaming you in the slightest because I believe that you are a good and honest young lady; however, we have been robbed, and I'm finishing-up my report for the police."

I should have kept my mouth shut and just waited, but I had to jump in there and defend myself and find out if he had figured out what had happened. I quickly interrupted, "Oh, no, Mr. Smith, that is awful. I am so sorry, and I swear to you that I never gave any gas to anybody for free!"

Mr. Smith looked at me sort of startled and puzzled, but then he smiled again and repeated himself, "I'm sure you never did. I'm also sure that the safe was not robbed because the gas stamps match exactly the amount of money from the till and safe. I have my own daily records that I keep every afternoon, so those figures are right. They match exactly. So, I know for sure now that it was actually gas that was stolen."

I looked at him nodding in agreement and murmured, "I sure am sorry, Mr. Smith."

Then my boss looked at me kind of funny and asked, "How did you know it was gas?"

He caught me in a trap. I had been exposed, and now he was onto my *guilt by association*. I just didn't want to lie to him, but I didn't want to get into any trouble either. If he figured I was lying, or that I knew more than I was saying, then he would get real upset and make me tell him everything.

Then the thought crossed my mind: "If Mr. Smith is really a gangster, then he could be very dangerous."

Well, Joey was a real sap and a sucker because he was being used by all his so-called friends, but I also didn't want him to get into trouble. After all, Joe wasn't selling gas and then keeping the stamps and money; he was giving it all away for free with no profit to himself.

So, I thought for a brief moment and then responded, "I know I never took any money or stamps, Mr. Smith, and I always put all the cash and stamps in the till until closing, and then I put it all into the safe. I always knew the money and stamps from my customers were right every night when I closed."

That was when Mr. Smith stood way-up and looked down on me pondering, "Miss Patsy, what do you know about young, Mr. Joey? Have you ever seen him come here in the late afternoon, evenings or nights during your shifts and maybe even come inside the office?

Here was a chance for an out. I spoke quickly and honestly but perhaps not thoroughly, "Mr. Smith. I never saw Joey take any stamps or money from the till or the safe. I don't think he would ever do that, or let me see him do it, anyway. And I watch the place pretty good, Mr. Smith.

That was as far as I could go, I thought. I didn't want to spill-the-beans on Joey, but if I got cornered, goodbye, Joey! I wasn't going to jail with him, or for him. Just about then, Mr. Beau walked in and spoke softly to Mr. Smith. I was starting to squirm a little but tried to compose myself. Mr. Smith was preparing to speak to me again and eyed me up-and-down one more time.

In a gentle but firm manner, Mr. Smith asked me another question straight-out, "Okay, Miss Patsy, one more question, and think about what you know or have seen. Did you ever see Joey pump gas for anyone and then put the money and stamps in his pocket? Beau here says that often Joey is here with you talking and helping out when your shift starts. Has Joey ever taken the cash and stamps and kept it to himself?"

Oh, dear lord, did I just get the break of a lifetime? I never wanted to lie to Mr. Smith, even if he was a gangster. Maybe especially I didn't want to *because* he might be a gangster, but I doubted it. I just didn't want to lie, and I didn't want to get Joey in trouble, either. I just wanted to get my shift over-with and go home. Right then, however, I just wanted out of that office.

I looked up at Mr. Smith, and he was studying my face and waiting for my answer. So, I carefully chose my words and spoke slowly and clearly, "No, Mr. Smith, I never saw Joey ever take any cash or stamps from people and keep it. Joey is a nice person, and he means well. I just don't think he would outright steal from you. I don't care for some of his mooching friends, but I think Joey is a nice person."

Darn! Why did I go and say anything about Joey's miserable, rotten, no-good-for-nothing friends. Oh, boy, me and my big mouth. I kept my eyes down and waited for Mr. Smith's reaction.

"I think that now I understand what happened, young, Miss Patsy," Mr. Smith calmly spoke. He finished his comment while nodding at me and smiling somewhat regretfully but approvingly. "It is all my fault," he offered.

"His fault?" I asked myself. What was happening? Was this all a trap? Was I a cooked goose, or a *chicken on the chopping-block*? What should I say?" I rapidly pondered all those questions, and decided to say the smart thing, *nothing*! "Just shut-up and listen for once, you big-mouth!" I yelled inside my brain.

That kind man then closed-out our discussion with a calm and understanding soliloquy. He studied me and then thoughtfully pondered his words carefully speaking in the gentlest of tones, "You see, Missy, I am to blame, young lady. I put too much responsibility on you and let you manage the whole show here all by yourself. That was very wrong of me, and I apologize to you for my poor judgment."

He's apologizing to me? What did he mean? He used *poor judgment*? I thought that that was what I had really done. I had trusted Joey, and I did it often and over-and-over again. Why did Mr. Smith think it was his mistake? Then I reacted smartly once more, and I kept my mouth shut again waiting for the punchline.

None came. Mr. Smith simply and clearly explained what he thought had happened: "Miss Patsy, you have done a splendid job here for these past several weeks. You did almost everything I expected," he added. "But it was too much responsibility for you, and it was too much to have you remember every night all by yourself."

I was a little confused, but I just stood there staring up at his face and listening to him. Mr. Smith was feeling pretty confident of his solution by then, so he continued with his expose': "During the past month's nights when you closed-up the station, Miss Patsy, you probably just accidentally forgot to lock-up the gas-pumps. The gas-pump registers don't match the number of gallons sold, stamps and cash now, so that should have been a sign.

"So, the best explanation is that you forgot about locking-up. It was *the pumps*. Bad people waited until you left, and then they came in and pumped-out as much gas as they could. Either Joey noticed the unlocked pumps the next morning, and should have said something, I might add, or he didn't want to get you into trouble. Maybe the thieves put the locks back-on and waited until the next night to come again. Who knows? Regardless, I never taught you well enough, and you just never quite got the total hang of it."

I was stunned. According to what I had just heard, Mr. Smith was not blaming me, but he believed the whole issue of stolen gas was ultimately, if only indirectly, my fault. My fault! Oh, no, I wasn't going to accept that line of argument mostly because he was just plain wrong. I had to defend myself. I was new, but I wasn't an idiot! And I wasn't to blame! I always remembered to lock-up the gas pumps, first thing every night! Then, do the money and stamp count and lock-up everything else. I knew my job, so I had to justifiably defend myself by complaining to Mr. Smith.

With every bit of courage that I could muster-up, I defensively spoke-out, "Mr. Smith, I always locked-up the gas pumps. Always. You taught me really well, and the day's counts of stamps and money were always right when I put them in the safe. No, sir, Mr. Smith, I always *locked* 'em."

Mr. Smith, Beau, and I just stood there for a moment like it was a checker game, and I had just made a bold move. Mr. Smith had to study the game board some more.

Scratching his chin and sort of squinting, Mr. Smith looked confused and a bit bewildered. "Well, that sure doesn't figure right. How did all the gas vanish, then? And the pump registers just don't read right for the number of gallons sold and the register's money and stamps. I don't get it. Maybe, it was just..." and suddenly, Mr. Smith was cut-off by Joey's loud voice.

"Hey, Mr. Smith," Joey hollered, "I think I see something wrong here." Joey was staring down at the storage-tank filler valve and holding its lock in his hands. "See here, Mr. Smith? I think this lock ain't no good! Somebody's been messing with it."

We had all gathered at the storage tank area and stood next to Joey looking at the lock in his hands. Joey continued his discourse, "I think this might be an answer too. This lock is bad. I had trouble opening it for the delivery guy earlier but finally got it opened and never thought much afterwards. Until now, that is. I just tried locking it again, and it won't do it. It's busted," Joey proclaimed proudly!

PROMOTIONS!

Mr. Smith was really befuddled by then. He just stood there staring at the storage-tank filler-valve, and then he looked at the lock that he had taken from Joey and studied it carefully. Next, he looked back over his shoulder considering the gas pumps for a moment, and then he looked back at the tanks, then the lock, then at me, and Joey, and so on. Poor Mr. Smith was just lost in thought and lost in a confused state-of-mind, it seemed. Finally, he just shuddered and gathered his thoughts to speak.

We were all watching him intently as he pronounced his decision with serious resolve, "We have a problem here with several aspects, people. It's like a snake with many heads, and we have got to cut-off all the heads. Perhaps, people are stealing right out of our storage-tanks. Others may be getting gas right out of the pump without us being aware. Somehow, the cash and stamps are okay from the till and match-up, but they don't match the pumps' registers or records. And according to the delivery guy's invoice, the amount of gas gone from the storage tanks is almost exactly the same as the amount of gas sent out through the pumps. Gasoline is getting out, and people are stealing it right under our noses."

Boy, Mr. Smith sure could talk when he wanted, and he was a good speaker too. I really felt sorry for him. He was so nice. Then, all of a sudden, something occurred which ended up shedding a lot of daylight on the case for Mr. Smith. A car drove-in and parked at the pumps.

All four of us were still standing there by the underground storage tanks muddling-over the day's confusing events. I was waiting for Mr. Smith to announce something else when it happened.

The impatient customer at the gas pumps started calling out loudly for Joey. "Hey, Joey, come on, hurry-up! I got places to go. Gimme some gas."

Right away, Joey was a little embarrassed, but he quickly turned and ran over to the customer. We all watched as Joey stuck his head almost all the way inside the customer's door window and stood there for a short time. Then Joey backed-away from the car, and the driver stepped hard on his gas pedal and charged out of the station and back onto the street speeding-off into the distance. A moment later, Joey slowly walked back over to us.

Mr. Smith was the first to inquire, "What was that all about?"

"Oh, nothing much. They just needed some directions to a party later, is all," Joey began lying with the first of his slip-ups.

"But we all heard the man, Joey," Mr. Smith started in. "He wanted some gas."

Joey couldn't help himself now, so he just continued *slipping*, "Yeah, uh, uhm, well, he couldn't because he didn't have any stamps. He forgot his stamps."

Mr. Smith just stood there staring at Joey for a while thinking. Then he turned and stared at Beau without saying anything. It seemed like an eternity, but then Mr. Smith looked right at me. Nodding again, that time Mr. Smith was ever-so-slightly smiling at his apparent insight. He looked like a whole dawning-of-understanding had flooded over his face.

But, he had an immediate plan-of-action, and Mr. Smith delivered it to us affirmatively, "We need to make changes, so here is what we're going to do: First, I'm getting all new locks for all the pumps, and the storage tanks, and the front office-door, and the garage door. I will have a set of keys, Beau will have one set of keys and another set will be kept by the service-station attendant for the dayshift and passed-on to the next shift, if necessary. At closing time, the attendants' keys will be locked in the office safe. The office-door will lock without a key. Either Beau or I will open the station in the morning and give the third set of keys to the day-shift attendant. Got it, so far?"

Wow! Yes, Mr. Smith was very astute and serious with his planning, I thought. He's a good owner and manager, I was thinking. But, Mr. Smith was not finished yet. He still had a couple more plans or bombshells to ignite.

He began this way, "Miss Patsy, you have been doing really good here, and I am very proud of you. So, now that we have the *stealing* problem resolved, it's time for promotions!"

What? Promotions? What was this man talking about? But, once more smartness ruled out, and once more I just kept my mouth shut.

Mr. Smith was smiling now. He looked chipper and sounded like he was on a roll. He was getting a kick out of his instant *Promotion Proclamations!* Now with a big grin on his face, he looked over at Beau and said, "Old friend, we are just working too hard and too much, so I'm going to do something that I've been mulling-over for a longtime now. I want you to work less but make more, so I'm giving you a raise to make the same wages but work two hours less each day. That's like a twenty-five percent hike. Is that okay with you?"

Beau just stared at Mr. Smith blankly and waited for the joke to end and the laughter to begin. But it didn't., and Mr. Smith wasn't through, yet, either.

"Beau," Mr. Smith nodded approvingly, "You have been very faithful and have worked very hard here for me. I really appreciate loyalty, so I want you to knock-off the last two hours of your shift, and just go home, or to a bar or to your girlfriend." Mr. Smith was grinning big-time now and continued on his roll, "Yep, you do whatever you want with your time, but we are closing-up the garage earlier from now on. Same pay, Beau, just less work. How's that sound?"

Never a man with many words, Beau continued to stare still listening for the punchline. After a bit, he started nodding and finally gushed, "Aw, thanks a lot, Charley. I really would like to be home earlier now. It's getting more daylight, and I can work in my garden more, and mess around with my tomatoes and get my summer garden ready." He was actually smiling.

And that was the first time I had ever heard Mr. Smith's first name. *Charley*, it was. Well, I honestly gave it more thought than just that. For instance, was it *Charley,* or was it *Charlie, or Charly*? Not that it mattered at all. At best, it was Mr. Charles Smith, but after today, I was committed to always using his last name and Mister, of course. He deserved the respect. So did Beau, Mr. Beauregard Jefferson, but we had a little different relationship. Lesson learned: Names were important, and their usage was too.

Anyway, my mind had wandered a bit, but when I looked back-up at him, Mr. Smith was really grinning ear-to-ear now. He began boastfully, "And now for our newest champion, Miss Patsy!" He had a gleam in his eye when he announced, "Your reward for your excellent services is that you are being promoted to *Day-shift*! In fact, there is no more second-shift. We are going to close this service-station down tighter than Babe Ruth's britches. I've been working too hard too, and I'm gonna start taking it easy right along with my buddy, Beau, here."

I was sort of lost, but I kept on standing and listening and watching. Mr. Smith was really enjoying himself so far, and he wouldn't quit, so then he began carrying on about me, "So, Miss Patsy, what do you say to the day-shift? No more nights here alone. No more nasty people watching for you to make a mistake or steal from you when they think you're not looking. You will be safe because Beau will be here, and he will help you close up the station when the day-shift ends."

Okay, now, I was a little bit rattled. He gave me the dayshift, and he mentioned that Beau would close up the service-station with me. But, he never mentioned anything about Joey. That was odd, and I looked over at Joey's face as he was standing there looking really confused. He kept shifting positions and fidgeting and looking around from one of us to another. It was Mr. Smith who was still grinning that finally broke the silence.

He just smiled broadly and quipped, "How do you like that *promotion*, Miss Patsy? And if that works out for you, then real shortly, we're just going to let you keep one set of those keys to yourself just like Beau and me. That way, you can open up the place in case Beau or I get lazy and decide to sleep-in. Soooo, whatdoyathink?"

Wow! Mr. Smith sure could talk a lot when he wanted to. I was still a little confused, so with one last glance at an obviously fidgeting Joey, I had to ask, "But, Mr. Smith, Sir, what about Joey? Are he and I both going to do the day-shift together?" I saw Joey's face light-up as he listened intently for our boss's response.

Here is where Mr. Smith really began shining. He was almost bursting with humor and glee as he progressed with his announcements and *promotions*, "Well, I'm just pleased as punch, Miss Patsy, that you care about our young, loyal hero here, Joey. No, Miss, the dayshift will be yours all alone except with Beau around and me, once-in-a-while. But this is the best part of all these rewards because Joey gets the biggest promotion of all!

Oh, well, this sounded better all the time. I was getting a little anxious and worried without Joey's name mentioned yet. Then I became excited waiting for the good news for Joey. Was he going to become our *boss*, or would he move into the garage with Beau, or what was it?

Mr. Smith suddenly took on a grave expression. He looked straight into Joey's face, and he calmly announced, "No, Joey, for you, *it's the big-time*. You have got the best promotion of all. I am sending, no, I mean *promoting* you to my other service-station on the other side of town!

"It's a big, beautiful service-station right next door to the ship docks," Mr. Smith continued still grinning but staring solemnly, "It's a great place, and it's big-time, I tell you. And best of all, I have got a terrific, huge Samoan manager there who will watch you and train you for getting your own service-station one day. Now, I can spend more time over here too, hanging out with my buddy, Beau. How does that sound? Pretty good, huh! You're big-time now, Joey."

I didn't know what to think right at first. Mr. Smith had made it sound like the harbor station had *streets paved with gold* and was really great, but watching Joey begin to squirm and clench his teeth made me wonder. He didn't look that happy. Then Joey just sort of muffled a response.

He spoke sheepishly, "Uh, thanks, Mr. Smith but I sort of like it here a lot too. The other station is a long ways away, and I don't know nobody over there. That's sort of a rough part of town, too, down by the waterfront and all."

Mr. Smith was smiling again but almost glaring at Joey now while he confronted him straight-to-his-face, "Not at all, my young, loyal and faithful attendant. You will love it over there. Miss Patsy will be just fine here, and she can handle the whole job easily now after your excellent tutelage. And you will be great over there. It's *big-time*! Oh, sure there are a lot of thugs and tough guys and all those waterfront crews, but you will learn how to handle all of them, for sure. Congratulations, Joey, you have made the *Big-time*! Hip, hip, hurray for loyal Joey!"

I thought I sensed a little bit of mocking from Mr. Smith, but I just assumed it went with Joey's promotion and all. A funny thing too was that while we were all huddled around together there listening to Mr. Smith's speech, some more guys showed up in a car that this time I recognized as one of Joey's *friends*.

I got a little nervous and looked over at Joey. He too had seen them pull-up into one of the gas-pumps, and Joey started getting a little squeamish. He started shaking his head at them, and with an underhanded back-wave, shooed them away. After a moment, they just sped-off down the street, and Joey turned back to the group looking a little embarrassed.

Joey apologized and offered, "Those were just some of my pals. They probably just drove-in to remind me about a party I was invited to go to with them pretty soon."

Mr. Smith had been observing with a grave, annoyed, and disapproving eye, but followed-up Joey's attention once more with a very slight smile and understanding nod as he quickly got back on track, "Of course that's what they wanted, of course, and that's okay, Joey." Then with a long, hard stare at Joey, Mr. Smith finished, "I don't mind. Not at all."

Then, Mr. Smith went into one of his long speeches again, "As a matter of fact, why don't you just go with them now? That's it! Tell them to come and visit you tomorrow at the other station where you'll be working. Mr. Manuia Lalago, Manny for short, the Service Station Manager there, will welcome them real nice. And don't you worry because Mr. Lalago is an ex-Staff Sergeant with the U.S. Army, and he will watch out for you and give your friends all that they deserve.

"By-the-way, that Mr. Lalago is a real bad-ass, himself. Got wounded in Africa fighting for General Patton and got his foot injured in battle, so the Army discharged him. But, he is one, proud, son-of-a- er, gun, and he can still kick-ass all day long and way-into-the-night. In fact, he loves to brag that the tougher the other guys are, the better Manny likes it. That's why I've got him over at that location. He loves it there, and he is very proud of it. Just like you will be too, Joey. He will watch over you like a hawk, don't you worry, my young friend. So, way-to-go! Congratulations, again, and go on home now, and go party with your friends. You deserve a little partying after today's exploits."

So much had been said. So much to take in. I was in shock and in awe of Mr. Smith. He had made up his mind, and he just laid it all out there as rewards for all of us. Then, he got one more quick idea and started laughing.

Mr. Smith suddenly blurted out, "In fact, let's all go home early. I'm exhausted after all this excitement. Miss Patsy, you help clean-up and shut the place down now with Beau and me. You still get your full-day's pay. He and I are going out for a drink to celebrate. If I were just a couple decades younger, or you were just a few days older, well, uh, I'd. Oh, never mind. You just get home to your sisters and tell them the good news: You're on *day-shift!*"

I started smiling and couldn't hardly contain myself. I quickly realized that now I could get up with my sisters and go to work the same time as them, and then get home when they did too. We could visit more and relax together. We'd be real family, and I just got a *promotion*!

We finished closing-up the place, and I got my coat and purse from the station office right as Mr. Smith was closing and locking-up the door. After I said my good-byes to Beau and Mr. Smith and started to make the walk home, I just felt an urge to ask one final question.

Mr. Smith was heading for his own car, and I remember quickly approaching him and politely asking, "Mr. Smith, do you think that Joey will really like his new job at the other service-station?"

That question brought the biggest and brightest grin from Mr. Smith all day. His eyes were twinkling, it seemed, but it was only momentary. Right afterward, he became very serious when he next stated, "Oh, I don't think I'll ever see Joey there. In fact, I doubt that I'll ever see him again... except maybe for tomorrow's Pay-Day!"

With that last comment, Mr. Smith just started laughing and chuckled all the way to his car and then while steering his way out onto the boulevard. I even heard him give a big, long *toot* on his car horn. He seemed very happy, and I was also in a weird, different kind of way: I was happy about the shift change for sure; I was really glad I would no longer have to deal with Joey's *free-gas arrangements* or his nasty friends bothering me anymore; but, I was still unsure about Joey's situation. Regardless, I still liked him.

That evening, I told my sisters the news of my *promotion* and how and why I got it. They were glad that I got the dayshift because we'd see each other more. Plus, I had talked about my issues with Joey to them before, and Jean had seen right through Joey's game. Jean said that Joey was doing favors for his other "clients" or friends because he owed them, or they would do favors for him or give things to him.

Jean was very hard-lined and seldom gave anybody any slack, so she flat-out said, "If your friend works for your company, and he is not taking money or gas-stamps but still giving away gas for nothing, then no-matter-what, it's still stealing, and he is still a crook.

"Who wouldn't like *free* gas?" Jean continued commenting in her matter-of-fact tone. But, then came her objective lesson to be learned. "Just remember, Sissy," she said, "No matter what, even if your boss is a crook too, taking gas or anything from that service-station and selling it, trading it or even giving it away is stealing. You can get fired *and* go to jail for that.

And if your boss is who Joey says he is, then Joey could get himself hurt really bad to boot, really bad. So, watch-out for him, and be real careful."

Jean always had a level head, and she influenced my judgment all the time. I still think often about Jean's *hard, but fair* practice for life. It was very hard, in fact. She left little room for playing, and none for just goofin'-off.

Sis Mary, though, was just the opposite almost. She always laughed a lot and tried to enjoy herself as much as possible. When she heard the details of my *promotion,* she thought the whole situation about Joey and his friends, and the service-station was hilarious. The idea of *crooks robbing crooks* especially made her laugh. She said that she even wished that she could afford a car so that she could get *free gas* too! However, later into my story, Sis just about fell-out-of-her-chair rolling-over in laughter about all the so-called promotions.

When I mentioned Joey's promotion was being sent to the Harbor area, she rolled her eyes and laughed, "Promotion, my eye! Your boss just wants to get him killed!"

The next morning at work went very smoothly. When I arrived, Beau was already there and had the office, garage, and pumps already unlocked and ready-to-go. I had deliberately come in early too, in order to greet him for opening and to figure things out, but Beau was extra-early. Later, when Mr. Smith showed-up, he brought with him all new locks and keys for every location and three sets each. Like he promised, Beau got a full-set, Mr. Smith kept one and the third key set was put on a pretty key chain for me to wear during my shift.

Right about midday lunchbreak, Mr. Smith came over to visit me while I was sitting in the office chair and eating a sandwich. He smiled at me as usual, and then he got sort of serious.

"Miss Patsy, I'm probably a lot smarter than I look," he began. "And I've been-around -the-block-a-few-times," was his way of telling me he knew a few things.

I watched him carefully to understand where this was going, and I continued to pay close attention to his words.

Mr. Smith continued, "I have suspected for a long time that gas was leaving this service-station without payment or stamps. I thought it was going on long before you got here, in fact. Truth is, I started getting suspicious not long after good 'ol Joey came to work for me."

Since the subject was brought up, I asked with interest, "Do you know if Joey showed-up for work over at the other site?"

Mr. Smith just smiled faintly and said, "No, Dear, I called, and he never did. I never actually thought he would. That is not a good area for Joey to be in, and I never thought it was. Joey is the type of fellow who looks for easy pickings', if you know what I mean. I wanted to get him to leave because I did not trust him anymore, but I didn't know how to go about it, and I didn't want to just go-on and fire him without sure proof.

"These are hard times for everybody, and I believe in second-chances for everyone. We all make mistakes, but it's how we deal with those mistakes which matters. Joey made many and got several chances, but he ruined 'em all. Hiring you, and then watching to see what would happen, gave me the reason to do what I did today."

That was when I got a similar *learning lesson* from Mr. Smith as from Jean. They both seemed like they were cut-from-the-same-cloth in their life philosophies. Mr. Smith continued explaining, "There are lots of good folks in this world, and there are plenty of different kinds of *bad people* too, Miss Patsy. It doesn't matter what folks do or how they do it, though. Good is good, and right is right, and bad is bad, and wrong is wrong. You have got to learn how to tell the difference of one-from-another."

Mr. Smith enjoyed talking, of course, but his words made sense, and I enjoyed listening to him. I continued paying attention:

"The gasoline truck-delivery yesterday was just the final straw when I could make my move and send Joey away. At first, I have to admit, I was confounded and very frustrated. I couldn't prove he was stealing, but my records don't lie. Joey was too slick to get caught on his dayshift, so I figured that he was continuing to stiff me for gas on the second shift, your shift, Miss Patsy. You see, that second-shift used to be Joey's. That was when gas-pump readings and ration-stamps and cash began to differ. The stamps and cash in the cash register and the safe always matched just right, but the gas-pump readings seldom did. Same as this time."

I began to understand that Mr. Smith suspected what was going on all along. I began to feel queasy because he must also have known about my relationship to Joey. I didn't speak, though. I just kept on listening and waiting.

Mr. Smith started-up again, "After a while, though, the second-shift was just costing me too much in lost gas, and I couldn't trust Joey anymore. That was when I hired you on the spot. I liked you, and you seemed like someone I could trust because you needed and wanted to prove yourself. Plus, that was Joey's *first* promotion.

I placed him on dayshift when Beau and I could watch him all the time. Then, I changed Beau's hours to start later in the morning and go into the early evening to help cover the service-station's needs and to keep a look-out. I opened the place, myself, and occasionally with Joey, every morning as usual and helped around until Beau showed-up. But, we both kept an eye on Joey.

"Everything went back to normal, so-to-speak. That is, until a while after I hired you. Between my suspicion's and Beau's observations of Joey hanging around the station and you more and more, we were both fairly certain of what was going on.. Two old codgers like us weren't born yesterday, by gum."

Mr. Smith kind of shook his head smiling and then looked over at his friend, Beau, in the garage, pointed at him and started speaking again, "That's a good man over-there, you mark-my-words. Anyway, you've been here already well-over a month now, and I needed to make changes."

Mr. Smith had been leaning on the counter and shifted his position, so I quick offered him *his* office-chair. He smiled at me and politely brushed me off, "No, no. Not at all. This is your lunchbreak, and I'm just talking it all up. I apologize."

I was quick to thank him and tell him it was no problem at all. I remember even encouraging him a little because of my curiosity and interest, "Please, thank you, Mr. Smith. You were saying? Please continue."

Oh, my boss liked good manners, and he smiled at my chair-offer and request to hear more, I could tell. I think I even scored some more points with Mr. Smith right then, and I even gave the Church Sisters back at school a silent "Thanks" for instructing us students with that good practice: "Good manners are always recognized by those you use them on and almost always appreciated."

So, now with a slight smile on his face, Mr. Smith began again, "I knew you were not giving-away or stealing gas, yourself, but Joey had to go. Plus, Miss Patsy, I was just getting tired of the whole thing, and Beau and I have been working overtime for too long to keep going with this nonsense. It just wasn't right. The evening-shift wasn't making decent money, anyway, and with the pathetic losses caused by Joey, it just wasn't worth keeping the place open. Maybe on another day it will have two shifts again, but for now, it isn't even necessary."

I caught myself with my mouth wide-open and gawking. Mr. Smith did know everything and all the time. Oh, thank God he had never seen or knew of me giving any gas away for free. I felt a great relief, but I could tell Mr. Smith wasn't finished yet. He still had more to say and more to teach.

"Young lady, all kinds of people from all walks-of-life are going to bump into you at times, and some of them are going to try and get something out-of-you or take something from you. You have to be vigilant and strong-willed. If you suspect something is wrong, then do not support it or take part in it or go along with it. If you can, don't let it continue, either. There are plenty of good, honest, hardworking, and faithful people you can trust to advise you with solutions to your dilemmas. Talk to them, ask them and seek their advice or direction for appropriate responses."

The next part of Mr. Smith's talk or lecture actually became an admission when he confessed, "I need to apologize to you, young lady, for a mean stunt that I sort of pulled on you. Let me explain: Do you remember, by any chance, a sort of rough-and-tough fella in an expensive overcoat and big hat who drove-up to the pumps in a sleek looking, silver gray, Chevrolet Town Sedan and then went ahead to beg and plead with you to have some heart and give him some free-gas to get where he wanted? I think it was a funeral, maybe?"

I vaguely had a recollection, but I shook my head and replied, "No, sir, not really. There were lots of those kinds of folks coming-in all the time. But, if Joey was gone or didn't come running-over and tell me to leave and then take-over their service, himself, I always had the same answer for them. I would just say, 'Sorry, no,' but that they could come back the next day and ask you."

"That's right, Miss Patsy, that's just what you told that big fella I'm mentioning," Mr. Smith admitted. Then he explained, "That man was what you might call "a set-up" because I sent him here. He was actually a good friend of mine who had offered to help me "catch-a-thief," if you know what I mean?

"That same man had actually come by earlier that evening when Joey was there supposedly helping you with your shift. He asked Joey the same question, and Joey told him to get lost and then jerked his thumb at you calling for you to deal with him. Joey actually passed that test but not the next one. My friend left and drove around-the-block and then parked across the street with a full-view of the service-station gas pumps and watched like an undercover detective or something."

Mr. Smith had lost his smile by then, but he continued speaking as he shook his head slightly, "After a short-while, another car pulled-in, and my *detective*-friend saw you start walking over to service them, but then Joey ran-over and apparently told you to go away. You did, and then my friend said that he actually watched as Joey pumped gas into the man's car plus into an extra gas can that he was conveniently carrying. When Joey was done, the driver just put the can into his car trunk, got into his car and drove away. That was it. No stamps, no gas and not even a thanks or good bye."

Then came Mr. Smith's clincher, the final point of his lecture, when he advised, "I still do not believe that you ever had an active-role in the gasoline selling or trading or giveaways. It saddens me to think that you may have known about Joey's stealing or cheating and never said anything, but I gave it up to inexperience and not knowing the ways of bad men."

By then, I was feeling a little queasy and afraid I might even upchuck my whole lunch, but dear Mr. Smith started in again and made me feel a little better: "When you said that you *never* saw Joey stealing, meaning keeping stamps or cash, that was when I knew and understood your whole story. You were being forced by Joey either directly or under–pressure to sit by and allow him to do what he wanted with my gasoline.

That was when I felt sorry for you and was mad at myself for putting you in such a position and disadvantage. Joey is a weak, conniving, and manipulative young man who took *advantage* of you. And I am so proud of you, nevertheless, for not teaming-up with him. You have true character. Joey is a bad apple and will rot someday."

I was so grateful by then that I could have cried, but I needed to cover all bases and clear-the-air, for my sake. So, I questioned Mr. Smith just to finish things, clear-up matters and understand all that had happened, "Sir, what about the broken-lock that Joey found with the storage tanks? Did gas get taken from there, like Joey said, do you think?"

Mr. Smith was a little amused, "So, you're still trying to protect that little rat, huh? Oh, okay, I suppose he was a smooth-talker, alright, so-it-seems. The storage tank lock being *broken* was just a smokescreen by Joey. 'Oh, look over here, instead,' he said. He was getting nervous, so he came up with what he thought was a clever distraction. Only, it didn't hold water, and it made Joey become even guiltier to me. The problem was not likely the tanks. It was the vastly irregular and inaccurate, pump-register readings.

"Joey messed with those locks, himself, and he broke that one too, and I knew he did because that was the very first place I ever looked for the problem earlier when the gas-delivery fellow gave me the invoice. Joey must not have seen me because I was upset but not making any noise or fuss yet. Did someone steal gas straight from the storage tanks, I wondered? Well, the answer was no because I had already closely studied all those locks. Every one of them were in reasonable condition. Could someone steal gas from them? Maybe. Leaving storage tanks open for easy stealing is the first and easiest way to get robbed of gasoline. It's the first place a crook would go. You gotta have good locks, that's primary."

I could tell that Mr. Smith was getting a little tired by then; however, he had concluded what he wanted to do. He had explained a lot of the details to help me understand what had happened since I was hired and even a little of the circumstances before I started working there. His explanations helped me with some important life-lessons. He had accomplished both: Understanding and appreciation.

Looking back now, of course, I have learned to understand those unfortunate, criminal-behavior effects of wartime-rationing and, of course, my own foolish naiveté. Mr. Smith wasn't only a teacher; for me, he was an understanding mentor, a nice combination. Back then, I think the main lesson I may have taken from Mr. Smith was, "Don't trust young men!" and "Nothing is free; there's a cost or price for everything we want to have or do."

I remembered Mr. Smith's *lessons* very well over the years, and his *lessons* were to help my judgment many times to come. In fact, to his credit, they still do. Of course, I never brought-up Joey's claims about Mr. Smith's and Beau's backgrounds. They never held water, and I would have been too embarrassed to ask about it. I'm pretty sure both Mr. Smith and Beau would have been very angry, over Joey's claims. Plus, that information would have been embarrassing to me too. It would have provided more explanation for my excusing Joey's criminal behavior. There would have been nothing gained by bringing it up.

As for Joey, well, I never saw him again. I never inquired either, but on that very next morning, which was payday, I overheard Mr. Smith laughing and telling Beau that Joey had called-in and found out that his check had been delivered to the new, Harbor Station, his supposed new workplace. Joey had gone over to the other site. Apparently, to pick-up his final paycheck. Mr. Smith was laughing by then and joking with Beau because, apparently, Joey had to have been outside the station watching and waiting for Mr. Smith to leave, and who knows how long that took. Then, once Mr. Smith had gone, Joey went into the service-station to collect his check.

I guess the story got even better for Mr. Smith when he mentioned to Beau about the other service-station's manager, Mr. Lalago. It was obvious that they both were getting a big kick out of the matter. Mr. Smith was even bent over laughing when he told about the tough time Mr. Lalago had apparently given Joey for quitting. Mr. Smith laughed that Mr. Lalago had really gotten on Joey's case, and even into his face. Apparently, though, after a brief, but loud and ridiculing, lecture, Mr. Lalago was pretty disgusted with Joey's tough-guy, inattentiveness.

Supposedly, he tossed Joey's paycheck to him and told him, "Get out of here, Small-time!" I figured from that story that Mr. Smith had already told Mr. Lalago all about Joey and Mr. Smith's "big-time" reference to Joey. Mr. Smith ended his comical rendition of Joey's paycheck visit by mentioning how Joey had just picked-up his check from the floor, and without any further word to Mr. Lalago, had taken-off running away.

In a way, I still felt sorry for Joey. I figured that he was just kind of mixed-up and was trying to seem or act like a big guy, somebody who was making big deals. He just hadn't realized that he was no match for those people to whom he gave gas. They probably mocked him too.

For sure, he was no match for Mr. Smith, Beau or Mr. Lalago. They all probably scared dickens out of him. Although I felt a little guilty and ashamed about letting Joey get away with giving away so much free gas on my shift, I accepted my naiveté and gullibility and took heed from Mr. Smith's lesson that it only mattered if we learned from our mistakes. I knew he was right, and I sure had…

TIME TO GO

Circumstances were going to change dramatically for me soon thereafter. From decisions by my own accord, I chose to say goodbye and head out for new horizons. After my fairly brief time with Mr. Smith, Beau, that Sears and Roebuck Service-Station, and Joey with all his *black-market* nonsense, Mr. Smith's kind words, support and spoken lessons stayed with me long after I was gone. I learned from him, however, and from Joey and from all those experiences working at that first job of mine. They all helped shape and develop my own character.

There was no doubt in my mind that those two consequential months had taught me a lot. I learned to stand-up more strongly against things I did not like or did not trust. I learned to watch out for other people and to try to become a better judge of character. It was okay to listen or follow those you really trusted, but without trust, there could be no following. Finally, I learned to stand-up and speak for myself more. If I felt like I knew what was right, then I was to stick to it, and to hell with anyone who challenged me.

My relatively brief experiences pumping gasoline in Cleveland turned out to be more of a serious growing-up adventure than anything else. It had been my first honest attempt to find decent work and my very first darn job at that. I had inadvertently and somewhat naively hooked-up with a seemingly nice, young man who turned-out to be, a rather seedy-character. I was inadvertently and temporarily ushered into the business of *black-market,* gasoline sales or just plain giveaway theft. As far as I was concerned, the people taking the free gas were just as bad as the one giving it to them. Because of the strict rationing in those days illegal gasoline and gas thefts, I had come to learn, were practically as common as regular, honest gas sales.

My lessons were costly too in more ways than just cash. One thing that I learned at that job was the value of real-life experience. Formal classroom education is very important, of course, but not enough credit can be given, or tribute can be said about the *school-of-hard-knocks*. For a naïve, sixteen-year old girl still a couple months shy of turning seventeen, what I had learned from that gas-station experience felt like a PhD in *Human Behavioral Studies*.

Gosh, did I learn a lot from *Professor* Smith. Sometimes, experience is costly, I realized, and those lessons learned back then have really stayed with me. Though I would try many times more in times ahead, I'd be much more wary in the future. Fortunately, however, way back then my brief departure into the *dark side* was short-lived.

THERE'S A FUTURE AHEAD

Finally, it was Spring all over. Cleveland was starting to warm-up a bit, and that was a nice change. Leaves were starting to sprout on all the city's once barren trees, and squirrels and birds were starting to romp and flitter around the park areas demonstrating their joy of the warming outdoors. I wasn't having to bundle-up so much for going outside and for work as much as before. I was enjoying the cool and brisk air so much more than the freezing, bone-chilling weather that that past winter had brought.

Jean must have been getting antsy too. She always seemed like a pent-up ball of energy almost ready to explode. Jean could not take long-and-steady very well at all. If a day went by that seemed too typical or quiet to her, then she started getting frustrated and bored. Jean could not deal with boredom at all. She needed to see, feel, and believe that she was marching forward, heading in the right direction, or taking steps toward reaching any of her distant goals.

Soon after Spring had sprung, therefore, our leader-sister, Jean, heard about a specialized, arc-welder training program and good-paying welder jobs available down in Mississippi for those who ventured there. Women were even being encouraged to apply through posters and radio-advertisements to take on jobs that men had left behind in order to go and fight for liberty, democracy, and the American way.

In many ways, the ads really worked because they made women feel needed and worthy. Factories and munitions plants and aircraft-building plants and shipyards were spring-up everywhere, but there was not enough labor to fill the necessary positions. Black Americans were encouraged to apply for work in those mostly city jobs. Other minority populations were reached-out to also to fill the jobs. But it was women who were the largest, easiest, and closest nearby labor force to focus upon.

Women were asked to step-up and do their part for the nation and the war cause. For women, however, patriotism and stepping-up were not the primary concerns of taking all those otherwise, previously done men's jobs. Most women were not trying to kid anybody. Times were difficult, and living expenses were costly. To us women, the new jobs mostly meant more money. Traditionally men's jobs meant higher-pay. More money meant more and better food on the table. Even higher-paying jobs meant a higher-standard of living for their children.

Before that wartime period, and throughout those terrible depression years earlier, few people would have ever expected women to work in any of those dirty, dangerous, and difficult construction and manufacturing trades. Those were "Men's Jobs!" Plus, with a workless and depressed economy, there were few jobs to go around anyway. But, then, when the war came, and men left to go fight in it, war-cause construction and manufacturing growth literally and figuratively exploded. High-paying jobs were plentiful, and there weren't enough *men* to fill the bill. *Women* were being referred to as: "America's Hope" and the "Strength, Determination and Foundation" of American will to win.

It all sounded nice on paper and in the radio airwaves, but reality truly painted a different picture. Women never started wars, well, mostly never. Men always went off to play in their foolish wargames and left the women behind to carry-the-load at home. It's been that way practically since the beginning of time. As a result, throughout history, women have always been left behind to *carry-on.*

These times after the big war started were the same thing. Yet, they were quite a bit different because of the war's pressure to develop a tremendous workforce at home and for those typically male-oriented jobs. Women who always stayed back and *carried-on* were now asked to step-forward and *carry-forth* with the nation's new necessary load of needed workers.

It only took a dumb second for women to see and understand the money factor. For almost all women everywhere in America, it was the money that counted. The men were gone, and it was money that paid the rent, fed, and clothed the children and paid for every other necessity and/or inconvenience that arrived. I really think that most of us women never had any doubts that we could do men's work. We just had to be told or shown what to do. Simple. Piece-of-cake!

We women have an ancient history throughout time of doing whatever was necessary to get a job done, whatever it may have been. Sick children with no man or male doctor around? Women took care of them themselves and got them healed. A young, pregnant mother needed to give birth with no male doctor around? Mid-wives carried out the procedure. Flat tire and no man? Fix-it yourself, or find someone who would, but get the job done. Hungry family with no man around? Wheel-and-deal, but put food on the table, feed the family and get the job done.

Women are doers and fixers. We have always *gotten-things-done*. We are fast learners and good workers too. We are dependable and seldom miss work due to inconveniences like hangovers, and such. Back then, however, with the big war going on, and so many men gone fighting and dying, countless job-opportunities opened-up everywhere. It just simply came down to basics for women: Money mattered.

Men's jobs traditionally always paid more than women's typical work. Therefore, what woman wouldn't rather trade in a job of washing, cooking, cleaning, serving, sewing, filing, or typing for twenty cents an hour, in order to get a man's job earning *thirty-five cents up to a dollar and more per hour* in certain construction-fields? Whoa! Move over, Buddy.

Make room for this lady! Oh, okay, right, Sis Mary wouldn't! That was true at first and for quite a while. However, she had some very good office and personnel skills, and a good attitude and charisma that typically got her higher-paying women's work. But, for most other women, darn right! Get a different job for more pay? Huh! We'd choose it seven days from Sunday.

So, anyway, back to my sister Jean's newest, latest, and greatest job-opportunity,… us sisters sat around the dinner table and discussed our situation. Well, the actual truth was that Jean talked, while Sis and I both diligently listened, and then Jean made up our minds for us. The money and conditions were going to be better, according to Jean. So, we all talked and got inspired by Jean and excited about some new welding-job venture she'd heard about.

I realized that I haven't even mentioned Duffy yet. Duffy was Jean's dog, and she adored him more than she did most people. Jean had gotten Duffy as a puppy to keep her company there in Cleveland right after Mary had left to be with me in Duluth. Her plan was to have Duffy travel with her wherever she went. Duffy was company, and he kept Jean balanced by making her focus on present situations because of his continual needs.

But Duffy was her quasi-protector and ally through thick and thin. He would do almost anything for Jean too. He was still growing, but he was a lap dog. He loved to sit in Jean's lap. That worked well enough while he was smaller, but not for long. Duffy was a white, Alaskan Husky, and they grow bigger. Also, it didn't matter where, Duffy was always ready for any adventure. So, it didn't matter if we were just taking a walk to a city park or heading out across a bunch of states. Duffy was ready to go.

However, Sis declined to go along at the end. She had a decent and stable office-job where she was just beginning to really enjoy herself socializing on-the-job and then socializing even more during her incredibly fun nightlife. Besides, previously, she had obligated herself to younger sister Colleen who still needed to finish school too. Sis was stable and carried-on quite a nice mail-delivery contact with Colleen. It was true that Sis Mary liked her sisterly-role and responsibilities keeping-in-touch with Colleen. She was always sending her things in the mail. With her contact and relationship with Colleen going-on along with her job and friends, I understood how Sis really enjoyed her lifestyle there in Cleveland and chose to stay instead.

Jean and I would take our chances on this next adventure together. Of course, Duffy was along for the ride too. He was our protector, but it was actually me-and-my-big-sister off on a wild, new quest. By then, she and I were the new hitchhiking partners, and that trip would just be the first of many adventures for the two of us traveling together. You gotta understand that Jean was my idol. I did so look up to her, and I felt excited and secure to be doing or going anywhere with her. It was going to be thrilling at the very least, I just knew it.

So, we packed our belongings, put Duffy on his leash, hugged Sis Mary goodbye, and lit out for our next hopeful and productive destination, the shipyards near Pascagoula, Mississippi. I was still way shy of seventeen-years old, of course, and I still looked far too young for any construction jobs. At that stage of our trip, I was just tagging along to keep Jean company, and watch over Duffy and help as best I could. We were like a couple of

Toms Sawyers on an adventure down the Mississippi River, only we were hitchhiking instead of rafting down that big, wide ol' river.

For hitchhiking, though, we both dressed-up more like young men so as not to arouse suspicion. We both wore full caps over our heads and covering our ears. I wore a coat with its collar-up so I could tuck-in my longer hair in back. Jean always wore short hair, though. It made her look tougher and more manly anyway, and that was the way she liked it. Heavier denim or cotton shirts and jeans with boots made us look like most of the other *hitchers* on the roads back then. Yep, we may have been a couple of girls out there with our faithful dog, but we sure looked like we were just full of all that *boyish charm.*

One issue was that we both knew I was still supposed to be in school somewhere. Yet, we were also fearful of any consequences were I to be found out and determined to be a runaway. It looked like my formal schooling was postponed for the time being. Getting another job real soon seemed much more important at the time.

At least it did to Jean. She wanted me to work so we could save-up money. I was less enthusiastic about having a job. Like they now say, "Girls just want to have fun!" It was the gosh-darned truth back then for most girls too, and I sure as heck did. Still do, for that matter. But, for cryin'-out-loud, I was still a couple months more from even being seventeen. I should have been having the time of my life. But, big baloney! I wasn't.

However, we were all together, Jean, Duffy, and me, and we were all heading out together on-the-road for new opportunities. We first followed the main highway along the Ohio River until it emptied into the Mississippi River. We would catch small rides in backs of pick-up trucks mostly because of Duffy being along. When not riding or having our thumbs stuck out, we would just walk along the roads or highway and talk about the sights around us. It was that or Jean would talk about our future. I think she did that so as to clear-up any misgivings or issues that she thought about. But we were good company for each other. Of course, there was always Duffy too.

Once we hit the highway going south, we followed Ol' Muddy all the way south to Pascagoula, MS. While hitch-hiking along the Mississippi River to the training-site, though, when we needed, we found cheap, basic lodging along the way. Things went well enough, and the trip was fairly uneventful. Mostly, the only events were when I got hungry. Plus, ice cream was my favorite treat, and I was always on the lookout for some.

I was willing to pay for it too. Why, I'd have gladly even bought Jean an ice cream if she had wanted. I still had money in my pocket from my time at the service-station, and I knew how frugal Jean was with funds. Hah! Frugal just isn't the right word. *Skinflint, squeaky-clean and tight wad* might be more clarifying. I knew she wasn't about to offer to buy either of us an ice cream treat. Yeah, that would happen like... never!

"Hungry?" Jean would ask. "Why then, just pick an apple off one of those trees we pass," she'd suggest... And then, a moment later, "Thirsty? Why, for heaven's sake, right there next to you is the whole, wide Mississippi River, herself! Just, jump-in, help-yourself and quench your thirst!" she'd scoff.

What she meant was for us to wait until we got to our next destination, or break for the day, and then we would eat. No, we did not need any frills in between. Well, almost, anyway. At least, sometimes, it seemed like that was her way-of-thinking. Jean was so goal-minded and achievement-oriented that she would never let minor issues like *starvation* or *dying from thirst* get in the way of her success.

I suppose now looking back at those times, Jean said and tried to do what she thought was right. She was so achievement-oriented, and she only did those sorts of things which would accomplish her goals. Hitch-hiking was a great example of Jean's character and thinking.

"Buy a car and pay for gas?" she'd challenge. "No way. Lots of people hitch-hike. It is a very common get-around. Let the car owner/drivers buy the gas," she'd argue. "Train rides or buses? My goodness! Don't you realize how many meals you could eat with that money?" Oh, Jean could stretch a dollar, alright...

CRAZY DRIVER

And yet, Jean was right in one sense. Hitch-hiking was a very accepted way of travel. So many folks could not afford cars, let alone gas, and oil, and tires, and repairs. Busses and trains travel cost less than cars, sometimes, but were still expensive means of travel. Thus, *hitching* was a very legitimate form of transportation. Like Jean used to say laughingly, "You got a thumb, and you can travel the world!"

Anyway, hitch-hiking, and a lot of in-between walking, worked just fine for us. Truth be told, I never really questioned our hitching rides. I was with my big sister, and Jean would always protect me. I always felt safe being with her. We caught so many rides together, and very seldom had any problems, especially in the beginning. Well, that is except for one anxiety-driven driver…

And that doesn't mean that we never had other worrisome or dangerous circumstances while hitching those rides. It was true that Sis and I had hitched almost all the way from St. Paul clear up to Duluth, Minnesota with no problems at all. Truth is that it was one ride that took us all the way because there wasn't much in between. Then later, when we were sneaking away and after the freighter ride, she and I hitched rides from Toledo, Ohio clear over to Cleveland with still issues, just nice folks helping out.

But by that time heading south to Mississippi, it was just Jean and me and Duffy. On the road with a place to go. Two would be fellas and their dog out hitching in the beautiful sunshine? We'd stick-out our thumbs, catch a ride, go the distance, get-out, and stick-out our thumbs again. Piece of cake! What could go wrong?

However, as I recall, it was our second or third lift along that Mississippi Highway that brought us our first case of extreme nervousness. At least, I was nervous and even a little scared, although, I'm not sure about Jean.

She said later that she hadn't gotten scared, but it was her plan right away and all along to eventually ditch the guy.

What happened was that we had gotten a couple of decent rides from Cleveland down to Columbus, Ohio on Rt. 71. Then came another ride all the way to Indianapolis, Indiana, and we had then switched over to Rt. 70 to go all the way to St. Louis, Illinois. That was where we would cross over the magnificent Mississippi River into St. Louis, Missouri and catch Highway 55 all the rest of the way south to Pascagoula, MS.

Well, it was that third leg of the trip on Highway 55 that found us some trouble. Things had started out alright. Our rides that far to St. Louis had been very kind and uneventful. We had done quite a bit of walking while carrying our luggage, and that was because it was a little more difficult to get rides with a big dog traveling along. But it hadn't been too bad. As soon as we were lined-up in the right direction and stuck out our thumbs, it seemed like right away some friendly person would give us a ride.

Like I said, mostly our more local rides were in pick-ups and such to make it easier for a dog. Made no difference to us. That first day, though, we laid-over in St. Louis right-off our Hwy. 55 and right near the big, muddy Mississippi River and spent the night in a fairly cheap motel. As I recall, Jean went in and got our room key while I hid outside with Duffy. Then she went to the room and opened the door, and I took Duffy on his leash and ran over and into the room to avoid suspicion or to get the manager angry because Jean forgot to mention anything about a dog coming along. "Nope. It's just two *people*, me and my little sister," she'd forgetfully mention.

That next day, we had an inexpensive breakfast meal in a nearby diner, and keeping Duffy on a short leash, we sauntered out to the highway and stuck out our thumbs. It wasn't but a few minutes that passed before a smaller truck pulled over for us. We ran up to it on the passenger-side, and I opened the truck door to talk to the driver. At first, Jean and I both thought we were in luck.

It seemed that our driver was going all the way to New Orleans, clear-past our destination in Pascagoula. I jumped in first along with my large bag onto my lap and squeezed over on the big, console seat. Then Jean followed-in sitting on the outside passenger's side with her own suitcase under her legs letting Duffy jump-up and lay on her lap.

Highway 55 stayed really close to the Big Muddy, and that river was always half the landscape. Corn fields, apple orchards and a variety of vegetable farms lay out on the other side view. I mostly focused on what was ahead of us or what was happening outside Jean's side window. I would have liked to watch the Mississippi River traffic, but I didn't want to stare into our driver's space.

All went quietly without much conversation between any of us until the *Great Weirdness* began. We were about an hour into our ride and had sort of left the Mississippi to go inland a little way away from it. Farm country aligned both sides of the highway, and it was getting to be sort of boring spectator sport. Then suddenly without any warning, or prelude or explanation, our driver started letting out of his mouth some ferocious growls and vicious snarls. That, in itself, was enough to waken both Jean and me from our drowsiness, but he was just getting started.

Our driver continued his roars and howling, and then, suddenly, he began crying out in anger and threats, "Ooooh, I'm gonna kill 'em! That dirty bastard, I am going to slit his throat!"

Neither Jean nor I had any intentions of inquiring into that poor man's emotional struggle, so we just sat there mostly staring at the highway or with eyes begging for the Mississippi to come back into view for preferred entertainment. For a little while, our driver calmed down. But, it was not to last. He obviously had more things on his mind.

Thirty minutes or more passed by, that seemed like an eternity, and then *Act II* began. Instantly, our driver let go of the steering wheel with both hands and grasped his head in seeming pain and anguish. He screamed out again, "Aaaah, I'm gonna kill him! Let me get my hands on him. I'll killlll him!"

Neither of us cared for details. We waited anxiously for him to regain his composure and retake hold of the steering wheel again. With hands tightly grasping our travel bags and eyes focused straight ahead, Jean and I shared later that we were both plotting our escapes and our getaways. We just drove on, though. Our driver drove, I mean, and by then he was shaking and rocking his head erratically sideways, back-and-forth. Next, he began grunting, and the grunts picked-up ferocity and loudness with each outburst. That was a man clearly on the outs: Like, out-of-his-mind!

Jean was the quick thinker. Rather than wait for our driver to start weaving all over the road while screaming in concert with his truck weaves, Jean saw a way out. *A way out* of that crazy-man's truck.

Calling to the driver loudly and effectively, but not angrily, Jean shoved me against the driver to help grab his attention and then bellowed out well over the man's hyperventilating gasps, "Oh, look! There's a restaurant! They've got to have bathrooms. Please stop and let me use the bathroom. I've got to go really bad!"

Well, go figure, our insane truck driver was also a real gentleman, after all. Somehow, he recognized biologic needs, and appreciating any special needs of a lady, or even a boy's, if that was what he still thought, Jean's mini crisis at once brought his mind back to reality. Apparently, that *reality*-check fostered a true, southern gentleman's spirit to attend to a lady-in- distress. Fairly rapidly, our driver braked, geared down, and turned his truck onto the offramp and directly into the restaurant's parking area entrance.

Once the truck came to a full-stop, Jean ripped-open our passenger's door and ordered me to bring my bag along as she practically leapt from the cab to the ground with Duffy and her luggage in her arms and began rushing for the restaurant entrance. I knew my sister well-enough. I knew that if she had really needed to go to the bathroom that bad, she would have told the driver a long time before to pull-over somewhere, even if it meant for her to go out behind some bushes or trees somewhere. That was not such a case, however. Jean was on the run, and she was bounding across the large parking lot from the truck-stop zone with her suitcase and Duffy bouncing up-and-down in her arms in unison. Right away, I understood her plan clearly.

I had already jumped from the truck cab with my bag-in-hand and quickly turned to the driver. Without mincing too many words, I called back to him and then slammed the door shut before the last mid-sentence, "Thanks for the ride, Mister. I'm going to go with my sister, and I think that we are just going to stay here for a while. We're not in any hurry, so we shall eat, rest (slam!) and continue on much, much, later... or even tomorrow. Thanks. Bye"

I ran off to catch-up with Jean inside the restaurant. Just as I thought, Jean was hiding behind a wall and peeking-out at the truck and me racing to find her. Once inside, I was huffing and puffing, but I looked at Jean and then joined her in her spying routine. We both just waited a moment, and then, sure enough, here came that crazy driver. Well, we didn't waste any time or chance of being cornered in the *Ladies Room*, especially with a dog in tow. Quick as two winks, we hustled through the restaurant with our bags and suitcases in-hand and headed straight for the other rear entrance/exit.

On our way out that door, Jean called over to a waitress cleaning a table, and used her quick-thinking again. "Tell that crazy truck-driver coming-in that we just left with some friends we knew," was her clever request. Then she concluded, "Tell him we are gone!"

We broke through that rear-exit and dashed around to the back of the building. After what seemed like hours again, but was only minutes, we started sneaking to the side of the restaurant where we could get a good look at the truck. Sure enough, after a few minutes, we saw our driver meandering back to his truck occasionally glancing back over his shoulder as to question something. I could have sworn I saw him shaking his head once inside the cab, but regardless, that truck engine started, and I almost peed my pants with relief. The truck slowly pulled-away and out onto the café entrance road, then onto the highway again and was gone. Our madness had ended.

Afterwards, we walked back to the restaurant front-entrance, tied Duffy to a post and went inside to find an empty table. We both simultaneously dropped our bags and flopped down almost breathless. That was finally when we both felt relieved, so we began giggling and smirking. I giggled and Jean smirked! A moment later, the same waitress Jean had called-out to help as we dashed out the back door came over take our order, and she had a few words to say.

"We've seen that kook in here before. He has always seemed strange to us before too. This time he just came in looking around the place and then went in and used the bathroom. When he came back-out, he was still on-the-lookout, so I walked over to him and told him you two were gone and were not coming back and for him to just keep heading up the highway. He left right after that. You're safe now. Hungry?" We were.

Indeed, we did have our share of mishaps along the highways of this wonderful and beautiful country. There would still be a couple closer calls while using our thumbs to get us around. All-in-all, though, hitch-hiking was relatively safe and quite common in those days. However, two young women on the road day-and-night was probably not the wisest of choices. But, when it was the only one, considering our savings advantage, we just pulled our caps down, kept quiet, smiled, and stuck-out-our-thumbs.

"WENDY THE WELDER" JEAN

Pascagoula, Mississippi

In no time at all, though, one more terrific ride down Hwy. 55, and we got to Pascagoula, Mississippi. Right away, Jean asked for information and directions and learned the location of the training-site. This time, it was all local traffic. After only a brief walk, a nice person in an older, large car picked us up and took us straight to the welding school. He was happy that we had our dog with us too. He said that he thought that was a smart idea.

Usually, it seemed like when we were in towns or small cities, the local folks picked you up right away. It was sort of like they were trying to show how hospitable they were. Pascagoula was no exception. Our car-ride driver, an elderly gentleman, seemed tickled pink when we told him of Jean's intentions to attend the welding school and then go to work in the shipyards somewhere there in Mississippi or Louisiana.

It was getting much later in the afternoon by the time we arrived, so Jean found out where it was located and went straight to the school-office, registered for the *free* welding-school, which was paid-for by another government-program, and entered the arc-welding training-program. Jean was going to start school the very next day. The program was individually based, so the fast learners could go through the curse even more quickly. If someone needed more time, then that was possible too, within limits.

So, right-off, we needed to find ourselves a home-base. The registrar's office-girl had told Jean about some special housing really close-by. We looked around in town, and after asking a few people a few questions, we found that very same place the office-girl had spoken about. It was cheap living nearby the school and was commonly used by workers and trainees. We were quickly established. Plus, we were grateful because they did not mind Duffy too much.

Our little apartment was part of a greater complex of all similar one- and two-bedroom quarters. We both laughed that we had been assigned a one-bedroom, one-bath unit with the Three-B's: The *bare bones basics*. It wasn't that we needed much, however. It was more like the place just didn't provide you with much at all.

When the complex manager saw Duffy, at first, she was hesitant. Then, she understood our situation, and Duffy was welcomed. We promised to keep him on a leash when out-and-about the neighborhood. We agreed to pay for any damages our dog may do too. That wasn't a problem for us because Duffy was very mellow. Very protective, but mellow to acquaintances and friends. We were going to be there for a stretch, so it was my plan to help decorate the place. Of course, I would do so minimally, so as not to upset Jean with any wasteful spending.

Jean's welding class was going to be a six-week program. She was to learn all the inner skills of arc-welding and metal craft. She was going to be very busy and likely very tired when she got home. Jean told me that she was going to go through the program as fast as possible. So, my job was going to be housemaker: Cook, cleaner, and bottle-washer. That would be easy enough for me, and it still meant that I would have quite a bit of extra time to myself.

During that brief period, however, because I had grown some, aged a little and had become a lot savvier, I just spent most of my time enjoying myself, while Jean worked. My sister was none-to-happy about the relationship, but I just argued that I was too young to work in welding, and it was just too dangerous for me to go to school. Nobody was going to hire me for such a short-term either, I reasoned. Plus, who was going to take dare of Duffy? I was the one, that's who! But, even still, I felt like I was stuck-in-the-middle again, and, I couldn't do anything to satisfy Jean's dreams!

At least, that was my complain. Therefore, according to *Patsy's Diary*, I was being forced to dilly-dally all day long in town due to our stressful and tenuous conditions and circumstances. After all, I was still just a mere sixteen-year-old girl who needed a little goof-off time. That contention, however, did not sit very well with my stern, ambitious sister, Jean. She had dreams for us, and I had better get-on-board, if I knew what was good for me!

It was amazing how I managed to fill in my days, though. Fortunately, we had our savings from working in Cleveland to cover our temporary expenses, so we were not down-and-out. We had no rent and utilities. I could afford to get a few necessities for our apartment such as a couple more plates and cups and dining ware. Our apartment came with twin beds and blankets and a pillow each. So, my main focus was on dressing-up the living-room portion, not the sleeping room. My goal, then, was to find the least expensive way to decorate and not upset Jean over careless, frivolous spending.

What fun I had. I took Duffy with me all the time and wandered all over that town and got to know it pretty well. I asked around the complex and found out where nearly everybody did their grocery shopping because the store owners lowered the prices way down due to the no-pay training circumstances. That was a good deal for us.

I also found a couple of hand-me-down shops, so I was excited to tell Jean how to get more cheap work clothes because she kept burning big holes in the ones she wore, an unfortunate aspect of her new work. I found several thrift stores too, so I got great deals on extra kitchen stuff we needed. I even found a couple of really cheap pictures to hang-up on the walls. They were both scenes of the Mighty Mississippi River with little riverside villages or river-life scenes displayed along its shoreline. They were inexpensive and very fitting for our adventure.

Mostly, though, I found time for myself. I dilly-dallied to my heart's content but still had dinner on the table when Jean came home. I was a good wife! I still got to have time to go window-shopping to my heart's content, while I walked Duffy, and I do believe that I bought just about everything in every store, at least in my mind, anyway.

It was fun, and so was wandering all around over by the Big Muddy wherever I found I could get access. There was so much business and industry going on right next to it. That river was one very busy highway. All kinds of ships, and barges, and big boats, and small boats, and even steamboats moved-up-and-down that water thoroughfare all day long and through the night.

Time seemed to pass very quickly, and six-weeks later, Jean completed her training. She was certified as an arc-welder and was assigned a position in the Pascagoula Shipyards to go right to work right away. Our conditions changed, however. We were at least temporarily allowed to remain with the school's housing program until they needed our space. Plus, now that Jean had finished the schooling, our government, free-paid housing ended. We had to pay rent then, although it was still quite minimal.

Wages were poor, though, and we were nearly destitute living with our meager housing conditions on Jean's low income. Wages were better, sure, but living conditions and expenses were higher too. Just like promised, Jean made more money now than ever before in Cleveland. The problem was that everything cost more down there too, so there was no getting ahead.

That's the way it is about the corporate world: For whatever businesses may pay in wages, other businesses know exactly how much to charge for living-expenses to get it all back. Fact is, I noticed that a lot of the *businesses* which supplied lodging, food, drink, or necessities were often owned outright by the very company, or by somebody who did their bidding. It was like a giant conspiracy. Big companies gave you jobs. Then their own businesses demanded all your wages for you to buy their products and support yourself with.

Years later, I was reminded of our predicament, and that of millions of others too, by the song made famous by Tennessee Williams, called "Sixteen Tons." In it, Tennessee sang about working all day for a company, but owing all his money to the *company store*. Wow! That sure was how we felt.

Before long, and for those very reasons, it really became necessary for me to go to work too and contribute to our cause. Alright, fine! Playtime was over! June was around-the bend, and that meant that same old cursed adage: What? No school? Then, get a job! So, it really was time. I had to go to work! Talk about sacrifice!

Wouldn't you know it, though? One week later, yes, that's right! *Only one-week later* after Jean had graduated from welding school, had gone to work in the Pascagoula Shipyards and we were moving-on already. Jean's brand new and first, professional-welding assignment on her new job let her hear some wild tales or word of new and better paying job elsewhere.

That is what lunchbreaks were for: Gossip! What jobs were going on where, and how much they paid.

My Goodness! We had been in Ohio with both of us working steady less than two-months earlier. By then we were in Mississippi and settled-in and working. Well, Jean was anyway. I was determined to find something useful to do and earn a living too, but Jean went-off to lunchbreak and heard about a new and much better-paying job in the State of Washington clear across the rest of the USA and way-up in the Northwest. I mean you couldn't go much further away without falling into the Pacific Ocean!

It seemed like Jean just wanted to trade in the Mississippi for the Pacific, or maybe it was a big river for a bigger ocean. Regardless, Jean always did dream big! In actuality, too, we really just traded in a huge Mississippi River, and its notable Pascagoula Shipyards, for the smaller, but still famous and dynamic Columbia River and its renowned Kaiser Shipyards.

But that meant that we still had a long way to go. C'mon Duffy, lets git! It was time for a little *thumb-action* again...

GO WEST, YOUNG WOMAN! GO WEST!

According to Jean, the shipyards in Vancouver, Washington, way out west, were apparently in grave need of arc-welders. Wow! Word sure got around, or else Jean had radar ears. But actually, I'm kidding around because that new place really sounded really interesting to me too. Maybe it was the area we were living in. Or, maybe it was the excitement of the northwestern part of the country that we had only read or heard about. Who knew for sure?

Or maybe, it was partly because I was getting bored with silly-dilly dallying around each day and taking Duffy for necessary walks two or three times each day. A girl may want to have fun, but after a while, for crying-out-loud, a girl can finally have too much fun, I supposed. Plus, I ran out of my own *goof-off* money from my earlier gas-station job fairly soon thereafter. It was a safe bet, I bet, that I sure wasn't going to get any *play-money* from Jean either.

Also, and now looking back and recalling, the romantic part of me liked to think that there was a special, sort of hidden, main reason we were heading out west. It was because, regardless of all the other plusses or minuses, going out west to Vancouver, Washington, or Portland, Oregon. simply meant another new adventure for us. Sometimes, you just had to go because you had a place to go. Sometimes, you just had to cross that mountain because you needed to see for yourself just what was on the other side.

However, I knew my sister Jean, and the real and true clincher for her was no doubt, *the money*. The wages that were being paid out west were *a dollar more an hour* than anywhere in Mississippi. We could hardly believe our ears. A forty-eight-hour workweek meant forty-eight dollars more in wages! After taxes, which meant over one hundred fifty dollars a month! That was crazy good! The money was amazing. No, it was glorious! Who wouldn't go? So, there was no argument about what to do: *Should we stay, or should we go?* Our bags were packed by bedtime, and we were off for our next opportunity at break-of-day...

Once again, we stuck out our thumbs. This time, however, we were going to have to hitch across seven states. Two young women, who might be taken for men, and their dog crossing half the country... That was us. A long stretch like that meant a few side roads until we could get ourselves onto that famous Highway 66 that would take us clear over to Highway 99 where we could turn north and go straight to our destination through California and then Oregon and into the State of Washington. No difference. A thumb-is-a-thumb to a driver, and a ride-is-a-ride to a hitcher, until they both get to where they are going.

Jean still had all the money from her past savings and a full-week's wages, so that meant that I was sort of along for the ride. But thumbs out, and with big smiles on our faces, we stood-out facing on-coming traffic trying to keep Duffy blocked-from-view behind us for strategic purposes, of course, and waited for a ride.

After one came and we went their full distance, then maybe we'd have to walk a bit to a new hitching spot. It was usually okay. Often times, a driver would appreciate what we were doing and drop us off at a really decent spot for our next ride. Those courtesies were really valued. Sometimes, we were dropped-off just because our ride was stopping-over someplace to visit a site, and we just needed to keep-going. So, we'd say our goodbyes, get out of the car and start hitching again right there. No problems.

Trucks were usually the best rides, though. Cross-country drivers would stop and pick us up because they wanted company. Often times, those rides would be going all the way across states to where we needed. Another advantage was that those guys usually knew the roads really well, and often times they knew all the good places to stop and eat cheaply or stay a night and get cleaned-up. However, one rule-of-thumb: Truck drivers do not stop at all the best places to eat. That is a fallacy. They stop for convenience sake, or because the food is cheap, not necessarily good. Once again… money ruled.

Many truckers would keep right-on-truckin' until it was time to find a place to pull-over and rest or to eat. When you are doing cross-country, those are the two key ingredients: Eat and sleep. Of course, the other subsidiary need is bathroom breaks. What was desirable was to time all three into the same time and place: Stop to use the bathroom, eat, and then sleep.

That was what Jean and I really wanted. When sleepy, truckers would just pull-over at their own special spots, climb in the back of their cab and sleep however long they needed. Jean and I weren't prepared to climb in the sack with them. Although, I am now fairly certain those drivers would have assured us there was plenty of room.

Of course, I may not have minded much because I hadn't the vaguest idea of what might have otherwise been on any of their minds. But Jean was savvy to them all. "No thank you," she would have said. "We have way different plans, if it's all the same to you."

So, given those circumstances, we needed inexpensive motels for a night's stay and a meal the next morning before heading out again. Of course, everywhere we went or were dropped-off, we had to cover-for or hide Duffy's presence. He was so loveable but still not the most welcome creature wherever we went.

Also, we were not camping, so the idea of sleeping under a truck did not go-over well with us. We weren't prepared for bad weather or bad animals wandering and sniffing around, either. No, the idea of a surprise rainstorm or some snarling, growling, and biting critters made us both the indoor kind of folks. A nice shower in a morning and a nearby restaurant's warm meal was just the ticket. If necessary, we would start-up again and stick out our thumbs and keep going. That is exactly what happened on one other unforgettable ride. Well, it was for me, anyway.

We had been dropped-off at a motel and coffee-shop by a driver who was just sleeping for a few hours and then heading-out again. We knew that we were somewhere in West Texas at that time of night. We thanked him for the ride that far, and then we left him and his truck to get a meal and check into a motel on the grounds for the night. We were somewhere in the beautiful, desert country somewhere. It was getting dark already, so it was pretty late in the evening. Our driver wanted to grab a fast meal in the café and then head back-out to his truck and the highway again. We decided to part company from him, get our room first, refresh ourselves, and then get a late-night dinner.

ROAD HAZARDS

It just crossed my mind, however, that while describing so many cross-country treks and freighter rides and hitch-hiking escapades, I may have left a false impression of mistruths, denials, extraordinary luck, or unfair exclusions of hard or bad times while on the road. So, I suppose now is as good a time as any to explain our less-than-perfect travel record. Truth is, in hindsight, we sisters were probably very fortunate travelers.

Oh, sure, we had gotten a weird ride from some crazy madman, but we had run from that without harm. Just our wits were frayed a little. By far, though, most of the time we were treated very decently by our countless ride hosts. However, the only logic and reasoning behind it was the lousy, economic depression and then that miserable, follow-up war. Lots of folks hitch-hiked or took freighters. If you couldn't afford a car, or gasoline even, then you *hitched*. Perhaps, now I can partially explain our fortunate and unusually good luck while traveling. It wasn't without thought and specific planning.

For one thing, we both were pretty much Tomboys. My sister Jean was rough, tough, and even talked with a lower, gruff voice. We both wore hats or bandanas and pants and shirts and coats when necessary. I have already discussed our travel garb, and Jean explained our travel behavior. One important criterion was that Jean would do almost all the talking. I was to keep quiet and keep my face and head down too, so as not to give-away awkward, embarrassing, or telltale appearances.

While traveling with strangers, there was to be little discussion of us or our backgrounds. Jean mostly referred to the future and our distant-travel destination. So, as much as I can now guess, most of the decent folks who gave us rides pretty much assumed we were boys or young men seeking better times elsewhere. During those years, looking forward and seeking better opportunities was very commonplace.

Nevertheless, life *ain't* perfect and neither was our "track record," so-to-speak. Now, please understand, Jean was a pretty tough cookie, as I mentioned before. Guys would have a very bad time on their hands if they had tried to "bother" her. And like I said, I dressed like a boy, kept my mouth mostly shut and kept my face down usually. And, for the most part, it worked most of the time.

Only a couple of times did the supposed "nice" folks giving us rides finally recognize that we were girls, and then the shock must have kept them mostly quiet. Plus, that was when often times either they, or we, needed to stop and take care of personal business. Lots of times, those were good places to say good-bye to our rides, thank them and get on with our own businesses. After a while, Jean and I would start looking for new rides again. We were never rushed and never hurried. We just tried to be careful, and most of the time it worked. Usually, things went along alright.

However, there were a few instances which come-to-mind when things got a little testy. Of course, there was that *crazy* nut-job driver who cussed so angry-like and drove so wild on that highway to Mississippi. After that there were still a few times I recall once we left Mississippi on our way to California and then on again to Washington that were not very pleasant or safe. Looking back, I now understand that I could have gotten myself into a lot of trouble back then. But, God's good grace, or my naiveté, probably saved me. Anyway, there are some stories of what I remember that happened during those *bad times*. I simply prefer referring to those ill-spent passages as *hazards of the road,* or just *Road Hazards*.

SCARY DRIVER

The worst incidences happened during our longest legs of travel from Mississippi to Los Angeles and then again from LA to Vancouver, Washington. Also, those real scares involved trucks and truck drivers. Third point, and most importantly, was the factor that because we were riding with long-distance, overland truckers, they only had one extra seat in each truck for a passenger. Therefore, Jean, Duffy and I were forced to split-up and ride in separate trucks, one following the other. But we made sure that both trucks had the same ultimate destination, of course. At least Jean was smart enough to figure that part out.

All went well from our last ride, though, and we went in for a night's sleep. Early the next morning, we were having our breakfast and had our luggage right there beside us in our booth. Right out of nowhere, a fellow stopped at our table and began talking to us.

"Good morning, Ladies," the man began. "I see you and your dog are hitchin' the highway. Which direction are you heading?

At first, I was a bit leery of the man. How did he know we were *hitchhiking*? Maybe our car was in the parking-lot. Then, of course, I realized that he saw our luggage next to us, and a car person would have left their belongings in the car's trunk, probably. Okay, then. Fair enough question. Jean was already a step ahead of me, though. She was already on the lookout for another lift to the next juncture.

"We're going all the way to California," Jean wasn't bashful with her conversations. "We've got family there, and they're expecting us right away. Why? How far are you going?"

"Oh, well, alright then," the man continued. "How about this? Me and my buddy over there, Willy, are goin' all the way to L.A., and we've got to get there by tonight. We got two trucks and plenty of room. We figure company will help us stay awake, and we can make better time that way. It's probably too crowded both of you in one cab, so splitting-up will make it easier all around. How about it? You gals willing to split-apart to get where you're going?"

"Yeah, we are," Jean answered for both of us, "but there better not be any monkey-business, or I'll let hell loose on you!"

The man stood straight upright in his boots a little started, "Whoa, there! Ain't gonna be no problems with us. We're family men and just want to get our jobs done. It's a long drive. I just figured company might pass our time better. If you're not up to it…"

"We are," Jean quickly responded agreeably. "I'll ride in your truck, and my sister can ride with your partner, Willy."

The man just laughed and concluded his offer, "Okay, then, we're happy to accommodate you two. My name is Howard, Hank for short. We'll be leaving in about twenty more minutes. That alright with you?"

"Hello, Hank, and thanks. I'm Jean, and she's Patsy. We'll be ready to go shortly."

I was thinking to myself, "Well, so much for my input. I guess I'm going to be riding in that other truck with, ah, Willy then. I suppose I should be glad Jean didn't beat-up the man before he could even give us a ride."

We were outside with our bags when both men walked-up that time and introduced themselves again. Hank spoke first, "Hello, Ladies. This here is Willy, and that truck over there is his. That one there is mine. Are you gals ready to ride?"

"We are," Jean answered again for both of us. "Which one of you is leading and driving in front of the other?"

"Well, we take turns," Willy jumped in this time. "Why? Which one do you want?"

"Patsy wants to be in front. That okay?" Jean had a direct way with words.

"Hank, guess I'm leading again. See you in LA. All aboard!"

I hadn't even spit out one word yet, and here I was all decided for by Jean already. I was in the truck, the *front* truck with *Willy*, and we were heading for LA. Then Jean quickly grabbed my arm and held me back a minute while the two drivers each headed for their respective trucks. Obviously, Jean had something to say to me. "Gosh!" I thought, "Maybe she wants my opinion…*now, finally!*"

She didn't, but she did have a plan. Leave it to Jean. Then she explained, "While you are riding up there, every fifteen minutes or so, hang your arm out the window and wave it around to tell me you are okay. When I see your arm, I won't worry. Got it?"

"Oh, gosh, oh, golly, Sister! You mean that you want me to say something now, or should I just wave my arm?" I started flopping my arm around wildly to emphasize my point.

"Alright, smart ass, just let me know you are okay, okay?" Jean was perturbed.

Of course, I gave in, "Sure, Jean. It's a good plan. How do I know when to stop?"

"Probably, the next time will be when you or he have to go to the bathroom. We can talk more then."

"Right you are,... again,... as usual," I smiled and lugged my bag over to my truck ride.

Right-off, we were off-and-running. My truck was in the lead, and all was well for a while with only a little bit of sketchy conversation between us. At least at the beginning...

Typical questions to get a dialog started came from Willy: "Where'd you two come from? Where you going to? Why? Any problems so far?"

I was still too ill-at-ease to converse much. I just replied with the basics: "Cleveland. LA. Work. Nope."

On this leg of our trip, Jean had decided to keep Duffy with her. Often, he rode along while sitting on my lap, but Jean wanted a turn this time, I guessed. Also, Jean had already recommended that I say no more than necessary. All I could imagine was that meant I had to pretty much keep my mouth shut all the time. I did love to talk so much. Alright, I'll deal with it. In the first interim, I focused on the fifteen-minute warnings to Jean. To help pass time, I kept a sort of mental track of time and fifteen-minute interludes. That was when I would stick my arm out the window and wave it around madly. I figured Jean would know I was exaggerating my *wellness*, but actually I was trying to make a point.

We should have had two signals arranged: One for *Happy!* waving and another for *Help me! I'm getting* **kiiiiiilllllld** waving! Arm *waving low*, everything is *go!* Arm *flopping high, I guess it's goooooodbyyyyye!* Oh, I suppose I got a little melodramatic at times, but *What if?* Anyway, as it turned-out, all I needed was a little while longer riding along with Willy to prove my point.

Old Willy turned out to be quite a talker, too. A regular Hans Christian Anderson he was, except that he added a diabolical mixture of Edgar Allen Poe and the Grimm Brothers with his talk too. "Hark the Raven, Nevermore!" became my mind-set. Han's diabolical and evil opposite whispered its messages into my driver's ears all along our highway path. Imagine one of Han's sweet stories being told by the Brothers Grimm, and then, just for fun, add some more real evil to it. Yes, indeed, Willy ended up having plenty to say. I wish that I had brought with me a magic wand that I could have just pointed at him, whispered a quiet chant, and turned him into a mute. No, that wouldn't be nice. How about a robot without a mouth? Yes, that would have worked.

Anyway, I had to put up with him, and he had quite a tale to tell, and all I could do was wave my arm around every fifteen-minutes telling Jean, "I'm having a wonderful time here listening to this man's horrifying tale of evil... Whoopy!"

And if I didn't wave my arm ever at all? How many sets of *fifteen-minutes* might pass before Jean noticed and did something? After just one set, I could already be nothing but a bunch of blood and guts and bones laying on the passenger's floorboards. And what about Jean? Why, we were split-up now, and who could ever tell what? Good ol' boy Hank might have, could have even killed Jean by then. Then what?

Oh, wait! No, that wasn't about to happen. First sign of foul play, and Jean would start playing dirty. Oh, goodness, I imagined all sorts of terrible things happening to that poor man. Oooh! Makes me shudder. No, Jean was fine. I felt better already. I'd just have to go on listening to this man's perverted story of hell-on-earth, and keep waving my arm, or not! That was the plan. Stick to it...

So, *Dirty*-Willy got to carry right on along with his historical references to Highway 66, much to my chagrin. I'll give you a quick catch-up and then tell you the rest as best as I can remember, at least up until the part where we... parted...

"It seems that Highway 66 had a long history of deaths by killings. All the cops from Dallas to Los Angeles were vexed out of their minds with so many unsolvable murders. People, nice folks like families, soldiers, young men, and young sisters hitchhiking together would just end-up disappearing anywhere along that route. Cops, Sheriff's departments, State Patrol Officers, and even government agents were all perplexed, confounded and vexed out-of-their-minds.

> "As soon as a new victim, or victims, turned-up missing, the multi-state reports would be out the very next day in all the local investigator's logs.
> They would all state the same outlines and references: "Another Dead Body Missing. Just add their names to the list and mark them down as *Six feet down* and *Unsolved*. We ain't never going to figure-out this case, anyway. Too bad. So sad. I'll tell you, from what I've been told, there must be dozens, no, hundreds, or, or, maybe even thousands of dead bodies all laying along this highway in unmarked graves. Terrible. Just terrible."

At this point, I was just starting to listen and go along with his story. I even imagined at first that he was trying to tell me ghost stories for entertainment. I was alright, so far. (Wave, wave, and wave to Jean. Oooooh, this is fun, I think). Anyway, *Mouthful-Willy* is just getting started.)

"Well, it just so happens that there was one case in particular that got the whole nation stunned and mortified. You might have even heard about it. It only happened just a couple months ago. It was in all the papers clear across the nation and had everyone just mortified and agonized over the discovery. Apparently, the killer, or there could have been killers, two of 'em in cahoots, who had gone-off and committed their dastardly deed and buried the two bodies in shallow graves, not too far from here, in fact.

> "But, these two murderers-from-hell, well, they slipped-up and left one of the dead body's shoe-tips still sticking-up from the ground. Just too lazy to dig a deep-enough hole, the fools! Authorities figured that most of the killings had been done during the bright daylight so that those evildoers could clearly

see what they was doin'. This particular evil act, however, must have been done in the dead dark of night, so they couldn't see no shoe- tip sticking-up from the bloody ground in that stupid, dumb shallow grave."

"Okay, alright. Enough is enough, and I've heard enough," were thoughts scrambling through my brain. Okay, Jean, notice that there is no *arm-waving signal!* It's time for a break. Someone else can hear how this disgusting story ends. Not me! Pleeeeeeese?"

Well, obviously, Ol' *Fleet-mouthed*-Willy could talk a lot more in fifteen-minutes time. I was sure of that. I was simply stuck like a captive audience to hear more. Jean, first chance we get, we're switching trucks! In the meantime, all I could do was sit-up straight in my seat, keep a corner of my eye on him and wait.

Wait for what, I did not know for sure. Wait for the end of this story? Wait to see what *Chilly-Willy* says, or does? Stop *waving* my arm and see what would happen. Jean, oh, Jean, do you see? Do you see *nothing*? That's the point. Tell *Hank* to pull-up alongside *Silly*-Willy and drive him off-the-road. Just let me out!

My mind was flip-flopping, "Oh, for heaven's sake, Silly, it's just a story, and *Big Mouth* is just trying to scare you, so let him try. Well, it's working! I've had enough of his talk, talk, talk. Silence is golden. Can't he be happy just staring at the desert? There's so much to see! Look at all that sand and, and, and plants!"

Slick-Willy is still talking away. I can see his lips moving and drawling words are still spilling out of his nasty mouth. So, what's up? I began listening again…

> "… and they finished digging-up the other body nearby the first murder victim. Autopsies and investigations proved that it was a sad, couple of travelers who had come to the desert area to experience the big outdoors. They had been hiking all through the local countryside apparently and must have stopped or been stopped by them two murderin' rapists.
>
> "Whichever way, those evil men had got that couple, it didn't matter none 'cause nobody ever heard hide-nor-hair of neither of them after that. That is, until the shoe was seen by some hitchhikers passing through. Why they was walking there

was never explained well except that they just loved to walk. Sure they did. They was probably killers, too. Who knows? Who cares?

"But that poor couple turned out to be a mother and her teenage daughter who was way across the country and probably tryin' to get back to Mexico. That was where they was from originally. Maybe they was trying to get to Las Cruces, New Mexico and then on to El Paso, Texas where they could cross over into Juarez, Mexico, home-sweet- home. But they never made it. Nope. Instead, they got bushwhacked by a couple of nice fellers on the outside, but pure, plain wickedness on the inside..."

"Alright, Jean," I began thinking ninety miles-an-hour again, "it's been at least sixteen or seventeen minutes already. What are you doing except nothing? Sleeping, probably. Oh, that's a big help. Okay. Just calm down, and let this loudmouth finish his make-believe tale. It is a make-believe tale, isn't it? I'm sure it is... It must be... Isn't it?"

"A sweet, kind mother and daughter just wandering through the wilderness picking- up cactus flowers and desert stones to take home and decorate their house with. Just so sad, the whole affair was. They had raped both of them women, well, the one woman and her grown child daughter. They had molested 'em both and beaten 'em and done all kinds of incredible things to their bodies.

"The bodies was all naked and such except for the one young lady. They had ripped-off all her clothes except for the one shoe. I suppose they was in a hurry. And that was their big mistake. Hurryin'. Stupid. Just plain stupid, I tell you. People like them have got to slow-down and take their time. Hurryin' always..."

"Hey, Willy!" I interrupted immediately once I saw a chance. "Look there's a diner up ahead, or a gas station, or something. Please stop, so I can use the Ladies Room. I've got to go really bad!"

"Well, you know," Willy answered back in a rush, "there's a real good restaurant only about fifty miles or so up ahead. Can you wait that long? And then I can finish my story too and tell you what happens in the end 'cause they never ever did catch them two killers, and they is both still on the loose. Probably still out there somewhere driving their trucks and doing this and that to whomever they want…"

"No! Now! I've got to go now!"

"Well, gee whiz! Alright, then. But, hurry back, so I can finish.."

Willy pulled his truck over to the road-stop just in the nick-of-time to make the turn-off and turned his truck up to an abrupt stop just past the coffee-shop/gas station. I held onto my bag and jumped to the ground. I ran full-speed into the coffee shop, panting like crazy and stood there waiting and watching for Jean to show-up. Hank's truck had pulled-in right behind Willy's and came to a stop. Alright, and hours later, it seemed, Jean climbed down from the truck and came walking toward me and the shop.

Once Jean was inside, I almost yelled at her, "I'm not riding with that crazy man anymore! He's nuts with all his killer, murderer stories, and I don't want to hear any more. I'm riding with you and Hank from now on!"

And that's just what happened too. We walked outside right after I did go to the bathroom. That *Nutcase*-Willy had managed to scare the devil out of me, and I could have peed all over myself in fright. Afterward, we walked straight-up to Hank's truck and both of us climbed-up inside Hank's cab and joined him and Duffy. Hank hadn't even shut-down his engine yet and was just sitting there waiting. Jean had me jump in first and she followed. I didn't ask. I threw my bag in the back of the cab and just sat there between Hank and Jean very quietly.

Jean said something to explain the circumstance, "I guess your friend scared her too much with some storytelling, so she wants to ride with us. That alright?"

"Why, sure. You and I were getting along so famously, we don't want to break-up our conversation. What's a little more company? Welcome, young lady. What's the matter? Oh, don't tell me. Was Willy telling his damnable stories of murders and rapists again. He is always doing that. Just loves to scare the dickens out of his passengers. A real storyteller, he is. A horror storyteller, that is. Tell me, did he talk about the poor Mexican mom and her child? Hope not. I've warned him before. Just like now, he's going to be driving a long ways all by himself. Serves him right."

Right for me, anyway. I had been filled to the brim with his terrible story alluding to all that filthy crime stuff. I was tired, though. Exhausted from having to listen to *Foul-mouthed Willy*. I remember putting my head on Jean's shoulder and taking a nice long nap.

When I awakened, we were in New Mexico somewhere. I was still tired, emotionally tired, and Jean and Duffy both needed breaks too. So, we asked Hank to stop at the next road-stop, and we would be parting company there. We were not in a hurry like Hank likely was. He still had to get to LA by nightfall, and we, I mean Jean, did not want to press ourselves that hard and especially in night. Just up-ahead we found a decent place that supplied everything we needed: An inexpensive motel for the rest of the day and night, and a basic, but delicious, home-cooked meal at a Mom & Pops Diner to rest and eat and collect our wits.

Hank didn't need any gas from Mom & Pop's Gas-Station, so it was a fast stop to let us all out. After saying goodbye to Hank, we went inside to meet Mom & Pop and take care of our business. Personally, I was just as happy not saying goodbye to Willy, too. When Hank pulled-over to let us out, Willy went flying on by, blasting on his horn and probably laughing his butt-off too.

DIRTY DRIVER

I can't say rightfully that that night spent at Mom & Pops Motel was the best sleep ever. On the contrary, they were very restless as I recall. I can still remember how my dreams that night were filled with horrifying creatures all wandering around various desert scenes causing evil wherever they crawled. Somewhere along the way in those dreams, there was a truck far-off in the distance just blasting away on its horn…

Something else that Jean considered as a safety-valve for us was her pet dog, Duffy. He was an all-white fur, Alaskan Husky Shepherd that was young and not yet fully-grown, but he did have a fantastic row of big, white, sharp, and pearly-white teeth. He also was very loving to kind people but extremely protective of us. Jean knew this, of course. So, when we made our transportation arrangements, Duffy almost always traveled with me while riding when we were forced to split-up and take different trucks together. That turned out to be a very good practice on our next particular ride. Dogs really can be a *woman's* best friend!

Early the next morning, we were all refreshed and ready to take-on-the-day. We greeted Pop outside pumping some gas on our way into the diner and then met Mom inside to fix our breakfasts. We were relaxing and enjoying our meal when all-of-a-sudden, Jean stood-up and made sort of a loud announcement stating that we were looking for any available rides to Los Angeles. A couple of truck drivers there who were also having a meal seemed willing to offer rides right away. Jean was getting fairly forward with her ride requests, but it was working.

Actually, too, that was where the first bad thing that happened to me (us) while we continued traveling through New Mexico. The second trucker who ended up providing a ride for us there at that Mom & Pops Diner/

Motel/Service Station actually came as a surprise. The first driver had been very receptive and willing, at first. Then he became questionable and seemed a bit indignant about letting both of us hitchers and a dog ride with him. So, instead he walked over to the table with the other willing truck driver and spoke for a moment. He then arranged for that driver who was following his same route to take me and Duffy along with him.

Before long, We were all loaded-up, and Jean was well ahead in her ride heading for LA, and I was settling-in for my own long drive. With my large carrying bag in back behind me on the driver's trucker's bed, I had Duffy stretched out comfortably on my lap. This ride was going all the way to Los Angeles, so it was a good distance for us and would get us all the way to where we needed to switch and get new rides heading north on Highway 99.

Interestingly, during our conversation and travel arrangements, however, both drivers also became aware that we were both girls. Perhaps, that factor had helped encourage them for taking us along. I'm not sure because they had both been willing even before when they still assumed we were both guys. Regardless, we all agreed and were soon on our way across the rest of New Mexico and then Arizona all the way to sunny California. I still remember watching the truck ahead with Jean in the lead and feeling all comfortable. All seemed well-enough for a while...

Hours later, in the late morning, and with my eyes getting very heavy, I began dozing-off. As planned and practiced before, I was to be very unsocial and talk very little with my head usually facing the passenger window and my eyes taking in the local landscape from the passenger's point-of-view. Duffy was laying across my lap also sleeping and was undisturbed at first by what was happening. With my head leaning up against the door window, I suddenly awakened with a startled jolt to a large, strong hand grabbing my knee and sort of rubbing it. Though uncertain of what was happening, I pushed his hand away roughly and spoke out loudly, "Hey, stop that. What are you doing? What do you want?"

The driver sort of smirked saying something like, "Oh, c'mon. Don't you like it?" Then he put his hand on my knee again and started moving it up my leg.

At once yelled at him again as I shoved his hand away, "What are you doing? Stop touching me! Don't do that!" Fortunately, it was enough noise and movement to awaken Duffy.

Two things now need to be explained. First, was good ol' Duffy coming to the rescue. He had sleepily let the first *hand-on-my-knee* incident pass without response probably because he was sleepy or uncertain, himself. However, his "protective" instincts had then taken over and Duffy was wide-awake. With the second incident and my second yelling, Duffy instinctively knew something was awry and began growling and baring his teeth. By then, the driver's hand was definitely in danger of Duffy's certain bite if not kept withdrawn.

The second *thing* needing explanation was my own behavior. I must now also emphasize that my past had never prepared me for anything like what had just happened. The honest-to-God truth is that I truly did not understand at all what the driver was trying to do with his hands on my knee. His silly questioning, "Don't you like it?" seemed absurd to me. Like what? What did he want? Of course not; it was weird. I truly had no clue.

After all, deep-down I was still just a good, little Catholic girl who had been kept in the deliberate darkness of naiveté by the Sisters at schools we attended. Oh, sure, we learned tricks and deceitful behaviors, but that was to avoid any cruel, harsh punishment from the nuns if we were caught doing something wrong. The topic of sex never ever came up. Thus, I had no clue as to what actually was occurring in the perverted mind of that nasty truck driver.

Okay, so anyway, back to the *incident* that had been going on. Duffy was growling, I was half-looking out the windshield and half-watching the truck driver with upset but curious eyes and the driver was, himself, getting all worked up into an angry state. Suddenly, he started slowing the truck down and pulling-over to a wide berth off the highway. He brought the truck to a swift stop, switched some buttons, flung open his driver's door, and jumped out. A little bewildered, I watched him stomp around the front of the truck, reach-up to the handle of the passenger door and swing the door abruptly wide-open.

Next, the driver stared at me intently and then growled menacingly, "You're either gonna put-out or get-out! What's it gonna be?"

I was still a bit confused and bewildered, but I very quickly responded to him with my squeaky, defiant tone, "You want me to get-out of this here truck, and then you're going to leave me and my dog out here in the desert without my sister? Well, I'm not going anywhere. I'm stayin' in this truck, and you have to take me to the place we agreed 'cause my sister will be there. And you'd better get going fast because they're way ahead of us now." And then I gave him my final, verbal, *coup d'état* thrashing, although I truly didn't fully understand what it really meant. I blurted out unhesitatingly, "And you better stop touching my knee with your hand, or my dog is going to bite you good!"

It actually took a couple more rounds to resolve the dispute. The driver angrily yelled at me to get out again, and I smugly and defiantly yelled back at him that I wouldn't. Back and forth it went until finally the driver got so frustrated that he just slammed my door shut and stomped around to the other side of his truck. He stared menacingly at me, and then perhaps a little more thoughtfully at Duffy, but he climbed aboard, switched some buttons again and pulled back out onto the highway. We were off again. The difference now was that there were no more looks, no conversation, and after a while, I even felt comfortable enough to start dozing-off again.

Hours later, and it was past mid-day by then, the truck pulled into another truck-stop for gas and food, and I quickly spotted the other truck getting refueled. Jean was standing right there and excitedly came over to check on us. Before she even got to us, I had reached around and grabbed my bag in the cab's rear and swinging it around me with one smooth motion, I opened the truck door, let Duffy leap-out and I jumped-out too with my bag-in-hand.

First, Duffy got his hugs, and then she asked what took us so long. I was really quick to fill her in on the details, and after I did, Jean walked over to her driver in a real hurry and had some conversation. He listened intently to Jean, and I could see him glaring and looking around a bit, first at me and then in the direction of my driver who had since gone into the restaurant.

Then, I easily heard his irritated and fuming response, "He did that? Why, that sorry son-of-a-b--ch! He did the same thing last year to a sweet, young Mexican girl who was traveling with her mother. I'm going to report that asshole, and this is the last time I'll ever double-up with him on a C-C (cross-country). He's bad news."

I remember being a little bewildered and thinking to myself, "Wow! He really got in trouble for trying to dump me off in the desert. I guess a deal-is-a-deal with those truck drivers."

Next, I heard Jean's driver follow-up with comforting news. He all but barked out new orders for us to Jean, "Get your sister and dog and stick them behind the seats onto my bunk. You both ride with me until we get to your drop-off in Los Angeles.

∞

I quickly surmised that there was both honor and dishonor among truck drivers. This nice driver, however, more than made up for the argument my driver had had with me. And now Jean, Duffy and I were all back together again and heading for California and then Hwy 40 heading north toward Oregon and Washington.

The rest of our journey through Arizona and on into California was very different. This time, we all became very talkative and shared information and hopes and dreams for the future. Our driver was actually from Texas, and he took runs every which way he got. It didn't matter to him because he said that he loved driving. He did add that he liked people too, but that there were some who were not so nice, and we needed to be careful. He was very kind to us, though, and even Duffy seemed relaxed and boisterous. He wagged his tail a lot and begged to be patted.

Our trip ended peacefully with fond farewells. Our driver had dropped us off at a decent enough Truck-Stop, but there was no motels around, so we just curled-up in a safe, quiet spot and slept through the night. The next morning, we got up early and used the gas station bathroom to clean ourselves up.

Then Jean and I easily worked our way through that new truck-stop to seek out some new transportation going north. It was very early, so we took our time, got some inexpensive food from the on-site diner, and then went to business. Well, actually, Jean went to work. I stayed with Duffy while Jean went one-by-one to the drivers as they were gassing-up their trucks. In no time at all, it seemed, she came running-over to me and Duffy.

"C'mon," Jean insisted, "I've got us two rides all the way north. They're both going to Seattle eventually, but we can go clear to Redding, California by nightfall with them. That's where they're stopping for the night. Hurry! We gotta go fast."

∞

MORE ROAD HAZARDS

I was happy, but not very surprised. Jean was really good at talking, it seemed. Jean picked-up Duffy and carried him over to one truck and spoke quickly to me, "Here's your ride. You and Duffy. I'll be in another truck up-front again. Remember: If we get separated, the driver has to take you to the Redding City Library. That is our drop-off point. I'll find you at the library. Got it?" Jean stared at me to see if I understood.

I nodded acknowledgement and then pressed to make certain, "Whoever gets to Redding first waits for the other, right?"

Jean half-smiled, and then smirked challengingly, "I'll be there waiting for you!" She quickly introduced me to my driver, and in no time at all, we were all up-and-running again.

My driver seemed pleasant enough. He whistled a little bit, talked briefly about how wet it was going to be up north eventually, especially in Seattle, made some small talk, and general conversation. Apparently, he liked to talk, or maybe it was just that he liked listening to himself. Or, maybe he was just bored, but I wasn't much help on the conversational end.

Mostly, I was still tired from the restless night before. It was easy to drift-off, and besides, Duffy seemed awake. This time Duffy was sitting facing the driver. Protective of me, I supposed. This guy was not going to be dropping us off early I felt confidently. So, I relaxed into my own comfort zone letting my mind travel to new destinations with new dreams filled with happy thoughts allowing me to just slip away.

I slept calmly and quietly, it seemed, for hours and miles and miles. I awoke yawning and stretching feeling refreshed and in a positive mood. I looked at my driver and he seemed a bit pensive, even annoyed. I noted that as far ahead as I could see, the truck with Jean was nowhere in sight. Maybe my driver was upset that he lost sight of the other truck. At first,

I was bothered, but I remembered our "library" deal in Redding. I was reassured momentarily.

Duffy wagged his tail energetically. He probably needed a bathroom break like I did. But I hesitated to say anything. I wanted a stop to be the driver's idea, but he seemed preoccupied. Yes, I was pretty certain the driver was miffed about something. He kept staring intently ahead, and then he would start turning his head one side-to-the-other and leaning over like he was looking out each truck-door window. Then the driver started shaking his head back and forth, back, and forth. I was getting nervous, so I decided to speak first.

"Sir," I asked politely, "I think my dog needs to go to the bathroom. Could we stop soon?" I studied the driver's face carefully to watch for his reaction.

"Aright," he replied, "but make it short. I'm real worried about that other driver and your sister's safety." He continued his surveying of the area and then took the first exit that came up and headed toward a small gas-station.

I was confused and asked of him, "What do you mean you're worried? What's wrong?"

The driver just muffled his voice while shaking his head, "Hurry up with your dog. We gotta get going and fast. It's probably already way too late."

When the truck ground to a full stop at a country gas-station and local market, I leaped outside with Duffy and ran to the outside latrine available for patrons. I was so nervous by now I could barely pee, but I hurried like I was told, and I let Duffy go does his business too. In a brief time, we were both climbing back up into the rig, and I rushed my question again, "What's wrong with the other driver, and what's not safe for my sister?"

My driver ground the gears, flicked some switches, and we were rolling again. He was shaking his head again then pronounced matter-of-factly, "That other driver is real bad business. Your sister is probably already dead. I've been looking all over to see any signs of blood or a body. That driver has probably already done her in and gotten rid of the body. It's looking real bad so far."

Naturally, I was terrified by his words. I began stammering and fighting back tears, "Why would he do such a thing? He looked like a nice person. My sister hasn't ever hurt anybody, but she can take care of herself. Why?"

Hours passed, and miles and miles flew by beneath us as I strained my eyes ever so hard staring ahead. My eyes began aching as well as welling-up with tears. I just didn't understand what was happening. The more I thought, the more afraid I was getting, so I just curled-up in my seat holding tightly onto Duffy and rode silently as the miles passed. The driver continued his fearful lurking, twisting, and jerking of his head back-and-forth. It looked like he was talking to himself a lot while shaking his head over and over.

From time-to-time, I could barely make out his almost whispered words as he continued speaking almost unintelligibly to himself. Finally, he spoke loudly enough for me to grasp his comments, "Oh, my God!" he almost whispered, "He's gone and done it again! She's a goner! A goner! Oh, no. OMG, oh, no! Oh, no!" he went on.

By this time, I was all but beside myself. The tears had started flowing, and I just held onto Duffy with all my might. Staring profusely ahead into the evening's coming dusk, and thinking rapid thoughts of what to do, what to do, "When we stop, do I jump and run? Can I trust anybody? If Jean is dead, killed, am I next? Oh, God, what should I do?"

The driver spoke again almost roughly and certainly unsympathetically, "We're coming into Redding in a little while, but we might as well just keep on going north. There's no need to stop now. Now that it's probably all too late, anyway."

Through my tears, though, I collected my thoughts and remembered Jean's and my absolute deal, "No, Sir, I have to go to the library in Redding. That was the deal." Tears of fear were flooding my cheeks, but I almost begged, "You've gotta take me there, to the library. You've got to!"

Again, the driver kept shaking his head and almost whining, "Oh, no, really we shouldn't stop. It's too late. Your sister's gone. It's over. It's over. Let's just keep going."

I'm gushing tears by now, but I was crying out loud, "No! You've got to go to the library! You promised. I've got to go there. Please?"

The driver shrugged his shoulders, and spouted with a definite sadness and almost apology, "Young lady, if that's what you want, okay then, I will. But I'm real sorry 'bout your sister. It's really too bad. Very sad. That guy is a bad, bad man. Terrible. Just terrible!"

With my face plastered against the door glass, I can remember peering into the slowly arriving darkness and straining to make out our location and any recognizable face, Jean's face, her driver's face, someone somewhere, anywhere. I was praying with all my might, "Please, God, please let me find Jean. Please don't let anything bad happen to her." Even Duffy was sensing something was not right. He kept trying to stand-up and was whining trying to figure-out what was happening. Even dogs get confused and fearful.

Surprisingly, my truck driver did what he had originally promised, and within a few minutes, though it seemed like hours at the time, I saw a building with a flag pole on it and another truck parked nearby. I recognized it immediately. It was Jean's truck! My driver had barely pulled-over to park when I jerked the door handle open and leapt outside with my luggage and Duffy practically mauling me as we bailed-out.

I had my suitcase with me which I nearly flung alongside me as I raced toward the entranceway. My head turned sideways to sideways, probably just like my driver was doing earlier, and my eyes were squinting to make out any shapes in the deepening dusk to notice anything. Fear, anxiety, and stress were swelling-up inside me like a volcano about to erupt, and I was feeling like I might vomit at any moment. I was truly scared.

Suddenly, from somewhere near the library building came a gruff voice, "Well, you finally made it! It's about time!"

It was Jean! Relief overwhelmed me, and I burst into full-fledged tears crying gratefully as I ran toward her ever-so welcomed voice. In a moment, I saw Jean standing there by a tree next to the driver of her truck ride. I didn't know what to think, but I bellowed out in belief, yet disbelief, "Oh, Sister, thank God you're alright. I was so afraid."

"What are you talking about?" Jean muttered, "Of course I'm alright," she continued, "I was beginning to worry about you!"

In no time at all, I relayed the whole story to Jean and her driver of the episode that had gone on with my truck and its driver. I explained completely about his behavior, all his antics and every comment I could recall. The words and story flooded from my mouth just as tears had poured from my eyes earlier. I was still almost shaking from the mixture of anxiety and relief.

Hearing every word, Jean had a very stern look on her face as she squared-off with her driver, "What's going on, anyway? What kinda crap was that for him to be saying to my kid sister?"

Jean's driver looked mortified. He seemed as shocked, confused and then frustrated as Jean, but he was quick to follow-up, "I don't know why. It was really dirty of him, and the fact is that he scared your sister over something bad that I was supposed to have done. There's nothing funny about that, and I don't like it at all. I'll be telling the company about this, you can bet on it. That guy is bad news. He don't deserve to be driving the highways. He gives us others a bad name."

Jean's driver seemed apologetic as could be. Jean thanked him with a curt, "Okay," and grabbed my arm pulling me along with her and away from the trucks. She looked over at the truck I had been in and mouthed some pretty nasty words at the driver who was pretending to be cleaning and checking his truck cab. We kept walking until Jean found a reasonably secluded place where we could sleep until morning. Once we were settled down for the night, Jean just shook her head, and said matter-of-factly, "That's it! No more separate trucks. We stick together all the way from now on. Enough of all their bullshit!"

The next morning, we got our belongings together and found a small market where Jean bought some basic food items for us to eat. I was with Jean again, so I felt safe, relieved, and even a little happy. The rolls and fruit and milk we shared tasted just delicious. Jean did mutter a few remarks suggesting that those two drivers were probably in cahoots with each other and were probably laughing together at their great joke terrifying a young girl.

I remember her spewing something like, "If one of 'em had tried to scare me like that, I would have terrorized him right back and threatened to kill him if he didn't find you safe somewhere. Boy, the nerve of those guys!"

That was my sister Jean's style. She didn't take any lip from anybody and especially from men. It probably had a lot to do with her upbringing. She had had a tough time with our dad, and they butted heads all the time. Jean lost battles over and over again until Bo and then she were finally kicked out. I think that was when she had finally won.

Anyway, the good news was that soon, thereafter, we were standing on the outskirts of Redding next to the roadside again with our thumbs-out. Finally, after a while, a nice couple in a decent pick-up truck stopped for us and gave us a ride all the way to Portland, Oregon where they lived. When we finally arrived in at their turn-off point, they stopped at a convenient place to let us off and where we could fairly easily continue on our way. After we had climbed-out with our belongings and Duffy and prepared to say our thanks and goodbyes, we could see the couple speaking to each other in the truck cab for another moment or so. Then both doors opened almost simultaneously, and the nice couple together asked us if we would like a ride through town and over the bridge to Vancouver, Washington.

We just grinned widely, thanked them immensely and jumped right back into the truck's bed before they could even change their minds. It reconfirmed to us, however, that there really were lots of very nice people around too. A few rotten ones didn't spoil the whole barrel of apples, after all. We had learned to just look more closely for good ones in the future like that nice couple.

So, I believe that all-in-all we did have pretty good luck in our travels with hitchhiking. There had been a few rough roads behind us, and there would still be some tough ones ahead, but most of our traveling times had actually been pretty decent and memorable. Besides, lots of folks hitched in those days too. It was understood and expected. And sure, we had to wait long periods sometimes while waiting for a ride. Sometimes, we even had lousy weather too, like rain and cold, while we were hitching. And, of course, we walked a lot. I mean a lot!

I remember times and places where we practically had to walk through whole towns to get to where we needed to be to hitchhike again. We had to walk from drop-off points to places to eat or sleep for the night many times and then back again to try and catch another ride. But we always got to where we were going, and we always stayed together. Now, we were finally in Vancouver, Washington to start the next chapter of our adventures. It was going to be okay, though. We both knew it, or at least hoped so, anyway.

DIFFERENCE A YEAR MAKES

Vancouver, Washington
Kaiser Vancouver Shipbuilding

We had made it! Cleveland, Ohio to Pascagoula, Mississippi to Vancouver, Washington, and we were finally at our destination. Both Portland, Oregon, directly across the Columbia River, and Vancouver were really thriving. Booming industries were going on along the riverbanks, and our destination of Kaiser Vancouver Shipyards was no exception. It was a huge, ship-building operation and its territory covered an enormous part of the riverside.

The ship-building industry, itself, was booming, and women were fairly readily accepted into the workplace by that time. It was the war period of late May 1943, and every construction aspect in the country which supported war cause efforts were in full swing. Almost anybody, including any hearty and aspiring women, who wanted a job could get one. I began thinking that finding work in Vancouver with Kaiser, or wherever, did not seem that difficult a task. I was approaching seventeen-years of age. There would have to be something that I could do. Piece-of-cake!

Then Jean and I had talked things over. We weren't going to get far without me working. One income supporting two people and a dog was not going to get us very far at all, even if the wages were that much better. Remember costs? Same thing there. Higher wages, but prices of everything were higher too.

It was pretty much a certainty. I was going to have to find some work. Jean had been hired right-on-the-spot after she showed her welding certifications from her Pascagoula Shipyards earlier job. That was a really good thing, but we knew even with her higher pay, we would barely scratch the surface for getting ahead. Finding work, however, might be difficult because I was still only sixteen years old. It was already mid-May, and my next birthday was close-at-hand. Jean considered things, and then naturally, my big, older, and smarter sister came-up with a plan.

Jean took my identity papers and changed, or forged, the dates on them by changing my birthdate to one year earlier, 1925. I remember teasing her about how she had really missed-out on her true-calling. Instead of a dirty, grimy, burned-up welder, she could have been a clean, slick, fancy-pants professional forger. After Jean's slick work, my new I.D. showed that I was closely approaching a birthday and *eighteen* years of age. According to my I.D, I was almost of legal age. That was the first part of Jean's *plan of action*.

Her next step was having me take my *new* I.D. and go to the on-sight, Kaiser Vancouver arc-welding school and apply for admission. Jean had me remove all my make-up and tussle my hair a little to give me a tougher appearance... like her, I supposed. Then, I had to roughen-up my attire to look like I could even do the potential job. Jean told me to stop smiling and try to look like I was older, wiser, and tougher. That was harder for me. I had gone through some experiences before at the service station but looking *older and tougher* was Jean's domain.

Of course, it must have helped me that Jean was already on-the-job. She surely even looked the part of a crusty ol' welder because of her rough and tough exterior appearance. Like I mentioned, they had snatched her up right away. Thus, as far as my welding-school admission experience was concerned, it turned-out not to be too difficult after all. Although I was actually only nearing seventeen-years old, the school clerks readily accepted my forged documents believing I was just a few days short of being eighteen-years. Obviously, in those almost frantic times, they must not have looked too closely, or dug too deeply or cared too much about my welding school enrollment application.

And just like that, right after that somewhat speedy application process, the arc-welding school accepted my application, and I was in. The program was apparently pretty desperate for welders, it seemed to me. My joke at the time was that: "It was a terrible sign for the war cause. We must be losing real bad because now the companies would just about hire anybody to get a job done!"

The shipyard was readily hiring even young women (girls), without much issue, to do all sorts of jobs involving physical labor. For any women that willingly chose to go into arc-welding school, Kaiser management personnel were grateful and encouraging. The school authorities took me right in, trained me in lickety-split time, and it seemed like almost right-away, I was prepared for my new vocation.

"FLASH" LEARNER

Of course, now I get to brag a little because looking back, that welding school seemed easy for me. Maybe I was even a natural, now that I think about it, but I picked-up their hands-on instruction right away. I was a quick study too because I learned all about different metals we might come across and which type of welding rod to use for certain jobs. They showed me how to grind-up and prepare metals to be tack-welded together and then how to weld-up nice beads.

I believe that I may have even become too sure of myself. I was just barely into the welding-school classes, and it was already my birthday. They all figured it was my eighteenth, but only Jean and I knew better. Anyway, I was doing a practice weld on a flat piece of steel and thinking ahead of myself and giggling over my *birthday* secret when I made a mistake.

Welders must always detach or remove their welding rod from the molten, metal puddle they are working-on before lifting their helmet to look around. I did not. My mind was happily daydreaming away on *birthday girl* thoughts while I was applying a weld. Apparently, I got distracted and just absent-mindedly flipped-up my helmet and eye-protecting lens to stretch or look around and *ZAP*! I got what is called in the welding trade as a *flash*.

A *flash burn* happens when your eyes are exposed to seriously bright ultraviolet (UV) light. Welders using their welding torches and welding rod attached are the most common source of these *flashes*. In the trade, they are referred to as *welder's flash* and *arc eye*. Flashes are just like sunburns of the eyes. They can be very painful for a period of time. Fortunately, our eyes are very quick healers, but even still, flashes are meant to avoid at all costs. Anyway, I had a short-day for that lesson, and I learned a very valuable lesson for my new craft: "Watch out for your eyes!" Happy Birthday to me!

I learned as much as I could and soon became fairly proficient at all angles of welding: Flat welds, vertical welds, overhead welds, and diagonal welds. I think they must have speeded- up my training too, because I was finished with training, graduated, and given my welding certifications pretty darn soon after starting, it seemed. Like I said before, I think I was just a real natural. Right away, I was congratulated and rewarded with my first, professional-welder assignment.

TEAM TERRIFIC

Our new bosses already must have known a little of Jean's and my background. They knew we had traveled all the way to Vancouver from Pascagoula, Mississippi looking for work. I think they even admired us a little. But still being aware of my youthfulness, they chose to team me up with my sister Jean for our first work together. Also, since most of the welding teams were manned by three welder teams, they got another new hire to join-in with us. We had become one of the many three-man teams assigned various tasks. Our unique difference was that ours was a *one man/two-women team*.

That new worksite at Kaiser Vancouver Shipyards was the actual place where Jean, our newly made friend and teammate, Thomas, who was also a new hire, and I cut our proverbial, welding-team performance-teeth as highly desired and valuable arc-welders for Kaiser Vancouver's shipbuilding, war-cause. We three worked as a team on double-bottomed, baby (mini)-carrier ships, and each of us had our specialty. When our team was assigned to any specific-welding tasks, we quickly organized the jobs: Thomas did all the flat-plate welding, I did all the vertical-welding and Jean did all the overhead-welding.

Our system and teamwork worked like a charm too. We were quick and efficient. We never got mad at each other over jobs or work. We always helped each other as best we could. It helped too that all three of us worked hard and fast and never wanted to fall behind the other two on a job. Over the next several months, our team earned a variety of verbal accolades and awards for our proficiency and achievement. It became obvious to everyone that we were good at our jobs, and we sure could produce.

There really is something to be said about teamwork. When each member knows the style and ways of their teammates, then it's less work and more like an activity, an association. It becomes second-nature to you to notice something that a teammate needs or is going to need. So, you automatically do what you can to assist without even breaking a sweat.

Just one example out of so many could be seeing that a teammate is going to run out of welding electrodes (welding rods) sooner than expected. Without any inconvenience, you just slip some of yours over to their pouch or can and then keep right-on going with your own task. So easy to make the whole job easier. It's the small things that count.

When it's truly teamwork, time passes so much faster too. The welding begins to flow ever-so-smoother, and you can just glide right on through a task or a day's work. Conversation is even more comfortable. The breaks and lunchtime become real relaxation, and you feel very contented being around *team mates*. When you become closer on a job by working with another day-after-day, you get to know the other team members and share with their successes and happiness and grieve over their losses and despair.

That was how it was with our team. Jean and I knew all about each other, of course, but as time passed, we both became closer to Thomas. We appreciated his skill and effort on the job and how he always carried-his-weight on our team. Thomas didn't just *carry* his weight; he *cared*. That made a big difference for the success of our team. We all cared. We cared about the quality of our work, our *craftsmanship*, and we cared about each other.

We learned a lot about Thomas on that job working for Kaiser Vancouver Shipbuilding. We learned about him as a worker and a man. We learned about Thomas as an individual and as a family-man. On-the-other-hand, Thomas learned a lot about Jean and me. He learned about our skill and abilities on the job as his teammates, as persons and as sisters, at that. He also learned about our pasts, our fears and anxieties, our dreams, and our plans. Come to think of it, we told Thomas just about everything about our plans to get our siblings all together again one day, and soon. He supported us completely.

One topic, however, that never came-up much during our conversations was ever mentioning our dad. Jean always cut that subject off very abruptly with a nasty tone. Thomas picked-up right away on that point, and as a true gentleman, he never pursued the issue. For me, I had still not gotten-over all my previous family abandonments, dismissals, and non-acceptance, so I was always willing to discuss our dad, or his aberrant behavior and cruel ways. I was still struggling inside for explanations or understanding. Regardless, Jean never wanted to talk about our dad or even hear his name mentioned, so that subject was always off-limits.

LITTLE ORPHANS

Unfortunately, also, wartime did not displace our family fears. It would not leave us and our families alone. Through mail services and occasional phone calls with Sis Mary, Jean and I continued to be appraised of difficulties back home with our dad and Edith and our youngest siblings. Times were hard for them all.

In fact, there was plenty of news all around. Sis Mary was happy, stable, and doing very well in her industrial plant secretarial position. We even heard that she had a special boyfriend already and was going steady with him. Brother Bo had completed his initial, military training in Pensacola, Florida and had been transferred to his first overseas base for further training and, ultimately, specified bombing missions over Italy and beyond.

It had always been the youngest ones which worried Jean and me the most. We were older, had already been out on our own and had learned how to take care of ourselves. Our youngest siblings, however, had been completely in the hands of Edith's care with complete dependency on our dad's support. It was not that I doubted Edith's care and attention, perhaps even love, for the youngest ones, especially Jackie-Boy and Jann. However, both Jean and I doubted seriously our dad's worthiness to continue supporting care for his family. He was not very dependable.

Jean and I worried about our young siblings' future with Edith and our dad. Wartime was difficult, and many families were struggling everywhere. Jean and I both agreed that we were going to have to plan and do something soon to help our younger sisters and brother. Colleen was thirteen-years old, Jann was eleven and Jackie-boy was nine by then. They were still too young to have to travel far-and-wide with their older sisters. We needed to be set up somewhere and then send for them all or go get them. Those issues, plus the fact that all three were enrolled in elementary school, made their care somewhat difficult to manage.

They were all totally dependent on others for their care. However, it was still our goal to have all of us McCord brothers and sisters living together and caring for one another. But with a constant barrage of new insight and reality-checks, we were beginning to understand the many difficulties of that occurring immediately. It would likely take several steps, or stages, to ultimately make that happen.

Colleen was the most advanced of the three younger ones, of course. She had already been working outside the house and on her own earning support-income for Edith. She was becoming fairly savvy of street life and its hardships, and she was maturing. In fact, we had already heard through mail and phone contacts with Sis Mary that Colleen was like a thirteen-year old going-on-thirty. We could assume that she was ready for a move very soon. In fact, she and Sis had been in regular contact, not just through special mail packages and letters, but with phone calls trying to arrange transportation for Colleen to go to Cleveland and live with her beloved sister, Sis Mary.

To begin our plan-of-action, then, we started with our first steps which almost always inevitably depended upon fiscal aspects. Sis Mary could not provide complete care for both she and Colleen plus any school expenses for Colleen in Cleveland. Therefore, Jean and I took funds from our savings and wired money to Sis in order to prepare for Colleen's arrival as soon as we got the details worked out with Edith. We used a Western Union Telephone and Telegraph Service right there in Vancouver, WA to wire funds to another office in Cleveland for Sis to receive and pick-up. We then arranged to continue wiring funds to Sis on a monthly basis as long as necessary to help contribute to Colleen's welfare once she arrived.

We already knew that Edith and our dad, of course, were both very partial to the littlest ones, Jackie-boy, and Jann. And our miserable dad was vastly closer to Jackie than any of the females in our family. Jackie was youngest, adored his mom and dad and was the epitome of health and vigor. After years of punishing his other son, Bo, for being so frail, malnourished, unhealthy, and rebellious as a young boy growing-up, our dad adored young Jackie-Boy.

He lauded all his attention and devotion toward his youngest, strong, healthiest, and supportive son. Jean and I knew that Jackie-Boy was going to be a really difficult case to manage because we understood those conflicts instigated with our dad over Jackie's potential departure. Once we resolved matters for our younger sisters, we would then have to reassess our actions concerning Jackie-Boy's rescue.

However, the time was coming to make our next move, so Jean and I prepared. It would involve a trip to Sioux Falls to deal with Edith and, hopefully, not our dad. We had already heard stories from Sis and our aunts that Edith had for quite a while been in very difficult times. She had all but been abandoned by our dad. Apparently, he had been forced, or not, to travel all the way up to Alaska in search of work. He was going to be gone indefinitely on a long-term, long-distance job. Edith had been very stressed-out trying to keep herself and the kids fed and cared for. We heard that she had really been struggling.

We called Edith in Sioux Falls, SD from Vancouver, WA to arrange for Colleen to go and stay with Sis in Cleveland. We figured that she would not put-up much dispute because of the financial hardship she was already facing tying to care for all three of the younger kids. Our phone call to Edith came so that all the rumors and gossip would be laid to rest once-and-for-all. We sure ended up getting the straight facts from Edith right there and then too.

Edith was extremely distraught in giving us her latest updates. It seemed that our dad had gone-off and left her all alone with the three remaining children. Edith said that she waited and waited for support money to arrive that would assist her with all her expenses such as rent money, food expenses for four mouths, utility costs, and personal effects funds. There had been some form of brief message from an Alaskan hospital stating that our dad had become ill and was trying to recover. Other than that, no additional news. Nothing from our dad ever arrived. No money, no phone calls, no contact at all, and furthermore, not even a decent word or explanation for his continued delays, or dalliances or inconsideration's.

Edith told us that she had become desperate to a point of extremities. She said further that she could just barely take care of herself through her friends and meager church assistance. She had been so devoted and supportive of the church before that the priests and nuns had stepped-forward to help her with minimal loving expenses such as aid with her deeply overdue, home-rental fees and modest living expenses. That minimal assistance could not continue indefinitely.

Edith continued to explain to us that after she truly had nowhere else to turn, she had finally been forced to deposit the children, all three of them, with the priests at the Catholic Church she attended. Arrangements had then been made, and Colleen, Jann and Jackie-Boy had been taken to the Sioux Falls St. Joseph's Children's Orphanage right there in Sioux Falls, South Dakota.

Another brief message had arrived for Edith, after the children were with the orphanage, which had shed more light upon our dad's circumstances. The message stated that our father had gone to Alaska in search of work and had come down with a very serious illness up there. Those were his conditions without any mention of ways or means for Edith to survive.

With no income sent home for Edith's support, and after literally months of struggling to survive, our stepmother could no longer afford care for the youngest children. Edith was practically helpless. She had all but been abandoned by our father. Due to our understandings, we actually never held any grudge against Edith. We all knew how tough times were, and we knew our father. Wherever he was, he was probably doing just fine, but his family members just had to make it on their own.

The agreed that the orphanage was probably Edith's last resort. After all, she had taken a liking to the youngest children never having had any of her own. In retrospect, it probably hurt her to leave the kids with the church. St. Joseph's Orphanage was a place that she could trust, though. It was also close-by being in the same city as she.

She probably trusted the priests and nuns there too because she was a very strict, church-attending Catholic, herself. She had earned respect and gone through all the local, typical rites-of-passage from the church. Edith was a good church member too, so the orphanage nuns had to accept her circumstances and do what they must in order to help her. The good sisters had obligingly accepted our younger sisters, Colleen and Jann, and our youngest brother, Jack. It was very considerate of them.

However, an orphanage was absolutely unacceptable to Jean and me. We wanted all us kids secure, loved and together. It was Jean's own, big plan, but she wanted us to work and save-up to buy some farm in Oregon or Washington. All of us McCord kids living together on that imagined farm would make us all happy, Jean had promised. So, Jean and I talked and decided that we had to go back home and rescue our sisters and brother. The next workday, we both went into Kaiser Vancouver's Main Office and applied for leave. We both received two-weeks each of *Family-Emergency Leave* to go back home to Sioux Falls, South Dakota.

Unfortunately, even with higher wages and me working too, our earnings were still sparse, and money was still scarce. Jean paid all our bills and kept most of our remaining earnings for our *future farm* savings account; however, shelling-out hard-earned cash for busses or trains was way too expensive to her. Besides, Jean observed, it was beautiful hitchhiking weather. We were both well-seasoned, so we would be traveling the inexpensive way again.

Fortunately, we had our workmate, teammate and friend, Thomas, to assist us with our plans. He quickly agreed to watch Duffy for us until our return in two weeks. I think Thomas appreciated the work we did with him which brought positive attention for his efforts too. He definitely was a key-member of our three-person team, so our notoriety reflected very well on him. It meant that he had a secure and comfortable workplace to continue working.

With our jobs and Duffy's care issues resolved, once again we stuck out our thumbs. This time we hitch-hiked back across the upper-northern and mid-states to South Dakota. We were both focused and certain of our goal: We were going back to rescue our brother and sisters. Of course, beyond that, our plans were sort of fuzzy. We were consoled, however, by the fact that what we were doing on that special trip was for our family's good, and we (Jean and I) were doing it together.

Our journey Sioux Falls went very quickly and smoothly. We were both pretty savvy hitchers by then, but we still paid attention to who and what was going on. With no Duffy along to potentially deter drivers from picking us up, our hitching tasks were mollified somewhat. Plus, we had learned the best places to look for good rides like truck-stops and cafes along the Interstate. We got to be pretty good at finding rides very quickly. A few times, we even refused rides if they seemed too suspicious or were not going far enough to help us much. Imagine that! We were so good, we even turned-down some rides in order to get better ones. We called ourselves the: *Picky-Picky* Hitch-Hikin' Sisters. Piece-of-cake!

KINNAPPING

It helped a lot too that a main route, Interstate 84, was used a lot by trucks and car travelers leaving the Vancouver-Portland area in Oregon and following along the Columbia River east across all of Oregon. So, we took that way to get us started, and we just kept on hailing rides right on through Oregon, Washington again, Idaho, Montana, Wyoming, and on into South Dakota until we were there near our onetime home. Once near our parents' home, it was obvious that we were not going to drop-in suddenly and say, "Hi!' to Edith, for that matter.

Plus, God forbid, what if by some twist of bad luck, our dad had actually come back home by then from his lengthy absence and was there to greet us. In two seconds, he and Jean would have been fighting. It was a moot point, though. Jean would never go anywhere chancing to run into him again. Our dad was a non-entity to her anymore, yet she did not believe in *tempting the devil,* so to speak. I realized that we all would be better-off if they were left alone and in the dark. Our plans were our business and none of theirs. We went straight toward the orphanage with no detours.

Being from Sioux Falls, we knew exactly where the orphanage was located. While living in town, we had often passed-by its huge, tall, wide, strong, and sad-looking, iron-gate with its concrete walls surrounding dull, concrete buildings inside. It was like a strong, solitary, and resolute military fortress. I used to wonder if the giant gate and walls were to keep people out or keep its inhabitants inside. To me, it sure seemed protected from the outside world. You might imagine that after we easily found the orphanage, we were somewhat surprised to find its enormous, steel gate unlocked. We walked right on through an open gateway without any issue or any announcement.

Once arrived inside, however, Jean spoke to one of the sisters and got directions to the head-office. We went inside, and within just a few moments, we were questioned for our business. After offering a brief explanation for our visit, Jean, and I both discovered immediately that our previously somewhat contrived plans were going to require some swift and new changes. First off, we were informed that only our baby brother, Jack and youngest sister, Jann, were still present. Our younger sister, Colleen, had already previously left the orphanage about three-weeks earlier and had gone to be with Mary in Cleveland.

That was quick. We had not been prepared for that news, but it was a bit of relief once we got over the surprise. The orphanage sisters had apparently received a letter from our Sis Mary asking the kind sisters to allow Colleen to join her in Cleveland as soon as possible. Sis had convinced the sisters that she would get Colleen back into school and take good care of her. Obviously, it had sounded agreeable to the orphanage sisters to do so sooner, rather-than-later, because they had already heard from Edith giving her approval. The St. Joseph's Catholic Diocese Orphanage had therefore accepted Sis's offer. Probably, it meant for the orphanage that it was one less person for those sisters to feed and to be responsible for, and their new arrangement with Sis still provided safety and security for Colleen.

However, we knew Sis Mary very well. Jean and I quickly talked between ourselves and surmised the same answer: Sis Mary was two-steps ahead of our plan all along. She had already made plans and arrangements with those necessary parties to help Colleen with her departure from the orphanage. Right away, Jean was concerned about Sis giving-up her official address in Cleveland.

When we approached Sis about it later, she bragged, "Of course not! The orphanage sisters have an incorrect address for me. As a matter of fact, I had arranged to pick Colleen up from the train station, so that's the address they have!"

Sis Mary was on-the-ball, alright. Two steps ahead. Obvious to us right away, Sis must have instructed Colleen to sit tight and that she would contact the St. Joseph's Orphanage sisters and ask for permission for Colleen to leave. To make things easier, by that time, the St Joseph's Orphanage Sisters had already heard from Edith who had given her permission and support. Mary then sent money to the orphanage for Colleen to buy train tickets.

Once transportation funds had arrived from Sis Mary, the orphanage sisters had allowed and assisted Colleen with purchasing train tickets from St. Paul to Cleveland. Sis was very professional in her speaking skills. She had certainly persuaded the orphanage sisters to allow Colleen to leave even sooner than we had expected. That action had made it a little easier for Jean and me to devise a new plan, but there were still other complications.

That was all well and good regarding Colleen. It actually put us ahead of schedule or simplified our plans. But it wasn't over, not by a long shot. It was going to be virtually impossible to get permission from either Edith or especially the sisters at the orphanage to release either or both Jann and Jackie. Both of them were still too young to travel unguarded. We knew that in a pinch, Jann was old enough and big enough to keep-up with us just in case we had to make a run for it. That was not the same case for Jackie-Boy.

Unfortunately, we recognized that little brother Jack was still too young to travel on-the-road with us at all. Besides, at only nine-years old, Jean and I both felt that a small child would really have drawn a lot of attention toward us while traveling. We would have been easy to spot in any crowd. Furthermore, as I mentioned earlier, our dad would never have heard of it. If we had dared to take Jackie with us, even from the orphanage, and therefore from him, he would have called-out all the cops in the world to go after us. He would have demanded in his pounding, authoritative voice that the police, FBI, and the National Guard all search over hell-and-highwater to find and retrieve his boy, and then he would have wanted us, his throw-away daughters, jailed for life.

Therefore, Jean and I understood fairly early on that we needed to leave Jack with the orphanage. When we finally got a chance to visit with him, we assured Jackie that our father and Edith would soon pick him up, though. He was so excited to see us that, naturally, he cried to see us leave, but we made him feel better telling him that our dad would be there right away to get him. With only little Jack to care for, we figured that our father would very likely, and gratefully, pick-up his beloved Jackie-Boy.

Also, by the time we had actually finally arrived in Sioux Falls, wouldn't you guess our surprise. We had quickly learned from the sisters at the orphanage that our father, Mr. Roy McCord, had in fact, returned from Alaska. We were also told, however, that he was still in poor health and could not afford care for his children. As long as Jann and Jack were being cared for at the orphanage, there was no sense rocking-the-boat, our father had decided.

With that news, we figured that having Colleen already gone, and then Jann out of the picture, there would only be Jack to care for under those new circumstances. Jackie-Boy would be a small bother to our dad, and he would probably be glad to have him returned without his sisters. Our brother would likely get picked-up by him soon after we were gone with Jann. Also, Edith would be happy to care for him. After all, she had raised him since he was one-year old, so Jackie was practically her own child. Lil' Jack would be okay.

That left Jean and me to plot youngest sister Jann's escape. We would have to lie to the orphanage sisters. Having been raised as staunch Catholics, and especially by our very strict and conventional, Catholic stepmother, Edith, you might think that lying would be difficult for us. Plus, it involved lying to those orphanage sisters to boot. As it turned out, that was hardly the case and never even an issue. In fact, we turned out to be pretty darned good at it.

By then, we were experienced at telling little mistruths, so actually a little lying came fairly easy for us. Lying about my age for a starter was actually a good start. Of course, everyone we practically ever ran into on-the-road would always hear about how we had been nearly starved from sheer deprivation and destitution. That *fat little fib* trick often got us an occasional free meal or snacks. Occasionally, it even got us some better rates for overnight motel rooms when needed. I would pull-out my empty pockets exposing them suggesting no cash, and then Jean would pay the bill for any discounted rate we received. Of course, Jean always carried most of the money.

Anyway, circumstances had now changed. That next time around required a quick-fix adjustment to our earlier-held plans. Since we were agreed to leave Jack, we would go about our plan for snatching and sneaking away with Jann with a little more sensitivity toward the orphanage sisters. As a full-fledged, twenty-one-year-old adult between us, Jean was almost always our spokesperson. As she faced the orphanage sisters and began speaking, I stood next to Jean with wide, almost tearing eyes yet promoted a pouting yet hopeful impression with my face.

Almost apologetically, Jean began requesting permission for she and I to take our youngest sister, Jann, out for a walk and family visit. We both admitted truthfully how badly we felt that our loving family-life had been so cruelly disrupted by the violent, life-changing war's conditions. We further explained that it might be a long time before we could see our sweet, little baby-sister, Jann, again.

We were so saddened, Jean explained, that we had already hitchhiked and traveled over fifteen-hundred miles in order to visit our siblings. Now, she continued, we were not even going to see our younger sister Colleen. She was gone, and only God knew how long it might be before we would ever see her again. Woe was us! Colleen had vanished to Cleveland somewhere and might be separated from us forever.

Then came the punchline when Jean pleaded, "After we visit with Little Jack, please allow us the courtesy of walking and visiting with our youngest of all sisters, little Jann. We need to share some private, sisterly advice."

In our minds, what we were attempting to do was not a crime, either. We weren't *kidnapping* anyone. We were *borrowing our sister* and then not returning her, that's all. It was *kinnapping* We put on our best act to persuade the orphanage sisters to allow Jann to visit with us off- grounds. We begged the sisters by explaining how we needed some quiet, private, and secluded time to say our good-byes to our *surviving* baby-sister, Jann. Of course, when I refer to "we," I mean that Jean did the talking and explaining, and I just stood-by next to her with a strained face pleading with agreement while nodding my head profusely.

Of course, the kind sisters believed our story. Of course, they did! It's in their nature to *believe*. They all looked upon us with complete understanding. Their emphatic agreement was obvious from their own synchronized nod-for-nods with my own head-bobbing frenzy. All the sisters held sympathetic smiles, as well they should. The sisters believed us, and we were sort of pretty good liars by nature too.

Besides, we McCord sisters had already had years of prior experience dealing with Catholic school sisters. They had been our teachers at the elementary and high schools we attended. There had been unauthorized and secret practice among student-populations to learn practical ways to survive amongst the nuns by fibbing, overexaggerating and when downright necessary, outright lying.

Little, white lies were foundational training at Catholic schools. Students learned how to appear like angels while in classrooms but play like devils outside of schools. It was paramount to last-man-standing survival practices. While interacting with sisters and nuns on school grounds and in classrooms, we learned how to barely survive or merely exist. However, when it came to the streets, we learned how to live and relish in it!

Anyway, once Mother Superior or Sister-in-Charge agreed to our plea by granting us an off-campus social-call, our plan went into full-blown effect. We three, pitiful, white-lying, and semi-sinning sisters calmly locked arms and casually moved down the entranceway drive toward the huge, fateful steel gate. Getting past that *great barrier* meant everything to us. It epitomized to us our goal reached, our escape zone's targeted bullseye and our quasi-race's end to our imagined finish-line.

We sensed that once we could waltz past that enormous, orphanage-inmate's *Guardian Gate*, we were likely to be home free. Outwardly, we appeared somewhat serious and morose; inside, however, we were all quietly giggling while our hearts pounded-out extra-anxious and rising palpitations. Regardless, both simultaneously reverent and tactful, we three *wander lusters* held our breaths while tip-toing right on out that foreboding and custodial entry-gate.

Once outside, all three of us simultaneously exhaled forcefully and started emphatically grinning together like a trio of Cheshire cats. After we had determined that we were finally out-of-sight of the sisters, we turned swiftly toward town and began running like hell.

Our own form of immediate religious affirmations were quickly cast-off, "Sorry, Sisters, but we're outa here!"

We blood-sisters were back together, and that was all that mattered to us at that time. We knew that we still had a reasonable amount of time to cover our deception before the orphanage personnel got suspicious and finally, started blasting on their revengeful horn of warning and castigation. Calling our dad, the family patriarch, would probably be the first outside contact.

Then both of them, Mother Superior, or Father Whoever, and our dad, would most likely be calling all cops, "Be on the lookout! Be on the lookout! Two desperados and a small child could be anywhere. Find them, arrest them and then return them for penance and punishment!"

We knew the sisters would calm down in time. In fact, in time, and in my own somewhat juvenile mind, I believed that one day, perhaps, we might make-up for our little ruse against those sisters and explain our circumstances fully and apologize. On that intensely sneaky and still *danger-zone* day, however, I recall that we were all pretty certain that we would likely never return there again.

Even with our little *ruse*, though, we knew that we had to make haste. We were sure that once the sisters realized how we had so cunningly and mischievously bamboozled them, at least Mother Superior would be furious. Her frustrated wrath might be tireless and unforgiving. We were also sure that absolutely and most certainly our stepmother and dad would be contacted by the angry nuns and advised of our ill-will and trickery.

Once the orphanage sisters informed Mr. McCord that our so-called visit was just a ploy to cover-up a kidnapping, or forced runaway of sorts, we knew that he was going to be upset. For Jean and me, from the very beginning, to have really planned on snatching Jann right-out from underneath their very noses, then high tailing it south, or east, or west, or, or, and disappearing somewhere with Jann, we knew would surely enrage him. Plus, eventually all of the sisters and our dad, would discover that they didn't even have an address. All they had was the address of the Cleveland Train Station. Oh, that would surely have tipped-over their proverbial *boatful of forgiveness*.

Jean and I knew that there would be several different, but contributing factors, which almost certainly would have incurred our dad's rage and then eventually his vengeful wrath. Factor one would be the renewed, sheer disobedience and challenge to our dad's supreme authority by Jean, and to a certainly lesser extent, me. He simply could not tolerate nor stand for Jean's relentless defiance of his supreme command. She had been ordered out of the house for good and never to return. In fact, she had been forced-out years earlier with only the clothes on her back. To deal with Jean's own form of retribution would have practically given him a seizure.

It had always been unnerving for the rest of us family to listen to Jean and our dad arguing and fighting. Their terrible battles simultaneously shattered household objects and our nerves. Growing-up, we often heard them *having-it-out* in practically all rooms of the house and at all hours of the day or night. It seemed like they were always yelling and roaring at each other. Jean was our oldest sibling and, accordingly, seemed always to be expected to do the most and be the most responsible. As a result, she got the brunt of blame and punishment for anything that ever went wrong with any of us kids.

Believe me, with seven kids at times, there was almost always something going wrong. Nevertheless, Jean's and our dad's battles were violent and scary to watch, and ultimately ended with our big sister getting thrown out of our home. We brothers and sisters all worried for her well-being back then. Our recent action, certainly to be signified as against our dad, would not mellow his attitude. Taking Jann away was paramount to kidnapping to him. He would have her head served-up on a golden platter if it could be.

Years before Jean's ousting remember that I talked about big-brother Bo's continuous hullabaloo walloping from our father. I use the term *walloping* because Bo told me, himself, that's really what it had been. Bo took a most severe *walloping* from our pa. Well, in actuality, it had been just another beating, one more in practically a lifetime of them from our dad. However, on that particular occasion, the beating was meant to put our brother in-his-place.

You see, at that time, Bo had only recently turned fourteen. From what I understand, he may have even challenged our father over some possible theft issue with Edith. Then he had defiantly stood his ground up against our dad. He had suffered terribly for it. The age of us kids meant nothing to our dad. Man, woman, child or not, nobody ever challenged our father in his own house over anything. There really was only one-way: His way or the highway. Period.

Anyway, as a result, Bo was almost physically thrown-out the front door when he had been sent to Father Flanagan's place. Of course, having heard earlier of his dismissal, Bo had run away. Naturally, he ran away, but that had only proclaimed his guilt even more to the authorities. Of course, he was caught soon thereafter and returned home. That was when, Bo confided in me later, that he knew for sure that he was leaving. He said that he had barely managed to hang-on to an old, worn-out suitcase which he had quickly jammed full of clothes and then tightly grasped in his clenched hands. That was when the police did our parents' bidding by personally transporting Bo off to Father Flanagan's Home for disreputable and disobedient young boys. There were no goodbyes or time from any of the others either, or with his police escort to take him away, Bo never returned home again.

After the war had ended, and Bo was honorably discharged from the Army Air Corps with medals of bravery, Bo backed-off his singular anger and stress toward our dad. I believe that Bo tried even then to reach-out to our dad and receive back some recognition or apologies or warming-up to Bo. It never happened. According to our dad's accounting, though, it had been "Good riddance!" Bo had been expendable, like Jean was a year or so later and Mary after that.

Sis's case wasn't so physically brutal as Jean's and Bo's cases were, but the sheer cruelty of his actions still deserved rebuke. Sis Mary challenged his authority, and Bam! Out the door she went. It would likely have happened to me, too but I never let him get the upper hand on me like the others. I effectively managed to simply stay out of his sight whenever possible. Regardless, once the war was officially on, I was certainly next to be gone. By then, however, I had managed to mature to a point that I chose to leave on my own.

So, anyway, all of this long-winded, repetitive capsulizing of our dad's violent angry side is to emphasize how we knew he would be explosively angry at us, and especially at Jean, for defying his authority still again. I actually had a theory that our dad, being a self-taught, radio-communications expert with minimal, formal education had always been forced to be subservient at his workplace. He could never be in a supervisorial position because of his lack of education. Therefore, he always had to take orders from everyone else because everyone else was his academic superior. Perhaps, that affected his ability to stay very long on any job, and it certainly may have affected his tolerance, or lack of, when dealing with his own insubordinate children. He could give us orders, and we had to obey. Or, there was a terrible price to pay.

It's just a thought, a theory I have. Yet, that issue, perhaps combined with very real physical suffering from actual pain that he had been forced to deal with, made our dad a very angry and, therefore, unhappy human being. So, he was definitely going to be upset over Jean's and my defiance. Taking Jann against his will was intolerable. He would want us, especially Jean, to pay a *terrible price* for that act of insolence.

Another factor that would truly upset our dad to no end was any condition which shamed him. He could not stand to be embarrassed or humiliated by others. After our dad's encounter with "Creepy" Karpis, and his eventual recovery, he grew to become very angry over the ongoing pain and suffering he was forced to contend with and the affect it had on him around others. He did not ever like looking weak or injured or incapable. Oh, the shame. And any embarrassment he was ever caused to feel was equally unbearable.

When Mother Superior or Sister-in-Charge of St. Joseph's Orphanage called to complain to our dad about how we had hook-winked them, he would have become excruciatingly shamed and angry as a result. Our dad was a very proud and boastful man. To do anything that tainted his image was inexcusable. Honestly, though, his potential shame or embarrassment was not because he really cared about us. It was just his persona, his image, that he really cared about. He was very narcissistic we kids learned to understand later as adults. Regardless, we were certain at the time that, even still, our father would be furiously mad-as-hell at us sisters for having embarrassed him before the orphanage personnel.

Later-on, just as we had planned and hoped, however, all us sisters became delighted and grateful to learn of another successful part of our plan. As expected, once our dad was given the troubling news of our snatching Jann, he did, in fact, go to the orphanage and pick-up Jack. So far, it had been good. Our plan had worked out just fine.

We never did find out about the orphanage sisters and their actual reactions; however, news reports of kidnapping and police searches for us runaways did eventually reach our ears. Being still being only seventeen by that time, technically, I was still a minor and, therefore, a runaway just like Jann. All that aside, though, it was fairly safe-to-say, we assumed, that the good sisters at the orphanage had probably cursed us more than they had ever prayed for our evil and delinquent souls. Yeah, they were probably a little bit upset with us, to say the least. Can I get an "Amen" to that!

In the meantime, back to our actual *hoodwinking, kid-snatching* effort, we were not off-the-hook yet. Soon thereafter, Jean and I presumed that we would be running from the orphanage and then running from the law. It would likely not be long before police authorities would be looking for us. We had to get going somewhere and fast. Nobody could exactly figure which direction we might go when they started looking, but we knew they would start looking.

Yet, Jean and I had over a week's travel time from our jobs still remaining for us both. Since we at least had Jann with us as originally planned, were together again and we had plenty of spare time on our hands, the three of us decided (Jean decided and Jann and I nodded in agreement) to go all-the-way and hitchhike the whole rest of the distance to Cleveland, Ohio. We were going to see our other sisters Mary and now Colleen and have a mini reunion.

Then suddenly Jean delighted us with a quick decision. Time was still on our side for a short while left, so she had an excellent plan. We all caught a city bus to the overland bus station and bought three tickets to Madison, Wisconsin. From there, Jean felt like we would have the edge to do whatever we wished. So, excited and self-assured, but vigilant on our lookouts, we three sisters hit-the-road again, and after a brief, overnighter in Madison, we took our time and hitchhiked our ways clear into Cleveland, Ohio.

It might as well have been all of our individual birthdays, Christmas, New Year's, Valentine's Day, and Thanksgiving all combined at one time. We were all thrilled getting back together again, and we talked non-stop almost all night and for the next night too once Mary returned from her job. Nobody could afford to miss much work, so Mary's office-job was important to her. However, after our excited, initial meeting and all the catching-up had finally been caught-up with, our five-sister reunion there in Cleveland left us time to get serious again.

Jean's and my leave-time away from work was running-out. We needed to get back on the highway yet again and hitch rides all the way back to our home and waiting jobs in Vancouver, WA. Our valuable employment at Kaiser Vancouver Shipyard as arc-welders was still very important to us, and we were still needed by our employer. However, as Jean and I readied ourselves for the return-trip, it really came as no surprise to us that Jann might complain.

Since we had snuck Jann out of the orphanage in the first place and then traveled all the way to Cleveland with her, Jann wanted to stay with us when we left for Vancouver. Jean and I readily agreed. It was best for all. Colleen was close to Mary, but she was enough responsibility for Mary already. Jean and I could watch out for Jann, put her back in school and take good care of her.

NEW ADJUSTMENTS

Vancouver, Washington

And so, once more, we sisters-three, Jean, Jann and me, vagabond travelogue-adventurers, stuck out our thumbs again. This time, however, was for a much more substantial trip. Now we were crossing about ninety per cent of the country by hitch-hiking. Fortunately, our journey was accomplished with minimal, trouble. Jann, after all, wasn't much bigger than Duffy had been. Jean and I just took turns, when necessary, having Jann sit on our laps.

We had enough time to spare, so we didn't need to worry about making the whole trek in one single, cross-country truck ride. We managed our trip with a couple of more modest in-state, family rides. Then somewhere in Illinois or Iowa, I think, we got one long-distance truck ride that got us all the way to Cheyenne. We had to get another ride after that because our driver was staying there too long. But, I remember that we spent the night at a fairly reasonable off-highway diner, gas-station, and motel, just like at so many other truck-stops along highways in those days. The next morning after breakfast at that diner, we got lucky and caught a ride going all the rest of the way for us clear to Portland, Oregon. Once we got dropped-off there, we did have a bit of a hike and struggled crossing the Columbia River Bridge. Yet, once inside Washington State, a local bus ride then took us to our standard bus stop only two blocks from our apartment.

After arriving back home in Vancouver, we got Jann enrolled in a local, public school using Jean's identification and our explanation of Jann's past educational background. She was accepted without issues. There was such a transient population at that time. Plus, throughout that very difficult decade before, the *depression* years, schools didn't question much if there were long distances involved for new incoming students. So many people were traveling across the nation, and many were heading out to the western states, especially California. For the school authorities to be told that Jann had bounced around quite a bit in school was not unusual news. They understood.

Of course, another helpful factor was that Jann had been a very good student. She was very composed and spoke to the intake-personnel with ease and effectiveness. Her new school was very satisfied with her 6th grade placement. We knew that it might become awkward in the future if her new school began tracking-down prior school addresses and information, like they had done with me and Sis Mary in Duluth. But Jean was an adult, and that likely satisfied the school record's office that particular time.

Back in our Vancouver apartment, we rearranged our modest conditions to accommodate Jann. Our basic studio was small, but it sufficed. Jean and I shared a bedroom, and Jann slept on a worn-out couch we had picked up from a neighbor. There was a small kitchen with simple wares, and we even had a private toilet in our apartment all to ourselves. It was comfortable and suited our modest needs. We visited Thomas and got our dog back too. Both Thomas and Duffy were delighted to see us. Things actually started out very well for all of us, and that was a relief after what we had gone through.

Settling back into our respectable jobs again was cordial and uncomplicated. Thomas had spent the previous two-weeks during Jean's and my absence just doing odd, repair-work or filling-in for someone else who had been gone for the day. He was happy to see us, and we three were all reassigned back together again as a team just like before. I felt pretty comfortable and relaxed with events so far. Finally, I was feeling genuinely peaceful inside. I was okay with where I was, and I felt needed.

I remember how I use to run through my mind all the different scenarios of sibling placements to help me keep track of where we were toward our goal of complete togetherness. By that time in early 1944, we McCords were still spread-out quite a bit, but we were all in reasonably safe and secure situations. Everyone was safe except our brother, Bo, who had been stationed in Sicily and Italy and was a flight-engineer on bombing missions. Sis Mary had been able to keep relatively good contact with him.

Bo was a trained mechanic for B-24 Liberator bombers, and he was also used occasionally as a gunner for defensive purposes during their missions. Obviously, Bo was the least safe of all of us McCord kids, but he kept in touch with us through Sis Mary, his twin sister.

Our youngest brother, Jackie-Boy, was secure too. As I mentioned, it had turned-out just like we had planned for him at that orphanage. Naturally, our dad became enraged with our snatching Jann right from under the noses of the orphanage's nuns. However, just as we expected, he took Jackie back home with him because he and Edith could more easily manage things with just him. Besides, Jackie was closer and more attached to both Edith and our dad.

Although we sisters did not like the fact of our brother still being under the influence of our dad, we had to accept his conditions at that time. We remained concerned for Jackie's well-being should he ever begin challenging our dad; however, we were comforted by the knowledge that Edith would surely be his security blanket and protect him from harm. Also, we were not aware of any physical cruelty of our dad toward Edith, unlike with our mom. Apparently, he respected Edith more or was simply more beholden to her. Regardless, we sisters continued our plans to rescue Jackie-Boy too, later, if not sooner.

To take another moment and talk about Sis Mary and Collen is simply fun and a pleasure. They were like two-peas-in-a-pod. Both of them shared the same interests, hobbies, and pleasing activities. Jean called Mary on a phone fairly regularly, although not enough to satisfy Jann and me. But we wrote to each other, and it was great fun to hear about all their exploits together. Mary adored Colleen and took her to the movies often, so they were both in seventh heaven. Jean's and my worst concern involved all the times that Mary left Colleen alone at their apartment while she was out gallivanting around Cleveland with her beaus. We even heard more about Mary's serious boyfriend, but nevertheless, things seemed relatively secure for Colleen with her big Sis.

I think that both Jean and I recognized that we had made great strides over the past several years. All of us were doing alright for the most part. Besides Bo's circumstances, there were no *Urgent!/Danger!* signs posted over any of us McCord sibling's faces anymore. Ideally, we would soon be able to gather all of us together, finally, and live the lives we had plans to make happen.

True, they were mostly Jean's dreams, but we were all included in them, so we all contributed. Well, actually, that wasn't the case. *I* helped contribute to Jean's dreams. *Me,* just *me,* and Jean. I was still okay with that, however, and I was very pleased that we were all more-or-less together and safe and secure.

WHATEVER YOU SAY, JEAN

At least, I was an important part of our Kaiser Vancouver working team. Through them I had become an actual breadwinner at home and an important part of that work team too. Once again, I accepted Jean's living-arrangements and strict rules that she had set up for us. Nearly all of our rules, *Jean's Rules*, had either a direct or indirect connection to fiscal matters. By that time, we had to, I mean *Jean had to*, budget for our sister Jann and all her new, additionally related expenses. Jean did not complain, but she did make the point that our savings would be lessened to accommodate Jann's expenses.

I remember teasing both Jean and Jann when I quipped, "Well, Jean, why don't you fix Jann's identification? Then she can go to work along with us, and our savings will grow even faster!"

At first, as I recall, I was actually a little bit concerned because only Jann was laughing at my snide remark. She had heard about Jean's and my little forgery trick. However, Jean took too long pausing before she finally grunted over the joke's absurdity. I really think that she took a long moment to actually consider the idea's feasibility and possibilities.

Anyway, Jean did go on to explain all the new criteria for our new arrangement: How much we would likely need to save from our earnings; how much we could spend; what sorts of things we were allowed to buy; and what we were disallowed to do or buy. Jean had devised a tough list for us all to live-by, and those were the *new guidelines* that we had to strenuously abide by.

Typically, Jean's *rules* meant that there would be no spending money on frivolous activities or having a good time. Jean's farm dream must have loomed so large in her mind that there was no space or place for anything else that did not focus or support that concept. Ice cream and movie theatre tickets were simply out-of-the-question. How could the waste of a melting ice-cream's cost or a fleeting, momentary movie's expense justify the loss of potentially owning a farm where all our dreams would be answered? I'll tell you, it was difficult debating with our older sister.

After a while, though, it was just mentally and emotionally exhausting how Jean was so rigid and unbending. I began developing many internalized, mental complaints thrashing about in my brain. After brief periods of frustration, however, I would get over whatever mental, fun-deprived issue that was bothering me. Eventually, I would go right back to carrying-on with all my responsibilities and duties. The nice thing that I continuously reminded myself about, however, was that we were surviving fairly well, even under Jean's somewhat strenuous circumstances. Plus, at least we were together. That meant almost everything to me.

During the following months, it was actually a very pleasing time for my own work career. I really liked my job, and I was liked and appreciated by my peers and co-workers. Sure, I was petite, but I was energetic and had learned my craft well. Not bragging, but I was a pretty darn good welder, and I seldom had any issues with my work. I even began trading-off with Jean and Thomas for more time on their angle of welding. It all came easy for me. I became extremely proficient at all directions of welding: Flat, diagonal, vertical, and overhead.

Heck, I *never* had any problems with my welding. I was that good, and actually, I became quite popular at the shipyard both on and off the job. I was way too young to go out drinking, but the guys were always teasing me to come along with them for an *afterwork refreshing beverage*. I would just laugh and wave them off. I knew they were all going out drinking, and I understood by then that some of the male workers were probably flirting with me after work. I never had the time or the money for that, anyway. Plus, I still was underage!

And, I could clearly hear Jean's imaginary voice bellowing in my ear, "WHAT? Waste *farm money* on booze? Are you out of your mind?"

Jean had me almost running home when work was over. For Jean, there was never a good time to be wasted on men or their wishes. It wasn't that Jean was unpopular at Kaiser. She just was not very outgoing and friendly. Jean was also very good at her job. Excellent, in fact, but she offered zero charisma to go with it. She came to work quietly, did her job privately, ate lunch alone, unless Thomas or I stayed with her, and went home immediately after work. No "Hellos" or "Goodbyes," just occasional grunts of acknowledgement or nods of affirmation. It was like Jean was trying to exist in a male-dominated workplace or society, and she felt like in order to do so, she had to revert to Neanderthal terms to communicate or survive.

For me, though, I was sprite, friendly, loved to joke around, and even enjoyed getting teased. When it came to work, however, I was all serious business. In time, I supposed that I even gained sympathy from some co-workers and admiration from a few of the male welders' wives. They all thought, "How can that little person do that hard, heavy job all day?"

"Shoot!" I'd just grin and laugh, "Piece of cake! I may be small, but I'm strong!"

Like I said before, sure I was petit for my size, but I still carried-my-weight. I lugged those heavy, long welding-cables long distances oftentimes to get to a necessary worksite. Wearing my full-leather welder's attire was heavy enough, but I carried my bucket of tools with me every morning going to my worksite each day, and I'd carry it all back to the change shack at the end of our shift to store it until the next day's work. My gear included burning torches and welding stingers, welding rod, chisels, hammer, wire brushes, and burning goggles. Plus, I carried under one arm my welding hood and my welding gloves in my free hand.

Some would see me *leathering up*, putting on all my protective leather gear, and seem surprised to see such a small, petit, woman doing that. I may have been more unusual or even funny to others to see me after work was over, and we would all be *leathering-down*, taking-off our gear to go home. On the grounds, I imagine that I simply looked like a smaller man going about his business. Throughout a shift, I would get dirty, and my face would become smeared with grime and sweat. When I walked around a jobsite, my hood was off, but my longer black hair was pulled-back, and a welder's hat covered my head. Nobody noticed anything until later after I got better known. That was when I would start getting all the hoots and hollers.

During breaks, or lunchtimes or even when just sitting somewhere studying my work, other workers, crew members and sometimes even strangers, brought me extra-food to snack on or eat. I suppose it was for courtesy's sake or just plain mercy that folks would drop-by to help fatten-me-up due to my slight build. I would grin at them, or laugh and always thank them, but I always thought it was kind of funny. Nevertheless, they all respected the work I was doing, every one of them, and apparently really appreciated the difficult circumstances and conditions I lived-with and worked-under. I was a young, little, no, *petit*, lady stick-o-dynamite handling my assignments on-the-job and struggling trying to survive, like everyone else, on the outside.

Of course, I had learned how to deal with most sympathizing observers and onlookers and how to take advantage of those circumstances too. With obvious, appropriate, and practiced behavior for any occasion that might arise, I mustered up whatever sort of look was necessary, and then I gratefully accepted or took all the help I could get. Although we had brought Jann back with us and gotten her right back into school again, she was still another hungry mouth to feed. So, like my sisters teased, and I laughed, and joked but agreed, "I milked the cow!" And how, I did! Blah-blah, squeeze! Boo-Hoo, squeeze! And I always graciously accepted any and all hand-outs with extremely courteous appreciations. Then I returned all those extra spoils back to our nest of sisterly and hungry eager eaters.

Fact was, though, I was relatively happy, even with that terrible war going on. I was well-liked at my jobsite and proud of my welding efforts at the shipyards. For the first time in a long time, I felt somewhat secure with myself. I knew it was partly because my sisters were nearby too, but I felt good that I was important to our relationship. I helped pay for all of our expenses, and Jann was with us. Her care was partially because of me and thanks to me. That was a very good feeling.

For once, I wasn't the odd-one-out, and a seemingly unwanted, extra-burden on our large family. Jean and Jann were my family now, and I was special to them. I was a serious breadwinner for us, and my contributions to my craft, my job, my country, and to my immediate family were important. I was loved and needed at home, and I was liked, appreciated, and needed at my job.

I can even remember tearing-up and crying a little back then. It happened especially when I paused at times and considered all the changes I had gone through in my life thus far. That was when I could really appreciate my new circumstances. The special feeling was so warm, and it felt so good inside. I felt pretty darn happy at that time, in fact. Life was good.

MANTRAS

Everybody knows that it is a special feeling to go to work every day and really be welcomed back on the worksite with warm and sincere greetings. Of course, Thomas was always nice and considerate, and Jean, well Jean was just Jean. She hardly ever even waited for our foreman to pass by chuckling to his own snide, remarking standard, "Good morning, Lady and Gentlemen." On some mornings, our foreman, or even his boss, might make a quick appraisal of our work-stage status and then nod approvals or give out a few, additional, verbal modifications. That was all to be expected. No problems. We adjusted, adapted, and reorganized to deal with any changes. It was all in a day's work.

Then, however, our Foreman, or *Boss Man*, we endearingly called him, would just smile and start-in again with his same, favorite, and daily preaching, "Okay, Kids, today, let's give another one to God and Country! F- - k the Nazis!" Or, "F- - k Hitler!" Or, "F- - k the Japs!" Or, "F- - k the Emperor! Our soldiers and sailor-boys are dying overseas; let's not get anybody hurt here today trying to help them win this f--king war. Be careful!"

He also enjoyed using his cursing slang attacks against *Hirohito* specifically or the *enemy* in general!" Once in a while, he'd even humor himself with an inclusive, verbal assault against *Mussolini* or occasionally even against Nazi friendly *Mexico*. It was obvious to us, that *Boss Man* got a big kick out of his sense-of-humor, so we'd always laugh or smile as he passed by to keep encouraging his good mood.

Jean, on-the-other-hand, was our own team *pusher.* A pusher is a foreman's helper that takes the details from a foreman's instructions for the day and keeps their three-man crew, or more, on task and on schedule. Jean kept us on schedule, alright. She would condense everything our foreman would say each morning into her own brief synopsis, "Okay, let's get going. Turn on your machines and grab your leads. Let's get this day over with!"

I always amused myself with the nearly opposite poles of their characters. However, both the foreman and Jean's attitudes worked for me. I liked to smile and, in a personal way, enjoy my work. Yet, I did take my job seriously. I liked what I did, but there was a no-nonsense aspect about the challenge too. "To enjoy doing a good job." That was my motto, my mantra. Sometimes, I remember even laughing to myself as I would mentally voice-out my *mantra* to my inner-self, "Today I will, *enjoydoingagoodjob. Enjoydoingagoodjob. Aahhmenn!*" It was a lifter-upper for me. Kept me content. Kept me happy. Kept me focused.

BLUSHING HEROINE

There was even a time on-the-job during an early production phase where I really got to *earn-my-keep,* as they say. Apparently, there was a fairly serious, design-miscalculation issue inside the double hulls of our ships being built. As I mentioned before, these mini carriers we were working on were in great demand by the U.S. Navy for the war cause.

Anyway, those *mini-carriers* were a double-bottomed type, and apparently, the engineers had come-up with a design that required every hull to have a small external flood hole. It turned-out, however, that that little hole was necessary for a teeny-tiny welder to climb through and do an absolutely critically required vertical weld on the inner-lining of the interior hull.

Every new mini-ship being manufactured there by the Kaiser Vancouver Shipbuilders had that same, unique engineering, design-flaw requirement. It was a big issue because of potential time-loss waiting for that inner-hull, vertical-welding phase to be completed so that the next part of the hull production could begin. Every new ship coming through was on strict schedules, timelines, and deadlines, so serious attention was given to that problem for production output.

Anyway, it seemed that the inspectors and bosses had determined a method and means to resolve the issue: If they could just find one, small welder to fit through that ridiculously tiny, flood hole, then possibly that welder could crawl or squeeze themselves over to the desired area, do the required vertical weld and accomplish the essential mission. Of course, what the engineers had not considered was the smallness of the access-hole.

Almost any welder with all their protective gear on could never squeeze through such small holes. That's where I came in, however. A company executive, an inspector and our foreman came over to talk to me and asked if I would try. I was most obviously the smallest welder in all the Kaiser Vancouver Shipyard crews and maybe in the entire world, I didn't know. But the company was in a real pickle, and I was rather quickly requested to attempt the fix.

After the inspectors and foreman explained the circumstances and extent of the job, I set my hood and gear aside next to the entry-hole and began trying to squeeze myself through that tiny hole that the engineers had designed. It was very difficult too, but once I had gotten one shoulder through, bent and squeezed some more, and then did a sort of Houdini contortion of my body, I managed to get clear through to the inside of the double hull for the vertical welding job.

Once inside the very small and compacted area, I reached back and took an extension light that was waiting for my grasp. Then with the entire area better lit-up, I managed to reach back and grab my welding lead, some welding rod, my hood and locate the necessary and vital work. In no time at all, I managed to size-up the job that the inspectors had talked about. I could clearly see the portion of the double-hull attachment which required a vertical weld to be completed.

Naturally, I advised our foreman and the inspectors of what I was doing as I fulfilled the necessary assignment. Quickly and efficiently, I did the required weld and then cleaned the completed areas with my welders tac, or flux, hammer, and wire brush. It really was not that difficult. Vertical welding was my specialty, so it was the same type of welding that I had already been doing for the company all along on other tasks. Piece of cake!

After that relatively short-period of time, I completed my task to my satisfaction and hollered to those observers outside that I was coming back-out and to pull out my welding lead, light, and hood as I approached the entry-exit hole. Then came the second hardest part of the entire job. It was again squeezing through that tiny hole. That next time was to get out, so it was very important to me. Claustrophobia, or something, I suppose, but I did not like welding in such confined areas.

However, during my exit or escape, in the distance while I wiggled, squirmed, squeezed, and contorted my body once again to get back-out that miniscule flood-hole that I had climbed through, I could hear a loud roar coming from behind me. At first, I was sort of curious over the unusual sounds, and then I understood what was happening... and their source.

It turned out to be a huge, thunderous ovation of clapping hands and cheering voices. Once I was finally able to hand-out the last of my welding lead, spare rod-canister, tools, light, hood and then squeeze myself out from the hole and turn around, I saw so many administration folks, various bosses, and crew members from all over the Kaiser Vancouver Shipyard who were there cheering me on. I was so embarrassed, but nobody could probably see my blushing, red face because I was so covered in welding smoke soot. The ventilation was fairly poor inside, so I imagined that my appearance may have cheered that crowd on even more.

Well, after that, I got lots more attention from all kinds of folks all over the Kaiser Plant. Everybody knew who I was after that, and I was offered plenty of handshakes, pats-on-the-back, nods and smiles and waves, and even a couple of flash-pictures were taken. The fix-it job that I had performed, I was told, probably saved the company hours and hours of valuable time. That kind of loss would have delayed Kaiser's entire production schedule. Of course, our labor bosses enjoyed mentioning that the lost time salvaged also saved the company a lot of money to boot.

One of Kaiser Vancouver Shipbuilding's top bosses spoke loudly and proudly to the listening and celebratory crowd. He praised me for how that specialty-job I did saved the company so much money and lost time by keeping that ship's production right on schedule. I even received a Certificate of Appreciation from Kaiser Vancouver head-office later on, and there were always lots more smiles and nodding heads of admiration and respect when someone recognized me.

"Look!" I'd hear someone call out and applauding from a distance, "There she is! There goes 'Whiz Kid', the Savior of Kaiser!"

What I didn't get, however, was a raise or even a money reward of some sort. I should have put them all on-the-spot right then when I had an audience, "How about a little extra dough to thank me, huh?"

Of course I didn't. I was way too bashful. Honestly, I didn't even think about it at the time. It was just my job, and I was doing it. That's all. Sacrifice! Sacrifice! Sacrifice! I didn't care, though. It was a job to do, I was able to do it and I was happy.

Now, Jean would have been a different matter entirely. Oh, I could hear her sounding-off while I shuddered with embarrassment, "Oh? Saved you so much, huh? Well, put your money where your big mouths are, and fork over some real tribute!" Of course, it was a moot point. Jean could never have fit through that tiny hole in the side of that ship…

Months passed. I continued daily to prove myself proficient at my welding tasks over-and-over again. Of course, I became Kaiser Vancouver's *go-to gal*, after that first fix, every time a new mini-ship product was begun. Back inside that tiny hole I went to fix that same stupid, designer error for those mini carriers. I was considered very trustworthy as a Kaiser Vancouver Shipyard employee, and I had actually become fairly popular and well-known due to my skill, enthusiasm, and youth. Even then, no one was at all aware that I was still only seventeen. Still actually too young to even be there in the first place! Jean and I continued to chuckle and smirk at our cleverness. Well, I chuckled anyway, and Jean smirked!

Jean was just more pragmatic. She approved of the extra-decent money that was coming into our household and going toward her pie-in-the-sky farm. I really enjoyed earning the money, but once I received it, I just handed all of my cashed check over to Jean, anyway We both figured, "What they don't know, won't hurt us!" I just giggled a lot and went to work each day with a big, very young smile on my sneaky face.

Then one afternoon at work, a really delightful thing happened to me. It was announced to everyone in the shipyard over the loudspeaker system that *little 'ol me*, Patricia V. McCord, was going to receive a noteworthy award from Kaiser Vancouver Shipbuilding Company. I was surprised, embarrassed and a little bit shy at first of becoming such a celebrity. But not that shy!

And what a surprise it turned out to be! I was singled-out from all the entire ship's construction crews at that Kaiser Vancouver Shipyard, and I was given the unique honor of *Christening* one of our completed vessels. With a little hoopla and lots of cheers to encourage me, I got to crash a bottle of supposed Champagne against the hull of the ship which sent it slipping down from its holding carriage and right into the Columbia River below.

To get a laugh from my audience just before I cracked the Champagne bottle against the ship's hull, I remember joking with the company executives, or teasingly pleading with them, anyway.

I pretending to whine in frustration and begged, "Oh, please, Mr. Kaiser, can't we just use water instead, and then let me take the Champagne home with me?"

It worked. I got the uproarious laughter I sought, even more. But it helped make for a very memorable day. That really was a highlight of my Kaiser Vancouver welding career. I was both proud and giggling happy at that time.

SACRIFICES

Unfortunately, wasn't there someone who once paraphrased that popular saying, "For every good time, there is always an opposite and equal... blah, blah, blah? It was true, it seemed to me back then. Good times do not always last. Wartime definitely had some serious disadvantages besides the horrific fighting involved. Rationing was still at full steam ahead and a continual frustration to everyone. There was little or no sugar for your coffee. In fact, there was very little coffee for your coffee available either. Everything was limited, and when something did come available, it didn't last long.

There was one particular glitch which was a relatively small factor, but an issue nevertheless, that caused a few ripples of frustration to swell at times. It was a fact that during much of that wartime period, housewives at their homes were free to go shopping anytime they needed. We sisters and other workers were always on our jobs and busy. Jann was in school, too, so she didn't count. Anyway, the problem was that because of our work, we missed out on a plenty good merchandise sales.

It was always easier and convenient for housewives to manage to get first and best choices of any meager store-pickings, including available meats. I'd be lying if I said it didn't bother some of us, but I certainly didn't begrudge or blame them. I would have done the same thing if given the opportunity. It was just the circumstances of the time and the demands of that blasted war we were in. Everything was focused on the war-effort.

And it wasn't just us, I knew. Everybody was forced to give to the cause, to sacrifice and do without some things that, prior to the war, we had really taken for granted. After all, those hard years of the 1930s, and then right up into the war's start, you'd have thought we had already given up so much and done with so little. But, the war just kept putting more and more demands on everyone.

Give, give, and give to the war-cause. Donate, donate, and donate to the war-cause. Do without, go without and forget about niceties, or pleasantries or decent food for the war-cause. Accept rationing for the war-cause and buy war-bonds for the war-cause. The government went on-and-on-and-on with its radio ads, billboard advertising, posters everywhere, and bulletin-board ads advising, encouraging, and warning us to pay heed to the contents of the messages.

We workers, and all the other folks at home, accepted the circumstances, though, and seldom complained. We all understood that our soldier boys overseas were doing the greatest sacrifice. So many of them were coming home crippled or even paying the ultimate price of dying for the war-cause. We all accepted the circumstances and just bowed our heads, prayed our prayers, and continued working and doing our expected parts for the war-cause. We all prayed for eventual ends to those miserable war fronts in the Pacific and in Europe to come soon.

However, there was one interesting, if not unusual, *free* thing that came to us shipyard and construction workers. It was included as one part of our workers contracts with Kaiser, and it subsidized by the U.S.A. government. The arrangement was that every month, we workers would get special, free coupons from our employer to use and buy ourselves new work boots. It was a fact, that workers could fairly easily tear-up and use-up a pair of work boots every month. Sometimes due to accidents or on-the-job burns, especially like with us welders, a decent pair of boots could last much less than a month. Occasionally, though, depending on one's work assignment or just the special care attributed, boots might last a little longer.

Regardless, I suppose that the government folks figured if they could keep us on our feet by replenishing our work boots, then we would just keep on working month-after-month. Nevertheless, the "free-boot provision" coupons were available to us workers every single month on an arranged date, and we were to use those coupons same-as-cash. Therefore, once we picked up our free coupon, we could go shopping for boots or foot attire at a Kaiser shoe and boot store, if we so chose, or we could go wherever else we chose too.

After a while, though, I was getting very tired of exchanging those coupons for another pair of boots. Month-after-month-after-month it was always time to toss-out old, warn boots and then receive a wonderful and magical coupon to use as trade-in payment for a beautiful, shiny, strong, and new pair of work boots. How exciting! To me, though, after a long while, it simply began symbolizing affirmation of another thirty-days gone by and another thirty days to go until I received yet another shiny, beautiful, wonderful, delightful, gorgeous, strong, etc., etc., blah, blah, blah, new pair of boots. We could measure our lives struggles and times against our coupons and exchanges for free, new pairs of boots.

I have to confess, after a while, it got down-right monotonous, if not frustrating. Regardless of *free* coupons and *free* boots, I was getting tired of work. I began bumming myself out to the truth that I was still only seventeen-years old, not even legal-age to work. Yet, I felt like I had been working my whole life. In fact, I was getting sick-and-tired of work, and more work all the time, and more coupons, and more boots, and the same ol' stinkin' new boots month-after-month.

It was always just boots, boots, boots, and more boots. Oh, they never thought about any *free coupons* to use for going out and having a good time for oneself. Nobody ever considered giving or doing something just a little bit special for us poor, fun-starved teens, it seemed. They had celebrations for good work, sure. They all would celebrate good deeds done on-the-job with hearty handshakes and citations and cheers. Well, I kept wondering why they didn't have some festivities and celebrate with some good, simple fun? Nope. It was always just the same things we heard, *"Cheers!* Now, get back to work and earn that *next new pair of boots!"*

On top of everything else going on in my sorrowful, underage, teenage, *girls-just-want-to-have-fun*, selfless, sacrificing life, Jean had always been ever-so-strict and firm about our money and paychecks. She always required that I give her all my cashed-paycheck funds to help pay our expenses. In exchange for my whole, two-weeks earned paycheck, I received back from Jean a pathetic allowance in which to stretch-out and use to buy all my personal items. I assumed that the balance of our combined incomes, after expenses, went toward our supposed future, family, pie-in-the-sky farm.

At least that was Jean's dream, and she made me try hard to believe in it. At least I did believe enough to entrust her with all my hard-earned money. I would get inwardly frustrated and upset because my *allowance* proffered by Jean was a mere pittance. That was my reward for two-weeks of virtual slavery to last me for the next two, whole weeks until I would receive my next miserable trifle on which to exist, it seemed. That was my life as I saw it: Work, work, pittance, work, work, pittance, and a new pair of boots! Then the same all over again.

I knew Jean carefully guarded-over our money, savings, and finances; I never worried about that. It was just that her lousy, chicken-feed *allowance* divvied-out was always spent so fast on my personal necessities that it was gone before I barely blinked. I was always broke before I could even go back to work. I never even had a spare dime for an ice cream, and I loved ice cream so much! And it was *all because of Jean*, I began feeling. No wonder I gratefully accepted all those pathetic, would be embarrassing handouts from all those sympathetic onlookers at work. No wonder people pitied me. I *was* pitiful…

NEW SHOES

Obviously, I was really getting irritable and tired of our whole arrangement. Perhaps, it's no surprise then, and may even be even appreciated, that by the next time those stinking, *free-boot coupons* were issued, I had had my fill of the gosh-darned war, the miserable work regimen and the strict rules set down by my overbearing, stingy and boring, big-sister Jean. Oh, it was terrific that Jean made all those plans for us which depended on hers and my combined wealth. Oh, sure it was great that all that combined money would one day be invested into a nice farm where all we kids could live together happily-ever-after. That was exciting and rewarding to consider and think and imagine about. But only for so long.

I cannot emphasize enough, though, that Jean was a real tightwad. She was a regular skinflint. Fact is, back then, Jean was so blasted frugal that she makes that modern, guru of personal finances advice, Suze Orman, sound like a weekday spendaholic and weekend, credit card binge spender. Jean's sort of advice was this: "Make money, save it and do without!" It was that simple. Jean had her dreams for us, and my sacrifices would never be enough. Although, to be fair, Jean applied the same rules to herself by sacrificing and going without too, no doubt.

In fact, Jean hardly did anything besides work: She would go grocery shopping and buy absolutely only essential food items, she would cook every other day for her turn, and she would sleep. That was it. Oh, yeah, and she always got her new boots once-a-month, and she collected my cashed paycheck funds every payday! Can't forget that. She sure-as-heck never did!

Anyway, Jean was like that. Obsessive, compulsive, focused, self-sacrificing, demanding of others to do the same, and determined. I actually believed that she would have made a really good nun except that she was an atheist. Point is, Jean figured everyone else needed to do the same and be the same as her. Unfortunately, Jean's mistake was thinking that I, her devoted, loving, little, younger, and follower sister was just like her.

She even taught us to always look down while we were walking somewhere because we might find some shiny pennies or nickels lying on the ground somewhere. Damn! To this very day, what do I do? Exactly! I am always scanning my surrounding grounds before me while walking somewhere to potentially discover someone else's loss:

"A penny found is a penny earned," she always preached.

Well, my point is that I *wasn't* like her, and all I wanted was just a little, *personal attention*. I understood the value of our work, I recognized the necessity of contributing to the war cause and I appreciated the meaning of giving, giving and more giving. But I was getting so tired of sacrifice, sacrifice, and more sacrifice to make all the others happen. My frustrations grew and built-up to such a point that for one month that was coming up, I quietly and secretly planned for myself.

My plan was relatively simple. It was not going to harm anybody else. It would only affect my well-being to the better and not cost anyone else any money, time, trouble, or additional sacrifice. My plan would just affect me. This is what is was: When I again received my new, standard work-boots, *free* coupon, I was going to do something else with it that next time. I would clean-up my old pair of boots, which were still in mediocre, thus satisfactory, shape, and continue using them for the following month. Then I could use my *free coupon* to get something totally different, yet something completely useful.

I wanted something nice, a *girlie thing*, instead of something for the war cause and for work. Therefore, instead of another pair of identical new boots, I decided to cash my coupon in on an adorable pair of ladies dress-up shoes. Just that one time, I planned and mentally promised, I would splurge on myself a little bit and do just that. My plan was no more than that. I simply wanted pure satisfaction and to treat myself to a woman's pleasure. I felt like I deserved it too. After all, I was, or had been, a celebrity! They owed me! Well, sort of, they did. I was awarded a citation, after all. Granted, it was a while back, but I was still climbing in those *hull holes* for the company every time a new, *mini-carrier* product was begun. I was still their *go-to gal*.

Anyway, the background for my personal fetish and desire was this: Every single day of my life for nearly the whole past year, while on our way to work, and then again on our way back home, Jean and I had to pass by this one particular shoe storefront. It was part of the downtown business area development near the river waterfront. Conveniently, the shoe store was close to our workplace, the Kaiser Vancouver Shipbuilding Company.

Jean and I always walked together from home to work. After work, we would usually hook-up and make the half-mile or so walk back home to our apartment together too. However, one morning I saw something in that *particular shoe store*, and I remained behind to look closer. It was a really nicely arranged setting of ladies dress shoes. All sorts of styles, colors, shapes, and designs. After that, each time I passed-by, I couldn't help myself. I had to stop and linger longer.

Going to work or home, from then on, I always let Jean go on ahead without me. I'd catch-up, if time allowed, or not. Whatever. Who cared? All I could think to say was, "Jean, you go on ahead. I'll catch-up." Jean would inevitably mumble something under her breath but keep on walking toward work or home.

That shoe store's proprietor must have found me obsessively curious, too. He had to have watched me each day going back and forth to work and home again, always stopping and staring, back-and-forth, stopping and staring, day-after-day just passing-by and pausing to stare at his women's shoe display. Then one day soon thereafter, I swear he must also have had a fortune teller's mind-set too. I say that because one morning he deliberately placed right there in the middle of his window-display, during that particular month of my *highest anxiety*,... the cutest, most gorgeous pair of dress shoes I had ever seen in my life, that side of the Mississippi.

They were baby-blue, high-heeled, peep-toe pumps with pretty little flowers on them, and I just loved them from first sight. In fact, I became almost obsessed with them. Seeing them right there every day in that shoe store window display, twice a day in fact, and right there within reach yet still on the inside of that glass presentation, was awfully stressful to a young woman. On-top-of-all-that, for the storeowner to go and put something so beautiful right there in the center of that wonderful, window display was downright painful for me.

To see those shoes sitting there day-after-day while walking past coming and going was cruel and unusual punishment. I was just a girl who wanted to have a little fun or simple satisfaction and never got any. But it was going to be alright, I plotted. Those beauties were going to be mine!

And so, the day finally arrived when my plan was put into action. Right after work on *coupon day*, I walked over and retrieved my latest, *free new boots* (foot ware) *coupon* from the Kaiser Shipyard Coupon Outlet Warehouse. Without any hesitation then, I raced back toward home before Jean could see me and arrived at that special shoe store early.

I hurriedly pushed open the glass door, practically leapt over to the window display and snatched that lovely item I cherished so much out from the window display. Quickly locating the storekeeper, I ran over to him and briskly shoved the delightful dress shoes into his hands. Almost breathless from the urgency, I begged the storekeeper for my own pair. He looked at me smiling and whiffed, "A 6 ½, yes?" and he was right.

Upon his noticeably swift return, I had already unlaced and ripped my boots and socks from my bare feet and prepared myself to put those new beauties on my feet for the final test. I think I actually remember screaming in delight from my joy. They fit perfectly! Later on, I imagined that that crafty salesman probably already had my shoes prepared for me all along and had simply set them right there, easily within his reach and behind the curtain in the back of the store. He had my number. He knew I would be back. What was that Kevin Costner movie line, "Build it, and they…?" Yes, that was it, "*Place them*, and she will come!"

Anyway, I quickly made my financial/coupon transaction with the smug, voodoo-practicing, mind-reading, witch doctor, storeowner, and I thanked him. I was back on my way home and even arrived before Jean. Once I dashed inside, I quickly flipped my untied boots off and dropped them at our work-boot spot behind the front door. Next, I ran into Jean's and my bedroom, and I hid my new shoes under our bed. Then, finally, I raced back into the living-room and plopped down on the couch so as to look ever-so nonchalant for Jean's return, and her sake and mine.

Naturally, though, and I remember like it was yesterday, a few minutes later, Jean walked through the doorway proudly holding onto her very own, brand new pair of shiny boots. After closing the door behind her, she turned to place her new boots where they belonged right next to my *worn and grubby boots! What*? Jean saw my *old* pair of work boots and at once recognized my ploy. Something in her mind was amiss. She was onto me!

I told you she was smart. It was like her brain was a magnet, and my new, beautiful dress shoes were made of steel. Actually, as soon as she walked into our apartment and saw my old pair of work boots lying there instead of bright, shiny new ones like hers, Jean immediately switched mental-gears and went into her tactical, search-mode. "Duffy! Go sniff-out those new shoes," I swear I remember her ordering her poor defenseless pet.

REBELLION

How did she guess it was new shoes she was looking for? I never learned why. It always became a sore point of discussion between us, so I never brought it up. But, I always wondered? How did she know? Maybe the storekeeper hadn't replaced the display pair yet that I had rudely jerked from their star position in the front window. Maybe Jean walked-by and noticed right away that they were gone! Maybe Jean was jealous! Maybe she wanted that pair too, and I got them first! Nawww, that sure wasn't it!

First, Jean started sniffing and scanning over our entire apartment looking here and there. Then, I could have sworn that I heard her drawing-in some quick-breaths, like she was a bloodhound or something, smelling for anything that reeked new. Her antennae were on red alert! Beep! Beep! Beep! Her built-in, mental radio-detector was following signals straight to the source.

Oh, she wanted my hiding-place alright, and she was certain that she'd find it. Jean was sniffing for treasure, it seemed. Only to her, it was like sniffing for sewage, which meant impetuously wasted finances. Something had triggered in her brain, and she knew exactly what I had done without me even confessing.

Would I be strong enough? Could I take the pressure? Or, her beating? Could I hold up to her onslaught of condemnation? My nerves were getting the best of me. Young sister Jann had already been home when I arrived. Watching my rushing antics first, and then Jean's peculiar behavior following, must have been a bit confusing to her. Sadly, I could not depend on Jann for moral or physical support. She was just too young and inexperienced around Jean to understand.

I sensed that I was beginning to sniffle and wondered if I was going to crack under pressure and break my impulsive, rebelliousness. Would I cry out, "I'm sorry! I did it! I kept my dirty old boots! Instead, I traded-in my coupon for a pretty little pair of the most beautiful, and gorgeous, and delightful, and elegant, and attractive, and delightful, and beautiful princess, and gorgeous, and, and fairy-tale-land shoes of all-time in the whole-wide-world...instead!" I was nearly fainting by then in my mind.

After I finished my imaginary sales-pitch, I entered into a meditative, plea-bargaining mode, once again in my mind, with a curt, "Aaaaaaaaahhhh, shucks! Please can't I keep them? I'll give you all my money from now on! No more allowances! I'll even stop eating! Aaaaaaaaahhhh! Please let me have them?"

But life is never that simple. We can't always describe or cry ourselves into favor, and cry-babies seldom get what they want. At least not from Jean! Well, maybe some of them do. Others might, but not me. Never me! In fact, I was the *only one* who never did! Everybody else *always got* what they wanted, but I *never* did! The mental, self-torture became agonizing, and I began wheezing for breath. I needed air! I was drowning in self-pity, or, or suffocating from frustration. Please, Lord! Help a girl out!

And just like I had previously imagined, choosing only the second place that Jean deliberately looked, the entryway closet being the first, she was on her knees and checking under our bed. Damn, she was smart! Dang, that was fast!

And oh, did she become furious? I actually think her body began growing,.. swelling ... enlarging! And her already puffy and angry face was turning blood-red! Honest-to-God, I was getting scared. Oh, and her powers! It was like she could read my mind too.

What was happening? First, the shoe salesman, and now Jean was controlling my mind. For Jean, there was no time for frivolity. "Life is a serious matter," I could hear her bellowing- out-loud in my mind, "and a person must pull-up their (new, shiny and coupon-free) bootstraps (pun intended) and get with the program. Life was hard, so get tough! Arrrrrrrgh!"

In a big, wide, and sweeping move, Jean reached deep under our bed and snatched-up my lacy, new shoes, without even the faintest glance to notice how stunningly gorgeous and delicate they were, and she viciously flung them at me.

Then, as if to crow like some greedy braggart, she bellowed, "Grrrrrrrr, I knew it!" and quickly followed-up her victory cry with her devastating declaration, "I caught you!"

It was as though she were sneering, growling, and grinning like that Cheshire cat from Carroll's <u>Alice in Wonderland</u>, but all-in-one and all at one time. Only, I didn't feel like Alice, at all. I knew what was going on because I was all too familiar with Jean's attitudes, values, behavior, and her antics. I had heard and watched her match wits with our dad on so many occasions.

In fact, right about then, she was actually reminding me a little of those arguments and battles that she'd had with our pa. "Alright, Dad." I began considering, "I sort of understand now." I momentarily wavered and then reconsidered, "But wait! No, no, that's not right. He was an a—hole, all the time!"

Anyway, the short of it was that Jean instantly demanded that I return the dress shoes the very next morning. There were no alternative options offered. I could only return them and retrieve my valuable *boot* coupon and then go get another pair of shiny, new, work boots,… like hers.

"Well, Jean, you have really flipped your mind," I thought to myself, "Why are you so upset and unable or unwilling to understand my wants or my real needs?" Then I tried relaxing and considered other factors. "Wow!" I thought, "Jean must really have had a bad day at work, or, or a bad day of the month!"

No, those weren't logical explanations. I had been there with Jean at work all day. There was nothing traumatic that occurred. Jean was the same as always. Grumpy. We simply did our jobs the same as always: "Grabbed our leads, did our jobs and went home!" Thomas was fine too. We had a successful day and ended our shift on a pretty nice note, I believed.

Back to Jean, though, I could still see her standing there growing more, still expanding, it seemed. I think she was inhaling and exhaling and huffing and puffing like she was preparing to blow-the house-down! It was that, or she really did hate pretty new things and shoes! Or, else she was deliberately trying to hyperventilate and pass out from exertion to express her true displeasure and disappointment with me.

"*Well, whatever!*" I screamed out-loud in my mind, followed by, "*Who cares?*"

And it was right then, at that very moment that something triggered in my brain. It was as though an explosive had gone-off in my cerebrum, and I reacted consciously to it and almost spontaneously.

"*Aaaaaaaaahhhh!*" I screamed in angry, independent defiance.

For the first time ever in my natural life, I had shrieked-out against Jean in my highest-pitched, whaling scream. And then I followed it up instantly with an absolute rebel cry, "*No! I won't do it!*"

Jean just stood there staring at me in shocked, wide-eyed confusion. I imagined her mind reeling under that great, unknown thought, "Wwwait, a minute! Wwwhat's happening?"

Jean continued glaring at me momentarily in her surprised and stunned state. Suddenly, she was having to deal with my dazing and impulsive negativity. For a few more seconds, as she stared-down into my insolent and convulsing soul, I believe she actually entered into momentary, paralyzed-shock. She stood there unwavering and motionless, like she was frozen-in-time and in disbelief. I could have prepared myself for her absolutely upcoming and violent fall-out, but I didn't.

Instead, I quick let her have the second blast of my defiant, shot gun lambasting rebelliousness. "*And you can't make me, either*!" I screamed at the top of my lungs followed by another quick bellowing, "*Aaaaaaaaahhhh!*" Opening that last necessary release-valve helped, I thought.

But, OMG! I was having an out-of-body experience! It was as though some highly sheltered, never-before-known, powerful, and independent *spirit-self* had actually risen and separated itself from my otherwise, weak, subservient, and fleshy-self and assumed powerful and commanding dominion over my previously pathetic body-and-mind.

For once in my life, for this first and singular time in my entire nearly eighteen-years of submissive and obedient existence, I had actually rebelled against my bigger, greater, all-powerful, and all-knowing Goddess-Sister.

I had never before done anything like that in my whole life. Well, except for when I called home and stood-my-ground telling our dad that I would not be coming home at summer's end. But, even then, they probably celebrated right after hanging-up the phone.

But there and then, that crazy time with Jean? That time? Over a silly pair of shoes? That was the moment when I had actually defied her? How did I, and how could I, do that? Jean was like my life-giver, my Northern Star, my past, present and future all combined.

Neither of us were prepared for my blistering challenge. It was like screaming at God! I was damned! I felt like lightning was about to strike me where I stood, and I'd better move quickly. And I hadn't even been able to wear my pretty new shoes yet!

"Maybe, I'd better run," I thought rapidly. "Grab your shoes and make a break for it quick before she grabs you!"

But wait! It wasn't over yet, either. Not by a long shot. That disagreement rapidly turned into our very own, first-and-only, full-scare, and full-scale war between us sisters. My emotional seams just seemed to have burst. The timing for the incident was all bad, or all good, depending on how someone looked at it. Everything was hitting me at once. Our situation with all its circumstantial pressure had just finally been too much, for too long and all for too little in exchange.

I broke. Simple as that. I had put-up with enough already. Too much: My job, Jean, no money, Jean, no fun, Jean, and now no cute shoes because of Jean! Enough was enough! All that misery coupled with my colossal fill of Jean's controlling behavior, and I simply could not take any more.

And so, at that actual moment, I think that I may have actually momentarily cracked. In that despondent state-of-mind, I broke, and it was only for those brief moments desperately seeking freedom and independence from everything. Everything including Jean, Kaiser Vancouver, and the whole, wide, miserable-rotten, war-filled world with all of its evil battles and constant, never-ending suffocating demands for sacrifice, more sacrifice, and my sacrifice.

Instantly, then, while throwing-out my crossing arms high-up into-the-air and announcing my forsaken disgust for all to see, I belched-out for all the entire universe to hear the finality of my utter collapse and pure disdain.

In my most shrieking proclamation, I screamed-out in a reverberating, sweeping shrieking referendum, "I quit! I'm going home!"

༺∞༻

Looking back, perhaps afterward when I paused to consider my new predicament, I may have considered my behavior, action, and words that early evening as a bit hasty; maybe even a slight, tactical error. However, I was emotionally lost, yet I was determined to find myself out there, somewhere else and on my own. Eventually, that decision evolved into other life-changing adventures for me. Only this time it meant that from now on, I truly was *on my own*.

ON MY OWN

I was by then a comfortably full, legal age at eighteen-years. It was Fall of 1944, and I finally had a little, extra money in my pocket. I made immediate plans to leave Vancouver and its Kaiser Shipyards, and Jean and Jann without much more forethought other than another departure, only this time it would just be me. That urgent trip to *go back home*, however, was going to be a little more comfortable.

I could afford a full, one-way bus ticket on Greyhound all the way to Cleveland. I would leave Jean, Jann, and Duffy there in Vancouver, and I would travel by bus to join my truly loving, sharing, supportive, and *Girls-Just-Want-to-be-Girls* sisters, Collen, and Mary. I was sure that they would understand my feelings and support me. If not, then I'd just keep on going... to somewhere else. I didn't care.

Still frustrated, upset and anxious over Jean's and my verbal battle, though, I decided to leave right away without any further discussion or potential yelling and begin anew on my own. Before bedtime, I had hugged Jann and explained gently that I needed to go back and see Sis and Colleen. I also reassured her that she would be just fine with Jean and Duffy and very safe and secure. I reminded her that our *great farm plan* was still binding, and that we would all be back together soon. I told Jann to keep studying and do well in school and that our travel plans together one day were still very important to me.

Several hours later on that extreme, life-changing early morning, I remember checking on Jann again. I covered her better with her blankets and kissed her goodbye one last time. After hugging Duffy and patting to calm him, I slipped out of our apartment while it was still so dark outside. Hurriedly, with two large sacks of my belongings in hand, I walked to our jobsite. I wanted to be there at the start of the morning shift to arrange for my departure, *my quitting,* and to make any necessary arrangements for my earnings pay-off including forwarding address to Cleveland at Sis's place.

One small, positive factor was that I had picked-up my latest salary paycheck the day before when the whole *shoe thing* blew-up into its, *my,* present state-of-circumstances. Thus, I possessed an entire two-week's salary from prior earnings, and I was still due an additional one week of wages to be mailed to me in Cleveland. Therefore, I was in a little bit of a hurry because I wanted to be gone before Jean might appear and make my departure even more difficult. It would likely have been a money matter, and that *mattered* a lot to Jean.

It was on the way for me, so I dropped-by the Kaiser Main Office early for a final good-bye. I didn't stay long because I needed to leave right away. I only got to see a few of the early-bird, dayshift, management team and office secretaries. They made me feel like I knew them all, however. I could tell that they were all surprised and somewhat disappointed upon learning of my leaving Kaiser Vancouver, but they all wished me well and safe travels. The bosses even thanked me for my *highly appreciated* work that I had done for them. I was blushing and almost in tears when I finished my goodbyes.

Walking to the nearby bus-stop with my suitcase in-hand of meager belongings but *including my new shoes,* I took the local bus to Vancouver's Downtown Area. I had to wait for a bank to open in order to cash my paycheck and then walk to the near-bye Greyhound Bus Station. Inside, I bought my cross-country ticket, and a few hours later, I was headed east for Cleveland and my other sisters for our sudden reunion…

Overall, things had begun moving rapidly. Earlier that day, I had reached and crossed the *no turning back* point. If anything, pride would not allow me to return to Jean's subjugation anymore. It could not be now that I had felt my own newly sensed powers of freedom and independence. I could not and would not return again to Jean's strict rules of governance…

No matter what *sense of power* I may felt at that moment, however, I was still certainly a little afraid and apprehensive from my abrupt actions and their potential consequences. My security blanket, Jean, was gone. Then I only had myself to depend upon. Sure, I had Sis and Colleen, but they both were deeply entrenched into their own lifestyles and needs.

No, I was on my own, and I would only have myself to depend upon from there on out. I can remember becoming completely exhausted over all my thoughts. However, sleep was an immediate remedy, even if only temporary. I was so emotionally drained and physically pained too because I had hardly slept at all that previous night. I needed to rest, and I soon fell asleep.

Unfortunately, when I awakened, I recognized that we were approaching Cheyenne, Wyoming. With such a short time to consider things, which was when I made an unexpected error-in-judgement, and another tactical, logistics error. Leave it to me. Oh, Jean, what did I do?

My folks, well, my dad and Stepmother Edith, and little brother, Jackie-Boy, were still living in Sioux Falls, South Dakota. Since my ticket allowed me to make transfers as long as I continued mostly eastward, I realized that I could take a transfer in Cheyenne and make a short detour heading northeastwardly to Sioux Falls. Since I could also jump-off a bus in any town and catch the next one at a later time, I decided to take that transfer, make a layover in Sioux Falls to visit my family and then continue from there straight on to Cleveland. Bad decision…

SISTER PROTECTOR

After a couple of city-bus rides to my folk's home area, I made the short walk in the late evening, to their front door. I had finally arrived at the same old house in Sioux Falls that they had remained living-in for several years, a new first. Unfortunately, even with my surprise, drop-in visit after several years absence, I was not very well received.

It was all too obvious that I was not welcome. Apparently, the lateness of the evening had attracted all three of my family's attention. Edith was caught by surprise by my knocking at the door, and after opening the door to see who it was, she muffled her greeting and cringed backwards leaving me to face my dad. One look at me and my father instantly began turning blood red while displaying obvious anger. He was incensed over the earlier happenings with the orphanage and immediately let his feelings be known.

My dad only cared about one thing when he saw me, and he demanded only one answer from me: Where was Jean?

He was enraged by her previous actions and strategy aiding Colleen's and then Jann's escapes from St. Joseph Orphanage. He was certain Jean was to blame for both their disappearances. I was surprised that he gave little accountability toward my own participation, and he never even mentioned my refusal to return home quite a while back. That was probably my good fortune. He wanted to have police authorities pick-up Jean for kidnapping. Regardless of her blame, I was still about to suffer his wrath.

My dad kept on demanding an answer to the same question over and over again. Each time I failed to respond or gave him a muted or vague answer, he would shove me backward. Eventually, he shoved me so far that I got cornered against two connecting walls in their living-room. Then he began pushing hard against both my shoulders and continued drilling me louder and louder with his same barrage of questions.

"Where is Jean?" my dad yelled into my face. Then he got even rougher, "Where did she go? Where is she hiding?" as I took his cruel slaps across my face and hard punches into my chest and arms.

He continued slapping and punching me with his violent inquisition and became even angrier and more brutal for each of my refusals to answer his questions fully. I cringed in fear as I watched my dad's temper begin seething while his face and blistered eyes contorted into vile, nasty glares because I would not comply and completely give up Jean's whereabouts.

After each angry and threatening question, I just meekly whimpered vague responses to try and mollify him or at least calm and settle him down. I said things like, "I'm not sure, but I think she went to Cleveland," or, "We split-up, and I went to California," and also, "I think Jean went to Mississippi."

After each angry and threatening question left unanswered or given vague responses, I took more and greater severity of his shoves and slaps and punches. It was as though all those years of disavowing me or disowning me or disregarding me all came to full circle. Now he showed precisely and directly how little, if any, feelings that he had for me at all. He truly did disregard me as a non-entity.

My dad had never hit me before that night. The few years that I had actually lived in the same home with him, I had always managed to keep my distance from him and keep my mouth shut while assuredly never deliberately defying him. That night, however, it became obvious that he planned to make-up for lost time and opportunity. All his disbelief in me as his own child, all his rage from embarrassment of how our mother had surely shamed him by lying with another man and all the torment he had gone through being forced to face and deal with me during the past erupted in his volcanic explosions of anger toward me.

The violent and cruel beating I took that evening in my dad's house there in Sioux Falls, South Dakota, and right there in front of my stepmother and little brother, Jack, must have signified to him some sort of necessary revenge: a mean, cruel violent behavior to dispense upon my body over my obvious disloyalty to him and clear loyalties to Jean.

Do you notice the little, *white-lies* strategy? True, I fibbed with the "not sure" answer but not with the others. At one time, they (Jean and Jann) did go to Cleveland, I really did go to California and Jean actually did go to Mississippi. The vagueness was, of course, that I was along on all those trips. He didn't need to know that. I suppose it's like they say, "The devil is in the details!"

After my fierce grilling and vicious beating, though, with tears flooding from my blackened and swelling eyes, and feeling like a human punching bag, I did manage to temporarily break-away from my dad's evil caging to find, and hug and hold my somewhat confused and frightened little brother, Jack. I just kept repeating softly in his ear, "I love you, and I'll see you soon. I love you, and we'll be together soon."

My corner vision let me know that my father was still getting madder and meaner. Maybe my comments to Lil' Jack about "… seeing him soon," and "… being together soon," were probably taken as threats or warnings. My father did not like to be tread on and especially by his kids. So, quickly releasing Jack, I grabbed my two satchels and backed-up as swiftly as I could manage. Then I quickly grabbed the front door handle, twisted hard to open the door, and while excusing myself, backed-out the front door to the porch, shutting the door again, turned, ran down the steps and path to the gate, and was gone.

"None the worse for wear," I thought to myself while wiping my face dry with my coat sleeve. I can remember chuckling out loud too as I paraphrased an earlier comment, "Well, that time at least *I* got out alive!"

I just could not understand why my dad was so mean, why he rejected me so deeply and why he hated Jean so much. I understood even back then that I would eventually physically heal after that vicious pummeling by my father. The emotional healing of my heart was another factor. It would probably take forever to heal if that soon.

Then, I had to smile at my own acceptable act of bravery. If it could seem possible, the one reward that I took-away from that *incident* with my father was the *silence* I had given for Jean's protection. For once, I had been able to help, I mean really personally help, protect my big sister Jean. Finally, someone had come to her defense, to her rescue. In a weird sort of distorted way, I was proud of myself.

"Hey, Jean!" I cried out loud, "I didn't break either. He didn't make me. I was there for you, Sister. Finally, someone looked out for you. I defended you, Jean!"

As I slightly staggered up the street right then, partially from the physical hurt but also from the emotional moment I was still in, I forced myself to stop and pause for a moment and collect my thoughts. Then, it happened. I could not help myself, but suddenly I broke-down in a gushing swirl of sobs and tears. I was letting-out all the anguish and fear and sadness and stress, and now pain, that I had felt all my life toward my dad. Now I believe that at that very moment during my *break-down*, I was actually purging my soul and spirit of all his negativity toward me. I was truly done with my dad in any remotely meaningful way.

I was feeling really disappointed, though, in the aftermath of that struggle. Rather than a preferred welcome and pleasant visit, I had been forced away under truly painful conditions. I continued down the sidewalk to the nearest bus stop. Once there I waited for the next local bus to take me back to the Greyhound Station. Once arrived, I just sat down and mused over my brutal mistake of visiting my parents while I waited for the next Greyhound heading for Cleveland.

Although I was happy to have seen Jack again and promised to see him soon, I was still rattled at my poor judgement for stopping to visit. Questions judging my decision-making capabilities flooded my already injured feelings.

"How could I have been so foolish?" I asked myself and then rattled-off a whole collage of poor-judgement challenges: "So stupid? Didn't you ever learn anything about your dad while still at home? How could you have been so foolish as to think your dad might have changed his ways after you had gone? Why hadn't you sought Jean's advice about returning home? She would have recommended against it, no doubt. Oh, yeah, going home was a big, fat decision that I made-up completely on my own. Not very smart, were you?"

Then I challenged my own capabilities of making it on my own, "Do you really think you have it within yourself to *survive* this cruel world by yourself?"

Then I began thinking about an odd, internal, light-headedness feeling I was having and realized that it was an actual sense of *freedom* that I felt. I was now feeling truly *free* since I had battled my dad to a finish and survived. Unfortunately, I also felt like I was leaving my parent's home with a sense of *good riddance* on both our parts. I was gone from them, but he was gone from me too and for good. And *that* was not bad…

Then, a pleasing and justifiable ending to that whole melee occurred. While sitting at that Sioux Falls Greyhound bus stop waiting for my own bus to Cleveland, I had an encounter with the Sioux Falls police. Two policemen on their regular beats were passing through the bus-station. Maybe my dad had just called the police station and reported my whereabouts to them demanding my immediate arrest for shielding a wanted criminal, Jean. Perhaps, they had already been given a heads-up to watch-out for me. I never found out. Maybe they even knew about the earlier *orphanage escapes* and were told I was a suspect and had been seen in the neighborhood again. Regardless, they walked into the bus station, saw me sitting in the waiting-area, and then, sure enough, stopped to question me.

They were pleasant enough, but they wasted no time in asking me all the direct questions to find out about me: Who I was; where I came from; what I was doing; where I was going; and the serious ones about why all the bruises on my face and neck.

Without giving-up an iota of evidence suggesting Jean's whereabouts, I practically vomited the entire rundown of my irregular visit at home with my dad. Once they had listened to my story, though, and saw more of my recent bruises to substantiate my claims, they chose to let me leave and go on my way. They even hung around the station until my bus arrived and watched until I had climbed aboard. I even remember how they both nodded to me as I stepped-up into the bus, and one of them even tipped his hat to me. It was like they were wishing me well and safe travels. They had been very nice to me, and I did feel safe then. I journeyed the final stage to Cleveland to be with my sisters Mary and Colleen without incident.

MORE FAMILY HISTORY

Cleveland, Ohio

Although I had already called and left a message for Mary that I was coming, Collen and she were still excited and happy to see me again. They were both horrified at my facial bruises. Mary, however, understood clearly and right away what had likely happened. She understood how my injuries had come about, and she was proud of me for my silence. Sis appreciated the beating I had taken to likely protect Jean and the rest of them.

As far as my leaving Jean and Jann and Vancouver, Mary also understood my issues with our eldest sister. She remembered how strict Jean had always been with her too. She even confessed that she had not gone with Jean and me to Mississippi partly because she knew she would have more fun with Jean gone. Of course, after that she also had to describe how much fun she had been having too. It was fun and distracting listening to Sis's sagas and not dwelling on the unfortunate recent past. She always made me smile. What a nice distraction.

Mary worked for a Cleveland manufacturing plant which primarily made parts for another nearby, aircraft-manufacturing plant. She worked in the office, though, because she could type and knew administrative duties from schooling. Plus, Sis had a little bit of teacher training, so she used that experience to get better office-jobs. Mary always like to dress and look pretty on her job too, instead of coveralls and boots and gloves and hardhats.

Sis always joked, "I am NOT an assembly-line woman; I AM a party-line girl, though!" True to her word, she was a party-girl too, and she enjoyed evenings going to parties and dances and movies and on dates. I was happy for her.

Thinking about it now, I believe that Sis Mary was also a *Rosie the Riveter*, sort of. I feel so now because she also had a job which was helping the war cause except that she worked in an office rather than on an assembly-line and manufacturing plant. In a way, if workers like her did not do their jobs, then we likely would not have had opportunities to do ours either. Also, if it hadn't been for the war, Mary would not have had some of her jobs because they were completely war related. It is sort of a moot point, though, because if not then, during those Cleveland years, Sis did eventually absolutely qualify later-on as an official *Rosie* in another city, Henderson, Nevada, near Las Vegas. It was there and then that she did an actual stint on an *assembly-line*. True, it had only been for a short while, a few minutes, I think is all, and she hated it! No matter, Sis was a *Rosie* too.

Mary used to laugh about it later on when she'd beam and give everyone around that huge, dazzling, re-lipped smile of hers and say, "Assembly-lines? Phooey! How is a girl supposed to show of her gorgeous, red-painted fingernails in *gloves*?" Our sister Mary loved to laugh, she loved to show-off, and she loved to make others feel happy being around her. She was great fun to be with.

Colleen, however, was still just barely into high school. Previously, it had been very easy, Sis Mary had told, to get Colleen registered into a public school near to their apartment in Cleveland. Colleen was a good girl and focused on her studies as she needed. In fact, it actually worked out well for me joining them and being there. Now Sis didn't feel so bad leaving Colleen at home so often while she went out and enjoyed herself. I would be there to keep an eye out for Colleen during evening times and we could become good company for each other.

I particularly remember that the first couple of days were nice. Mary and Colleen were off to work and school respectively, so I had the apartment all to myself. I rested, fiddled around, took short walks around the neighborhood, and even read a few, fancy-lady type magazines that Mary had brought home to occupy my time. One thing was for sure: It was very quiet, and I was not used to that at all. Fortunately, Colleen came home from school in the early afternoon, and we had time to visit and catch-up.

Sister Colleen was four years younger than me. Our middle brother, Jerry of course, had passed-away many years earlier, and Colleen and I had gotten closer because of his death. Jerry had been right in the middle of Colleen and me age wise, so while we were all young, we three had been like three-peas-in-a-pod. All of us kids had sort of come in groups, more-or-less, to our real mom, Marie Helms McCord.

The first group of us kids was made up of Jean, the eldest, and Mary and Bo who were twins. Jean was one and a half years older than the twins, and she practically raised them once she was old enough to hold them. Our mother, a good Catholic, was overwhelmed with child-rearing it seemed, and she was pregnant or continually caring for an infant all the time practically right up until her extremely untimely death.

Therefore, the older siblings always had responsibilities watching over the younger ones. The point is that Jean, Mary, and Bo sort of grew up together and were closer to one another. That point may actually help explain why the three of them were all booted out of the house by the ripe old age of at most seventeen-years. Leaving home and being split-up to live with other relatives until circumstances allowed, they also had all got back together for a brief period right there in Cleveland.

Let me refresh memories and details of my own circumstances again. I was in-and-out of the household because of what might be called a *temporary family-member*. Immediately after birth, I had been sent to live with our Aunt Annie. Years later, at around age five, I was allowed to return home for a short period of time until our mother's untimely death. That was when I was sent to another aunt's home, Aunt Kate. Of course, several years later, I went back home once again and lived with my family which then excluded y eldest siblings, but then included our new stepmother, Edith. What I'm trying to explain is that during those years before Mom's death and Jerry's too, Jerry and I had been very close. Years later with Edith there at home, I became close to my sister Colleen, and we did a lot together.

Then, all those years later, we became actual roommates, and it was nice to watch her growing and maturing. She had absolute goals of finishing high school and, if the war ended soon, go on to college. We talked a lot about our family and circumstances and dreams for the future. Colleen was very ambitious and was not afraid of hard work. She talked about the years with Edith when she had actually gone out on the street to seek work and earn money for Edith because our dad had been gone and sent no assistance whatsoever. I really enjoyed that relatively short time being there in Cleveland with her.

The only issue for me, anymore, was that I got bored really quickly. Sis was gone to work each day, and on many evenings and weekends she was out being entertained by her friends from work and elsewhere. Colleen was usually busy with school and homework, so she was studying much of the time. I needed activity, and I needed to help support myself. Getting a job was important and imminent. The cash I had in my pocket would not last long. I had Jean to thank for that attitude and discipline. I thought about her often at that time. I surprised even myself to realize that I had left her and Jann in Vancouver, Washington only a week before.

Jean, as the eldest of all us kids, was also undeniably "the leader of our pack." We other kids all followed her lead, but usually took her side as an original *silent majority* in the multitude of arguments and fights which developed in our family household. Most of those battles were only the ones I had heard about because I was dumped-off living with other relatives so many of those conflicting years. Nevertheless, when I did live at home for that brief period before Mom died, Jean watched over and led the rest of us kids.

Perhaps, now is a proper time to include another somewhat unusual tidbit of family drama. It involved my parents and all of us kid's births. So far, in telling all those chronicles so far of my family, I have mentioned the births and death of all of us. To me, it was always curious, if not fascinating to plot all of us sibling's births and realize quite a coincidence. We were all born so closely together and usually less than two-years apart from each other: Jean in 1922; Bo and Mary in 1924; me in 1926; Jerry in 1928; Colleen in 1930; Jann in 1932; and Jack in 1934. See what I mean? Poor Mom… Talk about keeping a Catholic barefoot and pregnant.

Another curious, if not dreadful fact involved our mother's passing following that pathetic, botched abortion. Had Mother gone through with her pregnancy, that next child would have been born in 1936. Interesting and unusual record. Nine pregnancies in fourteen years. Sorry, Mom. Our poor, dear departed mother. May God Bless her. In fact, regardless of what staunch Catholics, or anyone else for that matter, may believe, I believe God already has blessed her.

Back to more redundant and rehashing information about us McCord kids, though, Jean was definitely the eldest of all of us. There was also little doubt in any of our minds, too, that Jean was most likely the smartest of all us children. She also always seemed the most driven, ambitious, and angry too. However, we others loved to tease Jean about her intelligence, and we know she loved it.

"Jean, it's not fair!" we would pretend to complain, "When you were born, and they passed-out brains, you took them all! There were none left for any of us, meanie!"

I believe now that Jean argued, or debated, with our father so much that he must have truly resented her intelligence. No doubt he recognized that she was more intelligent, if not smarter, than he was, and it really bothered him. He was also a real male chauvinist pig. He despised Jean right from her own birth because she was a female. To him, the eldest always needed to be a male.

Furthermore, growing-up, Jean always saw another side to situations, and unfortunately, they almost always differed from our father's point-of-view. As a true MCP, he felt that women were supposed to stay quiet and remain in the kitchen, or in the bedroom. That was where they really belonged. Jean would do surely battle with any man over any of those conditions.

She was truly an early, *women's-rights* activist, only she never joined any clubs or organizations. Jean just fought all the male-sexist battles on her own. Sadly, she always let our father know about her viewpoints too, and she paid terrible prices for them at his hands. Jean was damaged and injured on the outside for all her time at home by our father from his beatings. All the physical injuries eventually repaired themselves in time. The greater harm, however, was the permanent damage our father did to Jean's psyche.

I believe that she grew-up mostly resenting all men as a result. Even she and my brother Bo would argue so much too and continued having sibling disputes most of their adult lives until Jean passed-away in 1993. I have believed for a long time, though, that their issues were mostly based on Jean's inability to ever accept what any man said. Actually, however, right after Jean went to live with Grandma Agnus, Bo chose to move in with them in Hayward, Wisconsin. They both remained there while attending college until Grandma's death a few years later.

That was when they first moved and lived together in Cleveland before eventually splitting-up and living separately. They both found different jobs working for war cause industries. Then, of course, Jean met Mary in Duluth for a brief period in order to allow Sis to attend school while she worked. That was when they had both shared that same attic-room as Sis and I did many months later. Then, Jean returned to Cleveland and Sis went with her in order for Jean to attend school again and for Sis to work. That was their arrangement for a while. About six months later was when Mary left Jean there in Cleveland to find me in St. Paul, Minnesota, and we took off for Duluth, MN together.

Of course, it was in Cleveland, when only a few months later, Mary and I had escaped Duluth just in-the-nick-of-time and joined Jean there in Cleveland. She had still been living there alone and working at an armament's factory. See what I told you? Jean, the original *Rosie the Riveter*! Later, of course, Jean and I left for Pascagoula, Mississippi and then on to Vancouver, Washington while Sis Mary got Colleen's help to fool the nuns and have Colleen join her at her apartment in Cleveland. Jean and I, however, got clever, sneaky, and devious and snatched Jann from the orphanage and had decided to first go on to Cleveland before heading back to Vancouver. Finally, I returned to be with Sis and Colleen there again in Cleveland.

So, hopefully from this little diversion of mine, you may have recognized the whole, full circle of events and times. In many ways, we all sort of migrated to Cleveland at one-time-or-another to begin, carry-on and fulfill our war year's work needs. So much of what happened to me sort of sprung from that city. I began my work career there, I returned to develop and improve my welding skills and job experience and perhaps the most significant event of my life as of yet was still to occur right there in Cleveland, Ohio. But, let's not get ahead of ourselves. That's another story for later.

WENDY DOES IT ALL

Several days had already passed, and I was getting itchy. Itchy and nervous. By that time, I had been working so much that a day without a job felt really unusual. I enjoyed my visiting with Sis and Colleen, but it was work that I needed. Not only did I want to pay-my-own-way, but I also wanted to prove that I could. Having left Jean and Sissy Jann, I wanted to show Big Sis that I could take care of my own self, pay my way, and take care of my own money.

By then, I was an experienced arc-welder with several certifications under my belt and a good record of work from Kaiser Vancouver Shipyards. I was pretty certain that with all that construction work going on in Cleveland, and all the welding demands, I would get a job fairly quickly. After just a couple days to relax and clear my head for this new city and my new family of sisters, I started looking for a new job.

It was still late fall of 1944. I remember that another Christmas was approaching, and it would be my first with Sis and Colleen together. Cleveland and the whole country were both decorating themselves for the holidays and just about busting-out-all-over with work and job-opportunities. Fortunately, arc-welding was in fairly high-demand, and openings for welders were advertised everywhere and jobs were readily available at multiple locations.

One place that looked especially good to me because of its near-bye location was at a Cleveland equipment manufacturing plant called Warner & Swasey. Apparently, they were a pretty big outfit working for the war effort building machine tools and such; however, they were also known for developing and building telescopes for astronomy studies. It didn't matter any to me. They were desperately needing and advertising for arc-welders, so I thought, "Why not? Welding is welding."

Early that next morning, I got cleaned-up and made myself look respectable for an interview: Hair styled nicely with minimal facial cosmetics and lipstick. To look the role, though, I was wearing a pair of Levi denim jeans and a long-sleeved, cotton shirt which was a typical welder's attire. Oh, yes, I was going to impress, alright. I was applying to become a dirty, burned-up welder for sure, but I was intent on showing the company that a produced weld didn't care who was behind that hood and stinger.

Wanting to feel pretty underneath all that heavy, awkward, and restraining gear meant more to me than the welder inside or behind the hood. Of course, it was a little bit of *Rosie the Riveter* braggadocio too. I enjoyed seeing all the placards, billboards and posters around town showing off all of Rosie's skills and asking women to join their ranks. There we were right in everyone's' faces telling them that women *could do-it-all. We could work hard all day and still look pretty, and then play hard all night looking gorgeous*! I figured at minimum, the least I would do was add a little color to otherwise drab and steel-gray lives.

I wanted to impress the job-site interviewers. While maybe surprising or shocking them, I also wanted to show my serious side. Inside a special folder that I brought along, I kept all my Kaiser Vancouver Shipyards arc-welding certifications, work-records, some cancelled check-stubs, and even some of the special-welding and job-related citations and awards that I had received. I would make that particular folder available to the company interviewers, if necessary, for their inspection and review. Additionally, I carried along a personal bag with my own short-leathers and welding-apron inside to show seriousness.

ARC WELDING 101

Leathers are the protective gear a welder wears to cover and protect their regular work clothes. Without them, a single day at work would destroy all your clothing attire from falling, molten-metal slag, fumes, sparks, flames, smoke, and general debris, and contaminants in the air. Usually, welders wore clothing underneath their leathers that was old, used and disposable, if necessary. Nobody ever said that welding was a nice, clean, and safe form of work.

On the contrary, even trying to be extremely careful, all welders absorbed their share of burns, blisters, and injuries on practically a daily basis. I already told you about my *eye flash* burn that I received when I was first in welding school. Well, there were a lot more ways of injuring yourself while welding too. *Welding* is a job that by its very nature was designed and destined, unfortunately, to harm a *welder*.

It is no easy task to take two separate pieces of steel, or metal, and weld them together so that they become one, single unit. There are a lot of issues involved such as types of metal, sizes of metal, thickness of metal, location, surrounding steel parts, or hardware, and even cleanliness of the area to be welded. A welder had to pay attention all the time. When welding, it was always important to stay alert about what was around you at all times and to closely mind what you were doing all the time.

Let me explain.

The ***essence of welding***. Wikipedia says: "Welding is a fabrication or sculptural process that joins materials, usually metals…, by using high heat to melt the parts together and allowing them to cool causing fusion."

The ***action of welding***, however, involves several stages: Two pieces of similar metal that need to be welded together first need to have the joining surfaces cleaned and ground smooth for a better weld; next, the welder chooses the correct welding electrodes, or rods, for the metal project. Welding rods are covered with a flux material designed to make a better connection between the rod and the molten metal. The electrode rod, itself, is used to add sufficient additional metal to the two adjoining pieces that are fit together.

The rod is then fit properly into the welder's stinger, or electrode holder. Next, the two pieces of metal are held closely together at the desired position and temporarily attached using a few small tacks, or tiny welds, spread evenly or regularly over the entire welding area. Then the welders use their own personal technique of touching the welding rod ever-so-carefully to the two metals being permanently attached causing a high-voltage arc and extremely intense heat that melts the two metal edges causing them to fuse together along with the small part of molten, metal from their welding rod to fill the gap.

The ***art of welding***, however, the craft, the skill, the expertise, itself, is found in determining all those *issues* previously mentioned like metal-type and proper electrode (rod), size of project, and thickness of metals to be welded, etc. Then it is in matching or *connecting those metals together perfectly* using *fusion* (the rod touching the metal which causes an arc and melts them), and doing so without causing any cracks, weak points, or holes in the final welded product.

It is said that when two separate pieces of metal are properly welded together, the welded area is even stronger than the original pieces of metal. In any case, however, there is hot, molten metal involved. That, in itself, should suggest danger.

For instance, slag is the crusty, covering part left over from a weld, and it is hot and molten at its initial point. Occasionally, and especially if a welder were not paying close enough attention, some of the slag could fall-off a weld and land right on any part of the welder. That is an example of the value of protective, leather gear which comes in handy absorbing all the burning sparks and molten-metal slag. The more exposed skin or regular attire covered by leather, the more protection.

Of course, another serious factor is the welder's positioning on any job. Sometimes, a welding task only requires *flat* welding on a smooth surface, and that was typically simple, with easy access and less danger. Another position was *vertical welding* where the welding remained directly in front of the welder and kept climbing up until the weld was completed. In that position, slag would fall-off and land on or near the welder, so it was necessary to be extra-cautious. Also, there was *diagonal welding* where the required weld went upwards in an angle. Hot, molten slag could fall-off, would fall-off, at any point in the weld.

Finally, there was *overhead* welding where a welder laid flat on their back and welded directly above themselves. Get my drift? Gravity was not your friend. Hot, scorching, burning, and potentially scaring, molten slag was absolutely going to fall directly on the welder. Thus, adequate protection was absolutely necessary.

Even with all a welder's protective gear and all the extra-special caution a welder might take, accidents still happened, and the unexpected might occur at any given moment without any warning. Once in a while, as an example, some break-away slag might fall-off a weld and somehow, someway, and mysteriously slip under your protective gear, or go down inside a glove you were wearing, or down one of your boots, or just unluckily land on an accidentally unprotected part of your skin. *Aaaahhh!* Talk about screaming and cussing and fast movements trying to remove the necessary gear or clothing in order to knock away the burning slag from the burning flesh. Every welder has got nasty, burning stories to share with curious listeners, and every welder has got scars to confirm, verify and prove their stories true.

That is why *leathers* were so critically important to the welder. They usually consist of a full, leather jacket, a full leather apron like chef's wear or a half-jacket where the shoulders, bib and short-back and long-sleeve arms receive protection. With those a welder also often wore either a full-leather pants or a half-cover for the waist and legs. Add to that some long, heavy gloves, a neck scarf, an optional, soft head-cap cover, some thick, protective-leather boots, and the *piece-de-resistance,* the welder's often personalized, welding hood, and the worker was ready and dressed-to-kill, so-to-speak.

Naturally, the typically personalized, adjustable, flip-up hood with its unique viewing shield of protective glass and extremely tinted-glass for viewing intense light produced from welding was critical. It was selected and adjusted just right for the particular welder or the particular job. The *hood* is what made a welder look like a welder. It was a unique and one-of-a-kind piece of equipment.

Typically, a hood covers the full face and top of the head and down below and under the chin. It also wraps around and covers both sides of a face clear back well behind a welder's ears. A *hood* also has adjustable points on both sides which allows welders to flip or lift their hoods completely up and raise them above their heads. That way a welder could easily inspect his work, lift it to have a desired conversation or do whatever might be necessary in order to prepare for the next weld.

WARNER & SWASEY ARMAMENTS

Interview

Anyway, back to my interview, I walked onto that Warner & Swasey plant site, saw the personnel offices but then continued through the plant-site seeking someone who looked like a foreman or supervisor. I spotted some men all huddled over a tall, slanted table and obviously studying some blueprints or something. I walked over to them and stood to the side waiting to get their attention. It was only a moment before the three of them all looked-up and over at me. Then like a choreographed dance move for synchronized robots, together they all gave me a complete, once-over check-out from my head to my feet and then back-up to my face.

Having their abrupt and complete attention after obviously interrupting their chain-of-thought, I addressed the group, "Good morning, Sirs, I am here for the arc-welding job. Can you tell me who to see?"

The head-honcho of the group, who just happened to be the tallest of them too, spoke up quickly, "Wow!" he said, "You're a welder? Well, I'll be darned." He looked me over again.

Immediately, I had my certifications from Kaiser available and handed them over to the honcho's outstretched hand. He looked them over and began shaking his head as he spoke, "Well, I am *darned*! The *shipyards*, huh? *Kaiser's too*, huh?"

"Yes, Sir," I responded, "I can do it all: Flat, vertical, diagonal, or overhead. We were building double-bottomed mini-carriers, and I got to do some time on the Liberty Ships just to say I did. All I need now is a job. I'm set to go."

Well, without much more detail, I can say that they were impressed and very happy to meet me. It turned out that I had good instincts because the honcho walked me straight over to the hiring office and introduced me to the personnel clerk. I was told to come right back the next morning to that same office door and I would be taken into the plant area and to an assigned station.

They seemed pleased, and I sure was. It looked like a decent place to work and getting a job that easy was reassuring and made me happy. I had a job that fast! My sisters would be happy too and impressed. Now, I would surely pay my own way. Besides that, at least presently due to some special project we were supposed to be on, we were working six-days a week with Sundays off. I figured that this job would work out just fine.

"MUM" WAS THE WORD

Everything started out well too. I met the same man the next morning as scheduled, and after the required personnel paperwork was completed, he walked me through the plant to a distant section. I learned that whatever was going on in that area was secretive and only cleared personnel could get inside. We had to pass through a special gate with a guard in order to get to my special work assignment. I was introduced to my new crew members, and they were all delighted to meet me and have me joining them. I got shown around the site, but I was told nothing about our actual project.

All the foreman could say was that our crew's job was sort of a hush-hush contract for the government. I was told absolutely nothing about the actual product that I would be working on. What the crew had completed already didn't seem like much, and with minimal structure in place so far, there was virtually no way to identify or recognize what the project would end up becoming. It sure didn't look like a mini carrier, that's for sure.

So, I just accepted the secrecy of the job, and let it go at that. My crew only had to complete regularly assigned tasks each day and then go home. Everything would be fine. Ignorance was bliss, so they say. Also, I had been placed on dayshift, so I was very happy about that. All I had to do was whatever my assigned task was each day and then go home. Gee! Piece-of-cake!

My job turned out to be fairly basic. Each morning, I met the other crew members near the front gate, and we would all be walked to our own, special jobsite by a management person. Since Warner & Swasey Plant Projects was a huge area, our crew had to be escorted through and past other areas of the plant and then through that guarded, special gate to get to any of those *hush-hush*, protected worksites. Once there, we were all showed what needed to be accomplished on our project for that particular day, including all arc-welding. My welding machine was not portable, so any specific tasks requiring my welding would always be setup in our work zone for easier and better controlled access.

As I mentioned before, everybody did their assigned jobs for the day, and then we all went home. The next shift, swing-shift, would come-in and pick-up where we left-off. Looking around that huge plant to check-out other *classified* worksites, I easily recognized, however, that we were all working on the same type projects as my crew was on. The difference was that the other crew's projects were in different locations, of course, and they were all at different stages of development. Some were at beginning stages, while others were at similar stages to our own.

I soon learned that nobody on our crew, or any other crews, for that matter, knew anything about our projects. Apparently, that *classified* program was working because nobody knew anything about what we were building or what we were working on or what we were doing. We were all scratching our heads and trying to figure-out what-in-the-world it was that we were making.

Having an inquisitive mind by nature, naturally, and right away I had to ask our boss what we were doing. He was quick to reply, "Oooohhh, hush, hush!" Still teasing, our foreman crossed his lips with his forefinger and whispered, "Shhhhhh! This is *Top-Secret* stuff you're working on, and nobody can tell you because nobody knows!" Then he'd laugh.

Honestly, though, at the time, I think our boss was a little frustrated too. I do not believe that even our bosses knew what it was we were building. Mum was the word.

LATRINE QUEEN

Anyway, a few days had gone by, and there had been no issues except for one: The latrine. Until I got there, it had always been a man's worksite. Few women worked in open, new construction, and almost never as welders. The war had changed all that, however. Now, women were needed in all types of manufacturing and development. They were still advertising for women to become *Rosie's,* and more-than-ever as welders. *Wendy the Welder,* at that. No matter, I was the first and only woman welder on any of those crews, at least in the beginning.

Thus, the only time there was a problem was when I needed to use the toilet, and some man would try to use it while I was. After a few embarrassing times, we all sort of adjusted to being a little more careful. The only difference was that the men only had to be careful about one little ol' me; I had to be careful about the whole darn lot of them! I openly admit, however, that my crew were all absolute gentlemen. They *pardoned* and *excused* themselves all over the place until it started becoming almost a joke to all of us.

"Good morning, Missy! Pardon me, please!" the guys would joke. Or they'd say, "Well, how d' do, Missy! Please excuse me all to pieces!"

I knew their joking was always a tease about the toilet's use, but we all laughed about it, anyway. I'm certain, however, that I got more flustered or embarrassed than any of them did. That is until they got used to me using their latrine. Like I said, in the beginning there were a few *awkward* instances, but the latrine was really the only real issue we had. I suppose I might now consider it *the calm before the storm,* because big, serious issues were to come later on, but just then, everything was fine. All was well, and we all got along very well.

In fact, I hadn't even been working there for too long before I'd established a decent routine. I'd get up in the morning, dress and clean-up was the first thing. My job was a little farther away by bus, so I was up in the earlier morning to compensate. Mary was up early too because she needed so much extra time for make-up and such. That was a slight advantage for me. Cosmetics did not go fare well with welding soot and smoke. Regardless, I went to work clean and fresh but with nothing fancy going on, not on my face nor on my body. My exposed skin and clothes suffered the consequences of a dirty, burning construction job.

Dirt and grime from the worksite and actual job would tend to exaggerate face creams, rouge, and lipstick reactions. So, a fancied-up woman-worker would look like a Dr. Jekyll to Mr. Hyde transition by day's end. At shift's end you might see some woman with large, black, runny eyes and a blood-red, dripping mouth to accent her overall tarnished and grimy-looking face-coloring. Not a pleasant picture at all: Scary, if not downright laughable.

Oh, don't get me wrong. I enjoyed making myself look pretty, but the latrine wasn't the best opportunity to do so. Plus, due to any potential interruptions that might happen almost anytime I used the men's toilet, trying to stay *lovely* was a lost, if not mistaken, art form. So, I suppose you could say that once I was at work, I looked the part I played. Nothing fancy.

My days usually went by comfortably. We all did our jobs and joked around during breaks or lunchtime. Often, we all laughed or teased about our secret-mission assignment which was *so secret* even Warner and Swasey didn't know a thing about it! But I was enjoying my work, and the days went by without problems except for an occasional, "Ooops! Pardon me, all to heck, Missy!"

Then, one Monday morning I got a humorous but absolutely delightful gift from all the crew and the bosses. First off, I was met at the front gate by a crew member, and then personally ushered through the plant and then through our *top-secret* work-zone gate entry and finally into our worksite area. There, I was unusually so cordially greeted by many other crew members as I walked to the welding machines to turn-on and reset my own preferred specs for my unit. Then I began gathering-up my tools and gear until suddenly, I heard someone call out my name.

"Missy! Got a minute, please? Come over here, please, would ya, for a minute?" The Foreman had called out to me while waving over a few of the other crew members too.

As I approached the group which was sort of assembling over near the latrine area, I noticed a large object way over to the side. It was covered over by canvas and set-up directly behind the assembled men. That was curious in itself, but the boss spontaneously calling me for a meeting was the real suspense. What was going on, and why was I the only one called out *by name*, or nickname? I was slightly embarrassed but soon pleased to find out why.

Our foreman looked really tickled and happy with himself as he spoke, "Gather 'round here, Lady and Gentlemen. You all know that we are all constantly apologizing and embarrassing our little Miss, here, and way too many times already. She is a darn good worker and keeps-up with every one of us every day. The only times we get slowed down, in fact, is when we dirty, filthy brutes have gotta go, and then we go and embarrass our little, lady worker here all the time. Well, no more!"

By that time, I was laughing and shaking my head right along with all the guys but still wondering where his talk was leading. Then came the moment-of-truth.

The Foreman and another worker on cue had walked over to the big, canvas drape, grabbed it by both sides and heaved, heartily yanking the canvas covering completely aside.

"Here's to you, Missy, and with all our most sincere apologies, etc. etc.!" the Foreman laughed as he introduced and welcomed the hilariously huge object beneath.

It was a large, somewhat crude but very nicely constructed *Ladies Only* latrine. You could tell *Ladies Only* because of the oversized and crooked sign which had been nailed above the doorway entrance. The crew had gotten together sometime after work and over that previous Sunday and had constructed the toilet and set it up at our worksite. They had probably built it as much for self-defense so as not to *embarrass* either of us anymore. No matter, I was just tickled by their thoughtfulness, anyway.

What it meant to me, however, was that I was really welcome on-the-job, and the boss and crew cared about me and my needs. Their kindness had moved me with their simple, yet very thoughtful gift. That *Ladies Only* latrine continued to mean a great deal to me for quite some time. Their gesture, although very sweet and kind at that moment, was to be relatively short-lived, however and become the focal point of a personal and serious uprising.

But that didn't happen until later on. Sometimes, circumstances can change which changes everything else around it. I suppose that's an example of life in general. Everything may seem just perfect at one point, and then one little thing can happen, and everything seems wrong and begins unraveling. In time, our situation would change right there for Warner and Swasey, and that would end-up changing everything else too.

But I was delighted at that time. No more bathroom interruptions. No more waiting in the sidelines for access to the one-and-only men's latrine. Now I had my very own, personal latrine just for me! Life got simpler and happier and better. Our jobs carried us right on through the days and coming weeks. I was happy and content with my life.

"I should have known better," I told myself later. All good things come to an end… eventually. All was well, alright, until one evening after work on a weekend relaxing when I just happened to learn something by accident, and lo-and-behold, all hell was to break-out!

HUSH HUSH

My job and our work was going along just fine. Each day I would be cleared at the entry-gate to go into the plant-site. I would follow the clearly labeled roadway and walkway to our section of the manufacturing plant. I remember always being in awe of the sheer size and construction and variety of the Warner & Swasey complex. It seemed like W&S back then was into everything imaginable. Every morning on the labeled walk that I would take to our designated work site before the guarded entry, I could look off in any direction and see new development and new construction going on. It meant another section was manufacturing something completely new and different from the previous section I had just walked past.

Our site and our project still remained the most secretive of all. I mean, I walked past one area, and it was easy to see and recognize that the crews there were making lathes or big machines which would then make small parts for other machines or equipment. Further down the specified walkway, and I understood that they were making some sort of giant telescope for observing space. The point I'm making is that every other area or section of development seemed to be no big, secret. Usually, it was fairly obvious as to what was going on and what eventual product was being built, constructed, or manufactured.

But, oh, no, not ours. Once you passed through the guarded-gate and entered into our protected zone, nobody could tell what the contraption was that we were working on? For one thing, not just anybody could even get into our specialized area. We workers would have to go through a proper entry-point, the guarded-gate, and there was always a security-guard or somebody to check-up on clearances for who was entering. That was all fine, but when I asked about the project we were working on, even the guards had no idea as to what was going-on, or what was even being built by us workers.

I learned quite a few of the different people's names who were around most of the time while I was there, and I was always friendly when I approached any of them. For instance, I still remember the guard at our second, restricted entry-gate with access to our special, *classified-site*. I especially remember our mutual teasing of each other. Often times, I would greet him with a big grin, "Good morning, Mr. Carson, How're we doing today?"

He'd always smile back and say, "Well, good morning to you, Pretty Lady, and I'm doing just fine, but I sure don't know about you!"

We'd both chuckle over and over again each day. Of course, we both had variations too. Like, for instance, I'd flip the greeting and say, ""Morning, Mr. Carson. I feel just awful today. How about you?"

Mr. Carson would quick reply, "Good morning to you too, Miss Patricia, and I was feeling terrific, but now you got me feelin' sad. What's the matter?"

My point about all that greeting silliness was that often right along with our morning hail, we would both quiz each other over our secret project. After saying hello to Mr. Carson, I might add, "I feel so bad, Mr. Carson because I don't know what-in-the-world I'm doing today. Have you got any idea?"

His quick response would always be something like, "I haven't got a clue, Mam. I don't think I'm supposed to know, so you can be sure that I'll be the last to know. It's hush-hush, you know."

Although our gatekeeper, Mr. Carson, always played along at that point, one difference was that he would never ask me what we were doing. I always figured that he was just fine with not knowing because it meant less stress. But I sure as heck was curious about our job. I was beginning to understand that maybe Mr. Carson had the right idea. It was sort of like that egotistical crack some smart asses use, "If I wanted your opinion, I'd give you one!"

That was a little like this job, it seemed. If the bosses or their bosses or their boss's bosses wanted us to know what we were doing, then they would tell us. Apparently, they did not care for us to know. Anyway, we just went on day-after-day with our sly little jokes or comments and continued to do each task as it was assigned for our mysterious, classified project.

And most days at quitting time, if Mr. Carson were there at the gate, I'd end the shift with, "Good day, Mr. Carson, and I'm still 'clueless.' No idea what I'm doing."

As always, Mr. Carson was quick with some sort of a reply, "Me neither, Mam. I have no idea what you're up to neither!" Then I'd grin, and we'd both laugh, and it always ended the shift on a positive note.

The joking and the comradery among all us workers went on day after day. Same old thing every day. Shift starts, we work until break. Back to work doing what we're assigned. Lunch break and some of us would sit around and chit-chat a bit. Occasionally, our work came up for question, and whoever was talking might offer an answer to the puzzle, "I figured it out! It's the insides of a submarine! Yeah, that's it. We're building this thing from the inside-out. Problem is, when we're done with the outside, we'll be stuck in the inside. So, then we gotta go to sea with it until we win, and someone can cut us out!"

The braver talkers would try to outdo each other with taller-tales, and the sillier they were, the better. We had contraptions like USA sponsored modern art getting ready for an International Exhibit, so it really needed to be really secret. Of course, the goofy worker with the idea was actually the *secret* artist who had designed the artful mess. Or, it was a giant beehive, and the company was going to start producing its own steel-made honey! Or, my favorite was the one about it being deliberately made to confuse the enemy, so that when we dropped it off in Germany or Japan, they'd spend so much time and effort trying to figure out what it was, that we could sneak-up on them from behind, kick their butts and win the war real fast. That got a lot of laughs, I remember.

But our corniness and silly, lunch-time pastimes always just showed that none of us really had the faintest idea of what we were really doing. It became: The Great Mystery to us all. It was sort of funny at first, then some of us got a little bothered by not knowing or not understanding why we could not be told or not know. After a while, though, the humor laid-off, and we just went to work… with no idea of what it was. We all simply tried not thinking about it. Ignorance was bliss. That was, of course, until one morning when I had to go and open-my-big-mouth…

'WURZBURG' NEWSREEL

The issue, or problem, began very innocently, at first. Isn't that the way it seems so often? You're just doing something quietly and minding your own business when suddenly, *Wham!* Right out of the wild-blue-yonder comes some screwball thing that just goes and messes up your whole day. That's sort of what happened to me. I was just relaxing and enjoying myself when something occurs which goes ahead and screws-up my whole day. Only this incident messed-up a bunch of days and got me into some serious hot-water for a while.

Anyway, here's what happened: Remember how *hush-hush* everything was on my job about the project that we were working on? Okay, fine. Now, all I did was go home for the nice day-off that we had coming. Because we worked six days a week and right on through Saturday, we had one nice Sunday off every week. If there was ever something really critical going on at the plant on some project, the company might have a shift or two or even three, dayshift, swing-shift and nightshift or graveyard-shift, come in and work on Sundays.

Only men were allowed to work on Sundays, though. I guess Women's Liberation in those days ended on Saturdays. That was where men drew a line. War, or no war, working Sundays and women would not fit together. That was almost sacrilegious. After all, Sundays were sacred, so only men could work and still salvage their souls. Thus, Sundays were saved for men only. Women could go to church, instead, and get saved there!

Well, regardless, I didn't care at all. I loved my one-and-only Sunday off, and I had my wonderful day-off coming. It was almost always a day that I really tried to relax and enjoy myself. A picnic to one of the city parks was always nice. Or, a day's outing down by the shoreline of Lake Erie was pleasant. Yet, the one thing to do that was an all-around crowd pleaser was, of course, the movies.

I could always count on company too. Mary and Colleen loved going to movies even more than I did. There were several really nice theatres located in downtown Cleveland. They were all arranged near to each other in what was called *The Playhouse Square*. Each theatre always played the latest and greatest films available. Very often, and always on a Sunday afternoon, all three of us sisters would go together, catch a bus downtown, and then walk over to whichever theatre was showing what we wanted to see.

One particular Sunday, there was a movie playing that all three of us were dying to see. I'll never forget that film either, or it wasn't because of how great the film was. Rather, it was because of what happened as a result of watching that particular film on that carefree spree we took on that pleasant Sunday. The film we all wanted to see was called *The Enchanted Cottage,* and it starred the gorgeous Robert Young and the funny but beautiful Dorothy McGuire. Anyway, it was supposed to be a big hit movie, and we all looked forward to seeing it.

Wouldn't you know it, though, but as soon as we arrived at the theatre and got in line to buy our ticket, Sis saw some friends of hers from work, and well, she just had to go with them because they were trying to attract some cute boys with whom to watch the movie. It was okay with Colleen and me because we would be paying attention to Robert Young and not Sis, anyway. So, with abrupt apologies and begged understandings, Sis Mary was gone, and Collen and I were left to enjoy the film together.

Here's the important catcher, though. Once inside after quickly buying our drinks and popcorn for snacking and finding some good seats up closer to the screen with great views, we prepared for all the other good things that came with a movie to view. At our modern, today's shows, all you get is over twenty minutes or more of local sales advertisements, theatre snack-sales pressure ads and lots of previews of coming-attractions before you get to watch the single film for which you paid to see.

Back then, however, there were lots of things going-on that were great fun besides just the movies. Of course, there were typical advertisements and coming attractions, but there were also usually two films to see: The main attraction and another movie of lesser fame or value. They were split up usually with an *intermission* separating them. Intermission time often had prizes and giveaways based on ticket numbers sort of like a lottery. It was exciting to see who might win, and it might be us! The prizes that they would give away were usually free popcorn or free movie tickets for upcoming films. It was fun.

The real kicker, and what made the movies event so special that day was what also always came with the film venue. Of course, there were always the famous, *episodic* programs where each week, the theatre would play another episode of an on-going, suspenseful, and dramatic show that continued-on week-after-week. Each week they would show a thrilling segment of a particular mini-series with a cliff-hanger closing at the end: "Will Captain Marvel be destroyed at the hands of the evil ruler? Or, will our hero find a way to escape and still save the world from ruin? Return next week to see the exciting, next episode in the ongoing saga of: *Adventures of Captain Marvel!* See you next week!" What a hook, but it was great fun.

However, all I've mentioned so far is a long-winded explanation to tell you about the best part of all, besides the movie, of course. It was the short and summarized *Newsreel* program that was provided at every theatre screening before the main attraction film was shown. *Newsreel* programming offered brief, highlights of special events, war efforts and anything of unusual or interesting value to the audience. Those *news* films would include high-lighted snippets of Allied or American Forces advances or victories, etc. They might provide a brief review, for instance, of a new car coming-on-line for the consumer public. There was always something special happening in politics, the arts or sciences that would be interesting to show to the public too.

Just about everybody had radios to tune into for comedy, drama, and suspense programs and for news and music specials. But those programs satisfied radio-listeners, not viewers. A few people were getting TV's, but they had very limited ownership and viewing capacity. The movies were a great place to go and catch-up visually on some interesting and noteworthy news items going on all around the world. I loved those segments and was always glued to my seat for their showings.

So now, I have just set-up the background information for what turned out to be a seriously crazy week coming-up for me.

The *Newsreel* program on that Sunday afternoon's showing turned out to be very interesting for me. At first they showed news highlights of

General Eisenhower and the Allied advances in Europe. General "Ike" was smiling and waving at a crowd from a car, and the theatre audience cheered. Then there was some item about the latest ladies fashions from New York City followed by some Hollywood actress throwing kisses to her beloved fans. All those stories were fun and interesting, but it was the next news item that absolutely floored me.

It was another *war news* highlight that time, and it was about an advanced radar-system that the Germans were developing. Apparently, their radar-system was supposed to really be assisting the Germans in their ground, military operations by watching for and tracking enemy military movements. High-level, big, and important stuff, I imagined. As the newsreel visibly displayed, and the film spokesman explained to us viewers, the radar-system's design consisted of a really huge, parabolic dish about twenty-five feet in diameter as a giant reflector. It was held-up by a bunch of vertical and horizontally intermeshed bracing and mounted on a really big railway carriage for transportation purposes.

I learned that their German Radar System was called the *Giant Wurzburg*. It was being built by some famous German contractor with that Wurzburg name, but I remembered hearing the newscaster mention the famous name of *Zeppelin* in the story. Everybody had heard of the big, airships made by him, and of the infamous Hindenburg disaster in the late 1930's. However, that Giant Wurzburg German Radar System they were showing on the theatre screen was supposed to be very superior. In fact, it was suspected of really assisting Adolph Hitler and his German Army in their efforts to conquer Europe and Africa... and the world!

Well, all I can say is to believe me. I was shocked and then amazed at those visually stunning pictures and film of that *Wurzburg Radar System* news story. It was an enormous, parabolic dish style radar used by the German's. It was big and round with dozens of crisscrossing, square-tubing forming its concave bracing which held a giant reflector dish. The carriage, itself, was enormous too in order to hold the dish and its framework. Yes, it sure was big, and it sure was amazing alright. And I recognized it right away. It was the *exact same thing* that we were building on our job at the Warner & Swasey Plant.

I was so excited to have finally figured out what we had been working on all that time at the plant that I felt giddy. Of course, I didn't know any more than anyone else at the theatre about the radar systems' full purpose or specifics or significance than what we had just learned from the *Newsreel* program. But, I was sort of self-satisfied and amused that I had at least recognized the thing. I couldn't wait to tell my co-workers and Mr. Carson at the gate about my discovery. I thought that it would be real fun playing another round of "What Is It, Anyway?" during our next day's noon lunchbreak.

Of course, I bragged a little to my sister Colleen sitting next to me. "Hey, what do you know about that?" I said matter-of-factly as I excitedly pointed at the theatre screen. Then I gave specifics, "I know what that is on the screen. I'm making one at my job. I do a lot of the welding on the one I'm working on."

After a bit, though, our feature film started, and I was just absolutely mesmerized by the movie's dashing star, Robert Young. The film was very popular at that time because it was about a war pilot (Young) who got injured and disfigured in war and ran-away in shame and embarrassment only to meet a plain-looking girl (Dorothy McGuire) and fall in love. By the time that film had ended, and our tears had been wiped dry and the next comedy film had ended too, we both were talking nothing but movies and movie stars. I had all but forgotten about that other theatre programming and especially that *Giant Wurzburg* news reel.

GAME WINNER

The next morning was a Monday, and I went off to work happier than usual. By then, I had thought of the *Newsreel* story about the German radar system, the Giant Wurzburg and Zeppelin thing. I chuckled again at the thought of playing our guessing game at work and then my surprise answer. I sure figured I was going to have *one over on them*. The simple and hilarious fact that their newest welder on the crew, and a young, eighteen-year old woman at that, had just figured-out everyone's business, had solved the great, mysterious puzzle on them all, ought to be worth a big laugh. Oh, I looked forward to their expressions… If only I could have known…

I felt giddy as all heck and light on my toes as I approached the second gatekeeper, Mr. Carson. I was smiling ear to ear when I addressed him, "Well, Good morning to you, Mr. Carson, and how are you on this beautiful March morning?"

"Well, hello right back at you, Miss McCord," Mr. Carson responded. Then he quickly followed with teasing, "But, I sure don't know who went and made you a weather reporter!" He smiled waiting for my comeback.

'Why, Mr. Carson, it's a beautiful day because I'll bet I know something you don't know," I teased.

"For goodness sakes, Missy, whatever could that possibly be?" Mr. Carson queried with a smile.

"Well, for goodness sakes," I started, "Mr. Carson, if I go and tell you, then you will know too, and I won't have a secret anymore."

Mr. Carson was obviously enjoying this little tit-for-tat, so he played along, "Yes, Miss Patsy, which is the solemn truth; however, then it would be a case of kind generosity rather than mean selfishness, now wouldn't it?"

How could I argue with that? So, I gave-in and proffered my secret? "Mr. Carson, I figured-out what we are building over there," I stated clearly and succinctly as I pointed in the general direction of my work-site project.

Now, Mr. Carson's smug sort of grin took a twist of surprise and curiosity with his reply, "Well, you don't say, do you? And whatever might that be?" Mr. Carson was very alert by then.

Just then as I began to respond, a couple other fellas from my crew were passing through the gate, so I waited to try and gain a small audience.

Mr. Carson nodded to the two workers as they passed through the gate and gave them both, simultaneously, a congenial but brief greeting, "Mornin'. Good morning."

The two men nodded acknowledgement but were more interested in seeing me there sort of waiting. I was quick to ease their curiosity by greeting them both and drawing them into my game with Mr. Carson. So, I played, "Good morning Mr. Joe and Mr. Henry." I almost always used *Mr. and* their first names, as they did mine, with the exceptions of our boss and Mr. Carson.

Both Joe and Henry picked up on the lead, and Joe inquired, "Good day to you too, Miss Patsy, and I apologize all over the place, but what in the world brings you here this early and then hanging around with this future, FBI agent and "Guardian-of-the-Gate, here?"

Joe was always funny, and he used to always *apologize* and *beg pardon* of me more than anyone else, so naturally, I laughed, and with that I began drawing the two of them into the game too by teasing, "Well, Mr. Gentlemen, I was going to wait until lunchtime before I became the winner of the *What the Heck Is It,* contest. But with circumstances and all, and Mr. Carson, here, just chompin'-at-the-bit to find out, I sort of supposed that I'd might as well go ahead and win the game right now!"

Joe and Henry both threw their heads back at the same time with a startled look of surprise and then a mutual laugh, but it was Henry who grinned and then begged first, "Oh, please, do tell us, Miss Patsy. Why, we won't be able to do a single lick of work now until you tell us. Oh, please, I beg your pardon!"

I laughed again, but since I knew it was getting close to the whistle blowing, meaning it was time to start work, I pushed on with excited hurriedness, "Well, okay then, Gentlemen, here it is: What we are working on, what we are building," I paused here to build-up suspense and anticipation and then continued, "... is a *radar system!* I remember looking around to check their shock or surprise, but they all just stood there with blank stares trying to let the answer sink- in.

Joe was the first to react with a squinting look, "Radar system, huh? Now that's a pretty good guess, alright, Miss Patsy."

"Oh, no, Mr. Joe, that's not a guess," I said emphatically. Then I proudly gave my evidence, "That's what it is! I know because I saw one when it was all finished, and that's what the newsman said it was."

Mr. Carson had been sort of standing back, but he smiled and interjected, "That's a good answer, Miss Patsy. You might just win that prize today for sure!"

I felt reprieved then and stood there smiling in triumph! I figured there would be lots more questions, though, but the fellows all still seemed a bit confused. I wasn't sure whether they were pondering my solution to the game being a *radar system*, or that a mere girl had come up with the answer. I realized momentarily that they all were just patronizing me and didn't really accept either premise: My solution, or that a young woman had actually come up with the answer to our daily puzzle.

Mr. Henry spoke-up, "If you say that's what it is, Missy, then by golly that's a fine guess, and until we hear the facts and truth, you have the best answer yet. But, I still think it might just be the insides of a submarine!" Joe and Henry laughed then and changed the subject to the day before and Sunday's activities. Turning away, they headed toward the worksite leaving me and Mr. Carson alone again.

"Well, I think that you just baffled them all-to-pieces, Miss Patricia," Mr. Carson said while smiling and nodding his head. Then he closed the conversation as he sort of jerked his head toward Joe and Henry and our worksite, "I guess you'd better just get over there and start finishing your *radar system* while they're all still befuddled and wondering about it. You have yourself a delightful day now, you hear?"

I was a little perplexed, and actually, I was a bit disappointed. I had thought that there might be some serious, "Holy mackerels!" coming from the group and maybe even some slaps-on-the-back for winning the whole, darn game, but it ended abruptly. Nothing more, so I just sort of shrugged and smiled in return, "You too, Mr. Carson. See you at finishing-time."

I headed for the job-site and was right at the welding machines hooking up my welding leads and adjusting the dials from the night crew's settings when the work-bell went off, "Beeeeeeeeep! Beeeeeeeeep! Beeeeeeeeep!" It was time to hit it again, go to work.

SHIFTWORK

I suppose that I should explain about the welding machines here and the shifts too. You see, there were three shifts of crews working on all the projects that Warner & Swasey had going-on at that plant. The place was really big, and every section, or department, or area, or whatever you want to call it, was separated by whatever machinery was used to do the particular job assigned to each department. Our section, or department, was really separated, though, by wire fencing and only one-way in-and-out. That was the special gate that Mr. Carson controlled.

Inside our area, we had our own, private-welding machines and equipment needed to do our jobs, and we shared everything: Power-source welding machines; long lead lines with the stingers on their ends; and basic cleaning tools (such as wire brushes, chipping tools and hammers too) with the other two shifts that were used to keep production running around the clock. There was the dayshift; that was my shift. We started at 7:00 A.M. and worked until 3:30 P.M. We took our breaks and our lunchtimes in small groups of each crew.

The second shift, or *swing-shift,* came in at 3:00 P.M. There was a fifteen to thirty-minute overlap so that any discussion of issues or problems could be sorted-out before their shift began its work. They worked until 11:30 P.M. when they gave-over the production to the third shift, or graveyard shift. That shift worked from 11:00 P.M. until 7:00 A.M. the next morning. Graveyard Shift got a paid lunchtime because it was that shift. Typically, they were already gone, though, by the time our dayshift began. The main bosses all worked dayshift too, so they could advise the various crews of issues were there any.

Each crew would work about two hours before taking a brief break. Lunch time was always a thirty-minute period. Most of the time, I would take my breaks with Joe and Henry, but there were about eight or nine other people in our crew which would take breaks with us too. Each crew on every shift was just told to make it look like some of the crew were working on the project at all times except at starting and quitting-time. Usually, when I got ahead of the other guys who were preparing any of the material or places for me to weld, that was when I would take a short break to use the bathroom. Or, I should say, "The *Ladies Only* latrine." That was also when any of us could take a quick breather usually around midday and run-over to the On-Plant cafeteria to get a sandwich or something to eat and drink.

As I mentioned before, with three shifts going there was always a slight overlap. Our crew would knock-off a little early to clean-up and roll-up our gear, and while we would be leaving to clock-out, the next shift would be arriving. It was pretty smooth, and there wasn't much time-stoppage between shifts at all. Two shifts would be passing each other coming and going. Only on Monday mornings were we coming to work without passing any nightshift who were just leaving. That was the case unless the company was running overtime on Sundays in which case… the men got to come in and work the special, higher-pay overtime hours.

After our crew's dayshift ended, and we were heading to the timeclock to punch-out for the day, the swing-shift was just coming in to pick-up and carry-on. I got to recognize most of the swing-shift crews members' faces, and even many of their names because I sort of stood-out a little, I suppose, and a lot of them teased me, so I remembered.

It was because I got known as the only female welder on that special, secret project, and I was sort of a small young lady, petit if you will, on the job too. Plus, all the crew members had special badges that we had to wear to identify ourselves and give us clear passage into the *special, secret zone*. It made Mr. Carson's job easier too because he could see the required badges as all the crews walked through his gate. Most everybody on both crews would greet me and bid me a good day if they saw me.

Of course, there were always complaints from one shift over another. Our dayshift complained about the messy area or the equipment not neat enough, or the welding machine settings all messed-up. `It was sort of our duty to complain because then our bosses figured we were into the job and trying to do it right. Of course, the swing-shift had to find something to complain about our dayshift too, and the nightshift complained about the swing-shift.

It sort of got to be a game in some ways. The fellas would try to think of creative ways to mess with the next shift too like welding a welding rod just sticking up on something out of nowhere. Sometimes, they would stick toilet-paper on it to warn that crew that there was none in the latrine. Or, they might write nasty notes and leave them dangling there just for fun. Some of the guys would hide the toilet paper from the latrines to be nasty, but nobody liked that trick at all when it happened to them. Those were just jokes between the shifts for fun and having a good time. All in all, it was a fun job until it was no longer fun. Right then, however, I seemed to really fit in, and the crews all liked me, and all was well. Well, for a while, anyway.

Anyway, swing-shift worked from 3:00 PM straight until 11:00 PM. They did the same thing as our shift, but just kept the project moving ahead. Once, every so often, the Foreman would come over and explain the next step or stage of our project, so we would clearly understand what we were supposed to do. Of course, the swing-shift handed over the reins to the next shift too, the nightshift. Everybody called it the *graveyard-shift* because of its all-night hours. They came on duty at 11:00 P.M. and passed-by the departing swing-shift while on their way in. They had to work all the way through the night until 7:00 A.M. when our dayshift came on. That graveyard shift was a tough one, I thought, especially when it got cold.

In those few, brief years during the war when I worked as a *Rosie or Wendy the Welder*, I never did have to work graveyard shift. I worked the swing-shift a couple different times when I switched from one ship assignment to another. Oh, yes, of course, it was swing-shift on my gas-station, black-market experience too. There was no doubt, however, that I liked dayshift the best. I could visit with my sisters then every evening, and it was nice to be in our family group.

TRAITOR AMONG US?

Well, now you know all about our shifts and what was happening with my own dayshift. What you don't know is what happened to me after I joked with the other crew members and Mr. Carson and told them all what the project was that we were working on. I felt kind of smug and proud of myself, and it actually did make a difference for me when I did my work. I could visualize what the final product was going to look like, and I understood better what part of the whole *radar system* it was that I was working on that day.

We were pumping those contraptions right on out too. We'd get one near completion as well as we could tell, and the next day it would be gone. We would be starting all over again on another brand new one. Each shift's crew would just catch a unit being built at whatever stage it was at when their shift arrived to take over production and carry-on with their job and its construction until the shift's end. It was actually only briefly that any of us got to see the whole totally finished product before that sort of skeleton looking thing that we had completed was hauled away to its next destination. And where it went, nobody knew at all.

Yet, I could not fairly and intelligently suggest places that that *radar system* was probably ending up…like with the military, for instance. It seemed logical to me, and that was part of the conversation that I had with the other crew members on that particularly eventful morning. As the morning edged on, and various crew members would walk-by as I was welding or busying myself, they would talk to me in turns. Sometimes, I had to pause from what I was doing, flip my hood up so I could see who was talking and then respond to their statement or question.

"Hey, Missy, Hank told me that you figured out what we're working on," came a comment from Bob, one of our other crew members. *Hank* was

Henry's other name or nickname. We all had two or more shortened-names or nicknames each, it seemed.

Behaving very seriously but testing to see if it was a prankster calling on me, I replied, "Hi, Mr. Robert, Yes, Sir, I believe I have. I saw a picture of a fully completed one, and the headlines for the picture and the newscaster who was talking about it both said it was a *radar system*. Of course, the story said the one I was looking at was a German radar system, but it still looked exactly like what we're doing." I held off there to see where his thoughts were going.

"You sure have come up with a real hum-dinger of an answer to our big puzzle here," nodded Mr. Robert. "Personally," he added, "I don't know what any kind of *radar* is supposed to look like in the first place, so I reckon we're all just stumped by your answer."

"Yup, that's what it is, Mr. Bob," I agreed. "It looks exactly the same as the picture," I concluded, "and a German *radar system* is what they called it. A *Giant Wurzburg*, it was. I'm certain of that."

"Well, how about that?" Mr. Bob said scratching his head. "So, you say we're building a German radar system, huh? Somehow, that just don't seem right. Guess we'll hear about it one day," he muffled his words as he continued on his walk. Neither of us knew or realized at the time, that we'd hear all about it and very soon.

Then I remember some fun the guys all started having with me. "Hey, Radar," one of them called out, "So, you went and looked at a picture-show, and now you think these here contraptions we're building are the same thing as what you saw?"

I took the bait but stood my ground. "Yes, Mr. Charley," I went right back at him especially because I knew who was hollering, "I saw a picture of a finished one, and that's what they said it was." I was not going to let them change my mind or make me feel foolish.

"Well, Miss Patsy," Mr. Bob retorted, "I seen a picture of the Taj Mahal once, and I was thinking that this was that thing, only much smaller, of course!" I could hear him and a couple others chuckling and shaking their heads.

I came right back at him, "Well, Mr. Bob, then you would be *thinking* wrong because I'm positive of what it is."

I heard a background of low-level laughter, and somebody whistled, and another spoke out in a mocking manner, "I'll tell you, Bobby, she sure got you. He haw!"

Then some other disagreeable crew member just laughed out loud and burst out, so everyone could hear, "Radar schmadar! We ain't building nothing for those lousy Krauts!"

I realized that I had been misunderstood, and anything remotely German was a very sensitive matter. I figured that I had better try to ease up the conversations and then just let the subject go. No need to stir up any muddy water.

I just sort of faced the other crew, and admonished myself, "I apologize, Sirs. I didn't mean to suggest we were making anything for the Germans. No, Sirs, this is ours. It just looks similar to what I saw, I think. That's all. I could be wrong too."

There was some additional mumbling and maybe grumbling, but I decided to ignore it. With that, I just went right back to work and stayed busy until it was time to take a short break for lunch. I took my hood off and cleared my welding stinger and laid it down safely over my hood. I looked around, and a few guys had already left. Mr. Joe and Mr. Henry (Hank) were already gone. They had probably gone to the cafeteria ahead of me, so I just followed suit.

I quickly walked up to the Entry-Exit Gate to leave our area and head for the plant cafeteria. Mr. Carson was on-duty, as always. I didn't stop to chat, though, as I often did. Instead, I just greeted him, "Good afternoon, Mr. Carson. Did you see Mr. Henry and Mr. Joe?"

"Oh, yes, I sure did, Miss Patsy, and they didn't seem all too social. They were talking way too loosely about your imagination, is what I could tell."

"Okay, thanks, Mr. C. I'll talk to you later," I said and started walking faster to the cafeteria area.

Once inside, I got a sandwich and a soda pop, paid for both at the cash register and looked for Joe and Hank. I easily spotted them across the room at a table, and they looked like they were engrossed in a conversation with some other fellows. I didn't want to intrude, so I headed for the EXIT. But, as I left the building, I turned to get one last glance at Joe and Hank, and I realized that the whole darn group of them were watching me.

They must have been talking about me and just noticed me, I figured. "Oh, boy, what now?" I wondered. Some of them looked upset.

I took my skimpy lunch in hand and decided to stay and talk things over with Mr. Carson. He was always nice to me when we talked. Maybe he had some answers or ideas about how I could mend-up matters with the other crew members. They were all obviously very miffed at me, and it had something to do with me suggesting somehow that we were building *radar systems* for Hitler and his Nazis and German Army.

OMG! I was ashamed and embarrassed that anyone might think that of me. My own brother Bo was overseas in the US Army Air Corps in Italy and bombing the hell out of the German Army. That much I hoped. How could I ever think that my own crew members might believe I didn't mind if we were building some sort of radar system that if given to the German's might detect where my own brother was flying and then help them shoot him down. It didn't make any sense to me. What could I do?

These were some of the rants I ran past Mr. Carson. All he could do was nod his head in understanding and let me continue venting my frustrations on his shoulders.

I remember feeling just dreadful and confused pouring my heart out to my friend, The Gatekeeper, "Mr. Carson, I need my crew to know that I never ever meant to insinuate anything like that or suggest we would ever help those stinking Nazis. What can I do?"

"Well, young Miss Patsy," Mr. Carson offered, "You might just have to let things go for a while. The guys will get over it and cool down after a bit. They just don't know what to think as of right now. But we'll all see our ways clear on this pretty soon, I imagine." Don't you fuss too much, Little Lady."

I was fussing, though. I had to work with those guys, and they were my guys before. Now there felt like a lot of tension in the air. Tension causes distractions, and distractions causes mistakes. On top of everything else, we did not need any mistakes to boot.

I had to try and find a way to resolve the whole darn matter. The other crew members needed to understand my feelings and my position. I decided that I was going to stand-up to them all and express myself clearly and completely. They all had to know just how I felt. Right after lunch break when they all came back to work, I would stand tall and *clear-the-air,* once-and- for-all…

SPY AMONG US?

I stood there leaning against the cyclone fencing with my mind adrift as Mr. Carson prepared to meet all the crew returning from their lunchbreaks. I was imagining how I might stand tall amongst the crew members and bare my open heart. To them. I envisioned them all in synchronized fashion completely understanding my feelings and grabbing me to hoist me up onto their shoulders and parade me around the grounds as the heroine that I wished to be ...

Suddenly, out of the clear, blue air, I was startled back into consciousness when I heard Mr. Carson muffle-out loudly a stressed call, "Uh, oh! This doesn't look good."

I shook my head back into reality and turned to look in the direction that Mr. Carson was staring. It was all the crews coming back to work like they were supposed to do, but with one big difference. They were all sort of in one huge mob. I am not talking about the other members of my crew, about a dozen or so total. I am talking about all the crews from all the *secret project sites*. There were at least a half-dozen of those other sites, so that meant like a mob of about seventy or more guys altogether and marching toward the Entry Gate, Mr. Carson and little ol' me.

If that didn't raise some hairs on the back of your neck, well just wait! Off in the distance about ten or so yards behind the *crew group* was another much smaller group following right-in-step behind my co-workers. This was the group that sort of bothered me and made me curious as all heck. But I decided to give all the guys and Mr. Carson a break and go off-down the walk to my own jobsite and kind of get-out-of-the-way. I did not want to be any part of anything rash. Not me.

As I high-footed it down the marked line to our sites, I looked-back over my shoulder to watch what was happening. I could quickly tell that no one, not a single guy of any of the crews was giving Mr. Carson a break at all. They all just crammed themselves into a final line right at the one-way gate with Mr. Carson all but shoved aside and pushed their ways through and continued their storming path toward all the *secret jobsites*… and me!

After all the crews had pushed and shoved their ways through the turnstile gate of Mr. Carson, I saw them all reform into their earlier mob group and continue down our designated path. This is where I also could note that the fellows in the front were not crew members that I recognized right-off. I did see Mr. Bob and Mr. Hank and Mr. Scooter and Mr. Harvey and several others I don't recall right now, but they were all sort of hanging onto the outside of the group; however, they were part of the mob, regardless.

Way-off behind them, I saw the other small group of bosses and some other guys I did not recognize stop for a moment and talk to Mr. Carson. Then I saw who must have been a leader of their group pointing to the gateway, then over at us, then back at the gateway, and then making a motion with their crossed-hands being flung apart, and then holding a pointed-up index finger at poor Mr. Carson like they were warning him, or something. It was strange, no bizarre.

By that time, I saw the crews all approaching my position fairly rapidly. There were no "Howdy, Missy's" or "Pardon me all to heck!" or "Excuse me, Almighty!" Not this time. If I weren't paranoid, I could have sworn that they had actually spread-out and mostly encircled me from where I was standing by my welding machine. I felt as though they were trying to surround me so that I couldn't make a fast getaway or something.

Then I remember thinking that this was all a big joke, and they were preparing to present me with a very special gift. After all, I had been the one to solve the big job-project riddle. Maybe after all this, they had felt remorse like they had with the Ladies Latrine issue, and now they were trying to make amends. Good. This was going to be just the right moment and pulpit for me to give them all a speech they would never forget. I was going to have tears streaming down their faces by the time I finished. They would be so overcome with guilt and remorse and then praise and appreciation, that they would hardly even be composed enough to cheer and applaud.

I could even imagine hearing their choruses of tribute echoing across the plant grounds, "That's our girl! She was right all along, and we were absolute bums not to accept her victory. Hurray for our winner! Hurray for our Miss Patsy, the Queen of Warner & Swasey, and the best darn welder of the whole war!"

I admit that momentarily, my imagination had gotten the best of me. I had taken myself to a point of being all worked-up into an excited frenzy. I was preparing in my mind how to accept all my accolades graciously. It was my next move, however, which changed the dynamics altogether. I went from *a star blowing kisses to her adoring fans* all the way to *an evil, menacing criminal on the verge of escape!*

All I did, however, was play straight into my imagination's plan of making a delightfully emboldened and empowering speech. I used the tongue on the welding machine as a projecting step in order to leap up onto the top of the welding machine. It was a perfect spot above my humbled crowd to begin my thoughtful and heart-warming soliloquy.

Only, it didn't happen as I so beautifully had envisioned. As soon as I made the jump from the tongue to the welding machine's top, there were a dozen cries that came out from the encircling mob, "Grab her! She's trying to get away! Stop her! Stop her! Catch that traitor!"

"Catch that what?" raced through my mind. "Oh, my God! What was happening?"

A bunch of the crowd all jumped forward to the machine and had their hands all grappling for my feet. I was beside myself with shock and dismay. I honestly didn't know what I should do. I remember some hands actually touching and grabbing at my feet, so my natural inclination was to kick back at them so that I didn't lose balance and fall. For a few seconds that seemed to irritate or support their ill claims and try even harder to knock me off the machine.

Even more voices became angrier, it seemed, at my resistance to the others below me with their grappling hands. In high-pitched frenzy, some yelled-out, "Knock that bitch off the machine! Get her down! Arrest that spy, bitch! Arrest her! Arrest her!"

Fortunately, a loud, powerful voice pushing through the group yelled out a commanding order, "Stop what you are doing right now! Leave her alone!"

Some did hear the order and responded at once, and a few sets of hands withdrew. Still, there were others caught-up in the excitement and turmoil who were mostly more intent on just really knocking me off the welding machine, like I had no right to be up there. Those hands continued with their persistent grabbing and grasping.

Another follow-up command came to my relief, "If you don't cease and desist, you will be fired! Now back-off and back-up!"

Fired was the magic word. Nobody wanted that on their resume. Well, they all knew they had good jobs, anyway. To lose this one would be a real rejection. At least that was the feeling I could relate to, and yet, when I considered that present activity, I began thinking about my own longevity and that word, *fired* very seriously.

What in hell was going on? I was absolutely in an oblivion. These crew members, my buddies just this morning, were now an angry mob, and they seemed to want my head. Why? What did I do? Were they all that poor of losers? The lousy male chauvinist pigs! Just couldn't stand a girl, a woman, getting the best over them.

"Well, f—k 'em! Uh, not literally, but metaphorically, anyway. Damned sore losers, all of you! Keep your f—king prize whatever it was; I don't want it anymore!"

Finally, I was able to put a face to the voice that warned the persisting fools of being fired. It was my boss's boss, the General Foreman. I can't remember his name, but I know he was a very nice man, and he appreciated me being there. I even recall him making some grandiose claims that my "... *presence there at Warner and Swasey was showing all of America what women could do under dire straits.*"

"Hah! I remember laughing at him. What in hell are you talking about? We *women of America* do "everything" under "dire straits" twenty-four/seven, day-after-day, week-after-week, and year-in-and-year-out now!"

Of course, I had met the GF earlier when I had been hired because he made it a point to meet me due to the unusual circumstances. Some jerk underlings had obviously already advised him of the political, and thus fiscal, significance of W&S hiring a tiny (petit, asshole!) *welder* as a real *Rosie the Riveter*! Or, now it was a *Wendy the Welder*!

That GF was also one of the men, the bosses, who had assured me that I would be safe and secure on this job. That was no doubt why I had been placed on *day shift* in the first place. I could tell that he was at least understanding of the dangerous situation-on-hand, and he was not going to let me get hurt at the hands of this vile, screaming mob.

"Thank you. Thank you," I remember thinking, "and I forgive your earlier revolting, sexist comments, at least for the time being."

That was the end of the "nice guy" routine, however. Right after that, the same GF ordered me, "Get down off our welding machine now!"

The men had backed away, and I was even pleased to see that Hank had come over to help me down from the welding machine. He may have been angry at me in the beginning and maybe he still was, but he was still a gentleman at heart. I did take his hand, though, and sitting- down on the edge of the machine, I slid over the side to the ground. I remember looking-up at hank's eyes trying to look inside his soul or mind, but all I could see was resentment and a little confusion. Well, that made two of us!

Then, yet another fellow from the small group stepped forward and seemed to overrule the GF for a moment. He looked straight at me and asked, "Are you Patricia Vera McCord, otherwise known as *Missy, or Miss Patsy or Patsy*?"

"Uh huh. Yeah, that's right. Uh, that's me. So, who are you, and what do you want?"

"My name's Hawkins," said the same man as he continued, "and we'd like to ask you a few questions in private. Will you come with us willingly, or do we have to use force?"

My mind was reeling, but I responded meekly, "Yes, I will come with you and the GF, but you still haven't answered my question, "What do you want?"

Hawkins replied calmly, "We have questions that we would like to ask you about extremely important matters. Would that be alright with you?"

"Oh, no!" I thought. "After all this time, my dad has finally got the authorities on me. They had to go and track me down at this highly secret, government-contract company. They must have traced my name through their audits, and now I am busted. When will that SOB get off-my-back? They are busting me for kidnapping Jann and Colleen. I am going to prison for life! But wait! I didn't kidnap Colleen. Sis Mary did that, and Sister Jean helped me! No, wait! I just helped Jean. It was her idea. I only liked the plan a lot, but she did most of the talking. I just nodded my head a lot!"

Then reason and rational thinking reentered my brain. Okay, now, why would all the guys be upset at me kidnapping my little sister from an orphanage. No, they would more likely applaud the idea. That means that it is something different. But what? It can't be that I was a truant runaway anymore. Heck, I'm eighteen and a half years old now. They can't hold that against me any longer…, can they?

Mr. Hawkins insisted once again, "Will you please come with us quietly?"

This commotion was going nowhere, and it was obvious that neither was I. So, I agreed but somewhat indignantly, "Alright, Mister Hawkins, I'll go with you and our GF, but this whole thing has got me bothered a lot, and I need some more explanation."

Some of the small group men all made an opening from the crew's group circle allowing me and the small group to pass through. As we did so, several *cat calls* came from the crews' group, "Hang the traitor! She's a Nazi spy! She's been laughing at us all along! Sweet talking all of us into working for Hitler. The bitch, spy! Hang her!"

As we left the *secret zone* and headed for the Special Gate and Mr. Carson, I continued hearing nasty callouts from the crew mob.

"Dirty bitch, Kraut!" the angry mob carried on with their hysterics. "F—king German lover. McCord, my ass! It's McKraut, no doubt! F—k her, and then kill her!"

They all really hated me now, and I had not done a single thing wrong to any of them. What is it about human nature? We are all nice on the outside, but then something happens which confuses us, or we can't answer it, so we automatically think the worst and become, vile, angry mobs? We act like that when we are uncertain, so we think the wickedest to be safe and become evil, just in case…

I stayed very close to our GF. He was not friendly, but he was civil to me at least. Considering all the others, I'd take *civil* anytime. We walked-up the marked walkway to the Entry Gate and proceeded passing through one-by-one. I was the third person through the gateway turnstile, and I looked up at Mr. Carson somewhat embarrassed, and my heart broke.

There was no teasing. There was no friendliness. There was not even any eye-contact. Mr. Carson just looked beyond me to the others passing through. Apparently, just like all the others, he had taken the low road and thought the worst of me just to be safe and had forsaken me too. I had done something that offended even him so much that even he could not abide looking me straight into my eyes! Cowards, the whole bunch!

What is it with people? Even people you supposed were your friends? I still had absolutely no idea what I was being harassed about, questioned about, and forsaken over, and all I got were angry stares and nasty epithets and cold, cold shoulders. And do you want to know the worst part of the whole sticking mess? What it was that stuck right in my throat and nearly made me gag later? It was the absolute fact that I began feeling so agonizingly bad inside over these trumped-up charges. I felt so horribly guilty over having apparently done something that was deemed by all my peers as so miserably despicable that I could not even forgive myself. My mind and soul began filling with immense disgrace and complete humiliation.

Continuing up the walkway, I looked around me and saw that all the small group's eyes were bent straight forward at their targeted destination, the Personnel Offices. I was marched directly to that entry door, and the first man opened the door allowing the rest of us to pass inside. The large mob of fellow crew members was ordered back to their individual worksites, but it hadn't been without additional nasty comments and dreadful accusations. One point that is worthy of attention, however, was that all the guys on my own crew did not actually get involved in the creepy, nasty mob mentality.

Sure, they were upset with me initially with that *Hitler's Wurzburg Radar System* information that I passed on to them. Without all the facts, and having a fervent anti-Hitler sentiment among them, what I said may have been a-big-pill-to-swallow. I understand that now. Back then, however, I just noted that, if anything, they still supported my *statements of innocence* and that I had learned everything from a trip to the movies. The sad and unfortunate part was that, nevertheless, they had shared that info with all the other ignorant and hysterical crews' members. Then feeling somewhat mollified by their sharing-actions, they just sat back and watched as hysteria grew into a fevered pitch, and *they did nothing* to quell the fever.

That was their shame; however, they, themselves, were never oppositional to me. They did not scream for my death or other things. Yet, they never would have won any *Good Samaritan Awards,* either. And what's that saying: *If you are not part of the solution, then you are part of the problem.* They backed my *innocence,* all well and good. But they might have just stood by and watch as I got crucified.

My can remember my imagination kicking-in again as I squirmed restlessly in my chair: "Tell me, Child," Warner and Swasey's, Designated-Site Priest asked, "did your experience give you empathy for Jesus's case before they crucified, or executed Him?"

"Uh, well, yeah, sort of, kind of., I believe," I hesitantly and meekly offered.

"Did it give you renewed appreciation for His Apostles' dire-straits circumstances?" the W-S-D Priest followed-up.

"Hell, no!" I screamed.

Inside that rather enormous, office-space room, there was one big, separated, and enclosed section over in a far end that the company bosses must have used for conferences, or special announcements, like for newspapers, or something, because that was where we went. There were enough chairs inside for everyone to sit and relax around a long, rectangular table. Also, there were large windows from the conference room looking-out to the rest of the dozens of offices, cubicle-space areas. However, as soon as all the men and I had come in and found our designated places, someone pulled the blinds closed. That way, I figured, their Spanish Inquisition wannabes had total privacy for their interrogation room. It was just all of them and little ol' me.

Remarkably, it didn't quite happen as I imagined, however. I was asked quite abruptly to sit down in one of the chairs at the table while most of the other men shuffled around the room finding positions for them to observe the examination. Apparently, it was the top brass fellows who all took chairs opposite me at the table. They included: Detective Hawkins, one of Warner and Swasey's top executives, our *loud-voiced* GF from the altercation earlier, and my Foreman too.

The four of them sat next to each other directly across the table facing me. The other men continued distributing themselves about the room expediently with two of them guarding both sides of the doorway exit. I had the distinct feeling that I was not going to be allowed to leave even if I should have so desired. What was up?

The W-S Company Executive was the first to talk. He seemed to look at me with a curious sense of disbelief and anxious frustration. Looking at me straight-in-the-eye, he calmly stated then asked, "We have reports that you have unsolicited and governmental secrets that you are passing-out freely to this company's employees. Is that true, Miss McCord?"

Now it was my turn to offer looks of disbelief. "I'm doing what?" I incredulously asked.

Then it was Mr. Hawkins who quickly butted-in, assumed complete control and began talking. He was calm, but you could tell he was just a little bit on edge. It was like he was acting nice, but he wanted to be very angry. It sounded as though when he talked, his teeth were clamped tightly together suggesting stress or urgency. At least he was talking, though. That, in itself, was a decent start.

"Miss Patricia McCord, may I call you Patricia?" he began earnestly.

"Yes," I agreed right away, "Everybody here calls me Patsy if you like."

"Alright, then, Patricia.," was his smug response as he continued in his somewhat arrogant manner, "We have received some very serious reports about you, and we are trying to get to the bottom of this issue. Are you willing to cooperate with us?"

"Yes. Sure. Of course, I am," I spoke out immediately. "But I still don't know who you are, and what you want from me."

"Then you are willing to answer any questions that I have for you?"

"I said, 'Yes!' I would. Who are all of you, and what do you want from me?"

Finally, my questioner calmly identified himself, "I am Detective Hawkins of the Cleveland Police Department Insurrections and War Crimes Department. Some of these men are your bosses, and the others are Cleveland Police Officers who are with me. We are trying to get to the bottom of a very perplexing problem. Perhaps you can help. Will you try?"

"Yes, I will," I responded exhaustingly. "Whatever you want, ask me. That's all I want to do is help. Ask. What do you want, for God's sake? What?"

He began, "You are an employee of Warner and Swasey Company Contractors. Is that right?"

"Yes, of course it is. You already know that. What is this, a joke, or something? Is this all a really elaborate *get even* joke because I won the prize and guessed the project we are building? Is that what this is? You guys all just got pissed at me for winning and are getting even with me by playing this elaborate hoax, question-answer game?"

"Just answer the questions, Young Lady. It is in your best interests if you do so. Now, we know that you are not a U.S.A. government employee, is that right?"

"Of course, it's right. I'm still only eighteen years old! I haven't had enough time to work for the government," I answered honestly.

"Well, Young Lady, your work records show that you've been working for a couple years already at government contractors' jobs. How do you explain that?"

"I don't know. They were really desperate, I guess."

"Or, you lied on your applications, right?" came my interrogators attempt at cornering me.

"What if? I needed a job, and I did a good job too. Just look up my records," I defended myself.

"Is that what this is all about?" I countered. "You are mad at me because I won an award with Kaiser Vancouver, and I was actually underage at the time? Well, shame on you. I know of several young boys who were only seventeen, and you let them into the military with their parents' permission. Some of them are probably already dead by now from the war. And besides, believe me, my parents would have given me permission too, if they had only known where I was."

"No, we don't care about that," answered Mr. Hawkins, "but we do want to know who you really work for. Now who is it?"

"Huh?" I was stumped there and then. What did they mean? All I could muster-up was a meek, "What? I work here, of course, for Warner and Swasey. What are you talking about?"

"You know exactly what I mean. Don't be coy. Who sent you here?" Hawkins asked a bit agitated.

"I sent myself. I saw the ads for welders needed. Nobody sent me," I almost whimpered.

"Look, Lady, let this go easier on you, and just tell us who you are really working for," the Police Detective continued.

"I don't understand," I cried-out in frustration, "I work for myself and to help my two sisters. Why do you keep asking me the same thing?"

Mr. Hawkins seemed agitated and turned to have a few private words with a few of the other men in the room. Finally, I heard one of the others say, "Let me talk to her. I have some questions of my own."

That man was in a business suit like the first questioner. He was probably another upper-executive type. He sat down on the end and across from me and began talking, "Young Lady, we are all here to help you. We don't want this to go down badly for you. But you have to cooperate with us. We want to know what government sent you over here to work at this plant and spy on the progress of our *secret projects*. Now, we need to know who it was that sent you here? Can you tell us that before it gets really bad for you?"

I was getting really frazzled, but I responded with as much effort as I could gather-up, "I already told that other man that nobody sent me here. I sent myself, and I'm not *spying* on anything for anybody. What are you talking about?"

Just as I was answering that last guy, the door flung open and two new guys walked in. One of them spoke-out right away with a demanding voice, "I'm Special Agent Carter Melrose (or something like that) and that is Agent (so and so). We're FBI, and we'll be taking over this case as of now."

"What's that you say? This is my case. I have it all under control," was Hawkins instant and surprised response.

Special Agent Melrose replied flatly and calmly, "We were called-in an hour ago by an Executive Vice-President from this site because this case is obviously of *national interest*, and that makes it *FBI jurisdiction*. So, please step-aside and take your little dog-and-pony-show back home to your little, Cleveland PD office, and let the big boys deal with this matter."

Detective Hawkins was really miffed, but he relented with a casual remark, "This is our town, and we're staying right here in this room until it no longer *suits us*. Is that clear to you?"

"*Suit yourself*," was Special Agent Melrose's retort. "You can *stay* as long as you *stay* out of the way. Is that *clear* to you?"

Wow! These two, grown-up little boys were having a down-right-for-real pissing contest, and it was *all over me*. Uhuh, wrong choice of words there. I meant "*because of* me. I was touched, but not really. I was simply getting more frustrated and stressed-out.

Special Agent Melrose glared at the first company executive until he got up and moved, and then he sat down in front of me while his cohort Agent So-so walked around the table and stood a close few feet away from me. I supposed that it was his responsibility to grab me if I tried to make a break for it.

SA Melrose calmly began his line of talking and questioning, "Good afternoon, Miss. It seems we have a pretty serious problem here. We all need to know who sent you for this job with Warner and Swasey. Who told you to work on their *special project* you have been on for quite some time now? You can help me out a lot, and then we can all go back home or back to work, if you just explain to us all *who* sent you to work at this *special plant* on their *special secret project. Who* was it, *please?*"

New face, same questions. Same face, same answers, "I *sent myself,* and those *guys* right *there* are my bosses, and they assigned me to weld on the project I am on. That's all."

"Well, Miss, uh, McCord," Melrose began again while looking at his notepad, "It says here that you have been doing a lot of talking today about the project you are working on. Is that right?"

"I don't know about a lot of talking," I explained as calmly as I could, "but I just told all the guys that I won the game because I knew what it was that we have been working on for so long. It was a game for us to figure it out, and I won. *I* figured it *out.* And now everybody has gone crazy and mean and gotten so mad at me for winning the contest."

"Well, you see, Little Lady," Special Agent Melrose spoke so patronizingly, "*that* is the *whole pickle,* right there. You have some very important, almost Top-Secret, caliber information, and you are spreading it all over the plant. You have practically incited a riot with the workers here because of your suggestions that *Warner and Swasey Company* is in cahoots with Adolf and his Nazis.

"How did you find out about the *U.S. Top-Secret, Radar Systems* that your crew has been working on? How do you know about *Dr. Wurzburg* and his *Giant Wurzburg*? Come clean with us now, Miss McCord, or it's going to be real bad for you. We need to know who sent you here with that information, and who are you really working for. So, who is it?"

Special Agent Melrose had gotten his face right down directly in front of mine as he spoke, and he was so close to me with his final question that he was practically spitting all over me. But it was Special Agent Melrose's last comments that made *everything clear to me.* They had absolutely no idea how I could possibly have known what it was we were working on unless someone else on the outside told me about it. That was the *who* I must be working for. Now, that I had figured out their *game of confusion* and knew how to beat them, I just decided to have some fun and spread embarrassment all around the room.

I began slowly, trying to build-up momentum, "Okay, guys, you all got me. Now I'm trapped, and I can't get away without confessing. I've got to come clean, so I might as well tell all the truth, and nothing but the truth, so help me God!"

I looked around the room, and what a range of reactions I could see. There was my boss, our Foreman, and our General Foreman whose eyes were bulging out of their sockets with shock, dismay, and absolute disbelief. I just imagined them both thinking: How could (I) have fooled them for so long, and I was so young, and so small too? Maybe they even surmised that I had been a spy against Kaiser Vancouver too, while I was sending reports back to the Third Reich all along about America's progress with their mini carriers. Regardless, their expressions were priceless. They deserved to be shamed giving-in and giving-up on me so quickly.

Then there was Detective Hawkins staring blankly at me and then at the Special Agent. His face was awash with surprise and then a hint of anger because he had been shown-up. Mr. So-Cool Special Agent had quickly taken over the interrogation, and right away, he had broken their suspect and extracted and divulged a confession from her. He looked as though he were thinking, "And I was so close to victory. She could have been my catch, and now he and his damnable FBI will get all the credit. It's just not fair." He looked just a tad surprised and sad.

I could easily see that several of the other cops, or bosses or whoever they were in that room all had big smiles on their faces. They were all so sure that they had just helped capture the *Mata Hari* of World War II. "She's another German spy, for sure, and we just apprehended her!" those fools thought in their warped minds. They were probably all gleefully preparing their bragging-rights speeches, "Yes, and we took down that filthy, Adolf-loving spy with only our bare hands and sheer intellect. No gunshots were ever even fired!"

Super-Agent Melrose and his Boy Wonder sidekick both had the same smug looks on their faces. However, I sensed a tinge of smug jealousy in the sidekick's smirk, though. It was likely due to the fact that because he never got to ask me anything, his Super Boss was going to get all the credit for my confession. He was shamelessly hilarious to watch.

But Super-Duper, Especially Special Agent Melrose's smug look was the best of all of them. His arrogant aura of superiority simply took the cake. He was the biggest winner, or loser, depending on how you looked at it. His false pride was obviously due to his self-centered belief of personal charm, confidence, and an innate ability to totally defeat of an Enemy-of-the-State using only courage, intelligence, and fortitude.

He sat there across from me just smiling and staring at me momentarily. He must have been a little surprised at how easily he had cracked the case. His self-assuredness made me want to gag and puke all over his self-conceited and self-satisfied victory.

Though, looking back, I believe that is just about what I did. It happened right after Special Agent Melrose asked his formal and final question, "So, who was it that sent you here?"

"Okay. Here's the skinny," I started-out, "I got sent here by *The Playhouse Square*. That's where I got the information."

SA Melrose was content with his capture but not with his information. "Go on," he chided. "Tell us more. Who or what is *The Playhouse Square?*"

"Don't you know anything," I dug, "Everybody around town knows about *The Playhouse Square* here in Cleveland." I began waving around the room at the other spectators, "You all know what I'm talking about. You guys know where *The Playhouse Square* is, don't you?"

Special Agent Melrose was thrown-off track. He tried to regain his footing, "So, who runs that organization, the, the, *The Playhouse Square*, and who is your contact?"

"Why, it's Mr. Simpson, of course," I continued with that smug look of satisfaction having returned to Melrose's face. "He runs the theatre there and is in charge of all the programs and movies that play there."

"Now we're getting somewhere," Melrose whiffed in relief. "How did he make contact with you to get the information you have?"

"Why, at the movies, of course!" was all I *smugly* replied.

"What, then? This *Mr. Simpson* character met you at the theatre and then passed along all the secret information about the *Parabolic Radar System*? Was that it? Huh?" Special Agent Melrose was getting confused and guessing by then.

And by then I couldn't help myself anymore. I was about to burst-out laughing at all of them, so I decided to choose my words carefully and spill-the-real-beans, so-to-speak.

"No, Silly-Sir. Mr. Simpson just runs the movies at the theatre there in *The Playhouse Square*. He plays the movies, and we all watch them. That's all!"

"What are you talking about? How did he get you the information?" Special Agent Melrose complained. He was getting close to hysterical now.

"In the film, Goofy, er, Sir" I began my attack. "Yesterday, while my younger sister and I were watching the Sunday Matinee Movies at *The Playhouse Square*, Mr. Simpson played the Weekly News Reel like he always does for every show. This past week's News Reel was an interesting film that told the whole story of Wurzburg, the famous designer of the infamous Hindenburg Blimp, who also designed his *Giant Wurzburg Radar System* for Hitler and his German Army. That's where I saw the same thing that we are working on, and I came to work and told everyone how I had discovered the answer to our *Hush-Hush Project*."

I looked around. I had my captive audience now. Every single one of them in that room had their jaws almost hanging on the floor. *Stupefied stupors* are as close as I could call them. There were a lot of, "Huh?" and "What?" floating around. Then they all started looking at each other to cover their embarrassment by looking to share it with all the others.

But I wasn't letting them off-the-hook that easy or that soon, so I picked-up where I left-off to rub-salt-in-their-wounds. Excitedly, I started adding to my assault on all their dignities, "Oh, the best part of the whole show, though, was not that stupid radar thing at all. It was that gorgeous Robert Young kissing beautiful Dorothy Maguire in The Enchanted Cottage. My sister and I just cried our eyes out. It was so romantic!"

"What are you saying? You saw it in the movies? Oh, for God's sake! Agent Burns, get your ass over to that theatre right now and check-out her story. This is absolutely ridiculous! Who in hell sent me here in the first place? I'll be the laughingstock of the whole G-D Agency! How in hell did you coppers let this situation get this far?"

Very quickly, Detective Hawkins had considered all his own options, and with a great sigh of relief, he smiled and said, "Gee, Special Agent Melrose, this *situation* was a National Security issue, so it has been your case all along. You said so, yourself. So, don't you worry at all. We here at the Cleveland Police Department are going to give you all the credit. You can bet your career on that!"

By then, the General Foreman and my boss, our Foreman, had collected their wits and began thinking about how to approach me. It was our Foreman who spoke-up first, "If this case is settled then, everybody in the whole, f---ing United States who goes to the movies knows all about our *Hush-Hush, Super-Secret Project* building *Parabolic Radar Systems* for the United States Military. Why don't we just shit-can the whole secret-project shit, and go back to work?"

"Just wait until I hear something from my Co-Agent," spoke the frustrated and stressed-out Special Agent Melrose. "Nobody's going anywhere until then."

A few members of the Cleveland Police Department in the room began leaving regardless of the FBI Agent's orders. It was sort of, "We don't work for you. We were never here. This is all yours!"

Finally, I was sitting there completely calm and feeling very *smug*. I let my imagination run amuck… again… as I considered all the ways that all the crews in the entire *Secret Project Zone* would react to the news. They would no doubt fall all-over themselves apologizing to me and trying to regain my confidence. And oh, was I going to make them feel sick with regret. I owned them! They were mine!

No, no, I wouldn't. I would take the *high road*, naturally, and forgive them all. Only I would do so with *silence,* by not saying anything at all. They had earned my silence. Even Mr. Carson was going to have to beg me to laugh at his charming character once again. I would just wait and see how things turned out.

After about twenty-minutes more of quiet, fumbling, mumbling and extremely small talk, there was a phone call for Special Agent Melrose at the Personnel Office Desk. A minute later, the embarrassed FBI Special Agent returned to our room looking ashen and practically helpless. His words were brief and succinct, "She's right. That news story has been there for week's now. It's old news. Let her go back to work. I want out of here. Apologies, Miss."

Apologies! I was only beginning to get those. But once again, I took the high road, "It's alright, Special Agent Melrose, but you guys ought to get out and go to the movies more often. You might learn something. May I be excused now to go back to work? I have some important welding to do on *our Parabolic Radar System*!"

"Absolutely not!" came that powerful voice that had rescued me earlier from those angry crew's mob. It was our General Foreman, and he continued, "After what you have been through, Miss McCord, you deserve all of our deepest apologies, and some sort of gift to make-up for our complete and shameful questioning and judgement of your character. Your *character*, by-the-way, remains spotless, I dare say. Please accept from me this small token. Go home right now, or go to the movies, I don't care, complements of Warner and Swasey, and take the rest of the day off with full pay. Would you like that?"

"Boss," I said, "thank you very much, and I am already gone. Would you please see to all my gear being set aside safely for me? See you tomorrow."

REACCEPTANCE

I'm not going to say that everything simply went *peachy-keen nicely* after all that bullshit, *Mata Hari* incident stuff. There were, as expected, several variations of *apologies* from all the *super-secret, special-projects* crew members we had been working with. The next day, however, it was so obvious how most of the other workers who had been part of the day-before, *mob-rule mentality* had deliberately taken the *low-road*. Once they learned the truth and understood the extremities of their ignorance, most of them were so ashamed and embarrassed that they tried to avoid all contact with me.

I, on-the-other-hand, was just fine. It's amazing how good, even righteous, an individual can feel internally against all sorts of enigmas claimed against them when they know they are innocent. I honestly thought about all those historically famous characters who had stood proudly up-against those ropes, or fire or firing squads which had taken their lives, yet they went to their graves with absolute, self-righteous indignations and certainty of their own assured knowledge of innocence.

That was a lot to manage, however, on a plate for an eighteen-year old. Anyway, I had no choice but to become sacrosanct. All the various crews' members had learned and realized the error of their thinking, and they had become embarrassed and ashamed of their responses and actions. The worst of the group's members slid back the furthest and had the least contact with me. Others who had not been so visibly vocal, over time had attempted trite contrition by acknowledging my presence in their realms of reality or workplaces.

My own crew begged my forgiveness with their actions. They welcomed me with open-arms and expressed how they had been-unsure-all-along but had hung-with-me-all-along until the end. My concern was whether-or-not they would have *hung-with-me* until the *bitter-end*. Anyway, it was *high-road* stuff, and I was ready to get back to work.

Some jobs, your work, has a special way of *setting-you-free*. Everything else cow-tows, or bows, to its demands or needs. All else is forgiven and forgotten. The most important thing in life is what is directly in front of you and demanding your full-attention and service. All else pales before it. That is the *magnificence* of *work-ethic*. I can't speak for other cultures, nations, or countries, but I am certain that every individual who takes on tasks for a boss, or some entity or just for themselves, puts their self-righteous signature on their individual effort exclaiming their pride-in-craftsmanship and desire of excellence. Don't you agree, or am I just being naïve?

I wanted to feel so proud of the excellent work and effort that my whole crew always put forward in our daily challenges of production. The thought went completely against my nature to consider that any of my crew ever considered that just *okay* or *satisfactory* or *mediocrity* was ever acceptable to any of our group. We all expected only the *best* from each other. Those were conditions that I always worked under.

My team, or crew, also understanding, believing, and applying those same work-ethics, made it easier for me to slide right back into work and begin carrying-on again. Nods of *approval* or *acceptance* occurred, and that was all that was important or necessary. Who cared about anything more? Plus, thanks to me, the whole damned, *shroud-of-secrecy* was gone, and now we could all just concentrate on production and output. Now everybody understood that we were just working on *whatever kind of radar systems* that, ultimately, would help us win the war against the f---ing Germans. That was what was most important. That was what we were all working for, in the end, after all.

Time passed, and things got back to normal. I was very pleased when even Mr. Carson reverted to his old tune and began teasing me again. He had a right to tease me, though, and I teased him right back. It was regarding his job-position at the *Secret Zone Gate Turnstile*. Mr. Carson teased me about almost costing him his job because there was no secret he was guarding anymore. I teased him right back that the whole sham had been a scam from the beginning because the company had, in fact, hired me in-the-first place to help get rid of his position.

I remember him pretending to weep and say, "Well, Missy McCord, now that you went and solved the puzzle, there ain't no secret no more, and now they don't hardly need me no more either."

I rebuffed him with faked sadness and drooping mouth, "I am so sorry, Mr. Carson. Really, I was just doing my job the best I could, and sometimes, the truth hurts. Don't worry, though, because I told the bosses they still needed you here to make sure none of us steal any secrets and try to carry them out right under your nose."

We'd laugh and get back to our business. Life became regular after that, if not just a tad bit boring. I believe that we were doing a good job because they kept-up production, and we were pumping those Radar systems out like crazy. Get one done and start another. Our shifts became very synchronized, and we worked well together. We all became so used to any project's assignments that we easily recognized every phase and picked-up on it right away and took it as far as we could each day. Quality and speed became our new mantra. We joked by figuring, "The faster we turn those *Radars* out, the more we'll learn about those *Germs and Japs* and the sooner we'll *kick-their-asses*!

DREAM FARM

Of, course, our jobs controlled only less than one-third of our daily lives. Everybody still went home and had to deal with all the other issues which faced each of them. I was no different. As much as I enjoyed and cared about my job and workplace, I still had all my other interests and obligations at home with my sisters and our apartment living. I loved my sisters, Sis Mary, and Colleen, so much and it truly was enjoyable sharing our apartment together. Although Sis continued her celebratory lifestyle away from home so much, she still gave us such hilarious stories and conversation to keep us all laughing and in good spirits.

Colleen was doing very well in school, and she admitted that she enjoyed public schools much more than the Catholic ones or St. Joseph's Orphanage school. She said it was mostly because there was so much more to talk about. Sisters at those other schools really practiced a lot of censorship and disallowed a great deal of interesting conversation and study as a result. Colleen said that she loved the *idea* of having more *ideas* to consider. It just sounded *more American*. I was proud of her, and I enjoyed helping her with her homework and talking about whatever she happened to be studying.

Well, that little discussion took care of explaining us sisters' homestand there in Cleveland, OH, but I realized that I haven't done a very good job keeping everyone informed about our eldest sister, Jean, and our youngest sister, Jann, and their progress. Typical of Jean, her life was always full of adventure and surprises. When it comes to discussing Jean's life, I'm afraid that a mere book would not do her justice. It's more like you need an entire book shelf, or a full set of encyclopedias. She was a dreamer and a schemer. I always admired her.

However, that is not to say Jean doesn't have her shortcomings. The main issue, I believe, is that Jean simply fails to recognize other peoples' shortcomings when compared to her own. She feels like everyone else sees the world as she does and that they can all handle all its pressures and circumstances just as well as she can. It's as if she feels that since she could sit down with Albert Einstein and have a serious discussion about *Quantum Physics*, then everyone else can too. Not true! She feels that if she can work a dirty, hard, and challenging welding-job, feed two people and a dog and buy a farm, so can her baby sister too. Not true!

That little insight into Jean's psyche makes it easier to explain what she and Jann and Duffy, the dog had been up to over the past several months. I had left them both there in Vancouver, WA and had come to Cleveland, OH to be with Sis and Colleen just a while before Christmas time. Right after I was gone became a very busy and calculated time for Jean. Looking back, I suppose an outsider might have been better at recognizing, however, how much influence I may have had on Jean. I'm not certain, but with me gone, Jean's attitudes surely seemed to change.

All of us sisters kept in regular contact with each other through the mail. Both Jean and Jann wrote to Sis, Colleen, and me on a regular basis. In return, Sis Mary, Colleen, and I all corresponded with both Jean and Jann to fill them in on our happenings and to ask about theirs. That was exactly how we learned of their most recent situation. I dare say, that I was surprised, if not downright shocked, by what we heard.

Sometime after I left Vancouver in November of 1944, and perhaps as late as the beginning of the new year of 1945, Jean fulfilled her dream of buying a farm. We knew she was going to buy one, but none of us knew where or when. We surmised that she had taken all the money that she **and I** had saved-up on that Kaiser Vancouver job, plus more that she had saved after I left, and she had put a down-payment on a small farm property just barely outside of Vancouver, WA.

Jean described the purchased property briefly in a letter to us as "... *nothing fancy, just the crude rudiments of a home on ten acres of land. But it has a lot of potential.*" She emphasized vaguely that we could also *easily* add rooms onto the *place* to accommodate everyone's needs, we could *easily* raise cows, and pigs and chickens, and we could *easily* have very substantial summer and winter gardens, and *easily* grow a small fruit orchard to *easily* feed us all very well. It was just a start, she reminded us, but it was a beginning…

When I heard about Jean's *farm* actions, my reaction was, "Yeah, it was *easily a beginning*, but how is she planning on *easily continuing* with it. There is no *easily* about that part at all. Taking care of a house is hard enough, but operating a farm, even if it is only big gardens and pigs, is a very difficult endeavor.

Apparently, my reaction was *spot-on* exact, too. The next letter from Jean about a month later showed how her mind really worked. For all Jean's well-intentioned plans for all of us, in-the-end, they were really all about her. Like I said, Jean was no doubt brilliant, but her mind was so fast-paced we meager others could not keep-up, and her plans were always in directions which served her interests first, foremost, and only.

Jean's 2nd letter was brief and to the point. She expressed how she had completed her dream's goal and had purchased the farm. Goal accomplished. Now that she had done that, there were still other dreams left unattended. She said that living on a farm, running a farm, and working on a dead-end job in the shipyards would no longer fulfill her life's dreams. Therefore, she had decided to leave the farm to all of us to do with as we pleased. Jann would continue to live there in the farmhouse, go to school and simply figure-out how to survive. Jann was twelve and a half years old, after all. According to Jean's thinking, it was time for Jann to grow-up and step-up to the challenge.

G.I. JEAN

Jean continued to rattle all our cages with that latest epiphany. Her *other dreams left unattended* confused me. Was little Jann one of those dreams because she had written about leaving *her unattended?* That was for sure. On-the-other-hand, Jean mentioned that she had to look to *her* future and determine what was the smartest move to make for herself.

Therefore, Jean continued in her letter:

> *"... I learned that American GIs could get the GI Bill after they are discharged and use the money for attending college. That is my dream, to finish college and develop a dynamic career for myself. So, I have left Jann on the farm, and I left Kaiser Vancouver and have joined the Women's Army Corps. I have been sent to Daytona, Florida for my initial training. After my discharge once the war is over, I shall return and use my GI Benefits to attend University of California at Berkeley in the California Bay Area...*
>
> *Hope to see you all there!*
>
> *Love,*
> *Your sister,*
> *Pvt. Jean McCord"*

Sis, Colleen, and I were all staggered by that quick, surprising shot to our guts. What we could not determine from her letter was precisely when she had left Jann all alone and gone-off to join the army. She was a Rosie, then a Wendy and now she was a WAC. But I was beginning to think she was *wacko!* Like I said, it was hard to follow in Jean's footsteps let alone follow her thought patterns. I'll bet she might have confused hell out of ol' Albert (Einstein)!

∽∞∽

If you were going to join-up to fight in the war effort, I suppose early 1945 was a good time to do so. The war effort was really starting to turn-up the heat for the Allied Powers in Europe. General George Marshall was top General for the US Army and General Eisenhower ran the entire show of the assaults in Europe. Together, along with other Western Allied Invasion U.S. Generals Omar Bradley and George S. Patton, the Brits' General Montgomery, the French Underground, the Ruskies' (Russians) General Zhukov attacking Germany from the East, plus all the other assorted Allies, they all drove Hitler all the way back, deep-inside his heavily bombed-out Germany into final, desperate defeat and Hitler's own suicide. Good riddance..

Adolph was being assaulted from all sides. We were feeling strong and righteous and beginning to sense the smell of victory in Europe. After Italy had been defeated, General Ike's complete focus had been on an all-out attack on Germany, the German Army and against Hitler and his inhuman, Nazi cowards. Even Brother Bo's Army Air Corps assignments transferred to partake in the southern European assault of the Western Allied Invasion of Germany from March into May of 1945.

Previously, Bo had participated in bringing about the ultimate destruction of Italy and defeat of its Axis Power Dictator. Bo played a heroic and courageous role in helping make Italy free and sane again, and *Big, Bad Benito* Mussolini was gone.

Side joke about Italians compliments of my brother Bo: Once Italy's despot Dictator Mussolini was captured, tried by newly the newly freed Italy's Freedom Fighter's Government, found guilty of horrific war crimes against humanity, and sentenced to death... Q: Who put the three, lethal bullets into Mussolini's executed body? A: Ten thousand Italian sharpshooters!

Okay, Brother Bo. That was for you!

In the Pacific theatre, General MacArthur was terrorizing the Japs. Island by island, beachhead by beachhead and across South East Asia, our US Army, Marines, Navy, Army Air Corps, and Pacific Warfront

Allies were also driving the Japanese back into their own, devastated-island nation. And, oh, goodness, they had no idea what was about to happen to them that coming summer in order to end the entire war once-and-for-all.

For the United States, the war had begun because of Japanese bombings of Pearl Harbor. It was going to end with our atomic bombings of Japan's Hiroshima and Nagasaki, using bombs unlike anything the world had ever seen, or has yet to see again during any warfare since then. It was cause for Allied celebrations, of course; however, it was cause for Japan's destruction, shame, embarrassment, and total surrender. Thank God.

FORGET THE FARM

A nyway, for us at that time, it was obvious that Jean was gone; however, we Cleveland sisters were by then very concerned about Jann. Jean was going to be very busy in the WACs and distracted for quite a while. In retrospect, too, none of us knew how long that war would carry-on., or how long Jean and Bo too would be away. They were both in *for the duration of the war.* We were winning, but that was all we knew.

In the meantime, Jann had to eat and have other basic provisions. She had to go to school. She had to feel a sense of security and stability. All those mandatory elements for a young child's life seemed very unaccounted for and highly likely missing. On top of everything else too, was Duffy, Jean's dog. Jean had obviously left Duffy for Jann to care for. What did Jean think Jann might do, share doggie biscuits?

There was only one adequate solution. Mary was highly needed at her workplace, so she said, but I did believe her. I could control my fate a little easier because the Warner & Swasey would only have to hire-in another welder or switch one from one of the other projects to our crew. My work was not a problem, plus was the fact that they all still owed me bigtime. They would let me go for a week, without pay, of course, but I had money saved up to cover the losses and expenses for traveling back to Vancouver, fetching Jann, and bringing her back with me.

So, I made immediate arrangements to take time-off for family-emergency. My bosses assured me that they would absolutely hold my job for my return. They really wanted me to stay with them. I felt good about that. Even my crew's members sympathized with me wishing me well for a speedy return. That was decent of them too. For a bunch of West Virginia Hillbillies who had traveled to a big city in order to make big money, they still were all decent examples of Southern Gentlemen. They knew how to treat a lady like a lady even if the lady was a dirty-faced welder at times. It was nice.

As I recall, I left toward the end of that week. It coincided with our very recent discovery of Jann's abandonment by our elder-stateman sister, Jean. I also figured that I would have a couple days to get to Vancouver by bus riding twenty-four hours day with various stops in cross-country, city bus-stations to change drivers and allow passengers to get meals and freshen-up, if necessary. Sleeping on the bus was no problem. I had learned how-to sleep-in truck front-seats crisscrossing our great country. A nap on a bus was a piece-of-cake.

I planned on getting to Vancouver by late Saturday. I would then use Sunday to gather-up all Jann's belongings and pack them into decent luggage. Once we had closed-up the farmhouse as best as possible, we would grab Duffy and throw-out our thumbs once again, if necessary. Duffy was a full-grown Alaskan Shepard by then, and it would be a big problem for riding on Greyhound. It wasn't like I could just ask the driver to pull-over for my dog to go do its business. They had their rules: No large pets. So, I had to make realistic plans for the three of us to hitch-hike back to Cleveland. A good fact was that I had plenty of money to accommodate reasonable lodging and meals for all of us on the way back home. We could take an acceptable amount of time to get to Cleveland. No rush.

When necessary, Greyhound Bus Lines had served us well. By 1945, it was already a thirty-year old company and the only national intercity bus transportation in the whole country. Greyhound could just about get someone anywhere they needed to go, or at least get them close. During those war years, Greyhound really boomed because they were a terrific means to get our soldiers and sailors all over the country to their homes, or sweethearts or military bases or ports.

This was going to be a very fast turn-around trip too. I laughed to myself and said, "Okay, this is going to be eighteen states in six days. Now, that was pushing it, but there they were: Ohio, Indiana, Illinois, Iowa, Nebraska, Wyoming, Idaho, Oregon, and Washington. Then I would grab Jann and Duffy and do the same trip in reverse except by hitch-hiking. However, hitch-hiking sometimes presented slight variations due to their own scheduled drop-offs and pick-ups. One could never tell, but one fact was true: We were all going to be putting some fast miles under our belts.

Greyhound had helped me not that long ago, and now they were going to help me one more time again.

Unlike my trip coming from Vancouver to Cleveland not that long before, there were not going to be any side trips such as brief excursions to Sioux Falls, SD to visit family. That was not a healthy idea. My arranged tickets from Cleveland would just keep me going straight all the way to Vancouver. A few stops at a few cities Greyhound Stations occasionally required me to change buses in order to maintain my route, but that was not going to be any problem.

I always used to tell the driver's what my plans were, and they were always kind to me. They kept me informed of where we were and what my next travel-step should be. If I happened to fall asleep, the Greyhound drivers would even wake me and advise me to change busses, if necessary, or get a meal or whatever. Their drivers were always very professional and gentlemanly.

After that short, unannounced advertisement for Greyhound Bus Lines, I can now add that just like it was laid-out to me by the ticket agent in Cleveland, as planned, I was dropped-off at the Greyhound Bus-Station in Vancouver right on time on that following, late Saturday afternoon. Thanks to Jean's letters and provided information, I had an address, and being a little familiar with the area, I generally knew which way to travel to find the farm. Just like before when I had lived there, I started catching Vancouver's city busses to get me near my destination. Those bus-drivers were very helpful too.

After the final, city-route bus dropped me off at the closest bus stop, I had to walk the remainder of the way to the address I had. It wasn't far. So many people all around the area worked at Kaiser Vancouver, so the city bus-system had gone to great lengths to accommodate all those workers. The bus routes were closely aligned and covered the territory well.

One aspect that was very refreshing to my view: No fences. As I gazed up and down the dirt and gravel road splitting-off the main, paved road into town, I could look far and wide and not see any enclosed front yards. Oh, sure, out back behind some farm homes I could see fenced and gated pens for farm animals. There were also property-line fencings separating one farmer's field from another to avoid planting issues. I even saw wooden fenced-in corrals for horses and livestock. All those made sense, but it was admirable and pleasant just to enjoy seeing all the farm yards open and receptive to each other without fences keeping each other in-or-out.

Farm houses and several barns dotted the distant landscape. Most of the other folks in the area appeared to have very large spreads of fifty, eighty or one-hundred acres each. Some of them were actively being farmed and there were crops in the ground. Others were growing hay and alfalfa for their livestock, and still others were left open and used for cattle, sheep, or horse grazing. Continuing, I saw Jean's property in the near distance. It stood out due to its size. As I casually strolled down that country road to the address I sought, I couldn't help but admire Jean's powerful will and fortitude. Right, wrong, keep it, or leave it, Jean's willpower and singlemindedness had forged this dream into reality.

When I finally stood on the dirt road in front of the little farmhouse, I recognized immediately that Jean had been right. The place was certainly the *crude rudiments of a home!* The fence line gave the appearance of a larger estate, however. Having spent so long in city living, I had forgotten what it was like to own a larger piece of property. Ten acres? Yeah, that was larger, alright. The little house was sort of barren and plain, though. It was a brown-colored, one-story, wood structure with four, medium-sized windows in the front, evenly spaced apart and facing the road. There was a large, plain, basic-wood front-door with a simple concrete walkway running up to it with a one-step, four-by-six-foot, square concrete porch in front.

The roof looked like it needed serious repairs, or else the previous owners simply couldn't decide on metal-sheathing, tarpaper, wood-shingles, or tar-and-rock for its covering. So, they used all four just to cover-all-bases. But, hey, down on the far-left end, it had a brick fireplace, so that did add a little texture and homeliness. Closing out that not too picturesque scene, however, were two rather lovely trees right in the front yard one on each side of the entrance walkway. One looked like a Maple, if I remember right, and the other was a very tall Douglas Fir. Nice. Reminded me of my fun, tree-climbing days in Duluth, MN as a small child. Made me wonder if Jann... Na, probably not!

From where I was standing, I could see a large note attached to the front-door. My first inclination was an *Eviction Notice*. Of course, it may as well have been because there was no way we others were willing or able to support *Jean's Farm Dream*. It began as a dream, but it was going to end as a nightmare. I remember making an analogy at the time with the Pacific War and Japan. Japan's war also started with a *Dream of Greatness* by defeating the enemy America at Pearl Harbor, but it ended as a *Nightmare* in Hiroshima.

Well, well, surprise, surprise! The note was not a "Notice to Vacate the Premises," after all. It was a message from Jann saying she had *already vacated the premises!* Apparently, Jann was temporarily living with the neighbors one house down the road. Stretching my head way backwards and craning my neck around to the right, I could see the closest neighbor's house not far away. Alright, that was really a bit of a relief. Jann was nearby, at least, and I knew I was headed there next.

Curiosity got the best of me, however, so I tried the doorknob, and it was indeed unlocked. Maybe Jann planned for me to live there in case I had planned on staying. But, obviously, she had *split this palace* already.

Lights did not work, so there was no electricity going to the place. Strange. Bill not paid? Power-outage somewhere? Who knew, but I was not planning on finding-out. There was still just enough daylight to make-out the interior design, though. Small, smaller, and smallest were the room sizes. The living-room with the workable fireplace, it appeared, was small but adequate for a family of three, maybe four persons. There were two smaller and smallest bedrooms each with a plain, single window looking to the outdoors, one to the side yard, and the other overlooking the ten acres out back. There was a small, but tolerable bathroom that worked. I know because I had to use it. There was running water too. No light to *watch* what I was doing, but there was water to *wash* what I was doing! Ha! Ha!

On the other end of the entranceway was a large opening leading into a typical, country kitchen. A simple, short kitchen counter with a sink and storage cabinets above, a wood-fed stove with four burners and a flu to release the smoke. And the *piece-de-resistance* was a decent looking, medium sized icebox to help keep things cooled… for several hours at a time! How about that? But then it needed more ice, I supposed.

Anyway, that quick walk-through was all I needed to see and know. Thanks, Jean, but no thanks. I was a little disappointed to realize that all those checks of mine given to Jean had been cashed and went into her *Farm Dream Fund* and had ultimately ended-up here. Furthermore, those funds were sure to remain here until an actual "Notice-to-Vacate" arrived. Then the bank who loaned Jean the money in the first *place* to buy the *place* got the *place* back to pay back their loan. Easy come, easy go.

Jean and I were both out our entire down-payment and any cash savings too. Somehow, I didn't think that was ever an aspect of Jean's *Big Dream*. I was pretty sure that was all, though. The timing of everything suggested that Jean had quickly changed her mind after she purchased the farmhouse and had probably never even made any monthly payments on the place. Why would she? She was a WAC in the Army! Adios, farm. Congratulations, bank! Goodbye, hard-earned cash!

I remember just shaking my head in wonder as I turned to leave and walk to the neighbor's home, "This was the *dream* that had inspired Jean all that time and kept her focused and ever-so-driven. It had been her guiding light, and it had kept me in-line behind her and following in her path."

In sort of a melancholy yet proud reflection, I recall further reflecting, "She had done it, though. Jean had achieved her dream even though now she was off dreaming something else again somewhere else." Where might we all have been without Jean's dream?

Then I just chuckled, started walking away and began singing out loud to my sister Jean, "How ya gonna keep 'em down on the farm after they've seen New York?" Thank you, Jean.

DOG GONE DILIGENCE

A few minutes later, Jann excitedly met me at the neighbor's front door. She pulled me inside their cozy front room and proudly introduced me to her caretakers, Mr. & Mrs. Sid, and Eva Franklin. They were a gracious, elderly, grandparent-type couple who warmly welcomed me into their comfortable home. Right away, Jann was ever so pleased to introduce me to "Teno," their dog. He was a big, lovable, and friendly Golden Retriever who seemed very attached to Jann.

I needed to ask right away, though, "Jann, where is Duffy? He wasn't over at Jean's farmhouse."

Jann replied somewhat frustrated, "Oh, Jean sent someone here weeks ago to pick Duffy-up and take him to his house."

"What are you talking about?" I shuddered.

Then Jann went into a credible but sad explanation which once more examined Jean's unusually compartmentalized mind. Apparently, after several weeks of her absence, Jean had arranged for a friend to drive up from somewhere in Northern California and pick-up her dog at that farmhouse in Vancouver for safe keeping. That's right! Pick-up Duffy, but not Jann!

Somehow in Jean's WACky mind, she had been thoughtful and courteous enough not to want Jann burdened with providing care for both Duffy and her. So, Jean had the dog rescued and left her twelve-year old sister there all alone to fend for herself. Or, more likely, Jean was worried for Duffy's poor sake and troubled that Jann might not provide enough ample and appropriate care for the dog. In either case, poor Jann didn't even have Duffy for company or protection.

And gosh, why hadn't Jean remembered that little sister Jann could have *easily* managed to care for herself and Duffy. Why, all Jann needed to have done was *easily* grow enough vegetables in her huge garden, gather enough chickens from her coop, milk the cows for enough milk, butcher pigs enough for plenty of chops and bacon, and pick enough apples from her apple orchard for her and Duffy both to live like a Princess and her Protector. Why not?... Hellooo? Hello, Jean? Are you there? Is anybody home?

The rest of the story is very basic, but rather pathetic. Just as we had surmised, Jean had changed her mind and plans. Once Jean had the farm dream achieved, it was no longer important. There were bigger fish to fry. I knew that it was also true that Jean had lost interest because I wasn't there to back-her-up, so-to-speak. She no longer had that blind-eyed, faithful, trusting, supportive, and assisting follower, me, to carry-on her dream. With all that huge, fulfilled dream then in her past, Jean made the U.S. Army her own next move. Somehow, however, Jean just figured in her complex and stridently self-serving mind, "If she (Jean) could do something, then so could twelve-year old, Jann too. She just had to grow-up a little."

Jann had continued living there at *Jean's Dream* farmhouse with Duffy for several weeks all alone. She ate all the food that Jean had left behind, and she picked fruit from neighboring trees to help feed her. Jann had some money that Jean had given her to buy basic staples from the local grocery a couple miles away. Jann faithfully continued going to school all on her own and, other than being lonely and frightened and insecure, she managed.

Then, finally, a man had shown-up at the farm and said that Jean had sent him. Jann told me that she was so relieved and excited to meet this quasi-family man. Jann added that she was a little nervous and upset about leaving on such short notice but prepared to leave with the stranger right-away. After all, *any friend of Jean's was a friend of hers.*

Jann confessed, however, that at first, she began pouting a bit. She believed that she was being asked to leave the farmhouse by a perfect stranger, and she wasn't comfortable with that arrangement. Jean had never said a word about this man coming to get her. Anyway, Jann continued, that once she adjusted to the idea and gratefully accepted the premise of not being alone anymore, immediately she had raced to her room and started gathering-up her clothes and belongings for the journey to wherever with this stranger.

However, there had been a great misunderstanding. With Jann standing right there before the stranger with her meager belongings dangling from anxious hands, the man finally understood Jann's intentions. Apparently, he was slightly embarrassed and felt somewhat awkward, but he needed to correct the confusion. It was certainly a dilemma.

Quickly, though, Jean's friend corrected Jann's unfortunate error-in-judgement. He clarified that Jean had arranged for him to travel all the way-up to Vancouver from Northern California *in order to get the dog, Duffy, not Jann.*

Jann told how the man did not dally after that. Swiftly, he put Duffy on a leash hanging by the door, grabbed-up the dog dishes, a bag of food, and then rapidly rushed-out to his car and stuffed everything, plus Duffy, inside. Without any further explanation, he climbed into his vehicle and drove-off. Just like that, he was gone and so was Duffy. No sympathetic, or empathetic goodbyes. No words of comfort or promises for a rescue soon. Just his car quickly in gear and an abrupt departure. Jean sure did love her dog. Adios, little farmer girl!

When I heard Jann's tale, naturally, I was in disbelief. Nobody does that to someone, and certainly not to a sister. And a nine-year old, at that! Oh, now wait! Nobody except a *Jean!* That was just part of her code-of-behavior.

I thought for a moment and considered, "OMG! Did Jean simply learn to do that sort of thing all on her own? Or, was her behavior inherited? Did our dad pass that inconsiderate, mean and tasteless behavior on to Jean?" No, I didn't believe so. The difference was simple: Our dad did that sort of thing and relished in the hurt or harm it created; Jean did it without wasting thought or consideration or remorse because, in her mind, it was the right, correct and justified thing to do.

Gee, what a *fatherly-like thing to do!* Our father, anyway. Today, I think they call it DNA. Jean couldn't help herself because it was in her genes! Jean and her genes… Jean's genes! God forbid! Oh, that's right. Jean is an atheist. I wondered if that was genetic too.

My mind was whirling by then, however. I thought about all of our Catholic training and other experiences, and I challenged Jean's thoughtless decision. I clearly remembered the Good Samaritan stories and about Jesus helping the needy. I recalled Father Flanagan's famous slogan from his Boy's Town: *He ain't heavy. He's m' brother.*

How could she, I pondered. Oh, yeah, it was all that *atheist* bullshit, again. My, how convenient! Their motto: Look out for yourself! And the other: Take care of Number One! And, of course, the Darwinian classic standard: Survival of the Fittest!

I started getting angry by then. I imagined Jean's rationale for her, "I had faith in Jann. I believed she could make it. If not, well then, it was simply *elimination of the weakest of the species.* That's all!"

Sorry, Jann, that was really terrible of Jean, I thought. At least, *I would have lied to you.* That was when I began stretching even my own Cathochismic learnings. Jann's situation with that stranger was a perfect example of what I figured was needed. *A big, fat lie!* That nincompoop, or Jean's lackey, could have used and should have used a little, creative-language mistruths to comfort Jann. There were literally dozens of suggestions or explanations he may have given Jann to encourage her and inspire her on to safety, self-reliance, and survival.

I easily put myself in his place offering a more appropriate response than, "Huh? Na, I just came for the dog!"

In my mind, I easily displaced Jean's, pathetic-fruitcake's discourtesy and substituted my own unique response for her flunky's dumbbell discourse. Instead, I quickly conjured-up a more enlightening elucidation to Jean's virtual abandonment in order to give Jann hope.

I would have lied. For me, that dufus messenger should have said something like the following: "Young Sister Jann, I am here to advise you that your loving sister, Jean, sends her warmest regards. She is off fighting Hitler at the moment and is risking her very life every day to maintain your safety here at home. In fact, the horribly dangerous missions that our US Army is sending Jean on daily require her to literally crawl on the ground smelling-out perilous explosives and vicious enemy. That is why she needs her dog to assist her.

"Duffy will join Jean and obey her every command. Then the two of them will team-up and *smell together…* So that you are *safe from harm*! Also, Jean must beg and scrounge for food from locals in the countryside or by picking fruit off trees. Oh, she is suffering, but she does so willingly for God and country. Er, well, for country, anyway, and she wishes you well… until one day, with God's, er, anybody's mercy, she and Duffy might return home and once again show you all the love she feels you deserve… PS: Jean further requests, 'Please send any remaining doggie biscuits along too because they may be the last good meal Duffy *and I* have for months to come!..."'

Sometimes, I rationalized, there really were situations and circumstances where a darn good lie was way better than... the truth... or even nothing. We've all heard the quip, "Truth hurts!" Well, sometimes, it's true! And silence can really hurt too. Believe me, I knew all about that on very personal levels.

At least a good lie can temporarily pacify someone or keep them confused long enough until they can get themselves readjusted. Or, maybe a great lie will even resolve the whole predicament, or even get them elected to the presidency! Or, better yet, if one lie doesn't work, then tell another even bigger one. Be original, though. Be creative. Keep 'em coming and keep 'em all guessing until the situation passes, or it's too late. If you get caught, then just tell another!

Best of all, get them madder, if necessary, so that they can *survive just for the hell of it!* Survive to *live for revenge*! Na. That's too complicated. Do it for *spite!* Yes, that's it! *Survive for spite's sake!* By God, it worked for me!

Another interesting aspect regarding Jann's debacle was that Duffy had, in fact, indirectly assisted with Jann's rescue. Every day, Jann would take Duffy for walks. Sometimes, it was to the market quite a way down the road. Other times, it may have only been to their road's corner where everyone's mailboxes were located. But it was during those times of walks, that the kind and thoughtful neighbor, Mrs. Eva Franklin kept noticing Jann and Duffy always alone.

After Jean had mysteriously vanished to chase another dream via the WACs, Mrs. Franklin had realized that there was only Jann and her dog, and no one else. Curiosity made her approach Jann along with her own dog, Teno, one afternoon. Initially, they met each day at the mailbox and let their dogs visit while Eva inquired about Jann's well-being. Jann said they got along famously, and Duffy was delighted to have another dog to sniff as a friend.

Mrs. Franklin kept-up with her light-hearted quizzing of Jann's circumstances, the kind neighbor told me later. However, Jann was very close-mouthed about her own situation. Jean had left her with such instructions. Anyway, Mrs. Franklin came-up with a plan. She knew right-away that the way to Jann's mind was through her stomach.

Just as she figured, whenever she offered Jann food of any sort, cookies, pie slices, fried chicken, sandwiches, or whatever, Jann was so appreciative that she devoured everything in sight. It didn't take Eva long to learn that Jann had been left there alone on the farm, and that she was just waiting along with her trusted protector and ally, Duffy, for family to come... Jann was just waiting... and waiting... and...

Finally, Eva began asking Jann to come over for dinner with she and her husband, Sid. Right away, Jann eagerly and gratefully accepted. After I arrived, I still never learned the Franklin's own circumstances, but it was obvious that they became very willing pseudo-grandparents for Jann. They were also equally disturbed as I to learn of Jean's friend who had showed-up to rescue Duffy, but not Jann.

That was likely the final straw that led the Franklins to eventually suggest and convince Jann to come and stay... temporarily... with them... until some family ever showed-up, like me. I am certain that in a small way, I must have saddened them with my arrival and having taken their little temporary Godchild away. Beautiful kind, warm and sharing people. Thank you, Mr. & Mrs. Franklin, for your generosity and care.

I dare say, circumstances changed radically right after that. There was no Duffy anymore, and as an indirect result, there was no farm anymore, either. In fact, with both gone, or longer holding us back, conditions had improved immensely. With no more farm to worry about, and without Duffy to burden or slow us down, it meant no necessary hitchhiking and no cross-country truck rides.

The trip back, all the way by Greyhound Bus, was a *piece-of-cake!* Two tickets, one *adult* and one *child*, took us all the way home to Cleveland without a *hitch*. (Pun intended.) The age-limit for a child's bus-tickets was ten and under, so I told Jann to just act like an idiot, and she was a natural! Terrific acting. Gosh, if she hadn't of been so smart, she might have had a real career in Hollywood! But no questions were asked anywhere along the journey. We saved a few dollars in bus fares and got to spend it all on extra ice-creams for us both. In a couple more days, we arrived back in Cleveland, and after a familiar city bus ride or two, we were at home-sweet-home.

Naturally, there was lots of catching-up to do, and four talkative sisters, Sis, Colleen, Jann, and me to do it. We stayed-up so late that night catching-up on all the current news. As expected, Sis and Colleen were both flabbergasted at Jann's abandonment story and delightful survival thanks to the sweet, Franklin neighbors. The next morning, Sis called her job to say that she'd be late a bit for family issues, and then she and Colleen took Jann to get her registered in an elementary school nearby Colleen's high school. Those two would bond again and stick closely together both to and from school. Four-out-of-five of us sisters were together finally, and life was good… for a while, anyway.

The next day was on a Wednesday, I do recall, because and I had only missed a total of five days of work, Thursday, Friday, Saturday, Monday, and Tuesday. My entire round-trip venture had gone timewise just as I had planned. I guess I had gotten fairly good at judging distances and travel times.

Anyway, I showed-up that next day, and I received a gala welcoming back. It was nice to be back. Mr. Carson was as delightful as ever, and I kind of noticed that my absence had sort of cleared-the-air somewhat. With my absence came an opportunity for all the hands to forgive themselves for their suspicious and deceitful thoughts and behavior. If I was going to be big enough to forgive all of them, then they were going to be big enough, and very willing, to forget about it all too. We easily slipped right back into our previous, congenial morning welcomes and goodbyes.

In fact, Mr. Carson's greeting that very day went something like this: "Well, Hallelujah and Loudi-Miss-Claudie, looks who's back? And it's just in the nick-of-time because it's gotten so quiet around here, since you left, that folks are just fallin'-asleep on the job! Welcome home, Missy!"

"It's nice to be back, Mr. Carson," I teasingly replied, "I have missed all you guys too, and I'll do my best now to stir things-up some more and keep everybody awake."

Little did either of us know that my response that Wednesday morning was almost prophetic. A few changes had occurred in the past week of my absence. Changes often bring with them adaptations and adjustments. Production changes had occurred as a result of my return, and some of those new changes were going to involve incredible demands for adjustments by everyone concerned.

More demanded adjustments would take place soon thereafter which changed the whole atmosphere and outlook of my job there with Warner and Swasey. Those West Virginia Hillbilly crewmates of mine were all thrilled to see me again, and being southern gentlemen, they welcomed their lady-welder back with warm, kind, and respectful open-arms. I appreciated their reception, in return. However, I was to learn some new aspects about that group of southerners which I did not appreciate, could not tolerate and which eventually all but turned-my-stomach.

I had grown-up a lot in the past few years. I was approaching nineteen-years of age by then, and I had learned a lot about work, life, and human nature. I had become stronger and self-reliant. I knew what I liked and what I didn't like, and I was no longer afraid to remain silent. I would speak my mind whenever I saw something interesting, useful, or wrong. Fairly soon, things were about to happen which absolutely forced me to speak-up, challenge the status-quo and force me to ultimately forge new chapters for myself which changed the course of my entire life…

GOOD IDEAS

When you are good at doing something, it doesn't take much from your observational powers to notice any variances, changes, malfunctions, and poor craftsmanship when compared to your own quality work. Just looking at something you make, you can tell right away if others' efforts do not match the excellence of your own. When I arrived at our crew's worksite, and I took a gander at the stage of development and craftmanship of our product, I could tell right away that our crew had been slower, and the work from the other shifts in comparison had demonstrated how much our team had been slacking.

I didn't need the Foreman to tell me how much they had missed me. It was obvious from the quality and production level that they had faltered and fallen down embarrassingly low. The crew seemed oblivious to the matter and just defended their present status as having been very awkward since I left because they had to use other crew's welders, or they, themselves, were shifted around to fill-in at other sites. In other words, our product, the radar system we were presently working on, had become a two-shift production just depending on the other two shifts, swing, and graveyard, to do the heavy work.

It also meant that our product, our *Americanized* version of the Wurzburg Radar System we were building, had fallen well behind in its production stage. Effectively, since I had been gone, the whole damned crew had fallen-apart. Without realizing it, I had been the driving-force that pushed our production. I told our riggers what parts to get and place where I needed them; I explained clearly to the fitters how to prepare the steel pieces and place them exactly where I needed them set-together and tack-welded; and I directed the others to move-ahead with necessary staging for future development for us or the next shift. The rule was for them to set-up and prepare always allowing me to chase and try to catch-up with them. Their jobs were always to be working steadily and having everything ready for my welding.

The Foreman and the General Foreman both knew our system, my system, and that was why they appreciated me so much. With me there, our crew was a well-oiled, finely tuned operation. While I was absent, outsiders were not able to step-in and automatically synchronize their actions to our own production methods. Our team fell-apart. As a result, our Radar System product was well behind in its estimated completion date.

Our GF and Foreman were very frustrated with their options to try and get our crew back on schedule. I could tell that. It was obvious to me. I knew a lot about production deadlines with all my time building the mini carriers for Kaiser Vancouver. I had expressly learned about and valued the several times that I had climbed through tiny holes to correct some bad welds and keep those mini-ships online and on-schedule.

That was why I went to see the Foreman and GF after work the following day right after I had returned. I had a simple suggestion to recommend to them and see if they felt it would work. My plan was simple: Add another welder to our crew to work with me. I could keep directing the others to do what was necessary, tell the new welder what to do and where and when to do it and I could easily maintain my own schedule of welding. If the crew did the fitting and rigging as I was certain they could, two welders could keep them running like crazy to have work prepared for us two welders to weld and complete.

After I explained my theory, the bosses stood there staring at me and then staring at each other as they paused to consider my idea. I could tell they were recognizing its expediency. It won't affect the other shifts because they will still have to pick-up where we leave-off. We shall simply complete a great deal more, close to twice-as-much production on any given day. Then I even had a deal-closer for them.

In similar words, I told them, "Let this change, adding another welder, be a trial, an experiment. If it is successful, our production will get right back-on schedule, and then you'll have your proof. If you want, or need, even more Radar Systems built, you can adapt our product's other two shifts into doing the same thing. If that works too, well, heck, you can add additional welders to all your production teams. Ultimately, you can adapt and increase production for all your crews and on all shifts into doing the same thing. Step-by-step."

The GF paused, shook his head and then said, "Miss McCord, you are one very clever young lady! That's a great idea! Wow! Two welders per crew to force the other crew members to work faster to keep-up. And if necessary, we can always add another rigger or fitter, that's easy enough."

I just smiled and said, "Sure it is. Piece-of-cake!"

The Foreman became more pragmatic, however. He warned, "The only problem will be finding other welders who can work as well with their crews as Miss Patsy does"

I quickly added, "That's no problem. Let the present welder, or the new one, no matter, be the pusher, or lead welder. He, or she, keeps the ball rolling and maintains the speed-of-the-line. That *welder-pusher* will make the others keep-up-the-pace and tow-the-line, or they will find themselves sitting around with nothing to weld. They won't like that because it will be a poor reflection on them.

"If they do really good work, then the crews will move so fast they will have time to relax and wait for welders to catch-up. And that is not bad. Welders already get paid more anyway for their welding skill; pay them even more for their *pushing* or management abilities." I smiled at that closing remark, and the bosses got my drift.

"If your plan works, Miss McCord," the GF smiled and stated, "you will be worth every penny and more. We'll start your plan as soon as we can hire a new welder. Nice idea. Nice work. Now go home and relax. Let's see what happens tomorrow."

"One last word, Sirs. *Competition*." I was on a roll, so I decided to unload a few other ideas I had been thinking about. Some were transplants from my Kaiser days. I thought that some additional ideas I had might work well right here in Warner Swasey's own form of high-production pressure, and war-cause environment too.

I continued on my roll, "You have a bunch of three-shift teams all building the same-type units. We are in a war, and things like output, successes and victories are what it's all about. Why not encourage the different crew-teams and shifts into competing with one another? I'm certain you already keep tallies. Schedules are critical, of course. Name winners of highest production by individual crews and best output for all three-shift combined crews.

"Only you bosses know the true results, so spread the winners around a little to make it more serious fun and competitive. Give winners simple announcement awards, or team citations or even free tickets to the movies." I watched the look on their faces to note if they caught my snide humor and then continued:

"It might make for smoother transitions from one-shift to another too. Add a little humorous gamesmanship to their work. Let shifts know from time-to-time how they are comparing to other shifts and respective crews. I believe it will give everyone more of a sense of contribution to this lousy, stinking war's end, and to our victory. Kind of *cheering* the workers on, sort of. It's a *We're all in this thing together,* kind of thing. Go Team America! I know it would inspire me."

I supposed that I had impressed them. They had stood there glued to every word I said. Both of their nodding heads suggested understanding and appreciation. The GF spoke out emphatically, "Miss McCord, you truly are a marvel. Very interesting ideas, you have offered. Our company has lots of work ahead for itself in the future. After we win this war, and we stop building Radar Systems for the war-effort, we shall be converting our plants and equipment to something else focused for civilian life. I'd like you to stick around and consider some sort of a worker, management-type position. For right now, though. Thank you, we'll talk more tomorrow and good evening. Go home and relax after your great return day."

It was a nice way to finish a day. Everyone likes feeling appreciated. I did, and I was hoping that some of my ideas might come to fruition. An extra welder was a no-brainer, though. I was certain that my crew could practically double our output with another good welder. I was a good and fast welder, but my crew had way too much time-off on their hands. Sometimes, they had to fake-it to look busy enough. That was not good for them or the company.

Working more, thus producing more, helped shifts go by more quickly too. It never minded to me because I was always checking-ahead, but then I'd refocus on my welding puddle and keep pushing it forward. I would get *lost in the light!* But I had my team keeping me busy, and I liked that. Time flew by.

I was hoping that my *two-welder* idea would work-out and happen. The *competition* idea was reasonable. It may not work during peacetime, though. Everyone gets complacent during those times, I imagined. But these were critical, war times and cheering all of us on to our own modest sorts of victories made sense to me...

What was that smart-ass's paraphrased comment? *For every good idea, there is an opposite and equal bad idea.* Well, I *had offered* some good ideas, and I really felt serious about them making a difference. I was anxious to test my theories too. I wasn't worried or even thinking about any of my good ideas backfiring. Both my ideas and I were filled with positive energy. They just had to work.

There was another popular axiom floating around back then that, perhaps, was to take hold here on this job with me, my crew, and the whole damned place: *It takes two to Tango.* Two people floating about a dancefloor in perfect harmony and unison to exciting music is awe-inspiring. One person spinning about on a floor dipping and tossing around without a partner probably looks hilarious, if not ridiculous. I had already seen Fred Astaire and Ginger Rogers Tango together in the film, <u>The Story of Vernon, and Irene Castle</u>. They were gorgeous together and brilliant while in each other's arms while dancing. The Tango was a specialty of theirs.. However, either of them alone while flipping and flopping about doing Tango moves might have looked foolish.

My unfortunate point is that good ideas must be nurtured by everyone. They must be accepted and willingly dealt with. Everyone on a team is relevant, and each player, or dancer, must have their respected place in the partnership, the union, to make the *good* idea or the *productive* dance flow smoothly.

Gee. I never thought about ignorant people, and worse yet, ones who could not dance, or worse yet, would not dance. Was I in for a surprise and another significant life-lesson? It was a lot for an eighteen-year old to deal with.

NEW WELDER

The next morning, there were no new changes evident. *Good Day Greetings* with Mr. Carson and the fresh, morning-air walk to my work site was exhilarating. My talk with the bosses the day before had given me ownership of my job, my work, my craft, and our projects. I really did want to see our team climb back into the running and increase our production rate. I even mentioned my idea to the other guys, and they responded well. They even said that if I kept pointing the way, they'd built us a Radar to the moon! I liked their attitude. They didn't want to feel 2nd rate either. We were better than that.

The shift ended and I had said my goodbyes when I passed through Mr. Carson's gate, and he told me that I was requested in the front-office. Of course, we teased each other about that. Neither of us could help it. With a set-up like that, however, automatically, I was the straight man, and Mr. Carson was the joker.

So, I began, "Why, Mr. Carson, whatever do you think I have done now?"

"Why, I don't have any idea, Missy, but those bosses sure looked a bit miffed."

"Well, what could I have ever done to make them act so angry?" I whimpered.

"All I can think of, Missy, is that since you've been here, they have been working lots of overtime just trying to keep up with you."

"Mr. Carson, do you know that I did go and give them some new ideas to help speed-up things around here?"

"I just can't say, Missy, but if that's the case, then maybe they are just going to promote you to President and take orders from you! That, or they're going to send you over to work with General Ike, himself, and let you whip them Germs and finish this war once-and-for-all. That, or their gonna get you out of here and give you a quiet office-job somewhere else. That, or they're gonna just fire your ass for being too smart, hard-working' and pretty! Their wives are jealous and probably told them to do it. I'm sure of it"

"Aw, Mr. Carson, you sure do know how to make a young girl feel… confused! Thanks for the tips, tough."

Having that little interaction with my funny and nice friend, Mr. Carson, no matter what, I was headed to the office in a good mood. We had a lengthy discussion the day before. I wondered if today's meeting had anything to do with it. Maybe they liked our talk so much that I was going to get a raise right away. In my mind, I remember already calculating various payroll increases to note their fiscal benefits. To be honest, I was *already* spending some of my new *raise* money too. *In my mind*, I was *already* worth it.

As I followed the clearly marked pathway heading up to the main Warner & Swasey offices, I know that I was in such a good mood that late day, I pretended to be following the *yellow-brick road* to the *City of Oz* to visit the wonderful wizard. He was the fellow that would give me more praise and a raise.

As I turned the corner around some stored oxygen tanks, up-ahead by the Main Entrance doorway, I saw four men standing together in a group talking. I recognized Foreman Mort and our General Foreman. And I had seen the one man as our Personnel Director executive; he was the same man who had taken part in that supposedly secret, Radar-System Inquisition. At least he had personally apologized to me afterward on behalf of the entire company of Warner & Swasey. Anyway, those three looked like they were chatting away with a fourth fellow. He was a tall man, dressed more like an executive than a worker, and he was black.

A black man, or African American, as we say now, was uncommon on jobs like those. In those days, some worked in cafeterias or as grounds clean-up, but never in the office-management or executive fields. It was just unusual, so it really caught my attention. This man was tall, like I said already, he was slender yet well-built, and well-tailored too. Plus, this newcomer was very-well groomed. He appeared as though he could be as official as might be.

I approached the group, and our Foreman was the first to spot me and welcome me to their group. He said while smiling, "Well, here comes our little fire-cracker now. This is the one I mentioned who cracked our whole spy-ring case all by herself! And now she's single-handedly trying to quadruple our entire production line! Mr. Jepson, this is Miss Patricia McCord."

I was already blushing, but I accepted their greetings and shook extended hands with each one personally. When I shook the new man's hand, he was introduced to me as Mr. Bartholomew Jepson from London, England. Mr. Jepson bowed slightly too as we shook hands.

I was quick and polite and responded, "Welcome to America, Mr. Jepson. You are a long way from home, but you sure are with a good ally. I enjoy going to the movies, and they show and tell us newsreels about your famous General "Monte" Montgomery. I'm glad he is on our side and even more glad we are winning together."

Mr. Jepson answered right back, "How about this? A skilled, bright, astute, and knowledgeable young woman too. I like this young lady, just fine. I am sure we are going to work together well and get along famously."

"Oh," I thought to myself, I've got another new boss to work for. I wonder what he's going to do?"

My thoughts were answered right away. The Personnel Director spoke-up and explained the situation, "I'm sure you both will get along just fine. Miss McCord, we discussed your idea yesterday, and we are moving on it right away. We do need your crew's project to get caught-up and back-on schedule. Therefore, we searched and found Mr. Jepson earlier today, and he is going to be your new welder. Mr. Jepson has all the welding certifications necessary and has assured us that he can do whatever welding assignments we require of him. What do you say?"

Of course, I was surprised, but it was because of those things I hadn't just thought about. First, he was apparently not an executive but rather a man-of-the-tools., a welder at that. "Wow!" I thought, "He sure isn't dressed for the job like I had been when interviewed." Second, he was going to be working for me, not the other way around. But mainly, I was flabbergasted by the rush the office had put on my suggestion. They really liked my idea. I was pleased and a tad excited over their agreement.

I had a humorous reaction, though, to hide my embarrassment, "Well, that's great, Mr. Jepson, but I sure hope you have something else to wear on-the-job!"

That got everyone all laughing together. Mr. Jepson added jokingly that he was surely on his way down to the leather shop that day, and I laughed with him again. The Foremen and Company man ended our introductions and discussion in a positive way. My new welding partner, Mr. Jepson, would start in the morning on that Friday.

I was to use that day to teach and break-in Mr. Jepson to the system and get the other crew members adjusted to *my* new plan. Then, the bosses agreed most importantly that I was to become adapted to the whole, new-system plan, myself. They were anxious to test my plan and theory and wanted to have a verbal report from me after a few days.

I agreed feeling a little bit anxious too, but I went home that evening feeling excited, confident, and content. I really felt strongly that Mr. Jepson and I would make my plan work, and the other guys on the crew would adjust and adapt too. They had enough time to manage it. If we coordinated our process, there would be no problems, I was sure.

At least that was what I had hoped for… What I did not know or understand was due to my lack of experience. I still had a lot to learn about human nature, or behavior. Reflecting back on that little, er, *petit* eighteen going-on nineteen-year old, I just shake my head now in wonder and think, *If hopes were horses, I'd have been riding sky high!*

Friday morning came early for me, and I was up before the break-of-day, cleaned-up, ate a quick breakfast of fried-egg sandwich and made the same for lunch. I was out the door just as my sisters were rising for their days. Loves and goodbyes hollered as I raced out the door, and I was on my way to work. I wanted to be there a little-bit early, at least, so that I could study our project some more and figure-out the smartest arrangement for Mr. Jepson and me to share our welding assignments. I wanted everything to go smoothly.

I was delightfully surprised to hear that Mr. Jasper was already on the jobsite when I got there. Naturally, Mr. Carson gave me heads-up, so I was already looking for him when I approached our own project-site. Fact is, as I walked-in, I had seen a man right in our staging-area where they unload parts we need and right next to the welding machines. He was doing a standard and typical, Stainless-Steel, diagonal, welding test.

Typical tests were done the following way:

Two narrow strips of metal about eighteen inches long by four inches wide are ground smooth and tapered on one length edge each and then set with tapered, ground edges next to each other, length edge- to-length edge (there is now a groove present) and tacked in a couple spots to hold them in position about one/eight inch apart. Those plates of steel are set on a base and angled at about a forty-five to sixty-degree, diagonal angle.

The test, therefore, is a diagonal-welding test. If a testing welder passes, they will have successfully turned those two, separate pieces of steel, or what-ever metal, into one finished plate of steel (metal) eighteen inches by eight inches. When the weld is finished, the tester uses his chipper tool to knock-off any attached flux and grinder to grind-down the weld on both sides to make it look clean, neat, and professional.

Sometimes, only one side is ground-down because often, a welder in unable to have access to both sides in certain, welding-project situations. That is why welders have got to be good at what they do. Once welders create their initial, tiny puddle of molten, liquid steel caused by the incredibly high temperatures from the welding rod "arcing" to the base metal, they use their own perfected method to keep rhythmically moving the puddle forward and completely through the thickness of the base metal and in the direction of the desired weld.

Often, both sides of a welding bead, the weld, are not possible to inspect. However, a welding-test examiner will check both sides of a test plate to look for a smooth, regularly flowing, progressive weld all up and through the welding line and completely filled-in and penetrating through the opposite side of the test plate without any holes, gaps, bulges, or bubbles.

Of course, different grades of steel exist and are used for varying projects. In fact, there are over 3,500 grade types of steel. They all involve the amount of carbon content in the steel. The more carbon, the harder the steel. The most widely used grades of steel have only 0.1% to 0.25% carbon content. However, most grades are generally just referred to as carbon steel. The type of grade, however, or level of carbon in the steel requires various precise types of flux-covered welding electrodes (rods) to do the job. Also, two other common, specialty-type metals used regularly in a variety of con- struction projects are Stainless Steel and Aluminum. Stainless Steel is often used when weather elements rust and damage lower carbon steels. Aluminum, used heavily in the aircraft industry, is strong and lightweight. Both of those metals, plus several other exotic metals like Titanium and Magnesium require specific and more specialized welding tests to verify knowledge and skill of the welder.

Once a completed test sheet weld is grinded down smoothly, there is virtually no way to see that it was two pieces before excepting by grinder marks. Paint it, and no one would ever know…if it was a successful test. A diagonal test is typically used because it utilizes, or incorporates, combined, standard- welding techniques of vertical and overhead. If a tester can successfully weld diagonally, then both those techniques are verified, and a test supervisor can be fairly assured that welder can weld most anything… within reason…

However, most welding tests, require an official X-ray of the weld. That test visually illustrates the true skill of the welder. An X-ray test will show-up any deformities or internal cracks in a weld that are unseen to the naked eye. Passing a weld's X-ray test provides the welder's certification for that type of metal welding only and only for that particular company.

SHOWING TRUE COLORS

The weld tester was all bundled-up in righteous welder's gear. This man's hood was down, and he was going-to-town on his welding test. I watched him for only a moment or two and could tell immediately that this fellow was, indeed, a welder. I didn't want to disturb him, but I did want to check his reactions, so I sort of snuck up behind him.

In a jovial tone, I spoke out to our man, "Good morning! I can't be certain, of course, with all that leather and hood covering you, but I'll assume you are Mr. Jepson under there?"

He didn't miss a lick in his weld, but jokingly retorted, "You are right, Miss McCord, but if I didn't admit it, and I just raised-up my hood, with all this smoke and suit all over my face, you might not be able to tell then either!"

A favorite joke of mine is the following: "I may be slow, but most of the time, I am at a dead stop!" I had to pause for a moment to get his refrain, but when I did, I gave him a hearty, thumbs-up belly-laugh.

I think Mr. Jepson may have appreciated my pause and liked that I didn't quite get his humor at first, but then I had to laugh and say, "Mr. Jepson, I can tell right now that you are silly. By day's end, we all look alike anyway! Welcome aboard."

Then I heard Mr. Jepson belly-laughing out loud, "So true. So true, Miss McCord, and now you are the silly one." He kept on chuckling, but he never missed a welding lick and kept on going until he was finished.

I went over to our worksite and began my inspection of our product, the stage we were on to continue progress with our Radar System. Mr. Jepson finished his test plate, cleaned-up his area, cooled-off his welding-test plate and prepared to deliver it to the office for review and X-ray inspection. One of the designated executives would examine, confirm, and verify that Mr. Jepson was the welder that he claimed to be.

I always smile when I think about that morning and how he walked past me chuckling some more and said, "Let me hurry this test piece over to the office and then get back really quick and start work here. That way, if I really blew that test, then I'll still have some time to mess-up this whole job here before they catch-on to me."

I remember saying something to him like, "Well, if you weld as funny as you are, then we're all in trouble. Good luck, I think!"

By that time, the other crew members were starting to show-up. That gave me opportunity to advise them of the new changes we had talked about the day before. To each member as they individually arrived, I simply showed them the stations for which each of them would be responsible. I told the ones who would be carrying-in new parts where they had to be placed. Finally, I showed the fitters where their sets-ups would be and how after they had tacked the pieces into position, they would be welded by me and the other new welder working side-by-side but slightly staggered with me just back a little to observe.

The new program for production was then in effect, and I reassured them all that our team was going to do just fine… Famous last words…

I had only just finished my little pep-talk when Mr. Jepson arrived back and smiled and greeted all the others. I introduced him to the whole attentive crew, "Gentlemen, meet Mr. Jepson, our new welder."

I smiled at Mr. Jepson, but as I looked about the faces of my team, I saw all the shocked, stunned and appalled looks on the crews' faces. I heard comments like, "What the hell?" and "Holy shit!" and "Oh, my God!"

My own immediate reaction was wonder. I thought, "Why is it when people get all surprised, they always turn to religious slang with their remarks like *hell, holy and God?*" I was confused by their reaction, but before I could say anything, Mr. Jepson just smiled and spoke.

In fact, he just ignored their impolite welcoming remarks, and just joked, "Well, I guess I sure fooled them over there (at the office) because they said, 'Get to work!' So, here I am, Lady and Gentlemen!"

One of our crew, I can't remember if it was Mr. Joe, or Mr. Henry or even one of the other nine fellows on our crew, but one of them said loudly and clearly, "Yeah, you sure did fool 'em 'cause yer face must a been all soot-covered, or ya still had yer hood on, so's they couldn' tell they was hirin' a nigger!"

The whole crew, minus me and Mr. Jepson, broke-out in uproarious laughter. One of them snickered out loud, "Jangles, you and yer mouth sure do take the cake, but you sure are funny, and right!"

Then it was my turn to become ghastly embarrassed and momentarily frozen with speechlessness. Once again, Mr. Jepson came to my rescue and spoke out, "Gentlemen, it is true that I am of African persuasion. However, I am also an Englishman first, but I have chosen to come to America during these troubled times to seek my fortune. Right here and today is my beginning. I shall try my hardest to keep-up with you and earn your respect."

Another member of our crew took a turn and spoke out rudely, "Yeah, well go *try yer hardest* cleanin'-up somethin' *respectable* somewheres else. We already got us a welder, and we don't need no nigger helpers."

One of the other more thoughtless crew members then jumped onboard that malicious attack and rudely announced, "Yeah, well, Ennnglish-Nigger, why don't you just go back to yer Englannnd, and get to hell outa here? We got us enough niggers here already and workin' in the kitchen!"

I was stunned, but I had heard way too much already. I spoke-out loudly and clearly to all of them, "I don't understand what got into you guys, but we have a big job ahead of us and Mr. Jepson is going to help us get caught-up. If any of you have any personal problems, then go talk to our Foreman or the GF.

"We are still way behind schedule, and we need to get more done and faster. Now please don't talk like that again. Let's all just work as a team and get our jobs done."

I was sure that my pathetic, begging message did not have much impact on those obviously prejudiced men, but it calmed-the waters enough for them to get started where the nightshift before us had left-off. I had heard about prejudice and had studied it in school, but I had never-in-my-life ever experienced anything like what had just occurred.

However, I refocused on the job-at-hand and then just reminded my crew that Mr. Jepson and I would be staggered apart with him on the inside doing the channel work and me on the outside doing the external parts and the ribs. I would do all my welding slightly behind and across from Mr. Jepson's position.

The riggers would be approaching around us welders from both sides with materials and assisting the fitters in front of us while setting-up the pieces in place. The plan was conceived to work very efficiently because now I would not have to keep shifting all the time: Moving-up and weld, then move-across and weld, then up, then across. It meant lost time. Two welders could just keep moving-up, weld, and move-up some more. Efficient and faster.

Throughout that morning period until breaktime, and then again up until lunchtime, I could hear random jokes or nasty remarks coming casually from the crew. They said things like, "Hey, Josey, I ain't never heard of no *nigger riggers*, have you? What about *jigger fitters?*"

Or, one rotten comment that was a disgusting take-off of Mr. Jepson's and my friendly joke: "Hey, Corny, you ever think that the reason they lets *niggers weld* is so's that they can stay all covered-up and nobody else can ever tell what they is?"

I was so ashamed and appalled and embarrassed by all their snide, nasty comments. I kept looking across to see if Mr. Jepson heard them. Of course, he did! I sure did. He never said a word to any of them, remained quiet and steady and welded like a professional man possessed. He easily kept-up with his channel and crew set-ups. Mr. Jepson was easily as fast, and no doubt as good, as I ever was. My idea was already looking like it might work. We were charging ahead with our production. The only low points were emotional with those dastardly comments that kept springing-up from several disgraceful crew members of ours.

When the first-shift whistle blew at break-time, I made it a point to sit-down next to Mr. Jepson. The first thing I did was to apologize for the horrible rudeness of the other crew. I didn't understand why they could say such cruel things to Mr. Jepson, or any other person, for that matter. I didn't want him to feel badly on our job. He was going to be a real asset and great help in turning our project around. I already knew that I needed him there. So did the company.

Breaktime, and then lunchtime a couple hours later, were opportunities for me to learn a great deal more about Mr. Jepson. His first response was an apology. He simply said, "I am sorry that you are so troubled by their comments, Miss McCord. Although bothersome, they are the rudiments of ignorance, and I know a little bit about *ignorance*."

"You do?" I beckoned. "How and what?"

"Well," he began, "on this job you call me Mr. Jepson, and you may call me *Bart,* if you like. It's short for Bartholomew Jepson. However, throughout many years with my last employment in London, England, I was referred to as Professor Jepson.

"What?" I exclaimed excitedly. "What do you mean *Professor?*"

He was a little proud as he continued, "Yes, I am, or was, *Professor* Jepson, PhD. I taught at University College London for eight years in their Humanities School. My specialties were: *Origins and Migrations of African Heritage.* So, you might imagine that I saw, experienced, read, studied, learned, and taught quite a bit about prejudice and ignorance."

"Oh, my God!" I answered. Oops! There I was too, *surprised* and turning *religious!* I needed to hear more, though. I was captivated, and from that moment on, Mr. Jepson became *Professor* to me. Throughout our breaks, on our welding jobs, and while just chit-chatting, *Professor* filled me in on many of his details…

He had worked long and steady at University College London up until recently. His classes had become smaller and smaller as a result of the war. Fewer young men or women could afford time to study about African cultures when the war needed scientists, and communications experts, and mathematicians, and language specialists. There was little room left for humanities. Plus, Professor emphasized, the war mostly required bodies, and his classes shrunk in direct proportion to Great Britain's demands and losses on the battlefields.

Eventually, Professor went on to say, his own classes, and thus his employment, had to be temporarily removed from the university's schedule of classes. Although he was told he would have his classrooms back after the war, he had to find alternative work. Professor decided, himself, that it was time for him to make a change. And a big change he made at that.

Professor said that he had read about construction opportunities, and especially with welding jobs, over here in America and researched it more until he thought it would be a fine change until or unless something better happened. There certainly were not going to be any professorships available over here either, he surmised. So, a major change in career direction was a temporary necessity.

He signed-up for a welding class over there and got certified in a London welding school. Then he bought transportation tickets on a freighter to New York, and then once arrived, he went through immigration and customs to get a work visa. From there he talked, asked a lot of questions, and looked around until he read on "Help-Wanted Bulletin Boards" and other news sources and recognized that Cleveland, Ohio had a lot of opportunities here.

Professor went immediately to a hiring agency, once he got to Cleveland, and was told to just sit tight but check-in regularly. He said that the very next day, he was informed of the job there with Warner & Swasey, so he confided in me that he believed it was *providence*.

Perhaps, he was meant to be here. So, here he was, an educated world-traveler, Doctor-Professor, Super-Welder Bartholomew Jepson, right there and working right next to me and in my crew...

I was so proud, I could just bust. The rest of our shift, I kept asking him more questions. I asked about himself, the war in Great Britain and how bad the bombings at been from that awful German Luftwaffe bombers attack. I asked him about his life before University College and his future plans.

Professor loved to talk, as I was sure most teachers and professors did, but I was an avid listener. Throughout that day, as he talked and I listened and occasionally asked follow-up questions, I became really impressed by what an exceptional person he was. I learned what a person could accomplish if they really put their mind to it. He even reminded me of Jean in some ways, except he was nicer to talk to.

The only times during the day that I was uncomfortable, however, was when I had to leave and use the *Ladies Only* latrine, or he left to use the *Men's latrine*. I could never be sure of what may have been said to him or about him by our other crew members in my absence or while he was gone. Although they had ceased from any direct insults to Professor's face,

I could still hear the guys snickering and making private jokes with each other at Professor's expense.

Before Professor's arrival, the other crew and I had joked and teased with each other all the time. It was fun and entertaining. I figured if I wasn't let in on any of their recent jokes, then they did not want me to hear them. Their jokes, therefore, were probably meant to insult and embarrass Professor.

When forgetting about those shameful guys words and attitude, and focusing on listening to Professor's stories, I learned what a truly fascinating, highly intelligent, and well-traveled person he was. I was glad he was on our team. He really added some class to us. Plus, he was an outstanding welder. On that first day of our project with our new plan, it didn't just go well, it went spectacularly. I knew the swing-shift was going to be stunned when they learned how much we had completed during our *newly planned* turn-at-the-wheel. I was sure that our bosses were going to be impressed too.

I can remember that on that day, for the remainder of our shift, anyway, I believed that the rest of our crew had started quieting down with their rude remarks. I thought too that the more they all heard Professor's stories about his life, and travels and experiences, they would be impressed too. I was hoping that they had all become ashamed of themselves once they realized what an amazing and accomplished individual Professor was.

It was a Friday, though, so I wanted to set the job-issues aside and look forward to a relaxing evening. Hopefully, the crew had calmed down with their terrible insulting comments, and our shift was going to start setting records the following week on production. Just one more day, the next day, Saturday, was needed to work-out any kinks, and we would have smooth sailing that next week. I even had a nice goodbye greeting for Mr. Carson.

I walked Professor to the gate after all the other crew members were already gone. It always took us welders a little longer to straighten-up and leave. We had more tools and protective clothing and gear to deal with. Anyway, I reintroduced Professor to Mr. Carson when we met at the gate, and they shook hands.

Mr. Carson said straight-out, "I heard some of that crap nonsense earlier today from those West Virginia Hoboken's. I apologize for their rude and unsavory manners, Mr. Jepson. Unfortunately, there are some individuals among us without any class at all.

"Please, kind Sir, no apologies necessary," Professor replied. My young, dear friend here, Miss McCord, is looking out for my interests with charm and grace. Together, we shall prevail and win them over."

It was my turn to butt-in, "I don't like the way they talk or the things they said. I am going to speak to the bosses about them and straighten this matter-out once-and-for-all."

"I dare say, Miss McCord," Professor professed, "you have the spirit of a ferocious thunderstorm, the character of a gentle-soothing rain and the charisma of a lovely rainbow. Thank you for your kindnesses and consideration, but we needn't bother management over those immature child-men. Hopefully, they will come around with your guidance."

"I hope so, and good evening, Gentlemen," I bid them both adieux, "and have a nice evening. Oh, Mr. Carson, I'm going to the movies again on Sunday. Don't know what's playing, but I bet I'll learn something new! Ha! Ha! We'll find out on Monday!"

"You are outrageous, young Missy, "Mr. Carson smiled back, "and I bet you will. I can't wait to hear about what trouble you stir-up over it. Have a fine evening.

I left right after that silly-serious chat and noted that those two fine men continued chatting-away until I rounded a bend toward the office. I was still planning to follow-through with my promise and talk to the bosses over that day's pathetic interactions. I suppose I was just too naïve and inexperienced to know or understand the ways of some people. All I knew at that time was that their words were disgusting, and I was horrified by that kind of behavior.

BIGOTS AMONG US

I was aware of the government's encouragement of blacks (Negroes) and other minorities as well as women to go into construction work in order to fill the void made from men gone-off to war. The *Rosie the Riveter* posters were great examples of that. Everywhere you turned were large picture posters of women flexing their muscles while wearing red polka-dot bandanas with blue denim shirts and blue denim (Levi's) pants. They were inspirational and excellent ads for women to take-over traditionally men's jobs.

The work agencies were also calling for other minorities, like blacks and Hispanics, to seek out factory and industrial employment. That stinking war did open-up a lot of opportunities for others back home. I used to read and hear about all sorts of ads calling for outside help to fill the enormous need for construction growth. I learned about those job opportunities from general conversations while working for Vancouver Kaiser, Warner & Swasey and from radio-talk shows, posters, and bulletins around town, and even from some of those movie-theatre News Reels.

The point is that I knew of our country's overall need and demand for construction workers in general, and especially for the minimally skilled *Riveters of Rosie fame* and welders (*Wendie's*) with any sorts of certifications and documentation. The same fact survives or exists even today. A good welder can find work practically anywhere and anytime. It was and remains a very valuable skill.

I could not understand how a company like Warner & Swasey could afford not to go to great lengths finding *and keeping* good welders. I'm not bragging, but welders, and good ones like me, can act somewhat aloof. They understand how valuable they are and often act a bit like *Prima Donnas* demanding acceptable working conditions. Professor was a good welder, maybe even better than me. Well, not actually, ha ha, but he was very good, and *valuable*.

The crew, our Foreman, the GF, and the Personnel Office executives should have been falling all over themselves to please Professor. You have to give deserved respect to your welders. The other positions, the laborers, fitters, and riggers can be picked-up and learned pretty fast by someone who pays attention. But someone had to go and complete a long, tedious training to become a welder. On-top-of-that, it was experience at your craft that made a big difference too.

Easy jobs were *easy*. *Hard jobs* were *hard* to find *good welders* to do them. It was like the Prima Donnas I talked about: "You better give them a cookie, or they might walk, and then your whole job stops…"

Our bosses should have followed-up on a new welding hire's placement and checked to see how they were doing. Were they happy or satisfied or content? Would they like a *cookie*? Well, no, I'm kidding, but they needed to know if the person they really depended on was still happy or *dependable*.

Our bosses needed to put a serious check on my crew and their attitudes. If they didn't, then that would make them all awful in my eyes. As far as I was concerned, that made all of them a bad reflection on the company. Because of them, Warner & Swasey would become a poor example of American equal fairness and opportunity for all.

I believed even back then that is what this country was supposed to stand for. To know that at that very time, black Americans and black Englishmen were fighting overseas and dying to keep America and Europe free, just didn't make sense for attacking others who were on our side and trying to help too. I didn't understand it. Maybe, Foreman Mort could explain and resolve the matter…

NO SUPPORT

A nyway, those were some of the thoughts that were running through my mind as I approached our bosses' office-quarters. I saw Foreman Mort over at the Blueprint Shack directly across a circular drive passing in front of the Main Office. He was bent over and all engrossed in some blueprint plans he had spread-out over a high-legged, slanted table. I walked straight-over to him to have a talk. He looked-up, saw me coming and seemed genuinely pleased. Good start.

A big smile spread across his face. He spoke-out to me even before I got up to him, "Missy, your idea seems to be working like a charm. Do you have any idea how much production your crew managed today? I dropped by a couple times just to watch you wildcats going. It was impressive. I didn't even want to bother you and slow you down. A few more days of that effort, and your product (the present, Parabolic-Dish Radar System) will be totally back-on-schedule. Good job."

I nodded appreciatively, but I was serious, so I changed the subject. "Thanks," I started, "much of today went well; however, there were some serious issues that you need to be aware of, though."

"Oh, yeah, like what?"

"From the first moment this morning, my crew said some absolutely disgusting, insulting, and embarrassing things to Professor, er, Mr. Jepson. I didn't know where it came from or what to do. None of us had ever met Professor before today. I didn't understand how they could talk to him so badly."

Foreman Mort, I think was his name, although as of that conversation, he became very forgettable, didn't even ask for details. He just said something like, "Oh, I'm sure Mr. Jasper has heard a lot worse in his time. He'll get over it. The boys were just having a little fun, that's all."

"*A little fun?* It was all at Mr. Jepson's expense," I explained. "He sure wasn't having a *fun* time, and neither was I. I was horrified at what they were saying."

"Well, Missy," Foreman Mort (I think it was short for *Mortician*) continued defending my crew, "you got to understand that those boys traveled a long way up here to get these decent-paying jobs. Before here, they had been killing themselves working in those West Virginia coal fields. Coming up here was a real Godsend opportunity for them. They're all hard-working, honest, righteous, and decent, good-ol'-boys. They don't mean no harm. They just got their own ideas about things that some other folks disagree with, that's all."

"If they're decent and righteous," I countered, "then they have got to leave Professor Jepson alone. They are saying hurtful things to him, and it is just not right. Will you speak to them?"

"Child," he patronizingly retorted, "if I *speak* to them about uncouth or unacceptable manners, then they are going to be mad at me. There are eleven of them altogether and only one of him, or two counting you. I can't risk losing eleven to justify one. Just let it pass, and they'll leave Jasper alone, if he just keeps his mouth shut."

"What?" I cried out, "Professor never said a single bad word to them. The only thing he said to me about them was calling them *immature, child-men,* and he was right about that."

Foreman Mort picked-up on my comment right away, "Mr. Jepson should know his place. He knows not to say any bad things about those boys, or they will mess with him real bad. Your crew is working hard and you're getting a lot accomplished with them. Now, just let that little incident blow-over, and tomorrow will be a brighter, new day, and everything will be just fine."

I wasn't appeased. If anything, I was more confused than when I first complained to our foreman. I didn't appreciate how *nonchalant* he seemed to act toward those *good-ol'-boys*. I went home that Friday very frustrated and upset over what should have been a rewarding and very successful day. All I could think of was, *I hope tomorrow will be better…*

Remember that earlier saying about *if hopes were horses…?*

Saturday morning came, and I left home without any goodbyes in order to let my sisters sleep-in. I was so wrapped-up in my imagined job crisis that I even forgot to make myself a lunch. I then considered that I might even buy my lunch at the cafeteria that day and offer Professor a cup of coffee, or something, to help mend any potentially broken fences. I left home quietly and was down at the plant as soon as I could get there.

Before heading to the jobsite, however, I decided to check-in with our foreman or GF before stating work. The nightshift was ending, of course, and its crews were all filing-out the gate in a rush for home, or wherever. They would have the choice of coming back-in that Saturday night for their next shift, or not. Because of church, and such, they could opt-out of that shift because it went into their Sunday. It also meant that they didn't have to be back until the following Monday night again. Three days-off! Nice break.

Regardless, my shift was about to start, and I wanted to clear-the-air a little more with my bosses. I didn't want any more issues during that day, or ever, with my crew and Professor. Just that stress hanging-in-the-air made for very uncomfortable work. The day before had me way over-sensitized to what anyone might have been saying to anybody or everybody.

Before Professor, I would listen-in nonchalantly to catch drifts of any jokes or something funny being said. Often enough, the jokes were about me, and I would laugh wholeheartedly right along with the crew. I had no false vanity or insecurities about anything said regarding my age, or height, or sex, or personality. I had already experienced practically the worse I could imagine, so nothing those silly characters said was going to embarrass me. Well, except for the Latrine thing. That was different.

However, with Professor there the day before, I caught myself straining to hear what was being said. I was so intensely involved and focused on what comments or nasty remarks any of those jerks might say to each other about Professor, or, God forbid, to Professor's face, that I was paying far less attention to our project goals. That, by the way, also addressed how well our plan did work because even with all my *listening stress,* our crew did a really terrific job.

I thought to myself, "Gosh, a day without those fools' nasty remarks raining-on-our-*production*-parade would let us destroy the competition, and we could do it in such a happy-go-lucky mood and team spirit."

I wanted the bosses to step-in, if need be, and calm the proverbial waters. It wasn't fair for me, an eighteen-year old, young woman to have to address all those older, grown men. Heck, some of them probably had daughters of their own my age, or older! Why would they take lecturing from me? I was their welder, true, but I was dispensable too. They probably didn't really care how fast we worked, or how far we progressed.

Why, the easier my crews' days went, the more rested-up they were going to be for spending money on Sundays, or boozin' every evening, for all I knew. I began worrying about consequences of their continued anti-Professor mockery. He was so vastly superior to any of them as far as decency was concerned.

That was when I started sensing all those ill-feelings which began churning in my stomach from stress caused by my crew's nasty words became reminiscent of all the bad emotions I had felt before directly, or indirectly, from my own, personal history of rejection. I truly sympathized for Professor. No, I actually think that I even *emphasized* with him. He wasn't accepted simply because of his *skin color*, and I had been rejected because, well, because …I was an outsider, or something. Unwanted, undeserving and an outcast, I was never *accepted* either… by my own father.

Anyway, I needed help from our bosses to straighten things out right away. We needed to go back to the good-old-days. The *good-old-days* with the *good-old-boys*… What a bunch of crap! But this was absolutely a matter for management, if ever there was one. For our *experiment* to work on that Warner & Swasey plant-site, there had to be peace-in-the-valley, first. The bosses and management had better come through!

At first, I didn't see any of the bosses or brass, the executives near the office doors. I wanted to talk to the ones that I was directly responsible to, though. Those were the main link, the conduit for change. I knew that my foreman and the GF had to go through higher channels in order to hire-on any additional persons. That made sense. Therefore, it also made sense that they were the ones to rectify issues with the crews' ineffectiveness or personal issues. Also, they were the ones who cleared my week-off to go get my younger sister, Jann. Surely, they were the ones, then, to clear-up this type of *family-emergency*. As a crew all working together in harmony, we were a family too, of sorts.

Just as I walked-up closer, though, right out the office doorway came the foreman and GF together. They were heading over to the print shack. I followed right after them and met them both by the shed. The GF spoke-up first, "Good morning, Miss McCord. We were just talking about you."

I had some talking to do too, so I jumped right-in, "I hope it wasn't bad, Bosses, but I do have some concerns of my own."

"Of course, it wasn't bad!" the GF stressed. "You are our star. We were just talking about what a difference a day makes! Your idea already showed strong evidence of being successful even after just one day. No, just one shift! Yours! We hope you can keep-it-up."

"Oh, we'll try our best, Sirs," I responded, "but I still have some other grave concerns."

The foreman was quick to pipe-in, "Are you still sweating over those Hillbillies? I told you not to fret any over them. They are all just a bunch of words, no action."

It's the words that hurt, though, Boss," I countered. When you have to think about bad words or feelings toward yourself, or someone you like or a crewmate, then you can't think about good work or producing more. The two go together. One either helps the other, or it hinders it."

"That's the point, Missy," Foreman Mort countered. "I said to just leave it alone, and the whole thing will blow-over. The boys are just adjusting to the situation and expressing their views. That's all"

Well, I don't want to hear any of their crap or nonsense today. It hurts Professor's feelings, and it sure hurts mine too. If I have to stop welding to start yelling at them to shut-up and be quiet, then I suppose there will be bad feelings all around. Please say something."

The GF took the upper hand then. He had a more satisfying response. "Mr. Kruper, here, and I have already spoken to several of the men on your crew. They assured us both that they were not going to say anything anymore to, or about, Mr. Jepson. They said that they were just having a little *back home* welcoming to a stranger, a Limey, at that. They just liked teasing the *new guy*, they said, to see how he was going to handle himself. So, don't worry. Your crew is just fine."

"Well, I hope so," I relaxed. "They sure had me going yesterday. I felt really bad for Professor.

"Professor?" the GF queried. "You don't say? Well, that nigger couldn't have been that smart if he's over here workin' with us!" The GF grinned profusely, "Kidding! Just trying to make you relax. Stop worryin'. Everything will be just fine."

My heart, which had just leaped out of my chest thanks to the GF's *joke,* started calming again, and I closed our conversation, "Very funny! I hope it goes well too"

As I walked back toward the *Yellow Brick Road,* the *arrowed path* to Mr. Carson's Gate and then our jobsite, I turned around just before going past and around the storage tanks to have a final gander and reappraise my bosses. I could tell right-away that they were up to something, but I couldn't be sure what they were saying.

I could tell that they sure were having a good time saying, though, whatever it was. In fact, they were both practically doubled over in laughter, or something. Then Foreman Mort slapped the GF hard on his back, and they continued their gastrointestinal, jovial manner. Or, or, maybe they were both so ashamed of GF's sudden, unprovoked, and tasteless joke, and of our crews' disgusting behavior, that they were both having embarrassment's stomach convulsions. No, I didn't think so. That wasn't it. I had experience that feeling, myself, before, and this was not the same thing.

EMOTIONAL ASSAULT

Good ol' Mr. Carson was always a ray-of-sunshine-on-a-cloudy-day. I saw him see me coming, and right away, that big, Cheshire Cat grin filled-up the entire area. "Good morning to you, Miss Patsy!" he exclaimed. "Whatever can you imagine that you would rather be doing than working on this incredibly... freezing cold, bitterly contemptuous Saturday morning?"

"Just fighting overseas," I retorted, "alongside my brother or sister and trying to get this damnable war over with, I suppose. Good morning to you too, Mr. Carson."

My somewhat snappy remark set Mr. Carson back a bit, and he responded, "Well said, Miss Patsy. I pray for safety and health for your family." Then he went silent.

I apologized, "I'm sorry, Mr. Carson. I didn't mean anything by that except that I can't understand why people don't get along over here while our brothers and sisters and kin are fighting over there and dying to boot!"

"My goodness!" Mr. "C" acknowledged, "You seem to have a heavy-plate this morning, Miss Patsy. Everything alright?"

"Oh," I began, "I haven't stopped worrying over those terrible remarks from my crew toward Professor. I hope today goes well."

"So do I, Missy. So do I," was Mr. C's helpless comfort.

I moved on down the lane toward our jobsite. As I figured, Professor was already there, all leathered-up and ready for the day's effort. Fact was, he could have even started without the rest of us because there were parts already assembled by nightshift for him to start-off with. I knew he was waiting for everyone to be there, so as not to seem like he was showing-up anyone. I still admired his gumption.

"Good morning, Professor! Are we ready for a big day?" I smiled halfheartedly.

"Every day is a big day for me as long as I'm still kicking on this beautiful Earth of ours," was his pleasant response. Then he continued, "However, I am not as certain the same feeling extends to you, Miss McCord. If you have to ask me about readiness, then perhaps you are not so certain, yourself."

Professor was so insightful, so intelligent and so smart. He knew what was bothering me without me having to say a word. Here was another place, another case, where the best things said were nothing. I was not going to drag previous drama and stress back through that current day's review and, thus, begin our new day by spoiling any possible redeeming spirits from our crew. Maybe the bosses were right all along.

'Sorry, Professor," I explained, "It was a bad night for me, a bit restless. But I am hoping for a wonderful day today. We are going to kick-some-butt today. I mean with our production, of course."

"Of course, you do, my dear, sweet optimist," Professor chuckled. "Let's give the heaven's some hell today! In a redemptive way, that is!"

As we spoke and while I suited-up, my crew started wandering in by twos or threes. It was a little odd because there was not the typical morning laughter that I had become accustomed to hearing. No morning jokes, or "Pardon me, all to pieces," like before. That morning it was very solemn without much address by anyone.

It felt like a Russian drumbeat for their woefully sentenced chain-gang workers: "Daa da daaa daaaa. Daa da daaa daaaa."

For fun, I started whistling that favorite jingle from <u>Snow White and the Seven Dwarfs</u>. "Wshhhhh shhh shhhhhhh! Wshhhhh shhh shhhhhh! "Whistle While You Work!" What a happy-go-lucky song, that was. I thought it might amuse the guys and get them all in a better spirit. Who could not start smiling to that tune?

I'll tell you *who*. My crew, that's who. Maybe it was my whistling, though. I'd been told by my sisters that my singing would make a songbird commit suicide. I had hoped my attempt at whistling, however, might be different on that morning. I thought that maybe they would all recognize my obvious armistice gesture, at least, and accept it as a welcomed peace- offering.

I was wrong. The crew all looked like they were about to perform a simultaneous self-slaughter. "Wow!" I reconsidered, "Maybe my whistling is that bad!" Perhaps, I should just shut up. Remember? Sometime, the best thing to say is *nothing*. I supposed that the same truth may be held for whistling too. Whistling, humming, or singing is just not for everybody. Some people hate it. Hate all of it. How did that paraphrased Lincoln lesson go? *You can hate some things all the time, and all things some of the time. But you can't hate all things all the time!*

Sorry, Abe. You were wrong! And I had proof. These West Virginia Hillbillies seemed to hate all things all the time. At least they hated things I liked. Come to think of it, these *good ol' boys* jumped right in line to join the Confederacy right after you were inaugurated President in 1861. Regardless of that war, or the one we were in, they still hadn't changed their tune. The only song they could sing or would sing, or whistle was their favorite Confederate refrain, "I wish I Was In Dixie." I was beginning to agree with them… I was wishing they were *all in Dixie*, myself, and not here.

We had a day of work ahead of us, though, so I started concentrating on that and just become very professional and business-like, if that was what they wanted. I pointed out some basic instructions to help them recognize where we were and what was needed. Then I just dropped my hood, cracked my arc, and started moving my molten puddle up the weld-line and losing myself in the light.

When you are welding, it is not like you are blinded to everything else around you. Granted, the small, two-by-four inch glass window with its heavily shaded viewing lens is to allow welders to clearly watch the intense light from their electrode as it continues its arc heating and melting the adjoining metals and joining them together using the rod's filler metal. The point is a welder can still see around their area besides the bright welding light.

It did not take very long for me to notice that I was catching-up to Professor while on the outside of our dish, and even beginning to surpass him. Something was wrong. Professor was having to spend his welding-time doing the fitters' work by setting-up his own parts for welds. I could even tell that the riggers were slacking-off on getting the necessary parts over to the parabolic dish in order for the fitters to do their jobs.

I paused my welding and lifted my hood. Looking around, I saw the crew here and there and scattered about looking busy but actually doing little or nothing-at-all. I was confused or misunderstanding something. I called-out to the crew, "Hey, guys, what's up? Professor, I mean Mr. Jepson, needs parts set up for his station to keep going. I'm passing him up here on the outside. Can you help him out and get him set-up?"

It was either the really rotten ass, Hank, or maybe it was the one called Curly because he was bald, naturally, but one of them called back, "Let him do it himself. He don't look like he's got nothin' to do, anyway."

There was a slight ripple of chuckles that quietly reverberated through the crew, and I had to speak-out. "That's not team-spirit, fellas. We all need to work together to get our production really going."

'Well, we don't need another welder," another tossed-out their ignorant opinion. "You was fast enough before for all of us. Why don't you just have that ni---, that African Limey do some polishing or cleaning-up or something. They're all good at that sort of thing. Then we can get busy and do the really important stuff we know."

I was debating. No, I was arguing with *flat-earth* mentalities. I remembered the quip, "Don't confuse them with facts. Their minds are already made-up!"

The job was everything, though. I had to try. "Guys, if we can catch-up with this product, we can easily pass-up everyone else in the whole plant with our production output. We could even win awards and stuff from the front office. We just have to act like a team. C'mon, fellas, can you do it? Will you try? For me?"

There was nothing left after that plea. I had laid my whole case at those ignoramuses' feet. I had resorted to begging them... for my sake. I had nowhere else to go after that.

Threaten them? Bad idea. One of 'em might have a gun in their lunch bucket and take it out and shoot me between the eyes. OMG! I could see it clearly. Me and Professor. Double homicide... No, it would be a *murder/ suicide*. I could see the headlines in the next day's paper... Or, no, I couldn't because I'd be dead!

But I quickly imagined how the headlines and bylines would read something like this:

"YOUNG HEROINE MURDERED BY NEGRO SPY!:

One of Cleveland's finest female arc-welders became a frantic, young, heroic, white girl when attacked and murdered by a gun-wielding, German, negro- implant spy via England. The (pretended limey and recent immigrant, kraut Bartholomew Jepson fired one-shot assassinating our poor, defenseless star, Patricia McCord because she had ever so courageously discovered the secrets of the German-built, Giant Wurzburg Radar System from the evil, Axis Powers and delivered them to the U.S. military.

Then, as eleven of Warner Swasey's most heroic, West Virginia, good- ol'-boys countrymen, and highly awarded, team-crew members, rushed the evil, darkey infiltrator, the cowardly, vile assassin took his authentic, M1911 Colt 45 Automatic Pistol, turned it upon himself and fired the remaining six rounds... all into his blackened heart."

Yeah, okay, I may have gotten a little carried away, but I was not thinking too highly or kindly of our West Virginia, good-ol'-boy hospitality anymore. But threats were out! Absolutely. There would be no Civil War II getting started here. At least, not on my watch.

No, it was going to be *back to the drawing boards* for next week. We'd have to come-up with some alternative. Replace the whole damned crew with other negroes? Sure, why not? No, wait! Women too! Yes! Send me some Wendie's! And some Mexicans too. Yeah, now we had something going. Heck even send me some Irish!

If we could keep 'em all sober, they'd be pretty good workers. And they made good cops too, just in case I needed some bodyguards... to protect me from *good ol' boys!* But they couldn't work on Sundays. No way. They were all Catholic, so they'd be too drunk to work that day. And not after St. Patrick's Day, either. No, they'd surely need that day off too because they'd never make it into work, anyway!

Oh, where was my mind going? These were not solutions. Only dreams, or demons! Besides, Foreman Mort and the GF like these *coal-mining rejects.* They're sensitive to their delicate feelings. No, we were just going to have to survive today, take a day-off to relax and reconsider, and maybe, just maybe Monday would be another day...

My thoughts mellowed to another favorite lyric, "Tomorrow, tomorrow, there's always tomorrow. Tomorrow's another day!"

Oh, *Annie*, I sure wish you were here…*so you could weld*! Or, maybe the other one? Oh, *Annie,* I sure wish you were here… *with your gun*!

Anyway, my thoughts were all going haywire. I had stopped paying attention to the crew. I had lapsed into daydream heaven, and I had not even noticed the ever-so-modest change happening. Who knows wherefrom some thin shred of decency had arrived and temporarily possessed my crew?

But for the remainder of the day, the men carried-on with their assigned roles. No doubt, they were all reluctant hero *wannabes*, but I didn't care. I just wanted them to do their jobs. I figured that it would just take time, and they would all become desensitized to Professor's darkly tanned skin compared to their own extremely red necks.

First, you change their deviant behavior. Then you change their corrupt attitudes. Demand and force a change with their behavior. Then you help them begin to work better together and eventually end-up liking each other. Success! Watch as eventual acceptance and inclusion slowly take their course, and everything falls into place. Oh, God Bless America! Only here can that happen. A *more perfect union* was our purpose. The *melting pot* of the world.

Okay, history/psychology-loving student, we get it. It was a start, though, a beginning, but I would take it. I was just afraid that the *falling into place* part might not happen before the war was over, or before the world came to an end!

But by then, I was finding closure to my distress. My haphazard, shoot-from-the-hip philosophy and derange-infected Hamlet soliloquy was taking effect: "Is it gonna be, or not gonna be? That's the miserable, rotten question facing us today!"

Slowly and steadily, my *good ol' boys* began shifting-over toward the dish with various pieces of product, and though they still sort of haphazardly tossed them up onto the dish., they were working again. A few others then climbed-up on the dish and set the pieces in place for Professor. Hallelujah! Amen! And pass the ammunition! We were going again.

Occasionally, throughout the remainder of the day, I still heard grunts or almost silently passive cursing, but I could not tell what the curser was cursing about. I just let it go. The GOBs were becoming docile, even civil. One less curse word meant one more step forward with our production, our product and with the advancement of world unifying society. Every great journey begins with a single step... Just don't step on me! Please?

Saturday ended quietly and calmly. I had not even gone to the cafeteria, after all to have lunch or buy Professor a coffee. Instead, I just faked lunch and hung-back at the jobsite milling around and considering the day's issues and efforts. After lunch, I could clearly see that we were accomplishing nowhere near what we had the previous day. But I could tell that if we continued maintaining that last brief drive we had done after lunch break, we were still going to surpass anything that just the crew and I had ever achieved. It was looking up. There was hope! There was always... tomorrow!

Ur shift ended, finally, and we all, well, Professor and I, and Mr. Carson too, said our goodbyes. We all looked forward to a relaxing, stress-free Sunday. I was already getting excited about going to the movies again. Thank you, Hollywood. You sure do know how to help someone escape all their troubles. For a few hours every Sunday, I could run away and escape to an exciting new place, or a foreign destination, and partake in some exhilarating, thrilling episode in someone else's life.

Oh, yeah, it was fantasy and escapism, but it was going somewhere and doing something where you did not have to dwell on all the crap in your own life. Yeah. Watch the crap in someone else's life! That was a relief, of sorts. No matter how bad you thought you had it, just go to the movies, and you were guaranteed that you could watch someone else having a way, way worse time. Anyway, hello, Sunday! Nice to see you again!

MENTAL ESCAPE

I remember that Saturday evening, too, like it was yesterday. In one way, I was a little bit happy about our production success on-the-job that day. It had been mentally exhausting, and that helped make it physically draining. But no matter, it had proved my point about being more productive, somewhat. We had still done more than with just one welder. But I was also still very bothered and skeptical about my crew's extremely slow-paced behavior toward accepting Professor. Time. We just needed time. More time. Yes, but such a waste of time!

To get all that out of my mind, I treated my sisters to ice cream that Saturday night. Of course, Sis just couldn't stay long with Colleen and Jann and me because she had a *hot date*. We used to tease her all the time because, according to Sis, all her dates were *hot!* "Yes," Sis would smile and say with that huge, gorgeous, sensual, red-lipped mouth of hers, "they are. It's just that they always *cool-off* by the next morning!"

Oh, goodness, Sis could get all we girls giggling and making rude and lewd faces over her comments. Sis Mary could make us all start laughing so hard, we'd all start choking on our ice creams. She was always the-life-of-the-party. However, that night, Sis had her own party to attend.

Jann, Colleen, and I went out for a little window shopping and then went back home. I was very exhausted from the last several days. But I promised my younger sibs a trip to the movies that next Sunday afternoon. We would go to the same *Playhouse Square* theatre as before with that Newsreel film about the *Wurzburg Radar System*.

I knew our Sunday film choice was going to be a good one because it starred the wonderful Bing Crosby as a priest in <u>Going My Way</u>. I suppose I was a good, little Catholic girl who always went to see movies about priests and nuns. In fact, remember me telling you that I went to see <u>Boys Town</u>

with Spencer Tracy and Mickey Rooney? Well, I did, and I also went the next year after <u>Going My Way</u> to see <u>*The Bells of St. Mary's*</u>, also starring Bing Crosby.

He sure made a nice priest, and he sure could sing. During those movies, I used to get myself all worked-up and jealous just wishing that any of my own priests had been like Bing. Oh, Bing, just sing! But then, like a good, little Catholic girl, I would mentally slap my face into holy contrition and get back into the religious spirit of the film.

Films were sure fun to see in those days. There weren't as many big movie stars, but the ones we had back then were huge; they were almost Godlike. Another fun fact was that for that film, <u>Going My Way</u>, Bing Crosby won the Academy Award for Best Actor in 1945. In another film during that same year, <u>Gaslight,</u> the beautiful Ingrid Bergman won Best Actress Award. Then, the very same year, the two of them joined together to do another Catholic smash hit movie, <u>The Bells of St. Mary's</u> in late 1945. See how Hollywood and Catholicism go together? They need each other like banks and money.

What's the point about all this silly, movie-trivia jargon? It's because of my sisters, Colleen and Sis Mary. Both their brains were so full of that trivial information, and they both could share plenty more from all kinds of years before. Colleen knew what color the beautiful actresses' dresses were in films and for Oscar's night. She even knew the color of all their lipsticks. Red! Oh, I just threw that detail in, myself, because it was the *only* color actresses lips ever were.

Colleen used to fill me-in on all the gossip about the stars and movies and directors. She'd be whispering facts to me faster than the films' own dialog. People around us were always, "Shhhhhh ing!" us, but that didn't stop Colleen. She was a fountain of knowledge, and her Hollywood-detail waters just had to flow. It was fun.

I was also anxious for the <u>Newsreel</u> film to learn what was happening with the war. No *secret weapons* were discussed, but the film short's host did let the audience in on all the Allied victories going on in Europe, and specifically in Germany. He told about the USAAF, what our brother, Bo, was in, and the 500,000 bombs it dropped on Berlin. Bo's unit from Italy had been called-up to participate in that all-out attack on Germany. How great, yet how vicious! And how dangerous. Please be careful, Brother, I always prayed.

Can you imagine, though? *Half a million* bombs dropped on Berlin in one battle. Later that year, of course, was when we heard about the one bomb each dropped on Hiroshima and Nagasaki, Japan. We were told then that Japan's destruction was far worse. Anyway, on that particular Sunday afternoon's <u>Newsreel</u>, the host also told everyone about the agonizing American battle taking place at that very time against the Japanese on some small island, Iwo Jima, and its horrible cost so far in lives for both sides.

I kept thinking, "Gosh, here we are sitting in these comfortable seats and relaxing and watching fun movies and interesting highlights of a battle that was taking place at the very time I was watching news about it. Poor soldiers! God speed. Apparently, thousands were dead already, and it was said to be one of the most violent battles ever, so far in the Pacific war. And the whole battle was all on a tiny, but very strategic island. Strange.

We were steadily winning the war against Germany and Japan, of the Axis Powers, and Italy had already been defeated. Yes, we were winning, but it was at a terrible cost in lives, casualties, and destruction. I remember praying for its end to come soon. Everyone was tired of it all. So much loss of life. So much destruction. So much waste. So much separation of families.

Anyway, that Sunday film was a fun and informative afternoon at the movies. I would certainly share any news I had learned with Mr. Carson and the others, but overall, it had been a relatively quiet and *peaceful* (poor word choice considering the war) day-off. I really needed the time away and the Hollywood escape. A time to cleanse the mind and soul, sort of. But it sure was evident that we weren't doing any cleansing in church. No, that sort of went by the wayside with getting-away from Edith. Religion and Catholicism were still important to me, but not the church attendance part. Maybe later on in my life, but not then.

Besides, I was getting anxious to have a good week on our project. I felt certain that we might even finish that product we were on, and best-case scenario suggested that we might jump right onto the next one and really show our crew's highlights. I wanted Professor to enjoy himself, and the crew to get to like him too. It was only right. He was from England, our best Ally in the war, and he was our newest ally on our team. I hoped all would work-out well. Hope… hope… hope…

DEVIL BE DAMNED

Monday morning came even earlier than the previous week. Of course, it did. We were heading into spring and summer, and days kept getting longer with earlier sunrises and later sunsets. It was nice, but I was excited and up to greet the day no matter what. Same routine as the Friday before except for the food. I ate oatmeal with toast and coffee, and I took the old standard of P&J sandwiches for lunch with a hard-boiled egg and an orange.

I looked forward to our thirty-minute lunchbreak, so I could chat with Professor some more about his life. I wanted to tell him a little more about mine too, although I realized my life was just starting in comparison. He had been around-the-block, and the world, a few times already. It was just pleasant to talk with him. I thought maybe we might even share our lunchbreak with Mr. Carson because he and Professor seemed to get along nicely.

I used to hang around the other crew sometimes and even have lunch with some of them in the cafeteria. That mixing sort of waned a bit after the *filthy, traitor spy* business, I was letting them get back on my good side slowly again. Now, I just didn't know what to think about them. I wanted to be friends, or at least always be friendly, but even my feelings had been hurt over their insulting behavior toward Professor the week before. I was looking for guilt and shame on their part, and their solemn requests for forgiveness and pleadings of contrition. Oh, how *Catholic* of me! Bing Crosby, it was your fault!

The first sign of something wrong came with my morning greeting with Mr. Carson. He was overly solemn that Monday when I arrived at his gate. He was nowhere near his typical jovial mood. I wanted to start our day with a tease about the <u>Newsreel</u> I had watched and wanted to report about; however, I could tell that he was not in any mood to laugh.

I still greeted him, but in more serious tones, "Morning, Mr. Carson, is everything alright?"

"No, Missy, everything is *not alright*. You didn't happen to see Mr. Jepson on your way in just now, did you? He was probably in the office. I'm sorry, Missy, but I do believe Mr. Jepson has drug-up. It seems your crew made it just too plain and clear to him that they did not want him around. So, he told me he was leaving and going to California."

"*Drug-up*? Why did he quit?" I was so startled at that news. "What did the crew say to him? Why would he leave? Things were getting better, I thought. The crew had stopped insulting him and shaming him with their comments. Why would he leave me?"

Mr. Carson was very considerate and gentle with his words as he attempted to console me, "Mr. Jepson, your *professor*, asked me to thank you for all your support and belief in him. He said that your plan, or theory, was a good one. That you should follow-it straight through and make a great difference with the company's production. He suggested that you just needed to hire another *more appropriate* welder that will make your crew behave more team-like."

"Oh, no!" I grieved, "What happened to him? What did they say to him that changed his mind? Foreman Mort said the Professor would get over it, and the bad words would pass. Why is he leaving now?"

Mr. Carson tried again to console me with his brief explanation, "Missy, it really wasn't any words that they *said to him*. I am so sorry to tell you, but it is what they *did to him* that hurt him so much. He cares for you so much, that he believed it was wiser for him to leave now and let you 'get that group of *deplorables* back under judicious control,' I believe were the words he used."

"Is the crew here now?" I continued to pry almost frightened, "Did they hurt him? Did they physically put their hands on him?"

"No. No, Missy, they didn't hurt him physically," Mr. Carson proffered, "And they didn't even say anything to him verbally. Sometimes, Missy, folks don't have to hit somebody or call them names to hurt them. Sometimes, they can do it so easily just by their simplest, cruelest actions."

"Whatever are you saying, Mr. Carson?" I was baffled by his words. "What did they do?" I practically cried.

"Missy, Mr. Jepson told me what happened, and it's just too despicable, too *deplorable*. You'll just have to go down there to the site and see for yourself. I am terribly sorry, Missy."

I was almost frozen in confusion as I stood there staring at Mr. Carson and then turning to look down the walkway to our jobsite. What was he talking about? Do something *cruel* with their *simplest actions*? What was I going to find down there?

With that final question burning a hole right through my brain, I abruptly turned-on-my-heels and started walking swiftly to our worksite. All the way there, with each step, I re-ran all the points, or clues, through my thought processing that Mr. Carson had given.

His hints flooded my mind: "...*plain and clear* they didn't want Professor around anymore? ...find a *more appropriate* welder? ...*nothing verbally*? ...*didn't have to hit him to hurt him*? ...(hurt) with *simplest cruel actions*?"

When I arrived at the site, all the crew were spread around the worksite like they were preparing to go to work. I knew they had seen me coming. They were all pretending to look sharp and busy at their preparations for the day's work. Nobody even bothered to say, "Hello," or "Good morning, Missy." Nothing. So, I spoke-up first.

"Alright, you guys, Professor just quit and left us. I want to know why. What happened?"

"Beats us," Mr. Henry was the first to talk. "That's a hell-of-a-sad-day when your welder just ups and drags-up and quits like that. Ain't that just like a nigger?"

'Shut your damned mouth, Mr. Henry. You're disgusting," I shouted at him.

The guys all started chuckling. They thought it was funny for a *petit* young woman to chastise one of their clan. I was so angry, though, that I didn't even care what any of them thought. Then it was Mr. Joe's turn to say something rash, and those two guys whom I had once thought were my closest friends of their whole stinking lot... were no longer...

Joe called out, "Why, Henry, I do believe our sweet, little welder just shut your *disgusting* mouth real bad. What we surely have here, I believe, is an honest-to-goodness case of *nigger love*. Do you all agree, or what?"

The whole crew exploded with laughter. I was so upset I couldn't hardly see straight. My face was no doubt blushed a deep red. I was fighting back tears of anger and frustration. I absolutely could not believe that other human beings could stoop that low. Those West Virginia, prior coal-mining Hillbillies were an embarrassment to all humanity for all I was concerned. They did not deserve to work on civilized city jobs, and especially not important war-support construction. Those jobs were honorable, respectable, and practically sanctified as the essence of what America meant, stood-for and was fighting in a world war with our troops dying to prove it.

I could feel tears of defeat welling-up behind my eyes. I sensed that at any moment, I might burst-out with a gushing torrent of blubbering raging-down from my eye sockets. I did not want any of those mean, cruel men to see me cry. It was obvious too that each of them by then had their eyes glued on my every move.

All I could muster-up, was a meager, "I think you all should be ashamed. Shame, shame on you all. How could you be so cruel?"

With that I turned slightly and headed for the latrine. At least there I felt like I could shed that emotional breakdown in privacy and not let them see that they got the better of me. I could feel all their eyes on my back as I stepped toward the latrines. Those callous and bad men were probably praying in their demented ways and watching and listening for me to break-down and wail-away like some forlorn lover."

Then the worst happened... As I walked, I looked-up and saw the horrid reality of that whole morning's matter. I stopped dead-in-my tracks, and I looked straight-ahead into the eyes-of-the-devil. The sheer, evil essence of those dirty men's souls stood-out and glared back at me like some fantastical screaming banshee.

I was stupefied, yet all-knowing at the same time. I was both shocked yet made stunningly aware simultaneously. I was angry beyond sanity's limits yet anguishing in a flood of pain and hurt. I felt ashamed of humanity and embarrassed by the pure cruelty of some people toward others...

There in front of me, up high above the men's latrine door was another sign, a revolting sign, centered and place above the "Men Only" which read: *White*. Next door, on my own personal latrine, and centered above the wording "Ladies Only" was another similarly evil sign which read: *Niggers and*.

Two signs, separate but of equal vileness, literally broadcast my crews' prejudicial, hateful, and discriminatory declarations like Nazi swastikas proudly waving over Auschwitz: *White Men Only* and *Niggers and Ladies Only*.

I was helpless. I could only stand there and keep staring at the signs in disbelief. I wanted so badly to believe that my eyes were playing tricks on me. I couldn't possibly be seeing and reading what I thought I was… Shame on me for even thinking so… No, even blinking and mentally wiping my eyes did not change what I read. It was there, it was true, and I was sickened.

All my anxieties over my crew, all my fears for Professor, all my stress over creating a real team-effort, all my hopes for success with our new project plan, all of it, everything came all at once building and surging-up from my innermost bowels. I felt deep abdominal pressure as everything grew larger and climbed up through my stomach and throat.

Instantly, in a violent gushing spray, I spewed outward in a deluge from my paralyzed and gaping mouth. I regrettably and shockingly barfed my stressed-out guts right there in front of my crew. Hell, it was in front of all the crews, and the whole damned world. I was sickened from the horrors and realities of humanity's inhumanity toward other humans.

Momentarily, I gathered my strength and rushed quickly into my latrine and spit-out the last holding remnants of stubborn vomit. I wiped my mouth and sweating face with tissue, took several deep breaths to calm my nerves and regain some stability, and I turned while stepping back-out into the morning's fresh air. My head was clearing by then. Not a calmness, but a steadiness, was returning to me.

Standing there momentarily while anyone curious continued watching me as I regained my composure, I stood-up as tall as I could and let my eyes scan fully over their faces staring back at me. Some of them were still chuckling. They had obviously enjoyed themselves immensely at my collapsing cost. But they saw me clearly and recognized that I was staring right back at all of them. Staring them down… down to the ground… down to hell, itself…

Then with a sudden and immediate plan formulated in my mind, with precise and swift movements, and in full view of that entire crew of human *waste,* and anyone else, I turned and walked behind the latrines, my own, to be exact, personal *Ladies Only* latrine. I placed my hands upon the upper, rear wall of the latrine. Its sides were built with just lightly joined boards with a couple one-by-fours crisscrossed to hold the shell together. I pushed lightly at first to test the weight and mass of the shed, and I sensed that it was relatively manageable…

Next, with all my strength and might summoned-up from all my anger and disgust, I shoved against that latrine shed's wall and felt it easily giveway to my force. The back-wall raised-up higher-and-higher to a medium point where I could feel its balance. I let my hands crawl down the wall putting more force on the bottom portion. With one final burst of power, fortitude, and adrenaline, I lifted, pushed, and shoved that *Ladies Only* latrine all the way up-and-over until it completely raised-up off the base flooring and fell crashing and collapsing onto its frontal-side and against barren earth. Shattering, splitting and folding-over into an ill-placed pile of lumber rubble, dust exploded from underneath and blew-out from all sides of the now destroyed latrine.

That *Ladies Only* latrine had been the *origin of my bonding relationship* with that crew. It had been a *symbol of mutual respect* and consideration. It was appropriate, therefore, that with my actions on that revolting morning, the true sense of my feelings toward that group of deplorable, unpatriotic, and unrighteous fools was made known to all. The only thing left remaining of our relationship, as I fully intended for visual and nasal evidence of my rightful and justified contempt toward them all, was that stinking, leftover, crap-hole filled with my own, personal sewage as a reminder.

As I gathered-up all my belongings, my leathers and hood, my bucket of personal tools and assorted welding-aids and held them on one arm, with my other free-open arm, I pointed over to that collapsed toilet while glaring-out over that ever-so-crude crew once again, and I attempted to stare each one down person-by-person, scumbag-by-scumbag.

Then in a calm, collected but forceful voice, I spouted, "That *shithole* is what I think of you all, and it is all that I leave you. You are disgusting human beings, and I am ashamed to have ever known any of you. Seek forgiveness from God for all your truly inhumane and repulsive ways because, otherwise, you are all surely going to burn-in-hell."

With that closure giving me impetus, I raised my head up high and marched-off toward the Personnel Office. I passed by Mr. Carson, and I said sadly, "My time here is over, Mr. Carson. I have more honor than to work with scum like them. W&S will find other welders, I'm sure. Who knows, maybe they will all deserve each other. For me, though, I am off for a newer and better adventure elsewhere. It truly was a pleasure knowing you, however, Mr. Carson."

For the second time since I had met him, Mr. Carson was without words. He stood there, mouth agape and moved his lips carefully, but without certainty, as he tried syncing a whispered, "Goodbye and good luck," to me.

I didn't stay to chat over that morning's deliberate end. From his control spot, Mr. Carson has easily heard and watched the entire episode. There was no reason to speak longer. He would hear about my further actions from someone, later, I was sure. And I was sure he would understand and overwhelmingly approve...

After that, I walked straight-up the marked walkway and straight into the Personnel Office. I meant to talk to no one else before I left. I did not want to stay and debate any more with the Foreman Mort or his also deplorable boss, our GM. I did not want to listen to either of their deceiving and contemptable opinions.

Both were likely just as lost and unworthy as those West Virginia trash workers that they oversaw. The pathetic, joking GF had no answers or solutions for me either. The company executives would carry-on with or without me. I knew that. It was still their task to make the place run effectively, or at least, function. They'd find another way, they had to. There was still a terrible war cause going-on that demanded their support. I would just support the war cause somewhere else. That was all.

I walked over to the secretary who handled personnel matters, and calmly said, "I quit. I heard there are a lot of better jobs elsewhere. Kaiser Shipyards at Richmond, California sounds interesting. That's where I heard our last welder, Professor Jepson, was going. Or, maybe I just may go anywhere else here in Cleveland. *Wendy the Welders* are wanted everywhere. Please send my close-out paycheck to my address on file. You have a beautiful day now. I sure as hell shall now!"

∞

With that, I turned and walked out the door and headed-back home for a relaxing and quiet afternoon all to myself. I would have a lot of thinking to do. Oh, sure, I was confident that I could go weld almost anywhere. *Prima Donna welders* were known to drag-up all the time for a variety of reasons: From getting upset, or for a different job, or better conditions, or more money, or new sights, or just for-the-hell-of-it. Whoever knew? I could choose any of the above and be justified to move on.

Yet, Professor's strength and wisdom had gently but quickly sprung forth, established and nurtured an idea in my head. It said that *I too might do anything else I set my mind to doing.* No, I wasn't going to give-up welding and become a university professor somewhere. I would be realistic, but I sure did feel like I could do so much more with my life, thanks to him.

Afterall, I had the whole country to see and try-out. Our Allied war efforts were becoming more successful. We were winning on both fronts against the Germans and had already whipped the Italians, thanks in part to my big brother. And we were steadily pounding on the Japanese and sending them crawling back home to their bombed-out island. Hopefully, there would be peace soon. Celebrations would be everywhere, and opportunities would abound. Who knew where my travels might take me? But I was definitely game for a change...

EENY MEENY MINY MOE

U nemployment didn't last long. Only one afternoon in our apartment sitting-on-my-butt all day, and I was as nervous as a priest waking-up in a cathouse. There were lots of jobs available doing all sorts of things for the war cause, but nothing that I was interested in. So, initially, I was a little concerned. Besides Warner and Swasey Construction projects, Cleveland was a central area for military-aircraft development. Even with minimal training required, still, I wasn't a *riveter*, like *Rosie*, and I understood that most aircraft were assembled with rivets.

But I was a welder and an experienced one at that. "Focus on what I can do, not what I cannot," became my motto. Of course, I was a little-bit spoiled, so I added: "… (not what I cannot) nor what I will not!" It only took me a brief research exercise to learn that arc-welders were in great demand all over the city. Newspaper want ads and bulletin boards all over town were advertising for welders.

There were lots of small, shop jobs doing smaller contracts for the government and paying smallest wages. There were auto-shop businesses doing bodywork for car-accident repairs also offering skid-row, low-pay. I imagined those jobs being designed or meant for security-minded, stay-at-home types. Jean had gotten me started in welding… at sixteen years old (almost seventeen). I had learned the craft well and paid my dues. Then *the* Professor had come along, and in two days, he had given me wings. So, okay, *maybe I was meant* for the aircraft manufacturing industry after all.

Besides, wasn't it a couple of Cleveland boys, Orville, and Wilbur, who started the whole *heavier-than-air* aviation experiment? They sure did, and it happened in 1903 at Kitty Hawk, North Carolina. By then, it was over forty-years later, and military aircraft had certainly become essential in warfare. Our brother, Bo, was helping to prove that with German bombing raids in his beloved *B-26 Marauder* missions. Brother Bo liked that plane, while many others didn't, but I can remember him saying after the war, "If it was good enough for *General Jimmy*, then it was good enough for me!" Apparently, General Jimmy Doolittle used a *Marauder* as his personal plane. However, Doolittle actually flew a B-25 Mitchell bomber when he led the first U.S. air attack on Japan, *The Tokyo Raid*, in April 1942, which made him famous.

Although Cleveland didn't step-right-up and embrace the Wright Brothers in the early 1900's, the city did later become a world-wide hub as a massive aircraft parts supplier for the WWII war cause and afterwards too. The huge Cleveland airport was great for equipment testing and flights, because of its uninhabited vast open areas. Within the city proper, early 200 different companies sprung-up to develop, manufacture and deliver parts for aircraft builders.

Unfortunately, because of typical, overcast skies, Cleveland did very little of the aircraft frame building. That was left-up to West Coast companies with all their continual sunshine. But Cleveland led the way with production of airplane parts, landing gear, engine development, and much more. If you wanted a job in aviation, Cleveland was the city to be in.

Since arc-welding was a significant aspect of aircraft manufacturing, I felt confident of finding aviation work. With my resume in-hand, I studied the aviation industry job ads and while fingering down the list, I spoke-out-loud to my *ambitious self*, "Eeny meeny miny moe: *Choose a place where* **you can grow.**" Or, there was my *show-off self*: "*Find some work where* **you will glow!**" Or, my *greedy* favorite: "*Pick a job that* **makes you dough!**" So, quickly I had my priorities: Aviation war cause, and making money. Low and behold! I spotted an ad right away: Manufacturing Government Military Aircraft: Welders Wanted: Best Wages Anywhere!

How could I possibly deny them my skills? The name of that new company was Federal Aviation Company, and they desperately needed arc-welders. It was on a Friday, and I went down to see them, put in an application with the Personnel Office and was sent over to the designated welder's desk. Right away, I was snatched-up and hired-on-the-spot pending any welding-test clearances and certifications.

You see, every company must certify a welder for competence before the welder can go to work for them as a welder. If a welder has worked for the same company previously, then that welder was automatically cleared. But a new company meant new tests and clearances for all new welders. Of course, if two separate companies were owned by the same parent company, then cross-referenced records often worked.

I had a variety of certifications from Kaiser and W&S, and those helped me be selected for Federal Aviation during the interview. However, I still had to test for all types of welding I may potentially be doing for them. Therefore, I was set-up for a welding-test early the next morning. The hiring interviewer pointed-out the place where I would find a Testing Foreman the next day. I was set to go. Piece of cake!

It wouldn't have mattered what test they put me up against. At W&S, I had been doing a lot of Stainless-Steel welding, and Kaiser Shipyards had been moderate Carbon Steel, but aircraft welding might require Aluminum Certifications. Fortunately, I was competent with that too. It wouldn't be a problem, I figured, because if I needed, I could brush-up a little on the materials they gave me to refresh my skills.

In any case, I wasn't worried. No doubt, I would be testing for all their arc-welding needs. I was so comfortable and relaxed about the job that I even began considering that, if I wanted, I could even have a career here. When the war was over, I had been told during the interview process by the excited and delighted interviewer, Federal Aviation would continue building planes for the government and could also convert over to civilian aircraft. Regardless, I was told that I could have a long career with them if I chose.

Well, as much as I liked it there, my work with FAC was not going to be my last job application. In fact, it wasn't even going to be my final, war-effort, construction job. However, what I can assure you, "My next welding experience with Federal Aviation Company became my *best, construction-job ever*, gave me one of my *best days ever* and changed my life *forever*."

ST. PATRICK'S DAY

Federal Aviation Company

I remember it as well as I do that Pearl Harbor Day on December 7th, well-over three years earlier. It was Saturday, March 17th, 1945, and it was *St. Patrick's Day*! Celebrations were undaunted, and enthusiasm reigned. Everybody was wearing green, and everyone was waiting for work to end, so they could go-out and drink all that green, Irish beer. Of course, I was too young for any drinking. I was still over two-months shy of being nineteen, but I enjoyed partying and celebrating and dressing-up for any occasion.

For my work attire that special *St. Patrick's Day*, I chose a green bonnet and scarf and bright green clothing under my welding leathers. When the shift was over, I knew full well that I'd have to go home and get cleaned-up. My bonnet and scarf and any exposed attire would likely be very dark and dirty. That was okay because Colleen and I would get re-dressed and go out for a fun time. Naturally, Sis Mary would be partying like crazy with all her Irish and Irish wannabe friends. It was a fun day for all.

Of course, I loved *St. Patrick's Day*. After all, I am a McCord, and I enjoy being Irish. Unfortunately, back then, I had a bit of an Irish temper too, and sometimes, my anger got the best of me. Those bums on my last job had gotten a little taste of it. Unfortunately, or fortunately, depending on how you look at it, some new fella at this job was going to get a little taste of it too.

That Saturday morning, I left home very early and in a good mood. Sis and Colleen were both sleeping-in, so I didn't disturb them. Carrying all my welding gear, I walked the short distance to the bus-stop on that *St. Patrick's*

Day. There was a brisk morning-air with a threat of rain clouds, but being dressed all in green, I didn't care. Regardless of what someone carries, it is a welder's hood that sets them apart from everyone else. That morning was no exception. I got lots of stares for all my green and my *hood*. I confess that I liked the attention. I felt a little different than most and a little bit proud. Even the bus driver was wearing green and nodded admirably. Everybody was all smiles and in good moods that day... so far... at least!

Although a Saturday and on *St. Patrick's Day* to boot, Federal Aviation Company was in full operations. All three shifts were obviously running because Graveyard was just ending, so workers were just heading-out the gate as I arrived. I was still a little earlier than expected, but the Welding, Test-Foreman Inspector was right where I had been told he would be, and he welcomed me right after I had identified myself. Women welders were still a scarcity, so he was a little surprised. I could tell, though, that he was more than surprised. He was giddy and interested, and it was not because I was dressed in so much green. I saw the glint in his flirtatious eyes, but I also saw the ring on his finger.

"No thanks, Boss. Business only. Where do I test?"

Foreman *Fred* was his name, and he was quick to recognize my *no-nonsense* attitude. He still took his time giving me the *up-and-down,* but then finally pointed over to a specific, welding machine in the yard. He told me to hook-up to it with welding leads there, if necessary, and use the work area across from it for my test. He added that all the equipment I would need was already there from the previous shift. I could gather-up what tools and welding rod I needed from the storage cabinet set right next to it. Of course, *Fast Freddie* had to add, "If there is *anything* else, you need, *please* come see me"

"Thanks. But I don't think so. I'll be fine."

While standing there as Foreman Fred was talking and pointing and eyeballing me, I casually began prepping myself and tossing-on all my leathers including raised-hood and gloves. By the time we were both finished, Foreman Freddie was all blushed, and I had bright-green highlights all around my welder's outfit. Other than the green, I looked like any of the other dozens of welders coming to work that morning. Leathered-up, it was hard to tell any of us apart unless you looked closely. At quitting-time, you had to look even closer.

I set myself up for my welding test: I walked over to the welding machine that Foreman *Fast Freddie* had designated and turned it to the "On" position; I set the Amperage Dial at about 130 amps, or appropriately for my welding task; I carried the welding lead and stinger over to the Test Area and set it safely aside; finally, I arranged the already grinded Test Plate Pieces for the test, dropped my hood and tacked them together properly… This morning was only a Stainless-Steel test, so it was basic for me. Piece of cake!

THAT "GUY" IS THE ONE!

The rest of the incident I am about to share then started-off like a comedy movie-clip: <u>Clash of the Prima Donnas</u>. Or, looking back, it was just silly or even hilarious! To think about it always makes me laugh and smile. It is a very fond memory that I have of one of the most important moments of my life...

After I had given a visual check of my test materials and was satisfied, I began again. Carefully, but casually, I bent over the test materials, dropped my hood and struck-an-arc with my stinger's welding rod. I was immediately engrossed with my test project. *Lost in the light,* I liked to say. I was intent on giving *Fast Freddie* a finished, test product that he would brag about to his sleezy buddies.

There I was just buzzing away and completely absorbed in total concentration of what I was doing. Suddenly, from behind and above me, I heard some irritated worker growling and demanding angrily, "Who in hell do you think you are using my (welding) machine?"

Without hesitation, I blurted back, "I'm testing, and I'm using the one I was assigned. Go get your own damned machine!" Then I flipped-up my welder's hood, turned, looked-up, and faced the irritated man's...strong, squared jaw... and rather handsome face, I must add, and stared back fiercely into his... deep, intensely brown eyes.

Instantly, that big, stocky, strong man realized that I was an angered, red-faced, petite, and annoyed female. Embarrassed, and instantly, red-as-a-beet himself, he bowed while apologizing, turned-on-his-heels and promptly walked hurriedly away toward the Foremen's Shack leaving me there to continue my test without any further interruptions.

I was done with the test in short order. I had ground down both sides of the test product plate, and it looked very good to me. After cleaning-up my work area, or that *other guy's*, I rolled-up and returned the leads, turned-off the welding machine and set the stinger in its protective compartment. Then I took my cooled-off test product back-up to Foreman Fred for its x-ray and examination. I knew it was good, but I was told to just hang around for the X-ray results to come back. I found a bench outside, sat down and waited.

When lunchtime came, I began thinking about a company cafeteria or snack bar because I had brought no lunch with me. Plus, St. Patrick must have been blessing all of Cleveland that day because those rain clouds had lifted, and it had become a very warm day, after all. I wanted coffee or something. I started searching around the grounds for a break-area when, suddenly, I was interrupted.

The very same man from the earlier, welding-machine incident had approached me smiling and began apologizing some more. I had calmed down by then, so it was my turn to blush. Maybe, I had over-reacted, and now I was a bit defenseless. He began teasing me about how cute I looked in *red and green*, like I was a leprechaun, or something. We laughed together, and he told me about a nearby, ice-cream parlor. Then he offered to buy me an ice cream to make up for all his rudeness. I said, "Yes!"

We had a delightful lunchbreak, and we both spent the entire time enjoying ice-cream and just chatting about work, and ourselves and getting to know each other. That *other guy's* name turned-out to be *Guy*, so I thought that was kind of cute. He thought it was funny that it was *St. Patrick's Day*, and my name was *Patricia*, so he stood-up and made a loud, embarrassing but charismatic, announcement renaming the holiday: *St. Patricia's Day*! Now that's how you win a good, little, er, petit, Catholic girl's heart.

Anyway, when the whistle blew again advising all that it was time to get back to work, we both agreed that the time had just flown by. We said our brief goodbyes and went back to our jobs for that afternoon's session. My test plate had returned and had been perfect, of course, so I was sent-off on my first assignment. They had me welding-up Stainless-Steel landing-gear for one of the many fighter-jet contracts they had. I confess that the rest of the shift went by dreamily. After work, I dare say that I walked back and dilly-dallied a little while around the test area just sort of casually waiting. After a while, though, it started getting crowded with all the next shift coming-in too, so we all went on to our homes. I was still excited, however, and practically rushed to the bus stop and then on to our apartment building.

A short while later, after had I arrived at our small apartment, Sis Mary, Colleen and Jann were still there inside. It was a Saturday night, so naturally Sis was *getting-dressed-to-kill*, and the younger ones were getting cleaned-up too and waiting for me to see what we might do. Anxiously and hurriedly, I gathered them all together in the living-room and joyously but seriously blurted out, "Sisters, who wants to go out and celebrate St. Patricia's Day with me? Today, I met the man I am going to marry!"

GUY HENRY (CHAPMAN) DORK

The man I was going to marry turned-out to be the way it was. How do those sorts of things happen? Beats me, but it was amazing. It was simply one of those feelings you get way-down-deep, and you just know it's the truth. We only had that first encounter which wasn't very pleasant or promising, although he did strike an intriguing pose in my mind. It was that Italian love-bolt of lightning, or St. Patrick teaming-up with Cupid's arrow or something that struck us, but it was *love-at-first sight*, and we both fell for each other. I may have *cussed-him-out,* or rather, *put-him-in-his-place,* but I couldn't help but think about him after that.

After that man had left me to my testing, I sort of regretted being so hostile. Why hadn't I acted a little more civil toward him? I remember thinking about mixed feelings I had of previous friendships and relationships with men in my life. I certainly had no relationship, or worthy one, with my dad. He usually seemed like he could barely tolerate me being around while I was growing up. In fact, I recalled that the last time I had seen him was when he had beaten me over Jean and very badly both outside and inside. I felt like a *whipping-post* for him.

I was a non-entity, or non-person, or at least a non-family to him that allowed his ill-conceived brutality to expose truth about his feelings toward me. He never loved me. He never wanted me. He never believed I was even his own child. In his warped and demented mind, I was the product of deception and an unfaithful wife. Essentially, my own father wanted nothing to do with me, and he rid himself of my disgusting reminder of disloyalty to him at my birth.

It was my mother who begged him to allow me to return home at five-years old. When I was thirteen-years old, I had pressured him to return home partly because of my contempt for *Georgie Porgie,* my intolerable cousin Rosalie's husband. and my dad's agreement surprised me, although he had been reluctantly put-on-the-spot. However, by the time that the war began, Jean, Bo and Sis Mary had already been dismissed, and I was easily the next reject in his mind. The war itself, its sacrifices and expenses were easy arguments to unload a non-family person to him and send her back to his ex-wife's family. That was the practical end of our ties.

Looking back, however, I can recall many instances of decent, upstanding men who had wished-me-well, or had watched-out-for me. Examples were the ticket-salesmen at the St. Paul Train Station and the nice policeman who had *looked-the-other-way* when I was running-away. Although I had a poor learning relationship on my first job with *Joey*, it was made-up for by the decent and supportive *Mr. Smith* and *Mr. Beau*.

Later, I did have a few, bad run-ins with some truck-drivers while hitching on the highways, but I also met some very fine, upstanding fellows. The men at Kaiser Vancouver were all fine, upstanding, and very supportive gentlemen, too as was *Thomas,* my workmate and friend. And I cannot forget the brief, but kind connection I had made with the *Professor* and the very nice and funny *Mr. Carson* at Warner and Swasey.

The point I'm making is that up until W & S, I had known some mostly decent and fine men, and I was proud to call them friends. Unfortunately, there were several others, mainly the West Virginia bunch and our bosses there of whom I did not think too highly. Then, on-top-of-all-that, I had begun my workday at Federal Aviation dealing with an incorrigible foreman, *Fast Freddie*. I guess you could say, my alarms were on, and I had no tolerance dealing with rude, impolite, or disrespectful men. That poor man who interrupted my welding test did not stand a chance against me. I wasn't about to take any more brash mouth from a man.

But then *Guy* had returned to see me after my rash disposal of him earlier, and that simply sparked a special kindling into igniting a fire burned which burned between us for fifty-seven years and his death at eighty-three in 2002. And it was because he did return, apologize, and proceed to sweep-me-off-my-feet. Although I had pronounced my imagined betrothal to my sisters the very same night as Guy's and my disastrous beginning yet repaired lunchtime that afternoon, it was all the days and adventures which followed with my sisters and us that really warmed us both.

Marriage was on the horizon, but it wouldn't happen for another eleven months. There were quite a few matters for each of us to get resolved first before we could finally *tie-the-proverbial-knot*. Getting all my siblings together was still a priority. Guy had promised his blessing and full-support, and that had meant the world to me. It helped, too, that my sisters absolutely adored him.

Guy was handsome as all get-out, and he was kind, courteous and a true gentleman always. Well most of the time, anyway. He said that he did get feisty at men who tried to push him around, and that especially might count on-the-job. Welders are particularly snooty about their gear and equipment because the quality of their work depends on exactness and preciseness. I absolutely knew what he was talking about. Remember what I said about *Prima Donnas*?

Guy wasn't one of those, per se, but he was a professional, and I had learned at Federal Aviation that he was the *Go-to* man when you needed some difficult welding done. All his professional welding life, Guy was respected and called-for all around the country for field-construction, Boilermaker welding. We had met as co-welders on a job, and for the first half of our married life, welding construction work would take him and our family all around the United States.

We were called modern-day *Boomers*: Workers and families who chased after the next, big payday wherever big construction jobs were requiring master welders. Guy was respected and appreciated wherever he went to work. Let's just say for instance, "I was a really good welder, but Guy was *amazing!*"

He was the type of welder that could surprise and impress you just by watching him. If you happened to walk-up behind him while he was doing a typical, vertical weld, on something, he would flip-up his hood, turn to talk to you while he was eating cookies, and all-the-while continue his welding just by listening to what was happening. In California alone, Guy was considered one of the top welders in the entire state. The Boilermaker Union Hall (job) Dispatchers loved to send my husband on jobs. That was one reason why we traveled do much.

Another example of his unique skill took place on a huge, coal-fired, power plant onetime. His anxious bosses called Guy to help, after some other welder had messed-up on a critical boiler unit. A defective-unit due to a bad weld had erroneously been put in place and completely welded and sealed-up to other components. The bad unit had defective welding that was nearly impossibly out-of-reach.

Guy studied the situation and then went-to-work. He took a couple of electrodes (welding rods) and attached them to end-to-end. He then bent the doubly long rods into a widely curved shape he needed to reach the *bad weld*. Next, using two small mirrors, he placed them so that used-together, they gave him a sighting of the defective weld. Finally, while stretched-out on the building's concrete flooring, Guy reached back behind the unit with his extra-long, radically bent welding rods, and sighting the needed welding location using the co-teamed mirrors, he correctly welded-over the bad welding and corrected the defective portion. Guy saved the company perhaps thousands of dollars in lost-time and additional payroll, and he earned the gratitude of the company with hearty slaps-on-the-back and resounding cheers. It sounded all too familiar to me. The life of a good welder…

Guy was a very interesting man too. As a young boy of nine, his father, Charles Chapman, had gone to the store one day in a small town of Ohio, and had never returned. There was gossip that he had been a minor-time hoodlum with gangsters around Cleveland during the 1920's and owed too much money to some bad sorts. Thus, Charles may have ended-up at the bottom of Lake Erie. Another gossip was that for the same reasons, Charles may have skipped town and never returned.

Regardless, Guy's mother soon thereafter met Cleveland's premier newspaper photographer for the <u>Cleveland Press</u>, Mr. Eddie Dork. In short-order, she married Eddie, and he adopted Guy and his sister and brother and changed their names to Dork. After only a brief period, guy's mother contracted a terrible disease and died. Guy was barely ten years old, and both his parents were gone, except that now he had a brand-new, adopted father, the famous Cleveland newspaper photographer, Eddie Dork. Fame was not his game, but Guy got along reasonably well with his adopted father for a while. He spent a lot of time watching Cleveland Indians baseball team games and selling popcorn there for a job because Eddie was the Team Photographer.

Father-son conflicts grew worse for Guy as he aged. Eddie was very popular and enjoyed Cleveland's adulation. Guy says that he didn't offer enough of it to his new dad, so they fought. He managed to escape stress for a while by practicing and becoming a semi-professional roller-skating dancer, but pressure and struggles at home with Eddie worsened. Eventually, Guy ran away at age sixteen and managed to get false, or forged I.D.s. He joined the U.S. Army in 1935 while still only sixteen, and he was sent eventually to the Panama Canal for duty. I felt his background had vague similarities to mine.

A side note is that for New Year's celebration 2002, and as an entire family adventure, Guy and I took our whole collection of children, grandchildren, and great-grandchildren on a ten-day cruise around the Caribbean Sea and into the Panama Canal. Guy showed everyone where he had been ordered in 1939, by his Army superiors, to point his rifles and aim at all Japanese crewmen aboard all Japanese vessels traversing the Panama Canal at that time. Of course, there were many structural changes, but Guy still had the distinct memories. Apparently, even then it was evident and ominous that war was imminent.

That same year, 1939, Guy severely injured his knee playing in an Army recreational, baseball game and was honorably discharged as a result. Approaching twenty-one years of age by then, he moved to Las Vegas and became a professional boxer. He was modestly successful as a fighter. However, he always said that his fight-game name was *Guy "The Big Dummy" Dork*, and it may have been true because it was barely paying his bills. After his final fight, when he had been bruised and bloodied severely but had still won the fight because the *other fighter* looked even worse, Guy left the fight game.

He had a girlfriend from there, and he knew he had to get *an honest job,* so he learned welding, and that carried him through his entire working career. However, a welder's lifestyle, apparently, was not exciting enough for his recent wife. She still loved and missed the glitter of boxing glamour and Las Vegas highlights. Guy always said that he liked the Vegas glamour and glitter too, but he hated getting his lights knocked out! Anyway, after a couple more years, his wife took their son, Richard, and left him.

Cleveland was home to Guy, and some of his family were still there. He moved back, made-up with his adopted dad and settled down as best he could in town. He began developing a reputation as a competent welder and never had problems finding work. With the war well underway by then, Guy ultimately established himself with an important, aeronautical engineering and aircraft component manufacturer, Federal Aviation. He worked there steadily after that… up until he met me. Then everything changed…

BASIC MAGNESIUM PLANT, INC.

Henderson, Nevada

Hip! Hip! Hurray! and Hallelujah! The war in Europe was over! It was May 8th, 1945, and the Germans and Nazi's and Hitler were finally defeated! Rumors had it that Hitler was already dead, maybe even from suicide. Who cared? A coward's way out was very befitting for him. Celebrations were going on everywhere you turned. Those were joyous and exciting times to be in, and I was sharing it all with my three sisters, Mary, Colleen and Jann and my boyfriend, *Guy Henry Chapman Dork*.

Around then, there was an incredible energy and excitement in the air. Summer was approaching as was my nineteenth birthday, and everything seemed optimistic. Employment opportunities were still booming everywhere. After VE Day there was a total focus on defeating the Japanese. Victory in Europe converted many war cause plants to convert to war munitions factories, and they were going gang busters. To defeat Japan meant *bombs and bullets.*

With the war against Hitler over, and victory in the war against Japan leaning heavily in or favor, it seemed like we were on the verge of the entire war's end and peace, at last. That was exciting because it meant that Jean and Bo would soon be discharged, and they could return to us. Young Brother Jack was still with our dad and Edith, and by then it was in Southern California. We sisters, and by then including Guy, made mental plans to have Jack join us soon.

One day, on little more than a whim, my boyfriend and future husband, Guy Dork, along with my three sisters and I, made another sudden plan. We all decided to head for California. From years of discussions before, we all had come to the belief that our futures lay there. However, we couldn't just make a journey there with all of us at once. We had to make a small detour and get there via Las Vegas Nevada.

Technically and legally, Guy was still married, and he had a son. By going to Las Vegas and setting-up a temporary home, Guy could file for a necessary divorce. That period would only take six-weeks to complete, and by doing so there, he could arrange to visit Richard and have him stay with us. When the divorce was final, Richard could come with us to California and the Bay Area.

Work was bountiful, so we checked the area and discovered *Rosie's* were still in great demand as were welders. Las Vegas was a major gambling and entertainment area, so it was not conducive to our family needs, so we chose the town of Henderson about twenty miles away. I remember Sis Mary excitedly laughing and saying that it might be the best of two worlds: Necessary work in Henderson and gambling, entertainment, and men in Las Vegas. Perfect!

Henderson, Nevada would be ideal because there was a large munitions plant there, so we could all work there who wished to do so. I decided that since my sisters were coming along on this escapade, I would spread-my-wings like the Professor had insinuated. I thought it would be fun to go to work in a munitions plant right along with my other sisters, Sis Mary, and Colleen, who was still only seventeen, but she could work in the cafeteria, or something. Also, Guy would easily find welding in any of the multiple steel-construction manufacturing plants in the area. Legal matters in Las Vegas also, and visits with Guy's son, Richard, would be simpler. All we had to do was get there. It would be the beginning of another adventure.

Initially, we all packed-up for our adventures, but only three of us went down to the Cleveland Bus Terminal together because we began with slightly different variations. Guy, Colleen, and I all took a bus zigzagging around the middle and southwest states until we reached Henderson. We had saved-up enough funds, so we were able to hop on-and-off to visit local tourist sights and stay-over in other towns to relax and spend a couple nights in motels for special meals and cleaning-up. Our plans were to eventually get to Henderson, and then we would find a reasonably sized house for all of us to live together. Mary and Jann were to join us in a few weeks.

They, however, had decided on a different route. Those two had really managed to bond, and in curios fashion, they had mutually agreed upon a special destination. They would get to Henderson a few weeks later, but they were going to do that trip almost completely cross-country. Both wanted to visit the Big Apple, New York City. Mary was excited to see Broadway and Fifth Avenue and Jann was thrilled to get a chance to see the Empire State Building and Statue of Liberty. They would be great company for each other, and their diversion would benefit them both. It would partially satisfy Jann's growing urge to begin seeing the world, and it would partially satisfy Mary's craving to see a central part the of world of fashion, theatre, art, music, and a cultural centerpiece of America.

Fairly soon afterward, however, we four sisters and Guy were all housed, as planned, in a nice and comfortable, partially furnished, three-bedroom home in Henderson. It was a nice house on a reasonably quiet street in a very decent neighborhood. There was plenty of room for all, and we even hoped that Jean might get discharged soon and join us. But, unfortunately, it didn't happen. The war was still on.

We all got jobs soon after arriving. Guy went to work across town at an assembly plant welding carry-all trailers for military equipment. Because of the cross-town distance to his job and several other reasons, guy bought his first car in a very long time. He had been using city busses and Greyhound for even longer than we had. But his cute little car served him, and us, well for our whole duration in Henderson, and then onto the Bay Area in Northern California.

Sis Mary and I both went to work in a munitions factory assembling fifty caliber bullets for big machine guns still used in Pacific War against Japan. That job became both of our qualifiers as definite, first-rate Rosie-the Riveters. I remember smiling and thinking about the Professor. I was doing my career yet a new and different way. I felt good about it. Plus, the money was good, and the work was very steady so far.

Sis Mary, on-the-other-hand… hated it! It just was not her style. She said she despised putting her gorgeous hair up in a bonnet. Having to wear coveralls was an absolute disgrace, too. She complained because she was made to look like all the other workers. Oh, how uncouth! How was anybody supposed to notice her curvaceous body and beautiful long, hanging hair and sumptuous lips with all that gawdy costuming on?

Anyway, after a couple weeks, she convinced one of the bosses to let her have a job in the office where she belonged and was an excellent office manager. I was surprised at her quick promotion, but Sis wasn't. She told us later that she had gotten a date with one of the bosses who helped her find her way. Didn't I tell you she was good?

Colleen was still too young to work on the assembly-lines or around any of the construction or office jobs. But it was no problem, because we had been advised that the plant had an enormous cafeteria to feed the thousands of employees, and they always needed extra help. So, just like that, Colleen got work in the cafeteria, and on many days, we would get to see her at lunchtime and have a brief visit. Colleen had known about working for many years ever since going out in the neighborhoods of Sioux Falls and finding work to help support Edith and the family during our dad's chronic absences.

Just like that, we were all busy bees. We were mostly all working together, and we left every morning together and came home together too. It was a bit of a walk, but the housing was built to accommodate all the plant workers. We were in good company, and we were happy. We were still right on track to accomplish our goals of being completely together again, the whole sibling clan, including Jean, Bo, and Jack. It was happening.

Jann was the only one who was too young to work anywhere. She was very pretty and looked older, but we were not struggling or pressed for forging more IDs. It was summertime, so we let Jann be the housekeeper. She cleaned-up around the house, and got dinners started for our return. It was a very comfortable arrangement…

Henderson's main industrial and, therefore, biggest employer was the Basic Magnesium Inc. industrial plant which produced magnesium for munitions and airplane parts. Henderson was previously called Midway City, but it had been recently renamed for Nevada's beloved Senator Henderson. Funny thing was that once the war was over, the US Army determined no more use for Henderson nor its military support aspects, so the whole town and lands all around were put-up for auction.

While Henderson was still thriving and booming with war munitions work and effort, we sisters and Guy really made the most of it. Our house became a very popular residence in the area. Back then, you see, it was very common to know many, if not all, of the neighbors on your block, sometimes a block over too. We sure did, and everyone around was always curious about what was happening at *Guy's Little Harem!* I dare say, there was excitement just about every day of the week and twice on weekends. Something was always going-on with us sisters, and Guy sure as heck had his hands full.

Here's a couple examples of what I'm talking about:

As mentioned, our place in Henderson, Nevada was very popular. Even the garbage-truck pick-up fellows liked to come-by and check us sisters-out. They would always swing-by our house on their route every Saturday morning with their garbage truck and dawdle at our house longer than necessary in order to flex their muscles and show-off their strength and dexterity. They would take turns reaching-over our full garbage can while bending, stretching, and flexing their enormous muscles, and then in one full-swoop, hoist-up that large garbage container and toss its contents up and into their waiting truck's bed.

Of course, all we girls would hear their truck coming down the street and laughing and giggling we'd hurry outside to watch them pass. Sis Mary, Colleen, Jann, and sometimes, even me, would stand around watching them faithfully from our front porch while swaying back-and-forth in our frilly dresses and overdone make-up while oohing and wooing at their heroic, majestic-strength machoism.

Even the envious driver stuck inside his truck would get into the act while sitting behind his steering-wheel. He would sit there smiling-widely at us in his sleeveless, tank-top t-shirt making Mr. Universe type, muscleman poses. They were all showing-off their male glory to us supposedly innocent and ever-so- impressed, sweet, and fragile, young ladies.

We bashful, shy, and teasing females, in return, would all resoundingly flirt back with smiles and giggles and wave. Only once, or twice, did I ever participate in my sister's outrageous performances, but I let Guy know that it was only a joke to me.

Well, regardless, it all became so much nonsense to just make Guy sick. He kept repeating that he "...would like nothing more than to walk-out onto our front yard one Saturday, garbage-pick-up-day morning, and right there in broad-daylight with all the neighbors watching,... pound the living-crud out of all those 'brainless, brawny, air-head, dip-shits' and send them all scrambling, crawling, running and driving-off crying for their bosses and mommies!"

But then he would repose himself, and reflecting further, he would add that he didn't "... because then nobody would come-by to pick-up our garbage. And this house of four women sure made for a lot of garbage!"

All us sisters would continue laughing and giggling at his comments, but I knew that I detected a bit of jealousy in my lover boy's mind. That was why I limited my own participation to Saturdays that Guy was gone or busy elsewhere. Like they say, "Girls just wanna have fun!"

Anyway, I guessed that finally Guy had simply had enough of those 'garbage- guys' moronic and flirtatious, he-man behavior. Guy always had all kinds of insulting names for the 'garbage group,' but, honestly, he argued, he just wanted to get rid of their ridiculous showmanship.

Finally, he decided on a way that he might finally get even with them, once- and-for-all. So, one Saturday morning, Guy went out-front to the garbage can already on the side of the street awaiting its pick-up. He then removed half the garbage can's contents and stored it elsewhere. Next, he took the garden hose and proceeded to fill- up the garbage can with water until the remaining garbage in the can began over- flowing.

Guy figured that would teach those 'garbage fools' a thing-or two when one of the unfortunate trios attempted lifting that can. Of course, Guy had already known that water weighs over fourteen pounds a gallon. With that garbage can half-full of water, therefore holding about twenty or more gallons he knew it would weigh approximately 300 additional pounds besides the overflowing garbage in it already. "Good," Guy chuckled to himself! "That would fix one of those soon-to-be herniate- jerks!"

Naturally, Guy had to go back-inside the house and sit down on the living- room couch to watch through the closed-curtains, so that he could gloat over his prank. Well, he got even more than he had planned. He told us all later that he had ended up watching the 'Fight of the Century' which made all his own professional boxing endeavors pale in comparison. All this reporting, of course, is from his own demented, spectator details, and from all his laughter, we knew that he had indeed enjoyed the view...

Continuing with Guy's own triumphant recollection, though: Shortly before the 'garbage-truck heroes' all arrived for their regularly scheduled pick-up time, Jann decided to amplify her sisters' semi-distant flirtations by bringing them all a little closer. Without asking, however, Jann borrowed one of Colleen's sexy-cute blouses to wear while she went-out to presumably wash Guy's car using the garden hose. Jann thought that she would get first-contact with the 'garbage hunks', thereby, one-upping her jealous sisters.

Lo-and-behold, Colleen came out about that same time with another bag of garbage to add to the already-full garbage can. She had also planned on timing her own garbage-delivery to the intended 'garbage-boys' pick-up time. She too was all dolled-up in a pretty, new dress for her own, personal-sensual effect. Unbeknownst to her, however, Colleen saw the full, garbage can, so she lifted her dress, raised-up her leg and using her foot stomped and stuffed and shoved the overflowing can's garbage down deeper to make room for her addition.

Instantly, Colleen let out a scream at her horribly soaked distress. Her leg, and once pretty dress, were drenched and dirtied by the sopping garbage. Furious and embarrassed as could be, she looked around for signs of her betrayer. What-do- you-know, but there was Jann wearing Colleen's precious and personal, suggestive blouse without asking, and Jann was just whistling-away, and hanging all-over the car hood for effect, and still with the garden hose hanging in her hand, she was gushing water all over the car and herself while she too waited to tantalize the 'trash trio.'

In a nasty, angry, and unholy rage, Colleen charged at Jann screaming, "You trampy thief! Steal my blouse, will you?" And with her livid threat still resounding throughout the neighborhood, Colleen leaped-upon Jann, and the two of them crashed against Guy's car falling to the ground in a furious, clawing, slapping, hitting, hair- pulling, and tearing feud. Then, in one quick, horrific yank, Colleen ripped her own blouse completely off Jann's upper-body which immediately turned Jann into a semi- nudist while simultaneously destroying Colleen's own, once-sexy blouse.

Shocked and dismayed, and by then fully aware of each's filthy, somewhat bloodied, and disastrously dressed conditions, they both let go of each other and raced back inside the house to continue their loving-sisterly brawl. "With perfect timing, too," Guy reported later in nearly hysterical laughter, himself, "the 'trash trio' had come around the street corner and were making their anxious, curious and hopeful way up to their favorite garbage pick-up place.

By then, Guy confessed later, with his sadistically cruel and outrageous sense- of-humor, he was almost rolling on the floor with his prophetic storytelling. It seems that just as Guy had planned, two of the 'compost kings' left the truck, walked into the yard and immediately began looking around for an audience while flexing their tanned, oiled and overabundantly-muscled arms. Then, also just as planned, one of the 'debris dummies' was elected to empty the unknowingly deceptive garbage can...

With one hand grasping the garbage can's handle-rung, the 'dumpster dummy' turned his head around still seeking an audience. Seeing none, never-the- less, for fame and promise, the 'debris-derelict' quickly and fiercely jerked-up hard to raise and lift the monstrously, over-weighted can. Instantly, the poor 'junk jerk' had let go the can, collapsed and was groaning and moaning on the ground as if he had obviously twisted his back into an agonizingly warped deformity.

In Guy's demented version, the other 'trash taker' laughed at his injured, buddy, co-worker's pain and then took his listless turn at hoisting the garbage can. He too was immediately paralyzed from the obscene weight. But he must have been the smarter of the two, Guy laughed, because he stuck his arm down into the bottom of the can searching for heavy rocks, or something.

Of course, his arm got completely drenched and cruddier, so he looked up started and looked around for someone's devilry. Right-away, he saw Colleen's ripped-to-shreds blouse laying on the front lawn right next to the garden hose still running water, and he put two-and-two together: The girls had tricked them! In angry, slanderous language and indecent gestures with their injured arms, the two 'garbage goofs' climbed back aboard their truck and were hauled-away to their next-door duty-station and vanished from Guy's intolerance.

Guy always admitted that he wanted to come outside and wave goodbye to the 'deflated dumpster dummies,' but that he was too busy rolling around on the living-room floor in hysterics! Oh, 'that Guy of mine' and his wicked sense-of-humor!

⁓∞⁓

Here's another silly anecdote demonstrating my boyfriend's (at the time) endless sense-of humor…

⁓∞⁓

Immediately after arriving in Henderson, Nevada, Guy knew we had to have a car. We were all working in Henderson, but trips to Las Vegas were common due to legal matters about Guy's divorce proceedings and arrangements to get Richard, his son. We all loved to go into the City of Sin for fun and entertainment too. When we could splurge to see them, many great entertainers would come to Las Vegas to sing or dance or tell jokes, and sometimes, all three during the same show. It really was a fun town, and it still is as far as I know, though it's been several years since my last visit.

Anyway, Guy bought a very cute, but older, 1930 Ford Model A with a Rumble Seat. When you lifted the trunk lid, it became the backrest of an exposed, outside seat big enough to fit two persons. It was ideal for all of us to go somewhere because three could sit in the front seat, including the driver, which was always Guy, while two smaller persons could sit in the Rumble Seat on the outside.

One day, Guy needed to go into Las Vegas for business, and Colleen and I decided to go along and join him for some later fun in the city. Mary and Jann were busy doing something else, so they were not interested in joining us on that trip. Guy, Collen, and I all climbed onto the front seat. It was summer and hot, and not too much fun in the sun's heat outside, so no Rumble Seat. We took off.

On the way to Las Vegas from Henderson, there is a very, very long stretch of highway that runs straight and flat and smooth and flows on and on for miles and miles. Literally, you can see for ten or more miles ahead on that single, long stretch of road.

Guy used to play with his loving automobile on the way to Vegas, or when returning home, by letting go of the steering wheel, and he would just let the car drive practically automatically all on its own. That Ford model had very stiff steering, so the wheels just held straight and true once they were pointed that way.

That morning, while we were zooming down the highway, Colleen and I were just gabbing away, lost in sisterly nonsense, and gossip and who remembers what else. Anyway, we were yakking and yakking and unintendedly completely ignoring Guy. He must have gotten dreadfully bored with our blabbering and never including him in any of our conversations. It was that, or he didn't like what we were talking about. He never said, and we never asked...

Regardless, that crazy character set the steering and wheels of his joyous Ford Model A straight ahead for that car. He next adjusted the throttle on his car so that it maintained its exact speed. Then while Colleen and I were comfortably turned-away from Guy in order to continue with our engaging babble and conversations of rapturous chatter, that maniac quietly opened his driver's car door, and silently slipped-outside.

Then while edging himself carefully along the running boards, he maneuvered himself along the side of the car until he got to the rear. Next, he reached back, twisted the trunk handle, and lifted the Rumble Seat upward into its proper position. Finally, he swung his leg up-and-over into the Rumble Seat Compartment and pulled the rest of his body into his seated position...

The next part is what is challenged: Guy says he sat there literally for miles upon miles, but Colleen and I swear we noticed his absence right away and were scared to death. We didn't know what had happened to him. Finally, we looked back, and there he was with that smug look on his face and laughing away in his typical hysteria. Funny! Funny!

The only evidence that Guy had about how long he had been sitting there was the fact that when he finally did slip back around and climb back into the driver's seat, we were just pulling into the outskirts of Las Vegas. But if he had fallen while climbing-out or later when climbing back-in, he could have been terribly injured, if not killed... And what about us? Funny! Funny! Ha! Ha!

WAR'S END

Las Vegas, Nevada

One of my favorite Henderson recollections was an unplanned and unscheduled trip into Las Vegas one day on August 15th, 1945. We decided to all drive in in Guy's wonderful and fun 1930 Ford Model A with a Rumble Seat in the rear. Sis and I sat with Guy, driving, in the front while Colleen and Jann sat in the rear Rumble Seat after it was lifted from the trunk lid. They were exposed to the elements like a convertible, but we in the front seat were all enclosed inside.

It was mid-August in the Nevada desert, so you can imagine that it was very hot. That was why the youngest had to sit outside. Age does have its merits. Anyway, we cruised the fifteen to twenty miles into Las Vegas and gratefully parked at the famous Frontier Hotel and Casino. We dashed inside to delightful cooling, and we began eating and drinking and gambling and having a wonderful time. Little did we know just how important our celebration would become.

A man came by taking photographs, and he promised to have one developed for us later-on for pick-up. To me the picture turned-out priceless. It shows the four of us sisters sitting in a booth in the Frontier's lounge area. That was the only picture we ever got for our time in Henderson. Anyway, that picture became special because while we were sitting in our booth relaxing, an announcement came over the loudspeaker to everyone. They announce that victory of Japan had occurred. It was V-J Day, at last! The terrible war was finally over. Two weeks later, on September 2, 1945, the Japanese formally surrendered. Everyone was screaming with uproarious delight and excitement was electric! It was Peace, at last! Jean and Bo could finally come home.

(L to R: "Patsy" McCord, "Sis" Mary, Jann, Colleen, and Guy Dork)
Guy's Little Harem!
Celebrating VJ Day (Victory Over Japan). August 15, 1945
Frontier Hotel and Casino, Las Vegas, Nevada

Right after the war ended with the defeat of Japan on August 15th, almost all the plants and war support businesses in town closed. Workers were laid-off and work just about everywhere around ended. The city of Henderson and all its collected communities fizzled and shutdown. As a result, property values all around there plummeted. We took our cues, however, and headed for California's beautiful Bay Area. That had been the plan to ultimately seek our fortunes and futures.

Years later, though, we would all laugh when we remembered about our brief but entertaining time in that area. After the war ended, and Henderson et al. was up for sail, surrounding area-lands all the way over to Las Vegas were selling for a mere $0.50 an acre. That's right! Fifty cents per acre. We laugh because we could all remember Guy scoffing and saying, "Fifty cents an acre? Hah! Who in hell would want to live all the way out there in that miserable desert?" *Fortunes* were hard to come by for my loveable Guy...

BAY AREA, HERE WE COME!

Steadily, and focused, we forged our ways up toward the Bay Area. We had a couple of delays, detours, and side-tracks, but we were all used to such things. For instance, we had gotten as far as Fresno when we were delayed. Guy had contacted his ex-wife again in Las Vegas, and she had given permission for Richard to finally join us.

We got a large-sized, furnished apartment there in Fresno to let the dust settle and get comfortable with Richard along with us. Guy drove back to Las Vegas and picked-up Richard to bring him back to us. Richard was the new-kid-on-the-block, and because my sisters all loved Guy so much, they took right away to Richard. He was *The Little Prince* around all of us for a while, so I was happy for him.

The main reason we stayed for a while in Fresno, besides for Richard's sake, was because we were waiting to hear from Jean and Bo. Our plans in the Bay Area were directly linked to their goals. Housing was available then, but with the War officially over, housing everywhere began to boom… except for Henderson! The Bay Area was getting pricier every day, and we were planning on depending on Jean and Bo to help arrange for housing for all of us.

That was when Jean finally caught-up with us. Her discharge, just like her enlistment, came out of Florida, so she had a long, cross-country, Greyhound bus-ride of her own. When she arrived there at the station in Fresno, Guy and I were there to pick her up. With all her sole belongings, guy's car needed all the storage space in the Rumble Seat he could get. Guy was extremely courteous to Jean, and they hit it off just great from the very beginning. Later, Guy told me that he knew that Jean was a lesbian right away, but he was such a gentleman. Jean respected Guy for that and she admitted years later that Guy was probably the only man that she ever loved. She loved him because of his *acceptance of* her and because of his love for me.

Jean remained so focused. We quickly got past our past differences of opinion, the farm, abandoning Jann, her dog Duffy, and new plans for making a stake in California's Bay Area. Jean's attitude was, "That was then, and we survived. This is now, and we shall succeed!" How could you argue with her? Complete focus on the present and future. Her one Catch 22? She had already arranged for Duffy to be delivered to her as soon as possible. Oh, Jean!

Jean had taken many tests in the WAC, and each test score elevated her positions within her military occupation. Eventually, she was a non-commissioned officer working in Army military hospitals as research scientists' assistant. That was where and when she decided to become a doctor. Of course, goals and plans change, as had Jean's.

After graduation from UCB with a master's degree in Biological Sciences, Jean dropped-out of Medical School and went back into research. Successful stints at UC Berkeley Medical Dept. and Lawrence-Berkeley National Laboratory came and went. Jean met the love of her live, Phyllis Manley, who was a UCB Art Master graduate. The two of them merged with Phyllis becoming a successful artist (painter) and Jean becoming a successful author while in Berkeley, California. Together, they combined their unique talents designing and building, with their own hands, several fantastic and architectural dream-homes around the Bay Area and Northern California. They lived their lives and traveled the world together until Jean's untimely death in 1993.

But back then in Fall of 1945, we had finally accomplished a significant goal. Finally, there we were. We five sisters were all together again just like we had dreamed, hoped, and planned for many precious years. It was so wonderful for us all to see her again. We talked and shared and gossiped until the wee hours of the morning. Of course, there was little arguing about who was in charge. Nope, it was Guy. I put my foot down, and Jean willingly accepted her secondary role to him. However, Jean noted that she would be the one getting us our housing. Go for it, sister! We're behind you all the way! And what can I say? Guy just had a way with women... even with lesbians!

As Christmas approached, we made our plans for a Christmas Reunion with Bo being discharged and coming to join us and little Jack, or Joe, as he preferred then, would come-up and join us. That was the icing-on-the-cake with Bo's and Joe's return. Ending-up on the East Bay side of the Bay Area in California turned-out to be a wonderful place for all of us McCord siblings to begin our separate, but new lives together. For many *ways*, it was the best move in the whole-wide world for me.

Initially, the *ways* were tiny, but they were four incredibly *significant ways* to be exact. Guy and I had four children born to us while in the Bay Area. My own future was certainly destined to remain there for a while. I had finally figured-out and begun the career I was destined to have all along: Housewife and mother to my stepson, Richard, and then five children of our own...

However, finishing off my sibling-family history, however, young Jack eventually joined us all in the Bay Area and completed his schooling there, including graduation from UC Berkeley. During that time and continuing throughout much of his life for a distinguished career, Jack had also followed his dream of joining the California National Guard. Of course, Jack as a youth, like the rest of us, had also done his own travels, the hard way.

He too, had grown-up fighting more-and-more, with our dad as he grew older. Teenage years were most difficult for him, and he too ended up running away at age fourteen. Our dad had decided to build a ramshackle vacation house in the Richmond hills in 1948. It was probably so that he could *look down upon* his now happy brew of children. Anyway, he was forcing Jack to work there, and Jack rebelled.

He ran away and hitch-hiked all the way back to... where? You guessed it! Cleveland, Ohio. Jack had heard of family back there somewhere and went in search of them. Anyway, eventually, he got caught by authorities, and he was put on a highly restricted, bus-station to bus-station trip all the way back to Berkeley.

Upon his return to California, Jack moved-in with all of us sisters and brother Bo. That date in 1948 officially marked the time that all of us McCord children were finally all together and living with one another. However, the first time Jack was with the rest of us, and we were officially and formally all back together at precisely the same time... was at Guy's and my wedding on February 8th, 1946. Our almost lifelong struggle, goal, and challenge to bring us all together had finally happened.

Jack still had more issues and plans. He had somehow lied about his age and managed to join the California National Guard at the ripe old age of sixteen in 1950. The rest of us were all well-settled in the Bay Area by then, and in fact, we all attended Jack's wedding that same year. Jack and his new bride immediately began having children there too. Under all his pressures, though, Jack also managed to put himself through UC Berkeley majoring in Journalism, and he started a long career as a newspaper sports writer.

Our brother, Tech. Sgt. Bo McCord came home from the European War a decorated hero and joined us all in Northern California. He had finally returned to us by that wonderful Christmas of 1945, right after his discharge. Both he and Jean had qualified for GI Bill housing, so the two of them initially put-up all the rest of us in government housing there in the Berkeley/Oakland Area. It was there that we all, including visits from young Jackie Boy, finally fulfilled our dream of reuniting our entire McCord siblings clan. In fact, we all celebrated it with Guys' and my wedding.

We all had survived, and we had finally mended our *war-torn* family. We had fought a dysfunctional father, depression, a World War, and even apart, we had stayed together in our hearts. We had, ultimately, won it all…

Wedding Day of Guy Henry and Patricia Vera (McCord) Dork

(L to R: Colleen, "Sis" Mary, Jann, "Patsy," Guy Dork, Lil' Richard, Roy McCord, Sr., "Bo," and "Joe" (Jackie) McCord)

Guy's and My Wedding and McCord Siblings' Reunion
Berkeley, California
February 8, 1946

WEDDING REUNION

Berkeley, California

It was February 8, 1946. We had been living in Oakland, California, and everything had come together. Guy and I had our very own little house above the city in the Oakland hills. It wasn't much, but we were very happy. Richard was still living with us and continued to do so for several more years. Even still, we continued living there in the Bay Area with Guy working as a welder and occasionally at other work just to change his routine.

Our wedding became the highlight of everyone's life, purpose, and goals. Finally, ever since our mother had passed-away in 1935, and I had been sent away to Aunt Kate's, our remaining family was once more reunited. We all had been separated from each other because of family conflicts and because of war for over ten years. Our family of siblings had been *torn apart* and separated from one another due to family tribulations and because of the war's demands. Guy's and my wedding brought all of us siblings back together after a decade of separation. We all were celebrating Guy's and my marriage, but it was extra-meaningful to us McCord brothers and sisters because we were celebrating the accomplishment of a precious and meaningful goal for all us siblings.

One unusual aspect of Guy's and my wedding was the fact that my dad had brought my little brother, Jack, all the way-up from Los Angeles for our wedding. Because of that good deed, Roy McCord was allowed to attend my wedding. However, he understood my grief with him, and his presence that day, when I denied him the right to walk me down the aisle and give-me-away during Guy's and my wedding ceremony. That honor went to my beloved brother, Bo McCord.

The second unfortunate part of my wedding is with our actual wedding photograph. My father was not invited to be a part of the picture-taking portion. In fact, he was not invited to the wedding, at all. However, typical of his stubborn and difficult character, he demanded to be included in the wedding-party photograph. You can see him standing between Guy and Bo with that arrogant look on his face. Bo said later that he was not comfortable at all, but that he *maintained his pose for me.*

Guy did not want any conflicts on our wedding day, so he asked me to make an exception. I agreed, but it ended-up being my greatest disappointment. My beloved sister, Jean, whom I wished above-all to be there with me, absolutely refused to be in the same picture with our father. I didn't blame her, but her absence turned-out to be my greater sadness and loss. Yet, she was a wonderful part of our reception after our father had left…

No matter, we all had survived the Depression and the War, and we had finally mended, more-or-less, and reunited our *war-torn* family of siblings. We had fought a dysfunctional father, struggled through a severe depression, survived a World War, and even *torn* apart, we had stayed together in our hearts. Ultimately, we had won it all…

CONFIRMATION

Oakland, California

A year after our marriage in February 1946, Guy and I had our first child. We named him David Edward after Guy's adopted father, Eddie. We still had Richard, Guy's son, with us and he was an absolute joy for our entire family. In fact, he was the ring-bearer for our wedding. He remained with us for a few more years until his mother came, took him away to live with her in Texas. Richard is still living there today after having retired from the US Air Force and teaching.

David was my jewel for the family. He was such a handsome baby, and he was the absolute spitting image of Guy. That was a very special reward for us. There was never any denying whose child he was. We all loved him, and he grew up to make us all proud and give Guy and me two wonderful grandsons.

Our next child came almost exactly a year later. I asked the doctors to let me bring our newest child home on little David's birthday, but they couldn't. I suppose the whole darn Bay Area had been too busy breeding like us. No room. But we brought David's brother home a day earlier, and there was a wonderful and blessed celebration upon his arrival. All the aunts and uncles were there to pay tribute and acknowledge the truth of a life-long held grudge against my father.

Our newest son became Daniel Thomas, and he was the spitting-image of my father, Roy McCord. After all those years of denial, dismissal, treatment like a non-family member, and begrudged associations, Daniel had proven, once-and-for-all, that I had been my own father's child. It was too late for forgiveness, though. It hardly mattered because my dad would never have asked for any. His false pride would never have allowed him to do so.

But I had gotten some satisfaction for my dad's mean ways when I married Guy. I refused to allow my father to walk me down the wedding isle. Instead, I was ever-so-proud to have my brother, Bo, do the honors. Our wedding picture does show my dad in it, but it was against my wishes. He barged in and demanded to be included. Guy would have very willingly excluded him, but we chose the higher-road, and to avoid any altercation, accepted his inclusion in the family portrait. Of course, one incredibly important member of our family who was absent from the picture, but very present for our wedding, was our eldest sister Jean. She refused to be seen in a picture with him. Such is life.

"Adventurers All," the McCord Sisters

(L to R: "Sis" Mary Johnson, Colleen McCalla, Jann McCord, "Patsy" McCord-Dork, and Jean McCord)

END OF THE BEGINNING

B eginning a couple years later after Henderson, 1947-1952, four out of five of Guy's and my children would be born right there in the Berkeley-Oakland Bay Area. Most of my sisters' and brothers' kids came from that area too. Pvt. Jean's previously written invitation had brought us all to California's Bay Area. Richmond-Oakland-San Francisco, all on the beautiful and beneficial San Francisco Bay, had been an important part of the war cause effort. By our arrival, the whole Bay Area was becoming a truly dynamic cultural, educational, industrial, and commercial hub on the West Coast.

U.C. Berkeley was there, and Jean wanted to get discharged from the USWAC to attend UCB and become a doctor. Bo wanted to get discharged from the USAAC and attend the California College of the Arts in Oakland to study art and then teach school. Sis Mary and Colleen wanted to fall-in-love, marry and raise their children there too, so they both did, and they both married US Navy sailors. They just adored men in uniforms, and those uniformed fellows sure loved them back!

Jann stuck around long enough to finish high school, and then she began fulfilling her *travel* dream by becoming a United Airlines stewardess. She began serious travel we had always talked about. Years later, Jann would earn her PhD from UC and practice in the field of Marriage and Family Counseling. Between United Airlines, her academic assignments and personal desire, Jann traveled the world.

Truth is, she and I would do a great many world adventures together too. In fact, at various times, all us siblings would travel to distant destinations together in varying combinations. Airplanes to distant, far-off lands took us on journeys to the United Kingdom, Ireland, all over Europe, Japan,

Southeast Asia, and China. Guy and I took a few months to travel and visit his own, special destinations: New Zealand and Australia.

Even my retired educator, Boilermaker welder, traveler, and writer son, Daniel, has traveled with me to so many destinations such as Hawaii, Northern Europe, China, Southern Europe, all around the USA, and many short and longer cruises in the Caribbean and California West Coast-Mexico destinations. We both are easy-going travelers, who both believe in: "…adventure," as he says, "…mellowed by relaxed, take-whatever-as-it-comes, and *see-what-you-can-while-you-can* attitudes." We both enjoy traveling with each other because our mutual motto is very Australian: *No worries!*

Of course, cruises were special too, and my children have all taken turns with me going- off visiting the Caribbean Islands, Latin America, Mexico, and up to Alaska. Trips, journeys, vacations, and just basic travel with my children has been a central, emotionally meaningful part of my life. And what can I say about travels with my siblings? Those amazing and unique trips throughout my life with various sisters and brothers, and of course, Guy, were all worthy stories for becoming books in themselves. Unfortunately, I don't believe there is a genre anywhere for *Hysterical Dramatic Humor!*

Yet, *life* is an adventure. Keep the dream alive….

Patricia Vera McCord-Dork
A true lover of God, country, family, humanity, and adventure"

EPILOGUE

Brownsville, California

The war had taught us many things: Frugality, family unity, hard-work, and conscientiousness would ultimately achieve winning results. Our difficult experiences throughout the war-period had proven that love of family came right along with love-of-country and of God. I guess we believed, "The family that fights together, unites together." We (McCord) children were close, and we wanted that feeling passed on to our offspring.

I believe that it surely did with my own children. After everyone's somewhat surprised revelation that I truly was a McCord sister, after all, and our mother's and my shame had been completely removed by my son Daniel's birth. Guy and I were on our way to duplication, duplication, and duplication. Daughter Barbara was born to us the following year in 1949, and son, Kerry, came along three years after that in 1952.

That was when Guy confided in me, and together we made the decision to uproot our lives and leave the hustle and bustle of city life. We moved up into the mountains of Northern California to a tiny, mountain community of Brownsville in Yuba County. Our children were essentially raised after that as country kids, and my daughter Barbara and her husband, Charles, still live there to this day.

A final child, our fifth and another daughter, Kelly, was born five years later in 1957. Although our other children all had big city roots from the Bay Area, Kelly was the first *all-country girl.* Today, however, both she and my other daughter, Barbara remain country-girls and live high-up in the hills, more-or-less, at opposite ends of Yosemite National Park in the California Sierra Nevada Mountains. They have taken turns watching-over-me while continuing to supply me with an abundance of clean, fresh mountain-air and the calming effects it brings.

Daniel began his teaching career in the city and has always remained down where the bright lights shine. He still loves visiting all of us up here, though, where his *other* roots, and part of his heart, still exist in the mountains. He remains a constant traveler spending as much time as he can in Puerto Vallarta with his wife, Angelina. She paints and he writes. He and I have traveled much of the world together, and I know that he is always up for another adventure somewhere in the world, whenever he hears the call.

Another side note worth mentioning is the pleasure of having finally received my high school diploma. While closing-in on his own retirement date, Son Daniel started one of the very first online, adult, secondary-school programs in the entire country, National High School. People like me, or others, who could not attend classes in person for a variety of reasons, were able to test, study and retest, if necessary, to fulfill requirements earning their diplomas. It was a satisfying accomplishment made even more special by my son's vision, effort, academic background, and business acumen.

As far as family-togetherness is concerned, to this day our extended families and children all continue to remain attached to each other. Cousins maintain continual phone and social media contact, and they all regularly plan family gatherings. I believe that perhaps they all appreciate and admire all those unique challenges faced by us parents and how we all managed to endure. I always hope that they all recognize the value of sacrifice necessary in order to keep families together and freedom on hand.

I am retired now, of course. After Guy departed this world in 2002, I have continued to live as an active Senior Citizen. I may be considered *old* by many, but I still consider myself a very active senior. I try to remain close to my past and present neighbors and friends, and we mingle together, and share our lives' stories and keep-up with each other's latest news. Fact is, it was visits with friends and family which ultimately brought the "Rosie the Riveter" Memorial Museum in Richmond, California to my attention.

My children have all heard tidbits of my own, as well as my brothers' and sisters' tribulations, and including their father's, through the Great

Depression and WWII eras. Often, they are shocked, surprised, fascinated, and impressed by our seemingly outrageous, youthful experiences and activities. My husband, Guy, and I have spent our lives traveling and chasing jobs and new adventures around the globe. Both of us remained *Boomers* at heart, although many of our family called us *Gypsies*. Both descriptions worked for me. To my delight, however, and to this day, many of our family continue their own, robust traveling plans. I think that traveling and adventure must be in their DNA by now.

A favorite expedition occurred in the not-too-distant past. Amazingly, thirty-four of Guy's and my immediate, family offspring all traveled together on a ten-day, Caribbean cruise over Christmas and New Year's 2002 celebration. Since then, many of us have joined together and traveled all around the USA and on other cruises. Occasionally, some even joined on world destination vacations. It seems they all love sharing unique experiences. A traveling-career side note which may even be worth mentioning is that several family members went on to become *Boomers*, themselves, as Boilermaker welders who chased big jobs all over the country just like we did.

Regarding unique travel and new experiences, however, one fun fact is that six years ago for my eighty-seventh birthday, many families showed up in Northern California to cheer me on for my first skydive. No doubt, lifetime experiences of family-ties, determination and courage had been gained from challenging and defeating so many difficult obstacles faced during those war years. They all gave me courage to attempt new and exciting opportunities. Experiences resulting from the war-effort years and challenges faced through those *Rosie the Riveter* and *Wendy* welding periods had developed my daring. My husband, Guy, learned to fly airplanes. I learned to jump from them? *Piece-of-cake!* With family beside me, it seems I can do anything.

More recently, however, I was denied another sky-diving activity by my doctor from his fear of heart-failure. I just thought, "Whose heart? Aww, if he dies, he dies!" In exchange, however, the pre-planned event became a Cousins' Jump Day. Six nieces and nephews plus my son, Daniel, all leaped from a plane, like I had done in 2013, to sort of congratulate me and each other and celebrate adventure. Besides, they were celebrating our entire family. The event may even become an annual spectacle. I sure hope so. Family, love, and adventure is good for everyone.

Finally, Daniel, surprised me with another fun and unique experience. We had the distinct pleasure of visiting and participating in an annual, Richmond, California "Rosie the Riveter" Memorial Celebration. It was wonderful, and with more than two thousand attendees, several of us original Rosie's were singled out as celebrities to honor. I enjoyed the welder's exhibit, especially, and all its special attention, and I plan on attending each year's memorial too.

Also, having shared some brief stories of my past connections to the *Rosie's* with their Richmond Memorial staff-members and other attendees, I was encouraged to submit my own "Home Front Story" to their "Rosie" cause. Therefore, my son, Daniel, wrote this story and did so for me.

The End of the Beginning

"May your lives be filled with travel and your travels full of life!"

ABOUT THE AUTHOR

D aniel Chapman's first love is travel. Growing up in a *boomer* family, where they followed his father chasing all over the country looking for the next, big job, Daniel's national travels were formidable by the time he left home. Even with his own stake at hand, our author continued to chase that illusive, yet potentially promising, goldmine of career experience, learning, and training. By the time he completed his second master's degree in Education Administration, Daniel had attended twenty-nine schools plus completion of independent trade schools.

No doubt Daniel developed and honed his love of travel experience from his parents and took his mother with him on multiple, globe-trotting adventures including Northern and Southern Europe, Turkey, China, Mexico, and even Hawaii. Always amazed and impressed by his parents' own childhood and youthful travels, Daniel began his own independent journeys right out of high school with a summer's solo hitchhiking experience throughout all of Europe. He has been back several times since to seek those unique, adventuresome, writing-subject materials.

Teaching is Daniel's second love. He says that he knew he wanted to be a teacher, a facilitator of knowledge, from his early youth. He laughingly recalls a second-grade teacher of his in a Texas school who one day gave him instructions on a particularly cold morning, "Daniel, git over there and shut that winder."

Then he smiles remembering his immediately sincere, truly thoughtful, and helpful correction for his teacher to become even better at her craft when he responded, "Teacher, it's *window*, not *winder*." Of course, Daniel laughs heartily when he admits that the teacher flunked him for second grade *for being too immature!*

Teaching was his calling, however, and Daniel spent thirty-two years in a variety of classroom environments from first grade through twelfth-grade, college-preparedness, honors classes. His greatest challenges and most meaningful contributions, however, came from over two decades educating at-risk youth in county and community correctional schools. His belief in the well-known mantra quip, *A mind is a terrible thing to waste* was modified for his liking: *A rescued mind is a life saved.*

During his educational career, Daniel did take a nine-year hiatus to follow in his parents' footsteps by becoming a four-year graduate from the Apprenticeship Program of the International Brotherhood of Boilermakers. He traveled the country as a rigger, fitter, and welder in huge constructions sites sensing the work and lifestyle his parents had faced during those years of the Great Depression and WWII. Although admitting to amazing times of adventure, danger, stress, feast, and famine, Daniel confesses that he preferred the classroom: "Those who can, do; those who don't want to, teach others *who want* how to do it!"

However, it was Daniel's travels, academic and trade careers, and adventuresome spirit that ushered in his attachment to poetry and eventual love of writing as a third career. During his classroom experiences, poetry became a viable tool and vessel for our teacher/author to share and reach his student audience with optional-thinking platforms and a means to showcase styles and love of verse. Daniel's retirement has become the means and forum to create new stories and poetry. With miles to go and many stories ahead, our author is always on the search for another tale to tell. "That is what we do," he says. "Writers write about life!"

'Take mine, for instance," Daniel grins. "My life is an open book. Read me!"

www.ingramcontent.com/pod-product-compliance
Lightning Source LLC
Chambersburg PA
CBHW021437070526
44577CB00002B/192